Innovation Mode 2.0

George Krasadakis

Innovation Mode 2.0

Designing Innovative Companies in the Era of Artificial Intelligence

Second Edition

Forewords by Alex Adamopoulos and Mathew Hughes

Springer

George Krasadakis
Dublin, Ireland

ISBN 978-3-032-00834-3 ISBN 978-3-032-00835-0 (eBook)
https://doi.org/10.1007/978-3-032-00835-0

This Springer imprint is published by the registered company Springer Nature Switzerland AG
The registered company address is: Gewerbestrasse 11, 6330 Cham, Switzerland

Foreword by Alex Adamopoulos: Building Companies That Live Innovation

There's a moment in every organization's life where it hits a wall.

Not because it's run out of ideas—but because it's run out of clarity. Clarity about what to focus on. Clarity about what to stop doing. Clarity about who leads the change, how to fund it, and how to bring people along. That moment—when excitement fades and fatigue sets in—is where most innovation efforts die.

But it's also the moment when something powerful can begin, if we have the right mindset and the right map.

That's what George Krasadakis offers in *Innovation Mode 2.0*. Not just a book but a blueprint for what it really takes to build innovative companies in today's world—companies that don't just talk about innovation but live it in their culture, in their systems, and in their everyday decisions.

George doesn't romanticize innovation. He doesn't treat it as the exclusive domain of creative elites or moonshot thinkers. He understands, like all seasoned leaders do, that true innovation is often messy, difficult, and deeply human. It involves challenging entrenched behaviors, rethinking priorities, and creating the conditions for new ideas to take root and grow. And it asks for something few leaders are trained to give: permission—for people to try, to fail, to learn, and to keep going.

What makes this book exceptional is its grounded empathy for both the people doing the work and the leaders responsible for making it possible.

Why this book—and why now?

We live in a time where the pace of change is dizzying. Emerging technologies like agentic AI aren't just augmenting how work is done—they're starting to shape what work gets done, how decisions are made, and what gets prioritized. In this reality, the traditional separation between strategy and execution, between ideation and delivery, no longer holds. AI can scan for opportunities, test assumptions, even generate product roadmaps. But AI can't tell you what's worth fighting for. It can't build trust. It can't rally a team around a shared sense of purpose. That still falls to us.

And this is where George's vision shines.

He sees artificial intelligence not as a threat but as a transformative enabler—one that, when combined with human creativity and good leadership, can compress innovation cycles from months to days. But for that to happen, leaders must rethink their systems, their roles, and their expectations. That's what this book prepares them to do.

The heart of the matter: leadership, systems, and belief.

Over the years, I've worked with some of the world's most admired companies, helping them rethink how they build products, develop talent, and deliver value. One truth that emerges again and again is this: innovation doesn't fail because of a lack of good ideas. It fails because the environment doesn't support the realization of those ideas.

George introduces us to the architecture required to change that. His framework—built around Opportunity Discovery, Validation, and Realization—isn't just process for process's sake. It's an intentional system that helps teams and organizations move from inspiration to implementation. It gives innovation a home, a rhythm, and a standard of excellence. And importantly, it creates clarity around roles—what leaders need to own and what teams need to be empowered to do.

But perhaps even more valuable is what George helps us feel: the belief that change is possible.

In a world where transformation fatigue is real—where leaders are exhausted from initiatives that go nowhere and employees are jaded from promises that don't materialize—this book offers something rare: a hopeful, practical path forward.

Culture is the soil, not just the scenery.

Innovation doesn't happen in isolation. It happens in environments where people feel safe to experiment; where failure is seen as learning, not liability; where curiosity is rewarded; and where the company's purpose is clear and compelling enough to warrant the effort.

As I've written before, if your leadership team isn't behind innovation, it's already failed—you just don't know it yet.

George understands this deeply. His chapters on culture, teams, and leadership read like a guide for human-centered transformation. He offers frameworks for building innovation "dream teams" not as elite task forces but as enablers who bring the rest of the organization along. He articulates the importance of language—why even defining what "innovation" means in your context can unlock alignment and momentum.

He also offers a lens of realism. Innovation is not always comfortable. It can feel slow. It can create tension. But those who persist, and who invest in the right systems and mindsets, build something enduring.

To the leader holding this book: If you're reading this, you're probably already asking the right questions:

- How do we keep up with the speed of change?
- How do we empower people to do their best thinking?
- How do we make innovation sustainable—not just sporadic?

Innovation Mode 2.0 will help you answer those questions. But more than that, it will challenge you to lead differently—to lead with empathy, to design systems that support learning, to model the behaviors you want your teams to adopt, and to build a company where innovation is not a side activity but the core of how value gets created.

Because the truth is, companies that operate in "Innovation Mode" aren't just more agile or more digital. They are more human. They listen better. They adapt faster. They serve more meaningfully. And in the long run, they win.

Let this book be your guide—and your invitation to lead that kind of company.

CEO Emergn
Tampa, FL, USA

Alex Adamopoulos

Foreword by Mathew Hughes: Solving the Innovation Enigma

I was thrilled when George Krasadakis invited me to write the foreword for the second edition of his groundbreaking book, *The Innovation Mode*. George has long had a keen interest in innovation, with his books *60 Leaders on Innovation* and *60 Leaders on Artificial Intelligence*, both of which I had the honor of contributing to, providing a rich set of insights into what the future may hold for innovation and technology-driven innovation. Innovation remains the one true enigma among organizations. It is essential and must be nurtured, yet as executives, managers, and entrepreneurs, we struggle to truly harness its potential. Why is that?

Innovation is the lifeblood of all organizations, and those that do not innovate risk squandering the future and falling behind more nimble, creative, and innovative rivals. No senior executive, manager, or entrepreneur wants to face that scenario. We do not choose to make decisions that limit or even cripple the ability of our organizations to create wealth or to survive. Instead, executives, managers, and entrepreneurs make well-intended decisions that may inadvertently close the innovation tap—be that by restricting the flow of ideas to what the organization knows best, limiting the space to be creative by choosing to refine what the organization has always excelled at, diverting resources to more immediate worries, or being so focused on the now that we lose sight of pioneering new frontiers. The innovative organization is something that needs to be constantly worked on and nurtured—it is a myth to think that past success inoculates us against whatever the future may bring.

The *Innovation Mode 2.0* is a powerful compilation of ideas that weave people and culture as the fabric of the firm, with innovation capabilities as the threads that knit together an organization's capacity to innovate. My metaphor here is deliberate. Using fabric to represent people and culture captures the foundational, interconnected nature of these elements in an organization; threads symbolize innovation capabilities as essential but flexible components woven into the larger system. A tightly knit fabric is resilient, just as an organization with the right cultural and human connections fosters innovation. Different innovation capabilities (threads) contribute to the fabric's texture and durability. Together, the organization's ability to innovate depends on how these threads are continuously woven and reinforced to enable people to innovate. The ongoing process of weaving innovation into an organization's cultural fabric ensures that it remains dynamic, resilient, and capable of evolving in an ever-changing environment. There is no finer pressure on executives, managers, or entrepreneurs now than to craft the innovative organization.

It is fitting that the tagline to the *Innovation Mode 2.0* is "Designing Innovative Companies in the Era of Artificial Intelligence." When I reflect on the Preface for the first and second editions, it is remarkable how the first edition correctly foresaw the pending rise of AI in our lives, work, and daily language. The speed at which AI-driven innovations have transformed the landscape of people's lives, the markets we serve, the products and services we provide, and the future for innovation begs an immediate question: What is next on the horizon that will change again what we thought we knew? Innovators will shape the future. With the insights in this book, I hope it will serve as a superb reference and resource for those seeking to design innovative organizations and spearhead the next generation of innovations, large or small, groundbreaking or gradual, that change the world around us.

The book provides an excellent overview and reference point about people, culture, and capabilities as the key pillars of innovation and practical ways to discover, validate, and realize opportunities on the road to innovation. I encourage readers to dive into these chapters and absorb the wealth of insights available.

Schulze Distinguished Professor and Professor of Innovation and Entrepreneurship, School of Business
University of Leicester
Leicester, UK

Dr. Mathew (Mat) Hughes, PhD

Preface to the Second Edition

Six years ago, I closed the first edition of this book with a prediction:

> "In a fully digitized environment powered by Artificial Intelligence [...] the focus shifts from running the business to pursuing opportunities [...] In the organization of the future humans will play a substantial role in forming opportunities through business creativity."

This future is now here. Artificial intelligence already powers essential business functions and redefines every part of the business that relies on digital operations. Yet this is just the beginning. Emerging Agentic AI is poised to transform how businesses operate: AI agents are autonomous software components capable of perceiving their digital environment, making decisions, and taking actions toward specific goals with limited or no human oversight. This technology will fundamentally change how companies operate, as AI agents will soon begin to take over complex workflows and accelerate decision-making cycles. At the same time, AI becomes more capable of understanding structured data and can connect to corporate data stores, identify patterns, answer business questions based on structured data, and generate compelling data stories that summarize various aspects of the business. AI dominates the business world: simply put, a well-integrated AI system knows what's happening inside the organization, what's happening in the broader market, and how the organization performs. By leveraging this rich and dynamic context, AI can enhance business operations, inform decision-making, and optimize processes. Beyond processes and optimization, artificial intelligence is entering more creative areas, rewriting the rules for corporate innovation.

AI joins the innovation effort not only as a *thought partner* helping human innovators shape ideas but also as an *extraordinary innovator*, capable of generating ideas and product concepts, building prototypes, and shaping strategies within minutes. Upon a prompt, an opportunity brief, or even a signal from the market, AI agents can use the company's full context, along with the latest market insights, to frame problems, propose solutions, and conceptualize products or even entire business ventures. While hallucination remains an issue, AI-generated ideas frequently demonstrate remarkable creativity and novelty. Considering the rate of progress, AI will soon evolve from a thought partner to a chief innovator, capable of *orchestrating* the entire corporate innovation process and optimizing multiple functions such as *market intelligence*, *business experimentation*, and *opportunity discovery*, potentially compressing innovation cycles from months to days.

Innovation disrupts itself. In this AI-powered world, the corporate innovation function faces a radical transformation. When AI enables anyone to generate brilliant ideas, shape strategies, and soon build digital products, the ability to *conceive* and *implement* becomes less important. At the same time, new competencies emerge as critical success factors for innovation: separating signal from noise, recognizing genuine opportunities, racing to market, establishing partnerships, and architecting smart in-market experimentation frameworks that maintain products differentiated. Consequently, a modern organization's most vital innovation capability is a scalable *opportunity discovery*, *validation*, and *realization* function—a "system" of talented cross-disciplinary teams powered by AI that can pursue multiple opportunities simultaneously. In this environment, innovation success increasingly depends on *in-market product growth* and ecosystem development, which involves connecting stakeholders, forming strategic alliances, building market trust, and driving momentum.

Beyond corporate boundaries, AI is fundamentally reshaping markets at unprecedented speed. As intelligence and knowledge become commoditized and available through simple APIs, established products and entire categories are under extreme pressure. AI services are displacing traditional digital products, sophisticated user interfaces are shifting to conversational experiences, and specialized applications are losing ground to comprehensive AI platforms. Moreover, this revolution extends beyond software: AI-powered robotics is already transforming manufacturing, logistics, transportation, and automotive industries, and connected devices will soon be powered by the most advanced AI models. What makes our era so special, though, is that these changes unfold simultaneously across industries and at an unimaginable speed, thus driving massive market disruption and, ultimately, the formation of entirely new ones.

At the same time, AI makes innovation easier than ever by removing barriers that once made innovation exclusive to well-resourced organizations. With an estimated 5.6[1] billion digital users and 20 billion connected devices[2] in 2025, businesses operate in a massive network of digital resources, a global "digital fabric" that provides data, market and consumer behavior signals, knowledge, services, and a *wealth* of digital building blocks and open-source software that can be used in the corporate innovation context: Humanity's accumulated knowledge is available through a simple HTTP request. This digital reality creates unprecedented opportunities for innovation by revolutionizing access to technology, talent, resources, and knowledge.

Advanced technology that once existed only in expensive labs is now widely available through API services that can be integrated into applications by anyone with basic programming skills. Cloud services and serverless architectures have simplified hosting complex solutions at scale, while modern engineering tools have shortened development cycles. Companies can access a global pool of talent

[1] https://www.statista.com/statistics/325706/global-internet-user-penetration/

[2] https://www.statista.com/statistics/1183457/iot-connected-devices-worldwide/

available through dynamic working models via online platforms, while Open Innovation enables strategic partnerships that can accelerate complex innovation efforts. With the current state of technology, it is easier than ever to grasp the dynamics of the global ecosystem and pick important signals regarding customers, brands, competitors, startups, and emerging consumer trends. When processed properly, these signals help companies—and their AI agents—understand their economic environment and discover *unmet* or *unimagined* needs.

While the opportunity to innovate is immense, competition is becoming increasingly intense and unpredictable. Our AI-powered world has removed barriers and blurred industry boundaries, enabling newcomers to build products rapidly using cloud computing, open-source software, AI coding platforms, and global talent networks. Competitive pressure intensifies from technology giants and startups across the globe. In this landscape, corporate innovation shifts from nice-to-have to *existential capability*. Organizations must prioritize a systematic approach to innovation, not only to launch new products but to reinvent themselves.

In this environment, innovation and adaptability are not just competitive advantages but survival traits, as companies will increasingly need to reimagine their core offerings or pivot toward new opportunities. Those companies that don't react fast are at risk of being displaced by AI-native competitors who can innovate faster. The pace of change demands not just adaptation but proactive opportunity-seeking: continuously sensing the global market and effectively pursuing high-potential opportunities.

This book provides a unique framework for corporate innovation, designed with artificial intelligence at its core. The first chapter introduces the core concepts of innovation by providing essential definitions and explaining the different types and styles of innovation. The next chapter puts these definitions into perspective—it presents the outlook of a modern, innovative organization and describes the most important failure factors for corporate innovation, ranging from *leadership failures* to *capability gaps* and *cultural blockers*. The third chapter explores the importance of people and culture in corporate innovation, describing the role of the *chief innovation officer*, defining a generic innovation executive role, and presenting the synthesis and responsibilities of the innovation "dream team," along with unique insights into innovation culture.

Chapter 4 presents the essential innovation capabilities, while Chapter 5 covers in detail the most important *innovation workshops* and how they are being reshaped by AI. Chapters 6, 7, and 8 present three critical, independent capabilities that shape the company's innovation core: *opportunity discovery*, *validation*, and *realization*, respectively. The opportunity discovery presents the idea assessment framework and how it is used by human and AI evaluators to flag opportunities; moreover, it introduces a novel, futuristic setup where AI *proactively* and *autonomously* discovers opportunities in the organization's context. Opportunity validation presents how to use business experimentation to obtain real-world evidence and produce insights-backed recommendations about the next best step of a business opportunity. The opportunity realization chapter explains the *AI-powered product development* function, starting with defining great MVPs and testing them in the market through fast product innovation and experimentation cycles. Chapter 9 presents a holistic *innovation measurement* framework that helps leaders understand the organization's innovation performance, orchestrate the innovation function, and steer the innovation transformation program.

The final chapter combines everything into a single, detailed *innovation masterplan*: it provides leaders with actionable guidance on how to empower their companies to innovate and drive them through a continual improvement journey to the *Innovation Mode*—the ultimate state where innovation happens organically. The chapter explains the architecture of the innovation program and presents the technological, cultural, and process-level change required to achieve the ultimate state of innovation. Through a system of six phases, the program introduces more than 70 activities, events, or innovation capabilities that gradually empower the organization to drive significant outcomes through innovation.

This book is designed for innovation and business leaders interested in establishing a powerful innovation function and transforming their organization into a fast, agile, and AI-powered company.

You will discover essential information, novel ideas, and unique insights on how to use artificial intelligence across the innovation process, events, and programs. You will learn how to design world-class innovation teams and structure organizations for innovation at scale, as well as how to build the essential capabilities needed to establish a powerful AI-driven 'innovation engine.'

Additional content on innovation, along with templates and other artifacts, can be found online at https://theinnovationmode.com

Dublin, Ireland George Krasadakis
2025

Preface to the First Edition

At the time of writing, it is estimated that there are 4.5 billion active Internet users along with 30 billion connected devices. We live in an era of unprecedented access to knowledge, talent, and digital resources. Our modern times are characterized by a massive, ongoing transformation that impacts every aspect of human life—from education and healthcare to entertainment, travel, and transportation. In the business world, digital technology drives an equally dramatic impact by changing the way we work, how we build products and operate services.

This revolution is the result of breakthrough innovations in many fields, such as hardware, software, networking, and technologies like big data and artificial intelligence. The Internet and the Web empower the formation of online communities and distributed teams that collaborate in entirely new ways. Movements such as the open source, open innovation, and open collaboration reshape the way we think about business. At the same time, flexible and remote working models emerge in the so-called gig economy, while entrepreneurship and startup initiatives are on the rise. This cultural shift, along with the general availability of some of the greatest technologies of all time, set the stage for radical innovation across sectors and geographies—and this stage is available to all, enabling relatively small companies, startups, or even individuals to disrupt the status quo and challenge established services and companies. Typically, these "outsiders" see the world through a digital lens and are faster in adopting the latest technologies; as a result, they tend to be more innovative when designing products, services, or business models. Consequently, established companies are at risk of being disrupted and outperformed. Corporate leaders realize that innovation is the only way to stay relevant and stay in business.

This "new order" in terms of technology, culture, and connectivity creates tremendous opportunities for both incremental and radical innovations. At the same time, the process of innovation itself is now faster than ever. Companies that have both the knowledge and the willingness to innovate have a distinct advantage over the established ones that take a more risk-averse position. Innovation-led organizations have the chance to stay ahead of the game and thrive. Companies that overlook the value of innovation or treat it frivolously will eventually get disrupted. Leaders need to transform their organizations toward a new model that incorporates innovation as a fundamental capability—fully embedded in operational aspects and well-aligned to the purpose of the company. To stay relevant, companies need to adapt fast and reset the way they work, communicate, collaborate, and pursue financial success.

The purpose of the book is to help business leaders rethink their corporations as agile, innovation-led organizations. At the same time, it aims to guide innovation leaders on how to design, initiate, and execute a robust transformational program. Through concrete proposals, original ideas, and best practices, it offers actionable guidance on how to drive the cultural and technological change through a structured transformation program and a continual innovation improvement process.

The book takes a holistic view of innovation—by examining the role of people, culture, technology, and processes. Innovation is seen as a fully integrated function that is powered by people and streamlined by technology. While it emphasizes the importance of culture, it also presents how digital technologies can redefine the ways companies innovate. The book introduces a robust innovation framework, a set of capabilities that empower the company to systematically capture market signals, spot opportunities, and react wisely through streamlined innovation processes such as ideation, prototyping, and experimentation. Furthermore, it presents a detailed innovation transformation program—a masterplan of work streams, events, and activities that help the organization move fast toward the Innovation Mode—the state where great innovation happens naturally, in an optimal balance with operational activities. By adopting the innovation-led model presented in the book, organizations can become more innovative and eventually gain competitive advantages.

This book is intended for business, technology, and innovation leaders. Readers will find essential information and unique insights on technologies, processes, and methodologies that can help them embed innovation into their corporate reality. Engineering managers can use this book to identify the technological components required to empower fundamental processes of innovation, such as ideation, idea evaluation, innovation measurement, gamification, and knowledge management. Innovation and digital transformation managers will find practical advice, ideas, and recommendations on how to design a winning innovation transformation strategy, inspire people, and grow a vivid community of innovators. Corporate leaders will get answers on how to measure success and orchestrate the end-to-end innovation process.

Additional content on innovation, along with templates and other artifacts, can be found online at www.theinnovationmode.com

Dublin, Ireland George Krasadakis
2020

Acknowledgments

I am thankful to Perikles Rammos, Alex Papageorgiou, Periklis Drougkas, Gaurav Kaila, Sergiu Hamza, and Alexandros Tzoumas for reviewing this work. Special thanks to Steven O'Kennedy for his valuable feedback and suggestions.

I am incredibly grateful to my family for their support and understanding and, above all, to Christina, Ariadni, and Nicholas—my source of truth and inspiration.

Contents

About the Author

George Krasadakis is a corporate advisor on AI, product architecture, and innovation strategy, with over 20 patents in artificial intelligence and related technologies. George has over 25 years of experience spanning start-ups and global corporations. He has worked with industry leaders such as Microsoft, Accenture, and GSK, where he held senior roles in technology, product development, and innovation. As the founder of four technology start-ups, including Datamine decision support systems, George pioneered AI-powered software systems that revolutionized operations for multinational clients across the telecom, banking, retail, and online sectors. His frameworks have shaped innovation centers and venture builders, creating environments where cross-disciplinary teams collaborate to convert bold ideas into breakthrough innovations. A published author and creator of the *60 Leaders* series on Innovation and Artificial Intelligence, George has also contributed 100+ articles on technology, product development, and innovation methodology to leading platforms.

List of Figures

List of Tables

Innovation (Re) Defined 1

The term "innovation" is arguably the most overused term in corporate vocabulary yet, ironically, one of the least understood. Hundreds of competing definitions exist: some focus on innovation as a *process*, while others describe transformative *outcomes* that disrupt markets. These varied perspectives often lead to confusion about what innovation truly means and, more importantly, how to systematically achieve it.

Clarity in terminology is essential for the success of corporate innovation: it fosters a shared understanding of the underlying principles and accelerates the adoption of related methods and practices. Using the right innovation terms in the context of the company allows leaders to communicate their innovation agenda and innovators to obtain a deep understanding of *what innovation is* and *how it can serve the company's purpose*. Solid, contextual definitions of innovation establish a shared language and provide the basis for an Innovation Playbook that enables the entire organization to engage with the innovation process.

In a modern corporate environment, innovation can take many forms. It may appear as high-potential *novel product concepts*, *inventions* that solve defined technical problems, or just *ambitious ideas* about new business areas and markets. Innovation may be *incremental*, found in specific features of an existing product, or *radical*, happening through expensive, long-term R&D programs. Innovation can also manifest as *novel business models* on top of otherwise conventional services or products or as new ways to *market, communicate, or grow* existing, non-novel technologies, products, and services. Due to the many forms innovation can take and the long lifecycle of innovation initiatives, it is not easy to spot innovation *as it happens*. The fact that even the most innovative and well-tested projects may still fail makes innovation tracking and measurement more challenging.

To address these challenges, companies should start by adopting a set of consistent definitions of innovation. Consistency in terminology is crucial for *measuring innovation performance*, which, in turn, allows effective *orchestration of innovation*. Moreover, having precise definitions for *types* and *styles* of innovation helps, beyond measurement, in shaping strong innovation narratives. Thus, it is of strategic

G. Krasadakis, *Innovation Mode 2.0*,
https://doi.org/10.1007/978-3-032-00835-0_1

importance to clearly state and communicate *what innovation is* and what *being genuinely innovative* looks like—not in a generic way but *contextually*, in your business environment.

In the following sections, we discuss existing definitions and their properties and, where necessary, introduce new ones. Contextualizing those definitions is essential to reflect your company's innovation principles, priorities, and strategies.

1.1 Novelty

Novelty, defined as the "state or quality of being novel, new, or unique,"[1] is essential for innovation. The actual verb *innovate* is defined as "Make changes in something established, especially by introducing new methods, ideas, or products."[2]

While the notion of novelty is straightforward, examining if a given concept is new is not simple: what appears to be a novel idea in the mind of an ambitious innovator may prove to be known to the team or the organization. Similarly, an idea considered groundbreaking in a corporation's microcosm may already be implemented elsewhere in the market. Organizations perceive novelty differently—some only recognize *novel-to-the-world concepts* as innovation opportunities, while others seek *novel adaptations* of known ideas from other domains or industries: well-known concepts *executed in novel ways* can still create a remarkable impact, for instance, through business model innovation, and, hence, are valid cases of innovation.

Tracking novelty helps companies identify patent opportunities faster and thus speed up the patent filing process. Moreover, it helps leaders understand and balance innovation portfolios by considering the *level* and *type* of novelty as one of their qualities. The Opportunity Discovery service described in Chap. 6 provides an early estimation of the novelty of ideas by tagging them as "New to the World," "New to the Industry," "New to the Company," or "New to the Product."

1.2 Invention

An *invention* is an idea, a solution to a problem that is *novel* and *proven workable* without necessarily being implemented. It may be just a detailed, validated technical description of a solution, a new, non-obvious way to achieve a goal. The key requirement is to be *novel*, "something that has never been made before."[3]

Inventions usually come in the form of a device or method that solves a specific problem or performs a task in a new and significantly improved manner. An invention may be enhancing a known solution by adding new elements, or it may be entirely new; it may refer to purely technological or scientific subjects or other

[1] https://www.dictionary.com/browse/novelty

[2] https://www.lexico.com/en/definition/innovate

[3] https://dictionary.cambridge.org/dictionary/english/invention

expressions of human activity, such as in social and cultural spheres. Inventions may occur independently of production and commercialization plans—the inventor may be solving a problem without having specific commercial goals or a strategy to exploit and monetize it.

1.3 Innovation as an Outcome

Innovation is more than *invention*: most innovation definitions include a condition on *execution* or *implementation* and accept as *innovation* a realized idea launched to the market and exposed to real users. For instance, according to OECD (2016):

> *An innovation is the implementation of a new or significantly changed product or process. A product is a good or a service. Process includes production or delivery, organization, or marketing processes.*

According to the same source, the product or service must be *implemented* and *available* to potential users to qualify as an innovation. Other popular definitions include criteria such as *success*, *widespread market adoption*, *proven impact*, and *successful commercialization*. These definitions work well at a macro level, for example, when measuring the level of innovation in a market, industry, or geography. Such macro views bound innovation to *impact* or *success*; they focus primarily on the *outcome* of a long development and commercialization process, seeking *novelty* that has been *implemented and delivered* to users with proven market *adoption*. However, when zooming into the business activities of a given organization, these definitions become less effective in tracking innovation due to the requirements for implementation, impact, and market adoption.

Consider, for example, a *product concept* that is mature, has verified *technical novelty*, and has successfully passed rigorous user testing, indicating that—in all probability—it *solves a major problem for a critical mass of users* in a *better and economically viable way*. According to the classic definitions, it cannot be measured as an innovation yet, as it has not reached the market and is not fully implemented—it does not meet the criteria of *adoption* and *exploitation*. However, in a corporate context, this is an instance of genuinely innovative activity: the *product concept* in the above example should be seen as a *validated innovation opportunity* that, if built and launched properly, may reach the level of adoption to qualify as "*classic*" *innovation*. Even if this product ultimately fails, it should still be considered an innovation initiative with partial success—a concept that progressed to a specific stage in the innovation funnel.

Hence, to track innovation *as it happens from* within the corporation, a more flexible definition is needed—one that can identify the *innovation potential* of less mature solutions before they reach the market. Considering that the journey from an idea to market is long and its success depends on various factors, some of which may not be directly related to the company's *ability to innovate* or *execute*, this definition should be independent of the *outcome*.

1.4 Innovation Opportunity

Typically, innovative organizations maintain portfolios of multiple promising concepts, which may be novel and high potential but not yet built or released in the market. Some of these may be tactical, while others may be part of ambitious programs tackling big problems or unarticulated user needs; they may be in a prototyping phase, awaiting a decision, or queued up for implementation and *may* or *may not* reach the market. We call these *innovation opportunities*, defined as:

> *An innovation opportunity is a well-defined, validated, novel solution that is estimated to be technically feasible, economically viable, and impactful for a critical mass of users.*

This definition is more flexible regarding maturity, novelty, and success since it allows non-implemented, early solutions to qualify as *innovation*. The term "solution" is used in its broader sense, referring to a defined and validated proposition addressing a specific *problem*. The latter should be presented as a structured problem, ideally articulated as a problem statement or a framed problem (see Chap. 6). The *solution* may point to a new product, feature, process, or service, and it may take various forms, such as a physical or digital product or an online experience. This definition requires the solution to be *feasible*, meaning that it *can be developed and offered* in a way that creates value for both its users and the company. Additionally, at least some of the essential aspects of the solution must be *novel*. However, as explained above, novelty can be defined with elasticity in the context of the company.

The above definition also refers to *expectations* of *viability* and *impact* based on estimations from the experts and acknowledges that uncertainty remains present. Failure is always a possible outcome, whether the solution is in development or when exposed to the market. Consistent use of this definition enables experts to assess early ideas, concepts, and proposed solutions through the lens of innovation and evaluate their potential. It also enables leadership to obtain insights into *how the company is innovating* and, as a result, better orchestrate the innovation process.

1.5 The Innovation Function of an Organization

The innovation function is the general *capability* that enables the organization to innovate consistently and at speed—it provides the means to discover and pursue *opportunities* and drive innovation *outcomes*. As defined below, the innovation function empowers the organization to innovate proactively while also sensing the market and reacting quickly and wisely to signals and emerging patterns from the global economic environment.

> *The innovation function is an always-on system of processes, services, technology tools, knowledge, and talent aiming to maximize the ability of the organization to discover and pursue opportunities.*

Beyond opportunities, the innovation function produces, accumulates, and diffuses *knowledge* and *innovation assets* throughout the organization. The "processes, services, and technology tools" mentioned in this definition refer to capabilities for capturing and evaluating ideas, sensing the market, rapidly developing prototypes, and running in-market experiments, as well as setting up and facilitating innovation workshops. In some cases, these services may be offered by specialized teams serving well-defined objectives, such as capturing market intelligence to inform the organization or conducting large-scale innovation workshops. "Resources" in the above definition refer to anything essential in practical innovation initiatives—from raw materials, equipment, tools, and hi-tech devices to communication systems and physical space.

The innovation function requires a well-designed framework with the right capabilities, processes, and resources, as explained in Chap. 4. The talent aspect of the corporate innovation function is covered in Chap. 3, "People and Culture."

1.6 Classification of Innovation

Given the various types and forms of innovation, it is essential that leaders consider the basic typology when defining their innovation strategies and agendas. Selecting the types of innovation that reflect your company's purpose and ambitions helps better focus and balance various innovation strategies through diversified innovation portfolios.

Classification of innovation can be done based on its *target—what the innovation aims to improve*—or its *intensity*, *the degree of change it seeks to bring*. In many cases, it is classified based on its *openness* or *the state of the target market*. There is a plethora of variations and combinations of typologies, which frequently lead to confusion regarding the underlying concepts. The following discusses a simple, structured approach to classifying innovation.

1.6.1 Based on the Target: The Object of Innovation

Innovation introduces new ways to improve *something*. Thus, it can be classified based on the form of its primary target—the nature of the object to be improved. According to the OECD,[4] there are four main types of innovation, *product*, *process*, *marketing*, and *organizational*, as described below.

- **Product innovation**: In this type, the innovation efforts result in a new product, good, or service or the improvement of an existing one by introducing significant and novel enhancements. A product in this context can be anything that may be offered to the market to satisfy a specific customer need—it can be a physical object, a digital product such as an application, or a Web experience. When tar-

[4] https://www.oecd.org/site/innovationstrategy/defininginnovation.htm

geting new products, this type of innovation typically has a long lifecycle, as it involves multiple stages, ranging from conceptualization and prototyping to implementation, launch, and in-market experimentation. It may require significant investments in production lines, development teams, research activities, and marketing plans.

- **Marketing innovation**: This type of innovation refers to *how a product is offered* to the market. According to the OECD,[5] "A marketing innovation is the implementation of a new marketing method involving significant changes in product *design* or *packaging*, product *placement*, product *promotion*, or *pricing*." At this level, innovation may come in novel ways of communicating and persuading potential users to engage with products or services. For example, it could take the form of a new interactive campaign, a cross-channel promotional experience, or a novel digital means of exploring a product's features. The purpose of marketing innovation is to present the company's commercial offerings in a better way and thus assist in opening up new markets, positioning products and services in better ways, and driving sales and growth. Based on the same definition, to be considered marketing innovation, such an activity must also be *new*—never applied before; it must be "part of a new marketing concept or strategy that represents a significant departure from the firm's existing marketing methods." Marketing innovation typically requires smaller investments and effort. Its implementation time is often short and usually does not involve technical implementation.
- **Organizational innovation**: This type of innovation targets the organization itself by introducing changes in how the company operates, communicates, and makes decisions. This type may refer to new means of organizing the work, executing and measuring progress, or new patterns of collaboration and contribution. It may come in the form of *more efficient systems*, *practices*, or *methods*. For example, it could be a new process for sharing information and gathering feedback from people within the company or a connected building that diffuses knowledge and information on plans, events, and the organization's innovation agenda via connected screens and interactive, personalized experiences.
- **Process innovation**: Innovation at the process level involves improvements of methods, techniques, and systems—it refers to "new or significantly improved production or delivery methods for the provisioning of services and goods."[6] Any new and non-obvious process or step that improves outputs by better handling the inputs can be considered process innovation. The improvements need to be novel, at least internally, within the organization's boundaries. Typically, such innovations impact the design and production methods, the distribution or delivery of products, supply chain operations, and the management of stock and organizational resources. For example, a company may introduce new operational procedures for a production plant or implement new systems that simplify the assembly line to improve throughput, increase quality levels, or reduce costs. Normally, this type of innovation is not directly visible to customers—it helps

[5] https://stats.oecd.org/glossary/detail.asp?ID=6871

[6] https://stats.oecd.org/glossary/detail.asp?ID=6870

deliver better products and experiences overall, but it is not necessarily apparent in instances of the product. Process innovation often takes the form of expensive, sophisticated technological solutions that combine software, hardware, or machinery. The rise of artificial intelligence and IoT introduces a massive opportunity for innovation of this type, as the available data and algorithms allow radically new ways of designing business or manufacturing processes. For instance, an industrial production line can be optimized by enhancing its telemetry and introducing real-time data processing, enabling production managers to make informed decisions. Beyond optimization, the production line can be altered and enhanced by incorporating "cognitive abilities," such as adding computer vision algorithms that verify the products' attributes and quality aspects. In this hypothetical scenario, the production line becomes, in a sense, "self-aware" of its own performance: through real-time insights from a computer vision algorithm, it can detect deviations from normality—in terms of the quality of the in-process products—and act accordingly, for example, flag a problematic product, re-route it for a fix, or notify the right team to intervene. In the same example, a new process may introduce the concept of self-checking, where the production system automatically compares current performance metrics against its historical data and predicts forthcoming maintenance needs or triggers troubleshooting for issues before they severely impact the process.

- **Business model innovation**: Simply put, a business model describes an organization's logic for generating revenues, making profits, or achieving success in a broader sense; it provides a holistic view by summarizing the end-to-end mechanism that creates and distributes value to customers. A business model comprises all the components that enable a company to run its business, a particular service line, or a product successfully. More specifically, it references the products or other offerings, the value proposition, along with the involved cost structures, the pricing, and monetization models; it defines how partner networks and distribution channels play a role in the process. Introducing new "logic" to any of these components or the whole model constitutes business model innovation. Usually, this type of innovation requires no new product or technology—it is defined on top of existing products and often a customer base.

1.6.2 Based on the Intensity of Innovation

Innovation can be classified based on the degree of change it aims to introduce to existing products, processes, or business models. Low-intensity innovations leverage established knowledge and less ambitious ideas, while high-intensity ones require new expertise and substantial investments. This classification enables organizations to reflect on, shape, and refine their innovation strategy, aligning expectations, resources, and programs accordingly.

- **Incremental innovation**: In this form, innovation occurs frequently but on a smaller scale, building upon current technologies or products. It can be part of a continual process that aims to improve an existing offering by releasing enhanced versions of known features or adding new ones. Incremental innovation is more conservative and less risky but also less promising in terms of impact. Still, while it does not drive transformative results, it helps maintain the competitiveness of existing products. In a digital context, incremental innovation can be fully embedded in the product development process: in parallel to scheduled development work, product managers maintain a backlog of novel feature ideas, which, given the fast iterations of the agile approach, can be prototyped and tested or even exposed as "preview" or "experimental" features to a small subset of the user base, at a fast pace. This way, the team gains insights into the expected performance of these novel ideas, makes informed decisions about their further development, and continually improves the product with smaller, more frequent doses of innovation. Unless the competition is faster or manages to successfully release a radical innovation addressing the same needs and market segments, incremental innovation should be sufficient to maintain proven products and technologies at the state of the art.

- **Progressive innovation**: This form of innovation targets significant advancements while preserving the core architecture and structure of existing products or offerings. It often involves new applications or combinations of existing technologies or solutions that customers recognize as better and more innovative. While less disruptive than radical innovation, it requires significant investment beyond product improvement cycles and incremental innovation. It needs specialized talent capable of identifying high-impact opportunities within or beyond current product scopes. Progressive innovation is typically powered by a dedicated product innovation team with different goals and increased autonomy, separate from day-to-day delivery or product backlogs. This separation allows for the exploration of more ambitious ideas while maintaining strategic alignment with core product teams. When executed effectively, progressive innovation can become a powerful driver of competitive differentiation and long-term value creation.
- **Radical innovation**: This form of innovation seeks to introduce significant changes to an established business model, technology, or process, often through the application of breakthrough technologies or scientific discoveries. In some cases, it replaces existing solutions or technologies entirely. Typically, it is the result of long-term, expensive, and high-risk investments at the technical and scientific layers. In many cases, it may also trigger marketing and business model innovations. Radical innovation is what typically attracts media attention—it is what consumers and the market perceive as innovation.

1.6.3 Based on the Style and Approach

Corporate innovation may also be characterized by its style—the approach taken by the organization, the level of openness, and how visible and accessible it is to people in the company.

- **The centralized model**: Companies that follow this model empower a centralized team to lead specialized innovation programs. This central team takes the form of technology labs or R&D departments that aim to deliver focused innovation, typically through expensive, long-term innovation technology or scientific programs. The centralized approach is effective in companies that require significant scientific expertise and technological breakthroughs, which depend on capital-intensive research programs. It comes with certain advantages, e.g., deep specialization and expertise, dedicated resources, leadership sponsorship, and strategic alignment. However, in some cases, it may create distance between innovators and the operational aspects of the organization. Moreover, it may become disconnected from the rest of the company, as employees from other divisions may not have opportunities to actively contribute to innovation. Consequently, the rest of the organization may feel like "consumers" of the ideas, inventions, and knowledge produced by the labs.
- **The decentralized model**: Modern views on corporate innovation advocate for an open, decentralized model where artifacts, knowledge, and resources are available to all. When following the decentralized pattern, innovation can originate from any team, and the knowledge produced is diffused across the organization. Of course, in specific industrial or scientific environments, specialized laboratories or research facilities may coexist as part of a bigger innovation program that connects them with the rest of the organization. With the right leadership and orchestration, this model encourages diverse perspectives, empowers the innovation culture, makes innovation more inclusive, and typically accelerates implementation.
- **The federated model**: This approach is based on a network of "innovation cores" established across the organization, which operate independently while orchestrated by an overall innovation program. The power of this model lies in adopting a consistent basis—innovation language, methods, and tools—across all the cores. This way, while each core maintains its autonomy and a local agenda, the network of innovation cores can be measured and managed as a single system. The federated model requires a central innovation team that provides governance, resources, methodologies, and strategic direction that power the embedded innovation cores. It combines the centralized model's advantages of deep specialization and strategic alignment with the decentralized model's local market relevance and inclusiveness. A well-implemented federated model enables organizations to maintain solid innovation strategies while accommodating the diverse business needs of different divisions, product groups, or markets. The federated model can help better plan innovation resource allocation across the enterprise, accelerate knowledge transfer between units, and drive the adoption of innovation methods and culture. However, it requires strong leadership, well-defined decision-making frameworks, and powerful technology, allowing smart knowledge exchange, strategic alignment, and collaboration across multiple organizational boundaries. The federated model is supported by the AI-powered Innovation Portal and the hub described in Chap. 4.

1.6.4 Disruptive Innovation

Disruptive innovations, as Christensen describes, are not breakthrough technologies that improve existing products. Instead, they are innovations that make products and services more affordable, accessible, and thus available to a larger population.[7] The disruption happens when a product or service enters the bottom of a market as an inexpensive and more accessible option, then moves fast, gains market share, and eventually displaces established competitors.[8] Disruptive innovations are usually driven not by established, successful companies but by outsiders such as start-ups. In this theory, market leaders do not respond to disruptive innovations when they first arise because they are not profitable enough and because their development can take scarce resources away from sustaining innovations.

1.6.5 Open Innovation

In our increasingly connected world, knowledge and ideas flow more freely than ever before. Digital networks have expanded access to information about the world's big challenges, enabling diverse communities to partner and engage in solving shared problems.

While the traditional approach to innovation emphasizes protection and competition, Open Innovation favors strategic sharing and collaboration, enabling organizations to connect and selectively exchange knowledge, form partnerships, and accelerate innovation processes in ways that create mutual benefits. Open innovation represents an evolution in how companies leverage both internal and external knowledge within their innovation processes. Formally defined as "a distributed innovation process based on purposively managed knowledge flows across organizational boundaries" (Chesbrough and Bogers 2014), this approach allows organizations to participate in an expanding ecosystem of knowledge creation.

This broader view recognizes that, for many organizations, innovating in isolation can be challenging and resource intensive without leveraging external resources. In addition to traditional practices, open innovation proposes the formation of ecosystems of companies, user communities, and research centers that selectively share and discover ideas. Companies may crowdsource problems, e.g., by asking partners, customers, or the public for solutions—a process which often produces valuable insights. Moreover, many large companies maintain patent portfolios, with a significant percentage remaining unutilized. In the Open Innovation model, these non-commercialized inventions could benefit ecosystem partners through sharing, licensing, or commercial agreements. However, effective ecosystem engagement requires a strategic approach to evaluate external inventions while carefully managing disclosure to protect competitive advantages.

---

[7] https://www.christenseninstitute.org/disruptive-innovations/

[8] https://en.wikipedia.org/wiki/Disruptive_innovation

Beyond knowledge exchange, Open Innovation 2.0[9] proposes collaborative approaches that aim to "drive structural changes far beyond the scope of what any organization could achieve alone" and emphasizes multidisciplinary ecosystems that bring diverse actors together. It replaces traditional silos with collaborative networks designed to maximize societal impact through shared vision and value creation. For instance, the Quadruple Helix[10] model engages industry, government, academia, and citizens as co-creators rather than passive participants, enabling innovations that extend beyond organizational boundaries. The model emphasizes the shift from producer-centric to user-centric innovation, placing end-users at the heart of the process from inception to implementation.

1.6.6 Social Innovation

We may also differentiate innovation based on its ultimate goal. For example, in contrast to business innovation, which focuses on driving success in terms of profits and market share, social innovation prioritizes impact and value at the societal level—it aims to introduce improvements in working models, education, access to health services, and community development. It may be driven by non-profits, activists, volunteers, or self-organizing communities.

The right approach to innovation—in terms of style, type, and pace—should be dictated by the company's strategy. It is the long-term goals, growth plans, and innovation agenda that collectively point to the appropriate balance between different types of innovation and models. For example, an organization's strategy can be translated into a roadmap that tackles named problems through different types of innovation, that run in parallel, with varying lifecycles: a company may be investing in radical innovation initiatives while accelerating its incremental innovation capacity to protect its market share and keep current product offerings competitive and profitable. By adopting a portfolio approach, companies can combine different innovation types and styles, addressing varying needs and business objectives.

Selecting the right mix of styles, pace, and intensity of innovation is one of the primary and most important responsibilities of the Innovation Executive, as described in Chap. 3.

---

[9] https://ec.europa.eu/futurium/en/system/files/ged/24-oispgopeninnovation20anewparadigm-whitepaper.pdf

[10] https://en.wikipedia.org/wiki/Triple_helix_model_of_innovation#Quadruple_helix_model

The Innovative Organization

2

Nearly every company on the planet claims to be innovative. It's hard to find a company profile or a pitch deck without bold innovation statements. In reality, though, only a tiny fraction of them are *truly innovative*—able to *consistently explore opportunities* and *deliver innovation to the market*. What distinguishes these companies is that they master both *discovery* and *execution*: they excel not only at *spotting valuable opportunities* through systematic ideation, assessment, and market validation but also at *realizing them* through fast, agile implementation, smart go-to-market strategies, and rapid in-market experimentation that drives adoption and growth. Some organizations are proficient at one or the other, but truly innovative companies bridge the two, creating a streamlined "system" that takes high-potential opportunities to market fast.

While conventional companies optimize for ambitious short-term financial targets, innovative companies aim for long-term success through systematic innovation: they remain highly *adaptable*, constantly exploring new opportunities rather than settling and relying on their dominant market positions. They maintain their edge through what we might call a "reflex advantage"—the ability to sense opportunities and respond rapidly. The key to this adaptive nature lies in having a strong connection with the market and the rapidly changing technological landscape; innovative companies are highly effective in capturing signals and identifying emerging patterns. This market intelligence feeds their innovation engines and inspires ideation and opportunity discovery. Doing this in a systematic way, e.g., by integrating artificial intelligence into various roles in this process, as discussed in Chap. 6, allows the company to maintain *a portfolio of opportunities* and benefit from its ability to validate them quickly and make the right decisions. Innovative companies evolve while in a loop of experimentation, learning, and improvement—a continuous process that leads to better results for customers, shareholders, the environment, and society.

G. Krasadakis, *Innovation Mode 2.0*,
https://doi.org/10.1007/978-3-032-00835-0_2

At the cultural level, innovative companies adopt a "new" way of working, emphasizing sharing, collaboration, and experimentation mindsets. People across levels challenge the established, cooperate, and contribute by sharing ideas and problems worth solving, testing their assumptions, and raising tough questions. These behaviors come naturally, as people believe in the purpose of the company and its vision and trust that innovation is appreciated by the leadership and used in "real-world" scenarios. In such environments, innovators know how to handle uncertainty and failure and can effectively balance big thinking and business reality as needed.

At the leadership level, executives demonstrate their support by accepting failure as part of the innovation process and acknowledging the value of continuous improvement through experimentation. They realize that the organization must systematically evaluate opportunities for better products, business models, or even new markets. This ongoing pursuit of opportunities is assisted by artificial intelligence, which helps establish a "nervous system" that senses emerging patterns and reacts by triggering the Opportunity Discovery process.

Designing a truly innovative company is challenging as it takes time and requires determination to drive significant *cultural*, *structural*, and *technological* change. True innovation goes beyond isolated programs, technology labs, hackathons, fancy collaboration spaces, and bold innovation titles. While all these are very important when considered in the right context, *operating in the Innovation Mode* refers to much more than that: a drastically different approach to running a business. Getting to the Innovation Mode requires both intelligent design and evolution: innovation is initially architected into the company's organizational design and its "operating system," but it then evolves naturally through fast adaptation and learning loops. The organization becomes smarter and more agile in every iteration as technology improves and the innovation culture grows across levels, departments, teams, and disciplines. The hierarchy eventually flattens—groups and divisions become less rigid and hierarchical, and the company performs as a single innovation engine.

When this transition is achieved, the need for special programs and ad hoc innovation initiatives gradually fades away: the innovation program blends with other business activities and becomes an integral part of the organization's foundation. Innovation endeavors get embedded in daily routines, in the standard ways of collaboration, decision-making, and product development. In this mode, the organization performs better, not only in terms of innovation but in every dimension, as a whole. People and teams communicate and collaborate more effectively by leveraging the embedded methods, accumulated knowledge, and the spirit of innovation to better serve the bold organizational purpose. When operating in this mode, innovation happens organically.

A company can be analyzed in terms of its *innovation maturity*, which reveals both its *ability to innovate* and its *attitude toward innovation*—for instance, whether it *produces* or *adopts* innovation. Some companies excel at inventing, discovering, and validating opportunities but don't have an "engine" for building and launching solutions or driving adoption. Others demonstrate a remarkable ability in building, launching, and iterating quickly with live experimentation toward product-market fit but have limited ability or interest in inventing or pursuing novel, disruptive opportunities. There are companies that follow a different approach and style to innovation. Instead of producing innovation in the form of technological inventions and novel-to-the-world concepts, they enhance their products and services by adopting cutting-edge technologies from the broader ecosystem. A company's ability to innovate can be framed using the Innovation Maturity Index—a topic we'll explore in depth in the following sections.

2.1 The Outlook of an Innovative Organization

Modern innovative organizations follow specific patterns and use special structures, methodologies, and innovation programs—these will all be covered throughout the rest of the book. But before we go deeper into the architecture of the innovative organization, let's examine the outlook of a typical innovative company—how they externalize their willingness to innovate and inspire people to engage with their innovation functions. Here is what some of the most innovative companies do differently:

1. **They have a bold, inspiring purpose**: Purpose-driven innovation organizations understand that meaningful work is a powerful motivator. Therefore, they consistently communicate their bold purpose. Their leaders become advocates for innovation—they live the purpose and lead by example by delivering authentic messages that demonstrate how innovation helps the organization achieve its goals.
2. **They empower curiosity**: Innovative companies value curiosity in every aspect of their business. They encourage people to ask the right questions and inspire them to challenge the status quo. Leaders demonstrate this principle by asking probing questions, admitting knowledge gaps, welcoming tough questions, and showing genuine interest in diverse perspectives.
3. **They invest in learning programs**: Innovative organizations realize that innovation requires both depth of expertise and breadth of knowledge. In this context, they invest in continual training of various forms—from regular, informal training sessions led by employees to formal educational programs led by internal or external experts. Some companies set formal learning goals and incorporate learning achievements in their employee performance evaluation schemes. Considering the pace of technology and the disruption caused by artificial intelligence, such learning initiatives are more important than ever.
4. **They acknowledge innovative behaviors**: Innovative companies acknowledge not only "winning" ideas but also certain behaviors that directly or indirectly link to innovation. Beyond success stories, they celebrate remarkable innovation efforts even when they don't bring the expected results. This approach enhances the culture and increases the visibility of innovation activities and achievements while also welcoming lessons learned from failures. This way, people engage more and contribute to innovation in various ways, eventually

getting rewarded, building their reputations as innovators, and advancing their careers.

5. **They maintain flat hierarchies**: Complex hierarchies slow down innovation and occasionally lead to silos, thus blocking the flow of knowledge. Innovative companies find ways to add flexibility to their structures, e.g., they encourage people to "skip levels" and connect with the right stakeholders. Flattened structures reduce the distance from leadership and promote collaboration across team boundaries.
6. **They provide resources**: Innovative companies ensure that people have the necessary resources to engage with innovation, including time to experiment, digital tools, equipment, and, occasionally, funding—*all* provided through fast, lean processes. They use effective funding and resource allocation mechanisms that balance strategy, planning, and just-in-time exploration of opportunities.
7. **They provide innovation-optimized office space**: Although the work model has undergone dramatic changes since the pandemic, innovative companies continue to maintain iconic innovation spaces designed for collaboration, prototyping, and innovation workshops. A highly collaborative office space can be valuable even in a remote setting, as it provides a good reason for distributed teams to come together and engage in hands-on, creative activities. A notable example in this direction is the Makerspace—a specialized office space that provides the means for both physical and digital prototyping—presented in detail in Chap. 6.
8. **They demonstrate their appetite for new ideas**: Forward-thinking organizations run ongoing programs that welcome problems and ideas and act upon them. They provide meaningful, actionable feedback to innovators, reward them for their contributions, and remain open to considering high-potential opportunities. These organizations leverage robust innovation management systems that extend far beyond "suggestion boxes" or "innovation campaigns."
9. **They provide an innovation sandbox**: Innovative organizations encourage people to engage with *special innovation projects* that address significant problems in innovative ways or by utilizing new technologies. These projects often operate with different rules, funding models, and expectations than standard business activities, creating a space where teams can experiment with new approaches, technologies, or applications.
10. **They make informed decisions fast**: Innovative companies address uncertainty and ambiguity by leveraging data along with robust decision-making frameworks that balance rigor and speed. They classify risks and, when necessary, utilize flexible approval processes to make decisions and move forward with speed while capturing their decisions and rationale for transparency and learning. These approaches prevent "analysis paralysis" while ensuring that important innovation investments receive just enough scrutiny.
11. **They celebrate failure as a source of learning**: They demonstrate in practice how to embrace *failure* by adopting a *portfolio approach* that balances risks and value; they apply the "fail-safe, fail fast" principle, and they regularly share both success and failure stories. Their approach acknowledges that innovation

comes with inherent risks and uncertainty; thus, it requires experimentation, which inevitably leads to some unfavorable outcomes. By framing failure as a learning opportunity, they develop inspiring innovation narratives that celebrate ambitious innovators and their bold experiments regardless of their outcomes. Through this approach, innovative companies create strong examples of what real innovation looks like.

12. **They encourage experimentation**: Innovative organizations promote the experimental approach and a risk-friendly profile by sharing business experimentation activities and inviting people to contribute. This way, people learn about specific experiments and their impact and, at the same time, understand the value of experimentation in the innovation process.
13. **They foster cross-functional collaboration**: Breakthrough innovations often emerge at the intersection of different disciplines and perspectives. Innovative organizations deliberately create structures and processes that bring diverse expertise together to solve pressing problems or frame big opportunities. They maintain physical workspaces, such as the Makerspace, along with digital platforms for knowledge exchange, supported by organizational routines that facilitate serendipitous networking and collaboration opportunities across functional boundaries.
14. **They connect to innovation ecosystems**: Rather than trying to innovate entirely from within, forward-thinking organizations build extensive networks with external partners, including start-ups, academic institutions, or customers. These innovation ecosystems allow them to access specialized capabilities, gain early insights into emerging technologies, and share development risks.

2.1.1 A Day Inside: How a Truly Innovative Company Operates

The previous section covered the high-level behaviors and attributes of truly innovative companies. But how do they work differently in practice? What happens during a typical day inside a modern, innovative company?

The short answer is business as usual. However, in these organizations, both "business" and "usual" take on entirely different meanings: having fully embedded innovation into their core operating model and mindset, innovative companies do business not only by running operations, developing products, and serving customers but also by continuously seeking, validating, and pursuing opportunities.

A glimpse into a genuinely innovative company unveils a fascinating synthesis of interconnected activities—a blend of operational, tactical, strategic, and innovation activities that are interlinked, balanced, and well aligned with the company's organizational purpose, vision, and mission.

Routine meetings, such as morning stand-ups or status updates, are naturally enriched with market intelligence and fresh, relevant ideas. Regular operational or implementation agendas on planning, progress, blockers, delayed deliverables, user feedback, or even customer support and operations are linked to innovation and occasionally feed into the process: people know that even routine chats or intense discussions and even debates can spark new ideas or frame problems that can be fed into the opportunity discovery platform and become instantly discoverable by others in the company.

Smart summaries of relevant business news and competitive insights flow naturally through corporate communication channels, keeping everyone informed about the shifting landscape of markets, competitors, and customers. People have clarity on how the company, its products, and services perform: business performance is precisely defined, measured, and shared via real-time dashboards available in the office space or through the Innovation Portal (covered in Chap. 4). Information about the company's overall performance is also highly accessible via real-time business scorecards. This way, people can easily obtain a holistic view of the company's performance while examining its specific facets, such as financial, product, innovation, reputation, and more.

Continuing our journey, the company's purpose and vision are clearly communicated across channels, together with its innovation agenda: people are aware of the important problems that need to be solved through innovation and the metrics that reflect success. The Innovation Portal presents "what the organization is innovating on," while unified dashboards showcase the business experimentation pipeline: progress, key learnings, and breakthrough moments that inform product development decisions and inspire further innovation activities. This transparency regarding the company's performance and innovation strategy leads to enterprise-wide clarity and alignment on the company's current state, goals, and key priorities across innovation horizons.

Between typical business activities, where employees manage their regular workload of emails, status reports, and administrative tasks, they also engage in lightweight innovation experiences, such as submitting just-in-time ideas for business experiments to improve a product. Distributed teams use the Innovation Portal as the home of innovation: remote and on-premises employees across all levels of the organization discover recent achievements, share ideas, explore opportunities, and volunteer for collaboration. At the same time, in between routine planning and review meetings, a cross-functional team prototypes a new concept, while a distributed team pitches their idea to stakeholders. Meanwhile, product teams operate their live products with innovation and growth in mind—they test their hypotheses and use in-product feature experimentation to learn and make informed decisions. In the leadership suite, between budget meetings and strategic planning sessions, executives interpret market intelligence signals, review high-potential opportunities, and ensure that the opportunity portfolio and the innovation agenda are up to date and relevant.

What's remarkable about this fictional yet realistic scenario is how these innovation activities blend naturally with everyday business operations: innovation is not a distinct process and does not happen as part of a special program or workshop; it happens naturally. The true differentiator is the vivid innovation culture, a collective mindset that transforms even the most routine moments into catalysts for creative thinking.

The general pattern for corporate innovation is clear, and the associated methods are well understood; the technology is available, and AI accelerates and simplifies the innovation process. This raises interesting questions such as: "How is it possible that so many companies still fail to innovate?" "Why employees don't engage with innovation?" and "Why are there companies that do not invest in innovation?" The following section delves deeper into the most important innovation failure factors I've identified across industries, markets, and innovation setups—organized into a simple model of six *deficits*.

2.2 Why Corporate Innovation Fails

The conditions to innovate look "ideal": modern methodologies and advanced collaboration systems are widely available; access to knowledge is easier than ever; there is a wealth of data, insights, software components, platforms, AI services, and frameworks that can be reused to build systems, products, or platforms fast. Although there appear to be optimal conditions for innovation, promising programs often fail to deliver satisfactory results. A survey by BCG[1] shows that only 30% of innovation executives said that their organizations were good at innovation, while a PwC Innovation Benchmark[2] found that "54% of innovating companies struggle to bridge the gap between innovation strategy and business strategy."

Corporate fragmentation is frequently mentioned in the literature as a significant factor contributing to innovation failure.[3] Many notable failures have been attributed to the lack of an innovation culture and non-optimal organizational structures. One of the most interesting cases is the downfall of Nokia: from being the world leader in the mobile phone market and, objectively, an innovative company, it declined from a 48.7% market share to 2.8% in just 6 years.[4] In a qualitative study (Vuori and Huy 2015), interviewing various Nokia top and middle managers and engineers, they describe a situation of "organizational fear" framed by "temperamental leaders" and "frightened middle managers" who were "scared of telling the truth."[5] This led to "temporal myopia—a focus on short-term product innovation at the expense of long-term innovation development." The company's research efforts appeared to be disconnected from its commercial front, leading to missed opportunities and, ultimately, poor decisions. Other reports identify *complacency* as a failure factor.[6] Although such situations are complex, with several factors at play, it is clear that the culture of fear and corporate fragmentation plays a significant role: it blocks information flows, discourages innovative behaviors, and slows down decision-making.

The following sections present a range of failure factors, organized into specific *deficits*, explaining how poor leadership, organizational design issues, or gaps in talent, capabilities, and market connection can fail corporate innovation.

[1] https://www.bcg.com/publications/2019/overcoming-four-big-barriers-to-innovation-success

[2] https://www.pwc.com/gr/en/publications/assets/innovation-benchmark-report.pdf

[3] https://hbr.org/2019/05/cross-silo-leadership

[4] https://statista.com/statistics/263438/market-share-held-by-nokia-smartphones-since-2007/

[5] https://knowledge.insead.edu/strategy/who-killed-nokia-nokia-did

[6] https://www.bbc.com/news/technology-23947212

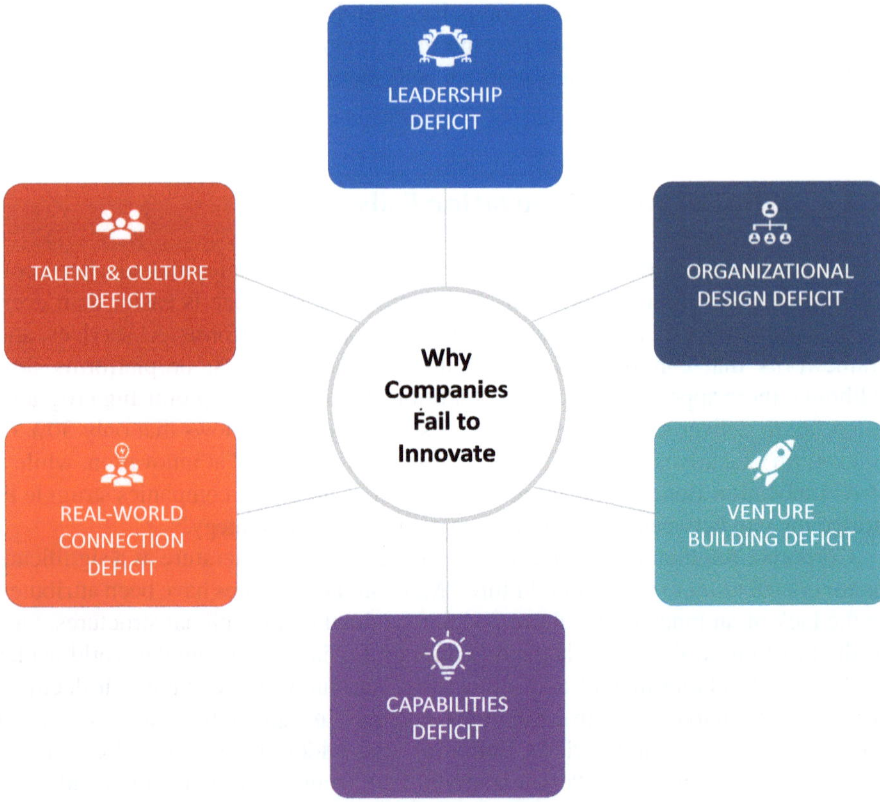

Fig. 2.1 A model explaining corporate innovation failure via six deficits

Figure 2.1 presents a grouping of various factors or patterns that contribute to innovation failure in a corporate setting. The grouping uses six classes of deficits, the primary one pointing to poor leadership.

2.2.1 Leadership Deficit: When Leaders Fail Innovation

While innovation success often results from collaborative efforts across an organization, corporate innovation failure always reflects leadership's limitations or poor decisions.

Senior leaders may fail innovation in several distinct ways: some don't engage with innovation due to complacency; others are willing to drive innovation but lack expertise in innovation leadership, making critical mistakes or omissions; and some have the willingness and knowledge but lack the necessary means or support from the C-suite. In all such cases, companies suffer from innovation blind spots, especially at the executive level. Even those leaders who genuinely believe in innovation and advocate for change may struggle to drive meaningful innovation if they don't have the C-suite's support and lack essential capabilities and resources. When this happens, innovators experience "empty" innovation promises, a lack of action, and no measurable outcomes. The following provides common leadership failure patterns or poor practices that impact or block innovation:

- **When leaders don't see the need to innovate**: This is also known as *complacency*—an innovation failure pattern in which leadership rests on past successes and becomes overconfident based on the illusion of invincibility. This typically occurs when established companies hold a stable or dominant market position: their leadership develops a false sense of security and a rigid narrative that dismisses competition and overlooks emerging trends. Thus, instead of exploring new opportunities for innovation, they focus solely on growing the company via established paths and business models. In this context, start-ups that might be entering the same market are seen as insignificant.
- **When leaders avoid risk**: Risk aversion, especially at the leadership level, creates major barriers to meaningful innovation. Business leaders often favor predictability and short-term success and view innovation as a risky luxury or a threat to disrupting operational efficiencies and progress toward their goals. Similarly, executives are afraid that innovation may cannibalize profitable products and services. This mindset is inherently unsupportive of innovation, as management incentives prioritize short-term financial performance over innovation. In this context, the dominant culture is incompatible with the experimentation method and the concept of *failure*. When the C-suite does not acknowledge failure as part of the innovation process, leaders tend to avoid decisions that might threaten their career progression. Similarly, employees tend to avoid taking risks that could be perceived as unnecessary. Such risk-averse attitudes and short-term leadership focus create a significant barrier to true innovation. In leadership teams with mixed-risk appetites, those who favor the status quo are typically the ones who dominate, establishing a culture that eventually suppresses innovation.
- **When leaders face first-mover anxiety**: Many organizations choose the fast-follower approach over launching new-to-the-world innovations. While it could be part of the strategy to wait for competitors to validate opportunities before committing resources, this unwillingness to enter the market first often originates from leadership's risk aversion. The latter occurs when leaders overestimate the risks of early market entry compared to the first-mover advantages. Leadership emphasizes potential failures over the opportunity cost of a delayed entrance.
- **When leaders are indecisive**: Lack of ability to handle the inherent uncertainty of innovation projects is an instant blocker for innovation. Leaders often don't have the skills or organizational support to make decisions under uncertainty, especially when "perfect information" is not available. Typical signs include requests for excessive analysis cycles before committing to innovation projects or a consensus approach in decision-making. These result in bureaucratic processes that slow down innovation and kill its momentum.
- **When leaders don't actively support innovation teams**: Senior leaders often fail to provide sufficient support or "protection" for innovation teams pursuing

projects that may be perceived as overambitious or futuristic. A lack of top-level backing and a poor framework for measuring innovation success exposes innovation teams to organizational resistance or *criticism*. The origin of the problem lies in false perspectives on innovation success: companies often use unsuitable metrics for tracking innovation performance, which triggers skepticism and criticism regarding the value of the program. Without meaningful executive support, innovation is eventually perceived as a side activity rather than a core capability essential to the company's future.

- **When leaders overrely on existing customers**: Business leaders who are overly focused on satisfying their existing high-value customers tend to develop blind spots and become risk averse. By prioritizing the needs of their most profitable clients and market segments, leaders may overlook opportunities and gradually develop a bias toward incremental product improvements rather than new products, services, or potentially disruptive innovations. While maintaining existing customer relationships is essential, allowing these established customers to determine the innovation agenda constrains the company's innovation and growth potential.
- **When leaders fail to understand the competition**: Many established companies fail to assess their competitive landscape accurately. Leaders often define their competition narrowly, dismissing emerging start-ups while failing to anticipate threats originating from other industries or emerging technologies. But even when new, emerging competitors are being tracked by the company, leaders often dismiss them based on their size, failing to acknowledge their dynamic and superior ability to innovate. This partial competitive view puts innovation at risk since resources and efforts are not applied in the right direction.
- **When leaders fail to connect innovation with the company's goals**: Leaders often prioritize highly visible innovation programs and events, such as fancy labs or workshops like Hackathons or Design Sprints. However, when done out of context, such events may only generate short-term results, e.g., ephemeral attention and superficial cultural improvements. Similarly, setting up expensive labs or a makerspace featuring fancy gadgets, devices, and tools may be impressive at first sight and add some value, but unless they are strategically positioned, they cannot move the needle toward a more innovative version of the company. When there is a lack of continuity and substance—e.g., the company fails to discover and pursue opportunities—such innovation programs inevitably collapse as employees recognize the lack of significance and disengage. Ironically, these surface-level initiatives can even damage the innovation culture since they may be perceived as "Innovation Theater."
- **When leaders fail to establish a continuous innovation process**: Insufficient leadership and orchestration of innovation typically result to "disconnected" efforts, with teams working and innovating in isolation, leading to inefficiencies, costly overlaps, and missed opportunities. According to a survey by McKinsey,[7] about one-third of leaders deal with innovation on "an ad hoc basis." This discon-

[7] https://www.mckinsey.com/capabilities/strategy-and-corporate-finance/our-insights/leadership-and-innovation

tinuous approach can only bring limited effects on the innovation outlook of the corporation.

- **When leaders measure the wrong things**: The absence of a robust innovation measurement framework is often a point of failure for corporate innovation. When an organization lacks clear definitions, innovation measurement becomes extremely difficult. Many organizations evaluate long-term innovation using short-term KPIs, while others rely on vanity metrics of innovation activity, such as the number of ideas generated, patents filed, and workshops conducted. Additionally, it is challenging for companies to quantify the indirect value of innovation, such as its cultural impact and organizational learning. Moreover, leaders frequently neglect to adopt a portfolio view when measuring innovation value—they don't acknowledge that some innovation projects will inevitably fail. Thus, they think in terms of *individual failures* instead of the *portfolio's long-term collective value*. In other cases, they don't recognize that traditional return-on-investment metrics are inadequate for measuring outcomes in the early stages of innovation. Applying financial metrics in the early stages of innovation projects not only misrepresents an opportunity's potential but also undermines the team's morale and the project's momentum.[8] Chapter 9 presents a thorough framework for measuring innovation holistically.
- **When leaders focus on short-term results over long-term innovation**: Executive teams are often trapped in cycles of quarterly performance pressure that fundamentally misalign with innovation's longer-term nature. This misalignment between innovation's lifecycle and corporate performance reporting is probably the most persistent barrier to corporate innovation.

This leadership deficit in driving corporate innovation often originates from a limited understanding of modern innovation architectures, methodologies, and leadership practices. Traditionally, executives are skilled in operational excellence and financial management but frequently lack the specialized knowledge needed to navigate today's complex innovation landscape. They may not fully understand how to design innovative organizations, build innovation ecosystems, implement experimentation strategies, or foster an innovation culture. This gap in innovation leadership presents a compelling case for the chief innovation officer (CINO) role or other leadership positions, such as VP or head of innovation. The importance of these roles and their responsibilities is explained in Chap. 3, "People and Culture."

2.2.2 Organizational Design Deficit

The structure of a company significantly influences its ability to innovate systematically, at scale, and speed. A good organizational design for innovation includes specialized teams dedicated to supporting specific aspects of the innovation function,

[8] https://www2.deloitte.com/us/en/insights/topics/innovation/corporate-innovation-program-report-and-key-takeaways.html

along with processes that encourage cross-team collaboration and effective knowledge exchange. The organizational design deficit occurs when the necessary elements are missing from the company structure or, worse, when existing features actively block innovation. Organizational design issues include fragmentation, excessive hierarchical layers, vague accountability models, and poor knowledge transfer mechanisms.

- **Fragmented organization**: Organizational fragmentation occurs when a company allows rigid structural boundaries that isolate departments, business units, or functional areas from one another. This fragmentation reduces communication, knowledge exchange, and cross-functional collaboration, thus undermining innovation performance. For instance, when R&D teams operate without a strong connection to product development and customer-facing departments, they may miss critical market insights that could inform important research or other decisions. This disconnect typically evolves when organizations grow without adopting frameworks that synchronize divisions through meaningful interactions, strategic alignment, and systematic knowledge-sharing activities. The phenomenon is often seen in larger enterprises with diverse, relatively autonomous product lines.
- **Overcomplicated hierarchy**: Hierarchical structures with numerous management layers create bottlenecks for collaboration, knowledge exchange, information sharing, and innovation efforts. When ideas and proposals must navigate multiple approval stages across different levels, momentum can be lost, and opportunities can be abandoned. Such environments prioritize established processes over agility and speed while concentrating decision-making authority at upper management levels. As a result, innovators feel disconnected and discouraged from engaging with the organization's innovation function. For instance, innovators often struggle to navigate organizational complexity and find the appropriate decision-makers to pitch their ideas. Or they cannot easily find teams or domain experts within the company to further explore their ideas and collaborate. In such environments, it is not easy to answer questions like "Who else is working on this?" or "What is the organization innovating on?"
- **Limited knowledge exchange**: Complex or poor organizational design often fails to incorporate channels and systems that enable and encourage knowledge sharing. Without structured pathways that allow insights and ideas to flow horizontally across functional boundaries, information remains in departmental silos—either inaccessible or undiscoverable by other teams. Organizations that fail to incorporate knowledge-sharing mechanisms into their organizational structure struggle to leverage collective intelligence and suffer from duplicated efforts and significant opportunity costs. This is both a cause and a symptom of the "fragmented organization": the absence of a framework for knowledge exchange reinforces the isolation of teams and divisions.
- **Ambiguous innovation leadership model**: Beyond individual projects, the lack of clarity on "who owns innovation" can severely impact corporate innovation

performance. When roles and responsibilities for functions such as opportunity discovery and execution, portfolio management, and orchestration overlap or don't have clear boundaries, people face increased ambiguity and communication challenges that can lead to accountability gaps.

- **Centralization vs. decentralization indecisiveness**: Organizations often struggle to design an optimal innovation model that works best for their environment. Debates on the topic are common in corporate environments, for example, regarding the centralization of the innovation function. When leadership is indecisive in this direction, there is a risk of confusion about who owns innovation and how it should function, leading to inefficiencies and, eventually, innovation blockers.
- **Perception of innovation isolation**: Regardless of their form, dedicated innovation teams—such as labs, incubators, and R&D departments—are often perceived as inaccessible and occasionally as *innovation silos* that are disconnected from organizational reality. Moreover, such teams that focus on *producing innovation* may be seen by the rest of the company as special or privileged. This perspective discourages collaboration and may lead not only to *perceived* but also to *real isolation* between the innovation teams and the rest of the company, thus negatively impacting the organization's innovation performance.

2.2.3 Innovation Capabilities Deficit

Even when a company is determined to innovate, it may be blocked by the lack of essential capabilities, processes, and systems required to drive innovation outcomes. Moreover, legacy technical infrastructure often prevents the adoption of modern product innovation practices, for example, when companies struggle to adopt patterns of frequent releases and in-product experimentation. When a strong innovation culture is present, but the technology and systems to enable innovation at scale are not, business leaders may experience occasional enthusiasm followed by frustration. Teams face execution difficulties related to the lack of tools, techniques, and systems, preventing innovators from delivering on their innovation objectives. More specifically, the most critical capability-related blockers of corporate innovation are:

- **Lack of a defined innovation function**: The corporate innovation process can become complex if not properly architected, managed, and orchestrated. Often, companies lack a defined, documented innovation function with clear goals and objectives, a robust leadership model, established funding mechanisms, and operating frameworks. Sometimes, business leaders invest in specific capabilities, such as a system to provide market intelligence, a platform to manage ideas, or technology for product experimentation. However, they often lack other essential ingredients or the orchestration layer that synchronizes all these components into a single innovation system. Such gaps or poorly designed processes can severely impact the corporate innovation function.

- **Legacy technology constraints**: Technical debt and outdated systems frequently slow down or even block innovation initiatives. For example, obsolete architectures, infrastructure, fragile interdependencies, and expensive-to-maintain systems consume significant resources and don't allow for bandwidth or technical flexibility for innovation: rigid product platforms, the inability to deploy product improvements fast, and the limited capability to establish effective customer feedback loops, along with data silos preventing a unified view of the business, severely restrict the organization's ability to innovate.
- **Resource allocation and funding challenges**: The way organizations fund projects and initiatives can be a major blocker of innovation. In contrast to traditional projects that follow predictable resource needs, innovation requires elastic budgets that can adapt as teams learn and pivot fast. Funding needs can appear unexpectedly in the innovation context, for example, when there is strong real-world evidence supporting the potential of an opportunity and the company decides to move it further for implementation. In practice, though, most corporate funding mechanisms are rigid, with annual budget cycles, inflexible allocations, and lengthy approval processes that cannot respond promptly to innovation needs. When innovation teams wait weeks or months for resource decisions, they lose critical momentum and market timing advantage. This misalignment between innovation's inherent uncertainty and traditional resource allocation approaches significantly limits the companies' ability to accelerate innovation and capitalize on those high-potential opportunities.

2.2.4 Real-World Connection Deficit

The real-world connection deficit occurs when a company lacks the means and practices to stay closely connected with its ecosystem—its customers, market, and technology landscape. This deficit appears as an inability to systematically scan the market, engage with customers, process user feedback, conduct business experimentation, and generally "listen" to the world outside corporate walls. Without these critical connections to reality, even well-resourced innovation efforts can fail. Common instances of this deficit include:

- **Poor customer understanding**: Innovation is often blocked by organizational blind spots and limited understanding of the customer. When companies fail to maintain a clear, unified view of customer needs, pain points, and user journeys, innovation efforts may end up solving the wrong problem or missing essential opportunities. Poor alignment or gaps in customer understanding are particularly prevalent in multi-product organizations, which often end up maintaining different views of the customer and disconnected user journeys. In such cases, where companies have a limited understanding of their customers, there is a risk that innovation teams deliver solutions that, while sophisticated and novel, fail to address real-world problems and provide customer value. This is particularly relevant when a technology function leads the innovation agenda.

- **Poor market and competition understanding**: When the leadership team has a limited view of the market and its dynamics, it may be challenging to set the innovation focus properly. Similarly, a constraint or inaccurate understanding of the competitive landscape and the broader ecosystem can lead to misalignment and ineffective innovation strategies. Without a comprehensive understanding of the market, innovation teams operate in a bubble, allowing outdated assumptions to influence the focus of their innovation efforts. In this context, even high-potential innovations can fail since teams may not fully understand how their offering fits within the broader ecosystem. Without robust market intelligence capabilities, organizations often discover market realities only after significant resources have been invested, leading to costly pivots or abandoned projects that could have been avoided through timely market insights.

2.2.5 Talent and Cultural Deficit

Corporate innovation requires specialized skills that differ significantly from traditional business functions. However, companies often fail to recognize that innovation expertise doesn't simply exist or develop naturally and that it requires strategic talent development, upskilling, external recruitment, and planning. When this happens, companies face gaps in innovation competencies, such as product design, rapid prototyping, product innovation, user research, and business experimentation.

This talent deficit is closely linked to cultural challenges—the shared values, mindset, and behaviors that enable innovation to grow organically. Organizations often struggle on both fronts: they lack certain specialized skills and the cultural foundation for innovation to thrive. These deficits appear in various forms and at different levels in the organization's hierarchy, as explained below.

- **Gaps in innovation leadership talent**: At the leadership level, companies need senior professionals who possess skills in innovation architecture, innovation program management, and product leadership, such as a VP of innovation or a chief innovation officer. When this expertise is missing, companies fail to effectively architect, operate, and orchestrate the innovation function of the organization, leading to structural problems that reduce the ability of the company to innovate.
- **Gaps in innovation management talent**: Innovation management requires competencies such as agile product development, product innovation, experimentation frameworks, lean approaches, venture building, creative processes, etc. When the middle management layer of the company lacks such expertise, innovation projects and initiatives often end up being managed by typical managers who not only lack the right skills but also possess a very different, operationally focused mindset. This puts innovation efforts at risk, as managers with this mindset rarely embrace innovation and tend to view it as a potential disrup-

tor of teams, timelines, and deliverables. This mismatch creates conflicts at both cultural and practical levels.

- **Gaps in innovation execution talent**: At the team level, where innovation actually happens, the organization requires specialized skills, such as agile development, user research, design thinking, software engineering, prototyping, and experimentation, along with skills and attitudes that welcome uncertainty, embrace change, and handle failure effectively. Gaps in such skills may result in poor innovation execution, as project teams may not be equipped to conceive, build, and execute projects quickly with a truly agile, experimental approach.
- **Limited diversity of thought**: The "collective talent" deficit is far more important than a lack of individual skills. This refers to situations where the organization fails to leverage the creative power of multidisciplinary teams due to skills gaps or a lack of experience in forming and leading the right cross-functional team for a given innovation objective. The limited diversity of thought and the absence of cross-functional perspectives limit the team's ability to conceive novel solutions and solve problems in a creative and collaborative manner.
- **Poor innovation culture**: A poor state of the innovation culture typically means that people don't trust the process or the company's commitment to innovation. They don't feel empowered to innovate, or they don't believe in the company's innovation promises—they may perceive it as "innovation theater." This cultural deficit creates a negative feedback loop: limited innovation outcomes trigger skepticism, which further reduces engagement levels in future innovation efforts. Without a strong culture, even structurally sound innovation programs face resistance from people that undermines their potential.
- **Performance reviews do not reflect innovation**: Innovation achievements and impact are rarely linked with employee performance reviews, career progression, and compensation structures. This creates a disconnect between ambitious innovation programs and employees' career objectives, failing to provide incentives for people to engage with high-uncertainty initiatives.

Attracting, developing, and retaining innovation talent establishes a solid foundation for success across the innovation cycle, from discovering opportunities to achieving market success. With strong talent supported by a vibrant innovation culture and robust capabilities, innovation programs can deliver transformative results. However, even companies with exceptional talent and a strong culture still need a powerful go-to-market capability that transforms validated opportunities into evolving, in-market products—as explained below.

2.2.6 Venture Building Deficit: Limited Ability to Execute

A company's ability to innovate depends on multiple factors, including structural barriers, funding, resource allocation, leadership support, talent, and more. However, what ultimately defines success is the ability to build, launch, and grow products or services—to reach the market, achieve commercialization, and gain customer adoption quickly. The following presents common failure patterns in this direction:

- **Lack of venture-building capability**: Many organizations lack essential innovation execution capabilities, including the ability to rapidly develop products, launch them, and drive them to product-market fit through fast improvement and experimentation cycles. When this capability is missing, great opportunities end up waiting for implementation or are outsourced to vendors or assigned to other teams with limited capacity or skill gaps. In the absence of a powerful venture-building capability, these half measures significantly decrease the likelihood of launching successful products in the market and achieving product-market fit.
- **Ambiguous innovation projects ownership**: Due to their increased uncertainty, innovation projects require strong leadership and effective decision-making skills. Very often, though, leaders fail to establish clear boundaries, accountabilities, and ownership models for innovation projects, which introduces friction and slows down decisions. Additionally, allowing multiple teams to overlap without a clear purpose can lead to communication delays, confusion, and unnecessary iterations, which can put the entire innovation project at risk. Clear, decisive ownership is essential for navigating the inherently uncertain path from concept to market success.
- **Poor handover protocols**: Organizations frequently struggle when handing over an early implementation of a product to another team for operation and further development. When *core* innovation teams develop innovative concepts without an agreed-upon handover protocol with the *receiving* product team, major disconnects can occur, for instance, misalignments and gaps regarding tech stack, product architecture, documentation, hosting environments, operational and support functions, and skills gaps. As a result, the receiving team may lack the capabilities, context, or bandwidth to carry the innovation forward. At the same time, the core team may have already moved on to new projects, putting continuity at risk. Without the early engagement of the "receiving team," structured knowledge transfer, and clear accountability, promising innovations frequently stall or fail entirely during this handover phase. This is why this phase is also known as the "valley of death" between research and development (R&D) and commercialization.

Given the numerous factors and patterns that may lead to corporate innovation failure, as well as the wide array of elements required for innovation readiness, a foundational question emerges: How can we measure a company's innovation state and maturity level? The following section introduces a model of seven levels—the Innovation Maturity Index—that helps companies assess their current position, perform a gap analysis, and discover what the next level of innovation looks like for them.

2.3 The Innovation Maturity Index: How Innovative Is Your Company?

Reflecting on the current state of innovation within your organization is essential, as it can unveil blind spots and lay the groundwork for a strategic improvement plan. The following presents the Innovation Maturity Index as a simple model that positions a company against a system of named innovation levels. This model enables leaders to assess the innovation maturity of their organizations, envision the next level, and develop a strategy for getting there (Fig. 2.2).

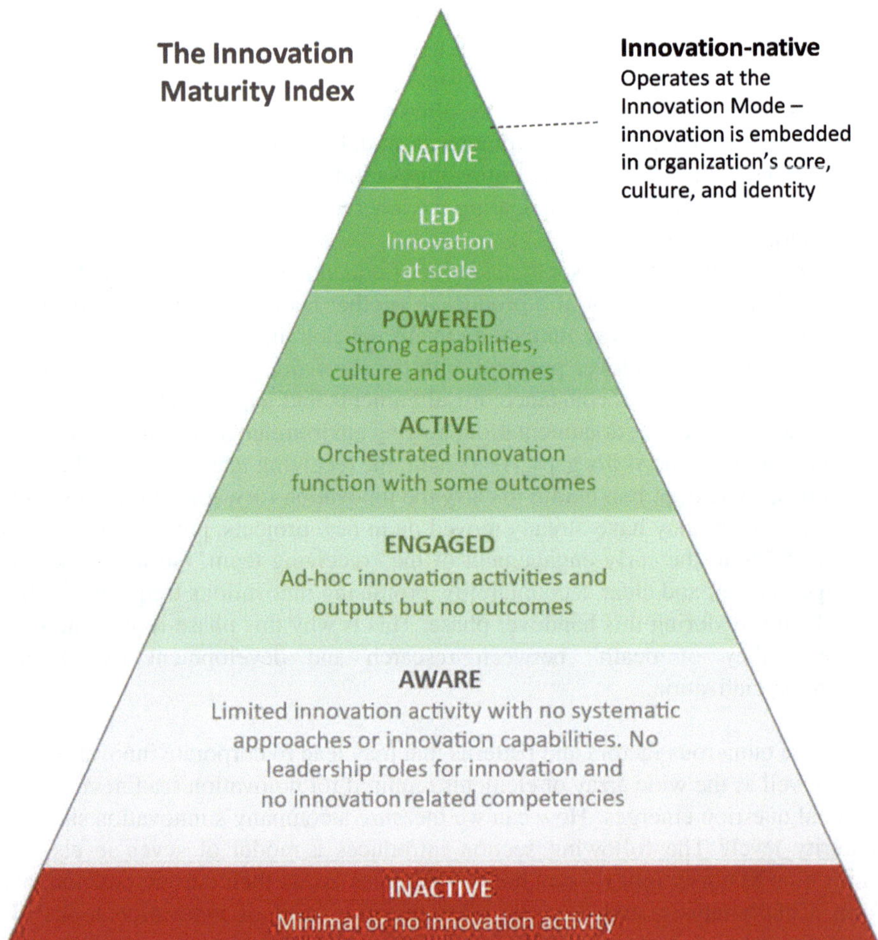

Fig. 2.2 The Innovation Maturity Index

The seven levels of innovation are defined as follows:

1. **Innovation-inactive**: A company at this level does not systematically leverage innovation methodologies, techniques, or tools, and there are no innovation-specific roles, teams, or capabilities in place. People are unaware of any substantial innovation activities happening in the organization and are not confident that innovation can drive significant value. The dominant culture is not compatible with risk taking, ambiguity, and failure, and the organization lacks the essential skills and competencies for innovation. Innovation is not part of the leadership agenda, and the company does not produce tangible innovation outputs or outcomes.
2. **Innovation-aware**: At this level, the organization is generally aware of innovation and its methods. The leadership talks about innovation, but there is no systematic use of innovation methodologies and techniques. There are no specific innovation activities except occasional isolated events or small-scale, informal initiatives organized by individuals. Innovation is not widely embraced as a means of improving outcomes and driving business impact; it is neither measured nor reported, and therefore, it is not an actionable item on the leadership agenda.
3. **Innovation-engaged**: Companies at this level engage with innovation and gradually adopt basic methods and tools. People are aware of innovation and see its potential; they participate in innovation workshops, such as brainstorming and ideation challenges. A small community of innovators is being formed and begins to drive knowledge exchange through informal events and initiatives. However, most innovation efforts are ad hoc and not part of a managed innovation function. Specialized innovation competencies are rare across the company, and there are no leadership roles to run the process. The company lacks objective innovation metrics and cannot quantify its business impact. Some innovation assets may be produced occasionally, but no concrete outcomes have been achieved yet.
4. **Innovation-active**: At this level, innovation is an integral part of the corporate agenda, and there is a strong, consistent message from leadership on its importance. The company has innovation leadership roles at the executive level but not in the C-suite. Innovation-active companies possess some of the essential innovation competencies and encourage people to contribute by sharing ideas and problems, as well as pursuing opportunities in both formal and informal ways. Innovators collaborate, pitch, or present their business concepts and join hackathons, workshops, and prototyping activities. However, there is no concrete narrative yet on how innovation drives the company's success. Innovation outputs and outcomes are limited and mainly focused on product or service improvements. While incremental innovation may be evident and valuable, it is not the primary driver of the company's success.
5. **Innovation-powered**: An organization at this level is not simply benefiting from innovation; it is powered by it. The company leverages an organized and well-

orchestrated innovation function to deliver better services and products in order to stay ahead of the competition. There is an influential innovation culture driven by an active community of innovators. People are inspired by the organization's purpose and constantly seek relevant business opportunities; they feel encouraged to experiment with new concepts and have the necessary means and resources to do so. At this level, the company measures all aspects of innovation performance to strengthen its ability to innovate through a continuous improvement program. A dedicated executive orchestrates the innovation function, empowering teams to innovate by providing advanced technology, methodologies, and strategic direction. Innovators are recognized for their contributions, and innovation stories circulate throughout the company. At this level, innovation happens in harmony with normal business activities, and the company is generally perceived as innovative. Innovation outcomes are tracked and regularly discussed at the C-suite.

6. **Innovation-led**: At this level, the organization has fully embedded the innovation process into its core business. It demonstrates an increased ability to capture market signals and react quickly by leveraging accumulated knowledge, specialized talent, and superior innovation capabilities. Innovation operates as a single system that enables rapid opportunity discovery, validation, execution and market launch. A company at this level benefits from innovation not only by making existing products better or optimizing business lines but primarily by reacting to significant opportunities for new products, new markets, and business models. Innovation is leading the organization to new business ventures.
7. **Innovation-native**: This is the ultimate level, where the company operates in the Innovation Mode. At this stage, innovation techniques, methods, and processes are fully embedded and adopted as part of the organization's operational core. Innovation is well defined in the company's context, and a fully automated measurement system feeds into the overall corporate performance scorecard. The company leverages the Innovation Graph—an AI-powered network of innovation knowledge, ideas, and opportunities. Artificial intelligence is integrated into the process, providing market intelligence, contributing ideas, validating opportunities, and helping the organization take novel products and services to market and drive adoption. While a C-level executive orchestrates the innovation function, innovation talent is embedded in every team across the organization. At this level, innovation is no longer a distinguishable program or activity of the corporation; there are no distinct innovation initiatives, as it is seamlessly integrated into the essential business processes.

Not all the above levels require advanced technologies—this depends on the organization's size, industry, and complexity. Smaller companies may be at higher levels in the Innovation Maturity Index, even if they are using basic technologies and standard productivity tools. What matters most is the purpose, the culture, the talent, and the leadership's innovation attitude. However, the larger the organization, the more advanced the technology needed to streamline and effectively orchestrate the corporate innovation function. This system of innovation levels is particularly useful for organizing a company's journey to Native (Level 7), where innovation is embedded in the organization. It helps set the goals and define the work streams required to transform a company from one innovation state to the next.

The following chapter highlights the significance of people and culture in transitioning to the Innovation Mode and addresses the deficits discussed in this chapter.

People and Culture 3

Innovation is powered by people. What brings people together is a culture of innovation—a system of *shared values* that enables them to collaborate effectively toward a common purpose. A *healthy innovation culture* is the inner force that drives the creation of novel products, services, and impactful innovations in the market. An *unhealthy culture* can be the single point of failure, even for the most well-planned, expensive innovation programs.

In a genuinely innovative company, all members are expected to innovate in one form or another. While there are numerous formal and informal innovation roles involved, as discussed throughout this chapter, we can broadly categorize innovators as *ideators*, *evaluators*, and *builders*. *Ideators* provide the big thinking—they contribute through organized ideation sessions and brainstorming events, but they also act independently by proactively framing and sharing ideas and opportunities. They are characterized by their passion for solving problems in novel ways and their openness to share, collaborate, and contribute to the company's future. *Evaluators* are skilled professionals who contribute to the *opportunity discovery* process by processing, assessing, and flagging ideas as high-potential opportunities, allowing them to be further reviewed by key stakeholders. *Builders* are those who *make things happen*. Their superpower is that they can take an early idea and envision the final product in the market—they can quickly frame and visualize complex concepts and lead the efforts to develop them further. Builders are not necessarily developers: while very often it is product managers, engineers, architects, designers, commercial people, or program managers who envision and lead the realization efforts, it could be any role in the company, provided that they have a good sense of both the constraints and the possibilities of current technologies. A builder, in this context, demonstrates a strong experimental mindset: they appreciate exploration, learning, and making fast, informed decisions versus rigid processes, detailed specifications, and perfectionism.

Beyond the typical innovation behaviors, senior executives play a critical role in innovation—they sponsor the overall program, contribute to shaping the innovation

G. Krasadakis, *Innovation Mode 2.0*,
https://doi.org/10.1007/978-3-032-00835-0_3

agenda, provide advice, and participate in steering the innovation effort. In a truly innovative environment, senior executives are also viewed as innovators who are closely connected to the innovation community and frequently interact with the innovation process.

In such innovative environments, business titles, hierarchical levels, and job descriptions are less important; it is the vision, ideas, and willingness to contribute that matter most. Leadership relies more on a powerful *vision*, *purpose*, and *influence* and far less on authority. People behave more as *partners* and less as *employees*. It is people's ideas, ambition, and energy that drive things forward: *innovation happens organically, driven by people and a bold purpose*.

Achieving this ultimate innovation state is challenging though—it requires a clear vision, effective execution, and inspiring leadership from an innovation executive or a team.

3.1 Who Should Be Leading Innovation in Your Company?

Innovation leadership in a modern corporation requires thoughtful organizational design that balances multiple competing priorities. While some companies thrive in innovation under the leadership of C-level innovation executives, others achieve the same through cross-functional teams or by embedding innovation capabilities across different teams and divisions.

"Who should be leading innovation in the organization" is a complex topic with no clear-cut answers. The "optimal" innovation organizational design for a company depends on parameters such as its industry, size, innovation objectives, and strategy. It also depends on the level of innovation maturity of the company.

Many companies don't have a dedicated position for innovation—they embed it in other roles. For example, especially in technology companies, it is often the CTO who leads the innovation efforts. Some organizations view innovation leadership as the responsibility of the chief digital officer or even the chief strategy officer.

Other companies have dedicated innovation leadership roles but not at the C-level, e.g., when the VP of innovation or head of innovation reports to the CTO or CSO. In other scenarios, innovation leadership is part of the C-suite through the role of the chief innovation officer (CINO), which is the most senior formal role dedicated to innovation. The CINO is typically seen in large enterprises facing industry disruption or corporations where innovation is acknowledged as critical, thus driving significant investment in innovation and digital transformation programs. The CINO reports directly to the CEO and has the authority and the resources to drive innovation initiatives and transformation across the company. According to recent studies,[1] approximately 30% of Fortune 500 companies have a senior innovation executive or CINO role, with a higher frequency in technology, healthcare, and financial services sectors. Having a CINO signals the organization's top-level commitment to innovation as a strategic priority. Moreover, it provides the space and

[1] https://hbr.org/2019/11/what-kind-of-chief-innovation-officer-does-your-company-need

support for organization-wide transformation by ensuring the provision of necessary resources, visibility, and strategic alignment.

Some companies take a drastically different path—they approach innovation leadership as a shared responsibility through "innovation councils" or "cross-functional committees" that have increased decision-making authority. This approach makes it easier to achieve buy-in from leaders across the organization since the model is inclusive by design and invites multiple departments to the process.

In other scenarios, companies delegate innovation leadership to *embedded teams*: they inject innovation expertise into the company's business divisions, thus creating *innovation cores* that contribute and coordinate aspects of the innovation process within their teams.

All the above could work under certain conditions, but they also bring important challenges and risks.

When embedding innovation leadership in other CxO roles, innovation may be seen as a secondary priority to the executive's responsibilities. Specifically, when the CTO undertakes this responsibility, innovation is often approached with a narrow focus and a tech bias that neglects other types of innovation, such as business model innovation. Similarly, when the CPO assumes the responsibility for innovation leadership, there is a risk of being overly focused on existing products and thus missing opportunities beyond the product landscape. Furthermore, the CxOs do not necessarily have the expertise or the required holistic understanding of the corporate innovation process and methodologies. In all cases where innovation is embedded into other CxO roles, balancing the strategic orchestration of innovation with day-to-day operations may prove tough and introduce the risk of limited organization-wide innovation success.

When innovation leadership is assigned below the C-suite level, leaders face different types of challenges. Roles like VP/SVP of innovation typically struggle to secure adequate resources without C-suite approvals. In many cases, they may not be empowered or authorized to drive significant organizational change. When innovation is not directly represented at the C-Level, the overall program may be perceived as an isolated effort or not strongly sponsored by the C-suite, and as a result, achieving general alignment and support becomes more difficult. Hence, this model could weaken the message of innovation, undermine the innovation culture and limit its potential.

The chief innovation officer (CINO) approach comes with different risks and challenges that are often associated with false expectations or misconceptions about the role itself. In many cases, unrealistic expectations for rapid transformation—both from within the C-suite and the broader company—can undermine the progress of innovation programs that, by design, deliver results over long timeframes and are also supposed to embrace certain types of failure. There are also "political" issues, as it is not unusual for the CINO to experience conflicts with other C-suite roles over ownership of certain initiatives or prioritization of investments. CINOs may be dealing with skepticism from other business leaders who don't value the potential of innovation programs and question their contribution. Furthermore, organizational inertia may be a significant obstacle when innovation leadership is concentrated in a single role, as other leaders may not feel part of the effort and, as a result, show limited engagement and support. In many cases, CINOs are under constant pressure to demonstrate measurable returns on innovation investments. While this is reasonable, it can become a problem when their outcomes are measured by inadequate or incomplete metrics that fail to capture all aspects of the innovation function and the opportunity discovery process.

The shared responsibility approach with innovation councils or committees suffers from what it entails: diffused and ultimately diluted ownership and accountability, as well as notably slow processes due to consensus as the decision-making mechanism. Without clear accountability and authentic drivers for innovation and change, companies may experience increased innovation activity but limited results, which introduces the risk that innovation efforts may be perceived as "innovation theatre." Additionally, members of such councils tend to prioritize their primary roles over innovation responsibilities, especially during periods of operational pressure.

Finally, the "embedded innovation" approach, where innovation expertise is distributed across business units within the organization, introduces the risk—or the certainty—of inconsistent innovation methods and gaps in knowledge sharing and cross-team collaboration. With this model, innovation results typically stay within teams or divisions, which may further worsen the feeling of innovation isolation and the sense of organizational fragmentation. Companies that follow this route face frequent disconnects, overlaps, missed opportunities, and partial results: the lack of orchestration makes it challenging to innovate as a single "system," thus impacting the company's innovation performance overall.

An effective organization design for innovation centralizes *innovation strategy and orchestration* while arranging a network of *innovation cores* throughout the company. Inheriting from the Federated model described in Chap. 1, this approach is based on *a dedicated innovation team* accountable for *steering the innovation efforts* and *enabling the organization to innovate* with autonomy, yet in alignment: innovation capability is present and accessible across teams and divisions.

3.1.1 Does Having an Innovation Leader Create Innovation Silos?

This is another misconception in the market—the belief that appointing an innovation leader signals a centralized innovation approach where the team is isolated from the rest of the company. This poor understanding of the innovation leader role makes organizations hesitant to establish formal innovation leadership, fearing the creation of an "innovation bubble" that is disconnected from core business realities. This misconception manifests in several ways: executives worry that innovation will become the exclusive domain of a specialized team rather than an organization-wide capability; business units are concerned about being underrepresented in the innovation process, while employees may believe they will be less empowered to innovate. Moreover, many organizations have witnessed the failure of stand-alone innovation labs that produced impressive prototypes but minimal business impact, further reinforcing skepticism about formalized innovation functions.

While the "innovation bubble" is a real risk that companies should be mitigating, it is not a result of having an innovation leader or not: it is the strategy and the overall innovation program that makes or breaks silos—not the presence of an innovation leader or an innovation team. On the contrary, a leader who is educated in innovation methodologies and organizational design can bring the exact opposite: they can utilize innovation methods and capabilities to unite the organization and break down silos. A skilled innovation leader and their team serve as enablers and orchestrators of the global, company-wide innovation process. Instead of centralizing innovation, they empower the entire organization to innovate: they provide powerful capabilities, methods, and consistent tools for *everyone to innovate* across departments and teams. They promote a culture of collaboration and knowledge exchange and reward behaviors that support it. Rather than owning or containing innovation within a specific department, they focus on empowering others to innovate more effectively. In fact, the above should be one of the key, formal objectives for this role. Understanding this distinction is crucial when organizations seek to enhance their innovation capacity through leadership appointments.

Before describing an approach for shaping the right innovation leadership model, it is essential to take a step back and define a generic "innovation executive" role, independently of its exact positioning in the organizational structure.

3.2 The Innovation Executive Role

There are different schools of thought and divergent perspectives regarding the role of the innovation leader in a corporation—it is perceived differently across organizations and industries: some view them primarily as change advocates and catalysts, while others view them as "venture capitalists" who manage a diverse innovation portfolio, making investment decisions and optimizing value creation. Others consider *cultural transformation* to be at the core of the role's responsibility. Moreover, as described earlier, various misconceptions make it difficult to obtain a single, widely accepted view of the innovation executive role. For instance, many believe that innovation leaders primarily serve the idea generation and opportunity framing processes, that they are the ones who invent and innovate at the technical level, or that the role is merely symbolic in motivating people. There is frequent confusion about innovation leaders focusing solely on creativity rather than methodical execution and the ability to drive innovations to market.

Here, we take a holistic view and define a generic innovation executive role with a clear mandate: *to empower the organization to innovate at scale and pace.*

3.2.1 Innovation Executive: Essential Responsibilities

The innovation executive is the *Enabler* and the *Orchestrator* of the overall corporate innovation function. They are the ones who envision the optimized version of the organization in terms of its ability to drive meaningful innovations to the market and create value for users, customers, businesses, and other stakeholders. They connect the innovation efforts with the organizational purpose and the company's strategic planning—they bring the C-suite, division leaders, product and technology leaders, and everybody on board to the innovation program.

Although they typically come with extensive ability to innovate and occasionally domain expertise, innovation executives and their teams are not meant to *produce innovation*; they exist to *enable* and *empower* the organization to do so. More specifically, I would say that the mission of the innovation executive is "to empower the company to thrive through the *discovery* and *pursuit* of new business opportunities." This mission requires the innovation executive to focus on three key areas: first, improving the organization's ability to spot and frame potential opportunities; second, enhancing the organization's capability to identify and validate high-potential opportunities; and third, driving alignment among leadership to invest appropriately in validated opportunities and successfully bring new products and services to market.

The innovation executive is responsible for onboarding the right talent, shaping the innovation culture, designing and optimizing effective processes, and providing the necessary technology to accelerate and enhance innovation. They ensure that the environment encourages the generation and circulation of ideas, promotes experimentation, and welcomes failures as a means of learning and continuous improvement. More specifically, the corporate innovation leader is accountable for:

- **Enabling innovation**: The innovation executive is responsible for architecting the corporation's innovation function and bringing in the right technologies, platforms, processes, and tools to enable innovation. This may include capabilities such as innovation management and collaboration platforms, market intelligence systems, experimentation frameworks, prototyping tools, templates, gamification systems, and more. Beyond technology, they are expected to design and run the required innovation programs, orchestrate workshops, and the overall innovation process, including communication and knowledge sharing.
- **Setting the focus for innovation**: The innovation executive must ensure that the innovation function supports and advances the organization's core purpose and strategic objectives. They translate broad strategic directives from the C-suite into the innovation agenda that describes specific focus areas and problems worth solving. This requires regular alignment with executive leadership, careful analysis of market trends and competitive dynamics, and a deep understanding of the organization's capabilities and growth ambitions. The innovation executive serves as the bridge between strategic vision and innovative execution, ensuring that innovation efforts remain connected to business reality.

- **Establishing a robust opportunity discovery capability**: A core responsibility of the innovation executive is the establishment of an end-to-end innovation process that accelerates opportunity identification and validation. They must introduce the right technologies, processes, and governance models to streamline ideation, idea assessment, and opportunity flagging. The innovation executive manages an opportunity portfolio that reflects the company's strategic priorities and balances different styles of innovation and focus areas.
- **Establishing an opportunity implementation capability**: Beyond generating and validating ideas, the innovation executive is responsible for establishing the essential capabilities—teams, systems, and processes—that can successfully implement opportunities, bring them to market, and drive adoption.
- **Fostering a culture of innovation**: At the cultural level, the innovation executive must introduce the right programs, events, initiatives, etc., to promote a genuine culture of innovation. This special culture—described later in this chapter—is built on top of a growth and learning mindset combined with openness, psychological safety, and the readiness to take calculated risks. The innovation executive is expected to lead by example and act as an innovation role model—to attract attention, inspire people, and gradually shape a community of innovators. They must also address resistance to change and help remove known cultural blockers.
- **Measuring innovation performance**: One of the key responsibilities of the innovation executive is to introduce a robust innovation performance measurement system. As explained in Chap. 9, such a framework is essential for driving a continuous improvement process for the innovation function and providing a comprehensive view of its health. The innovation leader uses this measurement framework to communicate the "State of innovation," educate the C-suite on the appropriate success metrics for innovation, and set meaningful expectations.
- **Connecting internally**: The innovation executive must be able to serve as a cross-functional catalyst, bringing teams and divisions together under an enterprise-wide innovation initiative. Unifying the company is a complex task that requires leadership, advocacy, technology, and mechanisms enabling smart knowledge exchange across the organization. The innovation leader and their team are accountable for introducing a shared "innovation language" along with unified innovation frameworks, methods, tools, and technology that make it easier for teams to exchange information and innovate in a cross-functional mode.
- **Connecting externally**: Beyond internal networking, the innovation executive is responsible for establishing strong relationships with external partners, including start-ups, academic institutions, industry organizations, and innovation hubs. This outward focus enables the company to benefit from open innovation strategies and pursue strategic collaboration and co-creation partnerships.
- **Providing innovation talent**: The innovation executive must identify, cultivate, and scale the necessary skills for effective innovation across the organization. This includes talent acquisition, upskilling through training programs, defining innovation roles, establishing career paths, mentoring rising innovators, and integrating innovation competencies into hiring practices. They should help func-

tional leaders identify and develop innovation champions within their teams while exploring alternative ways to access global talent through contractors or vendors.
- **Providing innovation resources**: The innovation executive ensures that innovation teams have all the resources required to support their initiatives and achieve their goals. This includes securing appropriate funding during budget cycles, establishing clear criteria for resource allocation, and creating mechanisms for flexible, just-in-time financing of promising initiatives.

While these core responsibilities remain consistent, their implementation will vary depending on the organization's innovation maturity, industry context, and the executive's position in the hierarchy. A C-level innovation leader is expected to emphasize strategic alignment and cultural transformation, while a VP or head of innovation might focus more on process optimization and portfolio management. Similarly, the CINO may have additional responsibilities, such as organizational design for innovation, shaping and funding R&D programs and teams, and specific investments.

3.2.2 Hiring an Exceptional Innovation Leader

Regardless of whether an organization adopts the C-suite or the VP-level positioning, exceptional innovation leaders share a distinctive set of abilities and core competencies, including:

1. **Mastery of the innovation process**: Innovation in a corporate environment can become chaotic, expensive, and occasionally slow. The innovation executive must be able to make the right interventions at the right time; they must know what innovation processes make sense for the organization, the required tech stack, the toolkits, templates, and other resources needed for real innovation to happen. They must be able to architect a powerful innovation function for the organization.
2. **Strategic thinking**: The innovation executive must be able to connect the company's purpose and strategy with the innovation initiatives and programs happening across the organization. More specifically, they must translate the corporate purpose and objectives into focus areas or a broader innovation agenda that serves as the guiding principle for innovation efforts. A talented innovation executive must be able to shape initiatives, programs, roadmaps, and projects that best support the organization's strategy.
3. **Deep understanding of technology**: The innovation executive must understand both the capabilities of current technologies and their limitations, as well as what is feasible now and what will become feasible within the company's innovation horizon.
4. **Superior product sense and prioritization skills**: The innovation executive must know how a product can be conceived, designed, validated, built, launched,

and operated. Moreover, as ideas, opportunities, innovation projects, and initiatives all compete for the same corporate resources, the innovation leader must be able to prioritize wisely through a balanced opportunity portfolio that serves the organizational purpose and strategy. Experience in actual product development, with a strong focus on product innovation, is a major success factor.

5. **Strong communication skills**: They must be able to speak "corporate," "product," and "technical" languages—an essential skill as a successful innovation leader must communicate effectively with product, technology, commercial leaders, engineers, designers, and the C-suite.
6. **Relationship building and influencing**: As innovation rarely occurs in isolation, the innovation executive must have experience in building strong relationships across the organization that help navigate politics, overcome resistance to change, and foster coalitions for innovation.
7. **Customer and market understanding**: The innovation executive must find ways to stay connected with customers and users to inform and guide the innovation efforts. They must establish mechanisms that sense the market, identify emerging customer needs and pain points, and translate market intelligence into innovation opportunities and strategies.
8. **Financial acumen**: Innovation requires investment, and a successful innovation leader knows how to secure and allocate resources effectively. They understand innovation economics, can build compelling business cases, calculate potential ROI when it makes sense, and make sound financial decisions that balance short-term results with long-term innovation potential.
9. **A special leadership style**: The innovation leader must be able to lead by example—being hands-on and occasionally serving as an innovator themselves. Seeing the innovation leader actively participating in the process is one of the most inspiring experiences that can further motivate teams and the community of innovators.
10. **Risk appetite**: The innovation leader must be able to shape a different mindset regarding the willingness to take calculated risks and how to handle potential failures in the innovation context.

Furthermore, a successful innovation executive must be adaptive and ready to innovate the innovation function itself: given that the cultural, financial, and operational states of a company change drastically over time, the innovation leader must be able to refine or adapt the innovation process and follow a data-driven, experimentation approach to improve and steer it in the right direction.

3.3 The Innovation Leader Dilemma: Appoint or Promote?

A frequent misconception about the role of the innovation executive is that they must come with domain expertise and actively innovate themselves. While deep domain understanding is essential, having extensive expertise is far less important than profound skills in innovation program architecture and leadership.

Following this narrow view of the innovation executive's role, organizations often promote successful leaders from their core business areas into innovation leadership roles. This approach is typically convenient and practical, as the promoted leader usually brings a deep understanding of the company's products, customers, and markets, strong internal networks and credibility, and knowledge of the organization's capabilities and constraints. This brings a sense of comfort for both the innovation leader and the organization.

However, based on experience in various innovation environments, this approach brings severe limitations: while domain experts in senior innovation roles can bring value in many ways—e.g., by generating great ideas, inventing, or leading idea implementations—they rarely have the knowledge and holistic view on how to transform the organization and enable others to innovate faster and at scale. *Innovating* versus *empowering others to innovate* are fundamentally different missions: the former requires domain expertise, while the latter needs primarily innovation methodology and leadership skills. Domain experts who lack formal training in innovation methodologies often frame innovation narrowly within their sphere of knowledge. Instead of developing a diverse portfolio of opportunities, they tend to focus on incremental improvements with an execution mindset rather than exploring more disruptive possibilities.

When the purpose is to make the organization more innovative through a transformation program, the best approach is to appoint leaders with strong experience in innovation methodologies, processes, and frameworks. These are the ones who can bring the best innovation technologies, tools, and knowledge together into a transformational program that will, instead of *producing innovation*, *empower the organization to do so* at scale. An additional benefit of the "appoint from the market" approach is that leaders can bring fresh thinking from outside the industry or through cross-industry experience. Furthermore, to strengthen this approach, any gaps in domain knowledge can be filled by getting the right experts on the team under the innovation executive.

3.4 The Innovation "Dream Team"

As established in the previous sections, the innovation executive has a challenging mission: to activate innovation and transform the company into a truly innovative and agile organization. To succeed, the innovation executive needs a "Dream Team," a high-performing, cross-disciplinary group of passionate innovators with a special mindset and a superior ability to inspire, influence, and execute.

The Dream Team is a "task force" consisting of visionaries who have a bias for action and are obsessed with success, but they also know how to fail and how to learn from it. Its members are seen as role models for innovation, mentors, transformation leaders, and advisors; they negotiate, plan, inspire, influence, and drive change. The common denominator for all members of this special team is the passion for innovation as a key driver for business success.

To operate at full speed, the Dream Team needs the right resources, increased autonomy, and exceptional talent. When forming the Dream Team, you should look for members who excel in innovation methodologies, strategy, leadership, communication, and program management. At the same time, each team member should have a deep understanding of the current state of the organization, along with its environment, including the industry, market, competition, and emerging trends.

However, as introduced here, the Dream Team of innovation is not supposed to *produce innovation*. Instead, their mission is to *enable* people, teams, and the entire organization *to do so*. This fundamental difference impacts both the setup of the team—there are no pure implementation roles such as software product development and related technical profiles—and its positioning within the organization. It is communicated as an *autonomous team* working across the organization to enable and empower innovation. It is crucial to emphasize the special purpose of the team—*to enable innovation* rather than *to innovate*—to avoid the misconception that the Dream Team is doing innovation in isolation. The team's fundamental mission is to *open up innovation* to everyone.

Throughout the book, we refer to this team by using the terms "Dream Team," "core innovation team," or simply "core team" interchangeably. The key responsibilities of this team are outlined below.

3.4.1 Responsibilities of the Innovation Dream Team

The innovation team undertakes a challenging mission: to architect a new, *innovative version* of the organization and lead the efforts to get there. This ambitious goal is translated to various responsibilities—they must be strategic and tactical to inspire and enable people. More specifically, the team:

1. **Leads the innovation transformation program**: The innovation program, detailed in Chap. 10, introduces capabilities, events, methodologies, and organizational changes that gradually elevate the company to higher levels in the Innovation Maturity Index. The team *defines* and *architects* the program according to the organization's needs and establishes a strong connection with the C-suite to ensure that the program reflects the company's strategy and ambitions. Beyond definition, the team *owns the program*—they lead multiple initiatives and orchestrate numerous implementation projects, communication events, workshops, and education activities. To lead such a complex program, the team needs increased autonomy to steer the efforts as needed, informed by a series of innovation performance metrics that reflect progress, engagement, and cultural aspects of innovation. They use data to quantify the program's impact and bring key insights, proposals, and action plans to the C-suite. When there is feedback, guidance, or requests from the leadership, the team updates the program accordingly to reflect new focus areas or strategic directions.
2. **Provisions innovation capabilities**: On the practical front, the team *delivers* the required capabilities—systems and processes that enable innovation to happen

at pace and scale. However, they do not *implement* these capabilities. Instead, they focus on *selecting* and *provisioning* the right ones and *driving their adoption* throughout the organization. For instance, the team may collaborate with internal implementation teams, vendors, or consultants to integrate technologies such as AI-powered systems to support ideation and opportunity identification, market intelligence tools to scan and comprehend the market, or tools that simplify the planning and hosting of Hackathons. They drive the selection and delivery process, but most importantly, they ensure successful launch and adoption through effective communication, training, and support. The *wide adoption of the innovation capabilities* is a critical element of the *definition of done* for the innovation team and a leading indicator of success.

3. **Operates the innovation function**: The innovation team manages the operational aspects of innovation. They maintain the innovation agenda, along with a unified innovation calendar, where they plan workshops and events throughout the year. They monitor feedback loops for actionable insights and manage the portfolio of innovation projects. The team also sets the right *cadence* for innovation: they adjust the frequency of big innovation events and workshops to ensure that the pace of innovation is right and that the balance between innovation and execution is optimal for the company. Moreover, they are responsible for setting up an effective communication mechanism, including channels, templates, content creation processes, distribution, and a framework for measuring effectiveness. The communication engine is vital as it must raise awareness about innovation events and activities without overloading people and generating noise. The right balance and intensity of communication are crucial for the program's success and, thus, a significant challenge for the team to address.
4. **Drives the culture of innovation**: The team plays a pivotal role at the cultural level. In addition to its strategic responsibilities, the team leads the efforts of growing an active community of innovators and cultivating a great innovation culture. They frequently interact with the community by providing feedback on ideas, mentoring teams, and listening to comments and suggestions from people across levels and departments. They inspire people and drive high engagement with the overall innovation initiative—they are seen as innovators, mentors, visionaries, and builders.

To effectively serve the above responsibilities and meet the demanding expectations, the innovation team requires multiple senior-level roles across disciplines. The team's structure, along with roles and profiles, are described in the following.

3.4.2 The Structure of the Innovation Team

The innovation team brings together senior profiles and various complementary skills, forming a special, cross-disciplinary "force of innovation." This team is special in many ways: it has increased autonomy, a bold mission, and the power and resources to drive organizational change. The members of this team have full trust and support from the C-suite to lead the charge toward a mode of true innovation. They bring a holistic view of the innovation function and clarity on where the organization should be heading, why, and how to get there. They are experts on innovation methodologies, new product development, business models, and organizational design, and they have the means to measure innovation performance and continuously improve the program.

The team's structure is flat: all members report directly to the innovation executive, who in turn reports to the organization's leadership, either as the chief innovation officer under the CEO or as a lower-ranking executive, such as head or VP of innovation, under another member of the C-suite. Alternatively, if you are embedding innovation in other C-suite roles, the innovation executive could be the CTO or CSO. For simplicity, we will use "Innovation Director" throughout the book to refer to the innovation executive, regardless of the leadership title (CINO, CTO, etc.)

The innovation director sets the *vision* for the new, innovative version of the company, shapes the roadmap outlining how to get there, and brings together the entire organization. They lead the innovation team and the overall program while building a strong network across the organization. Moreover, they partner with business leaders and help them adopt innovation methods and practices. In parallel, the innovation director educates the C-suite on innovation methods, macro trends, emerging technologies, and consumer behaviors. At the same time, they capture leadership's guidance and strategic priorities and reflect them in the company's innovation agenda. The innovation director empowers the team with strong innovation leadership skills along with tactical guidance and innovation know-how.

The exact synthesis of the Dream Team depends heavily on the industry, domain, size of the organization, and the company's innovation maturity level. As shown in Fig. 3.1, in one setup, there is a "core team" of innovation architects and orchestrators, program managers, and workshop facilitators framed by a wide range of roles, including market intelligence analysts, technology experts, content creators, and other specialists forming a dynamic, "extended team." The core team comprises senior leaders who are fully committed to the innovation program. Depending on the case, roles from the "extended team" could contribute "just in time" to provide expertise and advice, or they could be full time, dedicated to driving aspects of the innovation function. For example, the legal advisors may support the innovation function when there is a need for patentability assessment or to provide mitigation strategies for specific risks. At the same time, the MVP Dev Lead may be a full-time role—a product expert who takes validated opportunities and defines, builds, and ships minimum viable products.

The innovation team can be further expanded by the community of innovators who volunteer to participate in innovation activities and contribute to either specific projects or the innovation program itself. In some instances, the team can request support from the innovation community, thus gaining flexibility in managing peaks or sudden increases in demand for innovation activities.

Depending on the level of the organization in the Innovation Maturity Index and the scale of the innovation program, there could be multiple instances for some of the roles in the innovation Dream Team—leading to a structure where the core team

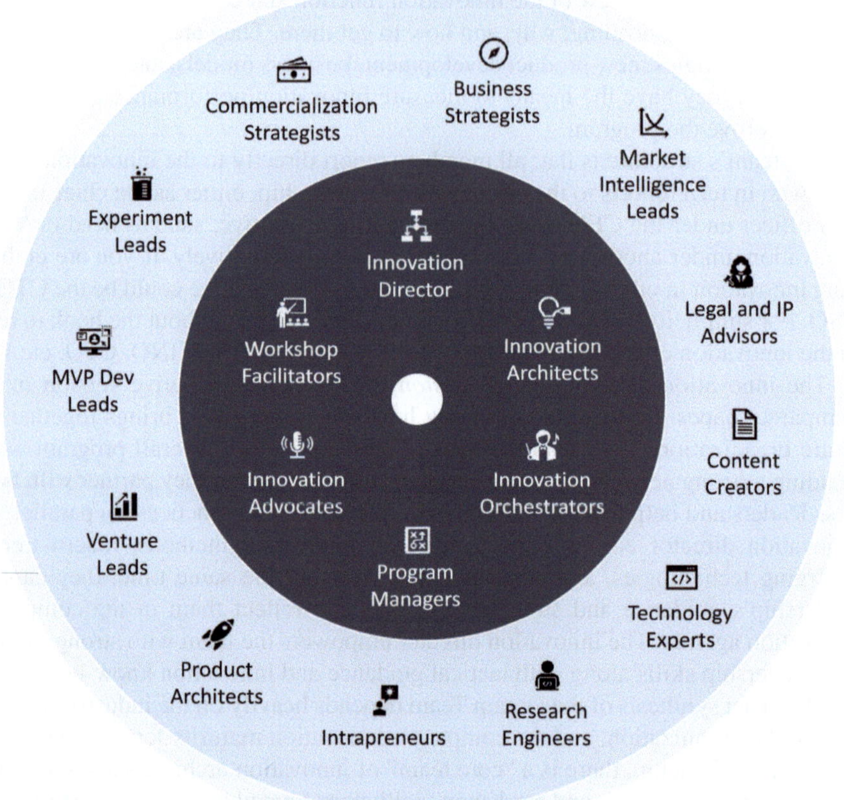

Fig. 3.1 The innovation "Dream Team"

is supported by "spin-off" satellite teams, focused on offering specific, narrow services, e.g., the market intelligence or the communication and content creation team. The following section details the Dream Team's roles, responsibilities, and profiles.

3.4.3 The Core Innovation Team

Along with the innovation director, the following five roles define an effective core for the innovation team—the foundation of the Dream Team that is powerful enough to kick off the innovation transformation program and bring the first waves of change to the organization.

– **Innovation architects**: This essential role is responsible for architecting the company's entire innovation function and the corresponding transformation program. Innovation architects are experts in innovation frameworks, methodologies, and organizational design. They create the *blueprint for corporate innovation*, a framework of innovation capabilities that empowers the company to innovate with consistency and speed. They regularly assess the company's technological readiness and identify gaps, required integration scenarios, process improvements, and automation opportunities, occasionally leading to new strategic innovation projects and initiatives. Innovation architects are also strategists—they shape roadmaps, make decisions on priorities, and define work streams and processes that are crucial for the innovation function of the company. They influence strategic decisions and how the company invests in innovation capabilities. Beyond architecting the broader innovation program, innovation architects are also viewed as engaged innovators, actively participating in and contributing to various innovation activities and events.

- **Innovation orchestrators**: In contrast to architects who focus on the big picture of the innovation function, orchestrators are responsible for operating and improving the innovation process. Their mission is to ensure that the innovation function operates effectively and contributes to the company's overall purpose. To do so, they monitor various "innovation health" metrics, regularly review the opportunity portfolio, and, when necessary, intervene with recommendations or drive broader "innovation steering" discussions with key stakeholders. For example, following a steering committee with the C-suite, they may revise the innovation agenda and adjust the strategic themes for innovation or introduce new problems worth solving. On another front, they are responsible for organizing the company's efforts in educating employees on innovation practices, behaviors, and collaboration models. In this context, they may organize an innovation academy program (explained later in this chapter) to serve educational sessions on rapid prototyping, experimentation, design thinking, and related topics. As with architects, orchestrators are also expected to lead by example, e.g., by actively participating in workshops, sharing ideas, providing feedback, and contributing to ideas from others. Typically, orchestrators come with a business or technology background, research and development experience, and a thorough understanding of innovation strategies, techniques, methodologies, and frameworks.
- **Innovation advocates and connectors**: Corporate innovation relies on people and culture, making *effective communication and networking* a critical success factor. The innovation team needs people who systematically advocate for innovation and, by sharing inspiring stories, demonstrate how innovation shapes the company's future. This special role requires passionate and effective communicators able to present and explain the innovation program, its goals, and achievements to attract attention and inspire people to engage. Innovation advocates should be able to navigate the organization's structures, products, business lines, and strategy, acting as *connectors—bringing* together talented innovators, teams, and stakeholders in the context of specific innovation initiatives or opportunities. Innovation advocates are typically strategists and generalists with a business or technology background combined with an in-depth understanding of the innova-

tion process, which enables them to connect big thinking with the real world. Occasionally, they may act as innovation advisors, helping teams adopt innovation methods, frameworks, and tools.
- **Program managers**: These senior members play a crucial role in the innovation transformation program. Program managers "make things happen" through the effective execution of complex initiatives and the timely delivery of innovation capabilities. They manage multiple parallel work streams and interdependent projects to accelerate the innovation process and make the organization more innovative. Unlike traditional program managers, they have strong innovation backgrounds and a passion for driving change in the organization—they should be seen more as innovation leaders and less as project or program coordinators. While they plan, drive, and measure progress methodically, they avoid bureaucratic approaches and focus on delivering innovation capabilities with speed and agility. Beyond delivery, they drive the adoption of capabilities by demonstrating the value of every single deliverable and the innovation program as a whole.
- **Workshop facilitators**: These are skilled innovators with a deep understanding of innovation methodologies, user research, and problem-framing techniques. Facilitators have strong communication skills and are experienced in leading cross-functional teams through structured ideation events that encourage diverse perspectives and creativity, such as brainstorming or Design Sprints. They are able to synthesize complex insights into coherent concepts and effectively visualize ideas through sketching or wireframing, thus making abstract concepts easier to understand—and all these in real-time, during complex and noisy innovation workshops. A successful facilitator not only leads workshops but ultimately helps participants identify user needs and shape solutions that address significant customer problems. To be successful, facilitators must possess strong interpersonal skills, empathy, and the ability to remain neutral while coordinating challenging conversations. Moreover, they must be able to help teams overcome common innovation barriers by managing group dynamics and guiding participants through the innovation process with confidence and clarity.

3.4.4 The Extended Innovation Team

The above six roles—including the innovation director—define the core of the innovation team and its starting state. However, as the program progresses, the workload for this team is expected to increase substantially. Thus, various new roles will be in high demand, e.g., product architects or MVP leads who can implement and ship innovative concepts to market. The following presents the "extended innovation team"—an additional set of key roles that make innovation actionable and accelerate its pace. These roles do not have to be acquired at once, and some could be offered "just-in-time," as a service—an approach that adds flexibility to the program, making the innovation team more elastic and adaptive. The most characteristic ones are:

- **Technology advisors**: These are technologists who bring deep expertise in various domains. They help the team understand the state of the art of the technology space and provide clarity on both the capabilities and limitations of cutting-edge technologies. They bring unique perspectives on emerging technologies and their relevance to the business. Technology advisors could come from various backgrounds, ideally covering software engineering, artificial intelligence, data science, computer science, and related fields. The defining characteristic is that they combine technology expertise with a profound understanding of product innovation and new product development.
- **Product architects**: This is a unique role that combines strong technical expertise with exceptional product sense. Product architects are capable of translating early ideas into concrete product concepts and then into solid technical architectures. Moreover, they assess the technical feasibility of new product concepts and identify ways that emerging technologies can maximize their impact. They also act as mentors by providing technical guidance to teams and individuals, helping them shape their products and identify the right technologies, third-party tools, and services to utilize. They typically come with a software background combined with a deep understanding of the new product development process and innovation methodologies.
- **Product managers**: These are senior professionals who know how to craft exceptional products and services. Successful product managers are very effective in identifying what features to build first, what a minimum viable product should look like, and how to define success for a given product concept. They are able to think both as users and entrepreneurs—they want the best experience for their end-users, but they also seek smart business models and monetization strategies. Typically, they go beyond implementation and aim for product-market fit through in-market experimentation. In parallel to product development, they contribute to innovation by connecting the organization to insights from the competition and global developments, identifying market gaps and potential opportunities. Finally, they play an essential role in educating the company on subjects such as agile product development, prototyping, and experimentation. Product managers may come from business, engineering, or design backgrounds, but in all cases, they demonstrate expertise in taking an idea through validation, product development, launch, optimization, and growth.
- **Opportunity validation leads**: These are senior professionals with expertise in product development and experimentation techniques. They own the validation thread for a given opportunity—they can determine if a concept needs to be validated in the first place and, if so, what the right path is and the combination of techniques to be applied. Moreover, they shape customized validation strategies that address the unique characteristics and uncertainties associated with each concept. They leverage various methods, including business experimentation with prototypes, which help generate meaningful insights for making informed decisions about the concept's future. For example, for a given concept, they shape the prototype to be built and define the target audience, timelines, success criteria of the experiment, and what happens upon success. Then, they form the

right team to build the prototype, launch, and operate the business experiment. They also play a key role in capturing, communicating, and managing the learning and knowledge produced through the experimentation process. The ideal candidate for the validation lead role possesses a strong background in product development and experimentation methods. They have excellent product sense, market understanding, and a deep knowledge of user research methodologies. Opportunity validation leads play a crucial role in the opportunity validation function, as described in Chap. 7.

- **MVP leads**: The MVP lead is responsible for *defining* and *delivering* minimum viable products with speed and agility. They may be thought of as specialized product managers with expertise in converting early concepts into tangible product definitions and building the corresponding minimum viable product (MVP). They produce well-defined Product Requirements Documents (PRDs) and MVP manifests, assemble the right development teams, and drive the implementation process. The MVP lead comes with a strong product development background, superior product sense, and a solid understanding of the experimentation process. They have good visibility of the talent and skill sets available within the organization, and they can work with partners and vendors to increase capacity and accelerate the MVP development process as needed. MVP Leads are foundational in the Opportunity Realization function, as described in Chap. 8.
- **Venture leads**: While the MVP lead role is optimized for building great products, the objective of the venture lead is to frame them as viable offerings or potential businesses. Following the launch of a new MVP, the venture lead orchestrates a continual product improvement process based on experimentation and data-driven decision-making. Venture leads support the in-market MVP with essential services and business functions, aiming to rapidly grow it and achieve product-market fit (PMF). They shape growth strategies, attempt growth hacks, run fast product improvement cycles, run experiments, explore potential pivots, and eventually form a justified view about whether and when PMF can be achieved. Moreover, they ensure that knowledge gained through each development cycle is properly captured and diffused throughout the organization, transforming individual project insights into organizational learning. The venture lead provides a critical connection between corporate innovation and viable business creation. They regularly connect with senior stakeholders to provide insights and recommendations, ultimately informing critical decisions, such as pivoting, parking, or sunsetting an MVP. The ideal venture lead combines strong business venture expertise with an entrepreneurial mindset. They possess in-depth knowledge of commercialization, business acumen, and expertise in monetization models and business model innovation. Their background ideally includes hands-on venture-building experience, with a focus on converting early products into fast-growing, viable businesses. Venture leads also have a foundational role in the opportunity realization function, as described in Chap. 8.
- **Legal advisors**: These are legal experts who understand the innovation process and its inherent uncertainties and introduce effective risk-taking strategies that help manage risk without slowing down the innovation process. They work

closely with innovators from the early stages of innovation projects to identify potential risks and compliance issues before they become obstacles. When such issues are identified, they offer practical mitigation strategies that help innovation teams strike a balance between regulatory compliance and innovation speed. They recommend effective, fast mitigation plans or work-arounds and help leaders understand the associated risks and potential impact—a valuable service, especially in complex, regulated industries. However, legal advisors must come with an innovation mindset and a thorough understanding of the innovation process so that they can apply a faster, more flexible legal review framework and more elastic decision-making processes. Instead of using general risk frameworks, they must employ adapted risk assessment tools specifically designed for innovation in order to *proactively assess risk* in a *pragmatic way* and help unblock innovation. Such frameworks should be optimized not to avoid risk but to frame it more effectively in the context of innovation—thus helping teams make informed decisions that unblock innovation without passively taking on significant risks, e.g., when running a small-scale experiment that may have theoretical but low-impact risks. Beyond risk management, legal experts—particularly patent attorneys—can accelerate the identification of intellectual property opportunities and ensure a smooth process for evaluating and protecting IP assets, thereby integrating IP protection into the innovation workflow.

- **Intrapreneurs**: Whether former entrepreneurs coming from the market or homegrown intrapreneurs, these driven, self-motivated individuals bring a start-up mentality and a different perspective regarding business opportunities. They are less constrained by the corporate reality and can think beyond its boundaries while remaining connected to the organization's purpose. Intrapreneurs bring the entrepreneurial spirit by connecting the dots, spotting opportunities, and demonstrating real innovation. They are typically individual contributors with increased autonomy to navigate the organization, shape proposals, and pitch for products and opportunities. Intrapreneurs are also viewed as advisors, mentors, and role models for innovation, inspiring colleagues by sharing their entrepreneurial experiences and big ideas. Their dynamic presence in the organization creates a powerful multiplier effect, as their entrepreneurial energy and mindset boost the growth of the innovation community. Intrapreneurs combine creative problem-solving with practical business skills, enabling them to navigate organizational complexities with speed and flexibility. They bring significant value in transforming the company into a more adaptive, innovative organization that adopts, to some extent, qualities from the start-up world.
- **Business strategists**: These professionals focus on identifying strategic opportunities within the broader ecosystem, e.g., market gaps, partnerships, and commercial agreements. They define and validate monetization scenarios and business models for emerging products and services, focusing on strategy and competitive differentiation. Business strategists typically have a strong commercial or product management background and bring a deep understanding of economic trends, market dynamics, client needs, and competitive landscapes. They help validate and prioritize opportunities based on their relevance to the strategy

and their commercial potential, bridging the gap between innovation initiatives and corporate strategy.
- **Commercialization advisors**: These are commercially minded individuals who bring expertise in translating early concepts into meaningful commercial offerings. They help innovation teams navigate commercial challenges and ensure that their innovations address real market needs, packaged in ways that resonate with target audiences. They help teams shape monetization models, create business proposals, design go-to-market strategies, structure commercial agreements and partnerships, and package, position, and launch products or services to market.
- **Content creation lead**: Systematic diffusion of high-quality content is crucial for building momentum for innovation and driving alignment across departments. The content lead is responsible for establishing a communication strategy and overseeing the underlying content creation and distribution process. They produce content that presents the essence of the program and demystifies innovation methodologies by showcasing success stories and highlighting learnings from experimentation initiatives. In parallel, they invite the broader community to contribute by sharing their innovation stories and updates. The content lead oversees and operates the Innovation Portal and the Newsletter as platforms for exchanging knowledge and educational materials, including guides, training packages, presentations, and workshop outputs. The content creation and distribution function is resource intensive, requiring a dedicated team. However, by adopting generative AI tools, processes can be streamlined and accelerated, allowing the content team to focus on strategic storytelling while AI handles repetitive tasks, such as routine communications, content summarization for specific audiences, and routine updates to the Innovation Portal, as well as drafting newsletters.
- **Market intelligence lead**: These are market experts who systematically scan the market, the competitive landscape, and the broader ecosystem to detect opportunities and potential threats before they become apparent. They utilize analytical tools to transform noisy market signals into actionable insights that inform various stages of the innovation process. They help the organization anticipate changes rather than reacting to them, thus reducing market risk or identifying untapped potential. Their contributions elevate the entire innovation function by accelerating the opportunity discovery and validation process and setting the focus of innovation.

Besides their formal roles defined above, all team members are expected to demonstrate genuine innovation behaviors and go beyond their job descriptions and formal responsibilities. In a truly innovative environment, they act as advisors, ideators, and evaluators of ideas; they educate, support, and inspire people and collaborate effectively to drive the innovation vision forward. In the same spirit, the team can be supported by the broader community of innovators or through the Guest Innovator program—a rotation scheme that allows employees from across the organization to join for either a project assignment or on a time-based arrangement and contribute to the innovation efforts. The latter not only brings elasticity and increases the capacity of the innovation team but also supports in action the notion of openness of the team—it connects the organization and breaks the silos. With this "elastic" setup, innovation becomes more inclusive and embedded in the organization while, at the same time, the core team reduces the risk of being seen as operating in isolation. These volunteering contributions are also connected to the innovation rewards program, so contributors receive the credit they deserve.

As the execution of the innovation program progresses and the company advances in terms of innovation maturity, the innovation team also expands. As shown in Fig. 3.2, it can grow across six main pillars: Communication and Content, Market Intelligence, Opportunity Discovery and Concept Testing, Execution and Product

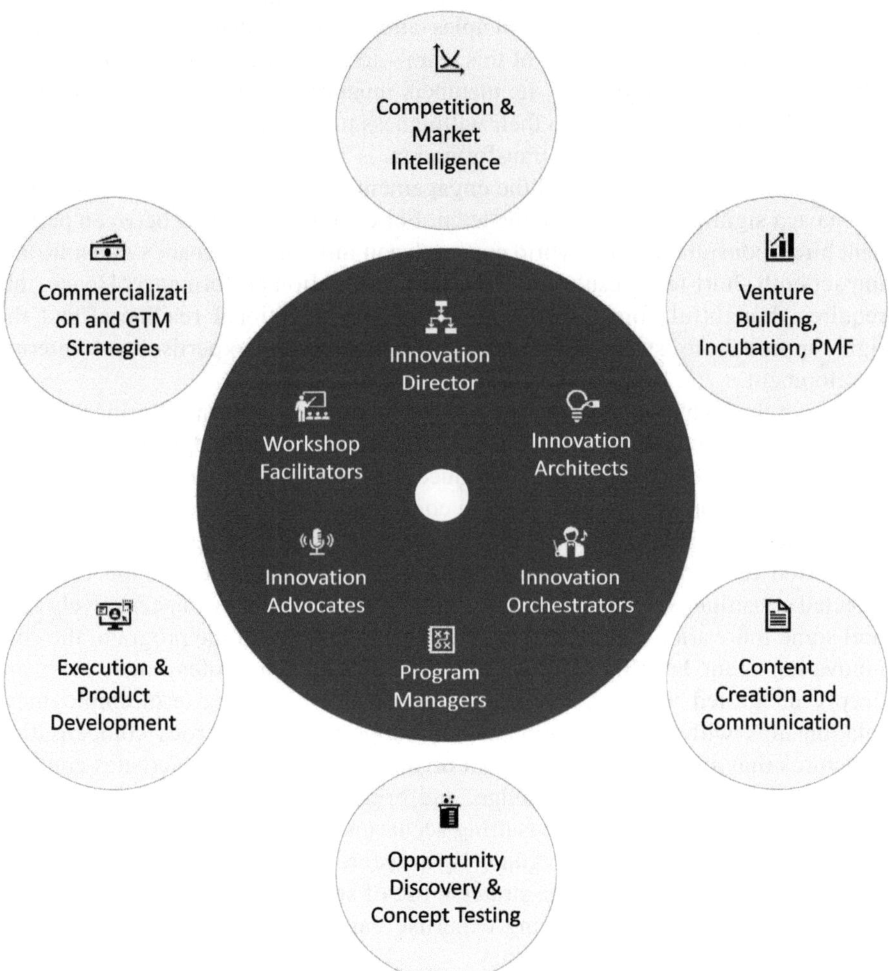

Fig. 3.2 The core innovation team supported by satellite service teams

Development, Go-to-Market (GTM) and Commercialization, Venture Building, Incubation, and product-market fit (PMF). These can evolve as stand-alone teams, reporting to the innovation director, each offering a well-defined service that contributes to the acceleration of the innovation process.

3.4.5 Sourcing Innovation Talent: Team Formation Considerations

Selecting the right talent for the innovation team is a key success factor for the entire innovation program. The composition of the team directly shapes its velocity, credibility, and cultural influence within the organization. While the team's synthesis and headcount depend on various factors, such as the organization's size and innovation maturity, there are key principles and strategies that apply to all cases. Considering the special purpose of this team—to act as the inner force, the core of the entire innovation program—its members must be carefully selected based not only on their talents but also on their willingness to commit to leading such a complex cultural and technological transformation.

The source of this talent and the engagement model are critical decisions that can have a significant impact on the team. For example, deciding between permanent hires, consultants, or a hybrid approach can influence the team's dynamic and impact both short-term results and long-term innovation performance. Hence, this requires thoughtful consideration of timing, organizational readiness, and the right approach to strike a balance between external expertise and internal development.

Setting the right balance between *internal* and *external* hiring is critical. While internal candidates can bring invaluable organizational knowledge and established relationships, external talent may introduce fresh perspectives from diverse industries and geographies that can challenge conventional thinking.

Another decision is whether to consider consultants for specific roles in the innovation team or proceed strictly with full-time employees. While carefully selected consultants with appropriate expertise and cultural fit can effectively support some innovation roles, especially at the early stages of the program, the core innovation team benefits significantly from permanent professionals who are deeply integrated within the organization. Establishing long-term employment relationships with key innovation talent, supported by generous compensation structures that align their success with organizational outcomes, creates continuity, accumulates valuable knowledge, and brings a level of commitment that is difficult to replicate through consulting scenarios. This approach ensures that the innovation function develops organically as a core capability rather than a temporary initiative. Nevertheless, the strategic use of specialized consultants and advisors remains valuable in covering expertise gaps or scaling capabilities during periods of intensive transformation.

3.4.6 Branding and Positioning the Innovation Team

The Innovation Team must evolve as a symbol that reflects the organization's commitment to innovation. The team should be announced by senior executives, ideally via a highly visible event such as an all-hands, to signal the start of a new era where people are empowered to achieve more and have a greater impact on the organization's future through innovation.

However, as explained earlier, there is always the risk that the rest of the organization perceives the innovation team as a separate, disconnected unit. In some cases, innovation teams may be seen as a benefit for a select few who enjoy exploring ideas and using the latest technologies in safe conditions without the pressure of production and operations-related tasks.

To address these risks, it is essential to emphasize three ways that fundamentally differentiate the innovation team as approached here. First, it is not a typical innovation team—it is not set up to *produce innovation*. Instead, its purpose is to *inspire*, enable, and orchestrate innovation, *empower* people and teams to innovate, and *make innovation inclusive*. Second, the team is designed to operate as *a hub* that connects to all parts of the organization, thereby bridging gaps, removing silos, and ultimately shaping a dynamic community of innovators across the company. Third, it emphasizes educating people on innovation techniques and encourages everyone to participate in the innovation process. Through systematic information sharing, real examples of how the team enables innovation in action, and effective talent rotation schemes, the innovation team eventually becomes a true hub for innovation with a universal presence across the company.

3.5 What Makes a Great Innovator

Being innovative is primarily a matter of mindset and a special attitude. Successful innovators demonstrate creativity, a risk-taking appetite, and a willingness to learn. The most successful innovators I've worked with are self-motivated, proactive individuals who go beyond their job descriptions and demonstrate a growth mindset—a way of thinking that promotes continuous learning and improvement. True innovators view *failure* as part of the learning process, and as a result, they are more open to trying new things and ideas and appreciate the importance of the experimentation process. They are comfortable with uncertainty and ambiguity and know how to test their assumptions.

In a corporate context, anyone can adopt this mindset to a certain extent—no specific background or expertise is required. However, there are certain professional traits that complement this mindset and enable the role model of the "true" innovator.

1. **Deep understanding of the organization**: A key factor that boosts the ability to innovate is the "connection" with the organization and its environment: true innovators relate to their company and its mission; they deeply understand its purpose, and they can see how it is positioned in the market and against competi-

tors; they follow the market dynamics, the global trends, and significant developments that may directly or indirectly affect the company.
2. **Great collaboration attitude**: Innovators need to be effective collaborators and team players. They realize that successful innovation outcomes require many great minds to work together. Thus, they are open to different views, welcome contributions from the team, and use their talents to help others develop their ideas as needed.
3. **Good understanding of the technology landscape**: While technical expertise is not required, having a justified view of modern technologies and associated capabilities is beneficial: it helps discover new ways to solve problems and understand what is feasible and what is not. Moreover, being technology savvy enables the innovator to connect with the right domain experts, speak their technical language, inspire people, and drive execution faster. Familiarity with modern methods, practices, and tools such as agile engineering, design thinking, prototyping, and experimentation is also beneficial.
4. **Product sense**: The ability to conceive products and solutions is another vital element for a true innovator: they can *think as a user*, apply empathy, and envision and articulate products, solutions, and services that address real problems and have the potential for commercial success.
5. **Entrepreneurial attitude**: True innovators realize the scarcity of resources and the importance of setting the right focus and prioritization. A true innovator uses data to make bold decisions and is ready to assume ownership and accountability. In fact, there is an overlap between the intrapreneur's role and that of the corporate innovator in that both focus on creativity, new ideas, and high-potential initiatives aligned with the organization's purpose. While the intrapreneur is usually an assigned role, the innovator, as defined here, is a behavior and a mindset that can be, to a certain extent, inherited *by anyone in the corporation*.

Most of these traits can be acquired through training and regular interaction with more experienced, active innovators. However, not all of them need to be there for every member. In an innovative organization, individuals complement each other and form powerful teams that collectively demonstrate these traits.

Identifying and empowering those true innovators in an organization is essential—they evolve as role models and act as mentors and intrapreneurs, leading by example and influencing others; they demonstrate genuine innovation behaviors, attract and inspire like-minded talent, and, thus, help drive cultural change from within and accelerate the formation of an active community of innovators.

3.6 The Innovation Culture

The innovation culture is *a special, collective mindset that encourages the exploration of novel ways to improve business outcomes*. It is a delicate construct that reflects *how people perceive the innovation process* and *how they feel about it* collectively; it reflects the dominant mindset, the general attitude toward *change*, and the *willingness to try new things* in order to serve the organizational purpose.

Corporate innovation requires an optimal mix of knowledge, strategy, technology, processes, and *culture*. From these ingredients, culture is the only one that *cannot be acquired; it must be developed* through a long process of inspiration and leadership powered by authentic messages and real examples that link innovation with the company's purpose. The culture begins to evolve when a critical mass of people engage with the innovation function as a means of pursuing the organization's purpose.

You can tell that the innovation culture is present when there is a *willingness to pursue new opportunities* and *readiness to disrupt the status quo* with the intent to create value for customers, the company, and the world. When the innovation culture is in a good state, people are proactive in spotting, framing, and pursuing opportunities that can serve the organization's purpose and goals. Innovative teams are driven by an *inherent curiosity*—a continual questioning of not only *how* things work but also *why* they work this way. In truly innovative companies, this force of improvement, the *propensity to novelty*, comes from within, from the collective state of mind.

The culture of innovation is a mindset that evolves on top of the following six principles, as shown in Fig. 3.3:

1. **Trust**: Great ideas require combined expertise and cross-disciplinary talent to be converted into innovation. To achieve this collective effort toward impactful innovation, people need to trust the process and feel safe to share their ideas, plans, ambitions, and knowledge. An increased level of trust is necessary in all the following ways:
   - Employees trust that the leadership believes in innovation as a means of achieving the organization's vision and purpose.
   - Leaders trust employees and their business judgment; they provide them with increased autonomy, resources, and flexibility in investing their time and energy.
   - Innovators trust each other. They know that their ideas are valued and that their contribution to others' ideas is always recognized. Innovators know they eventually get the credit and recognition they deserve for their contributions.
   - People trust the opportunity discovery and innovation process. They know it is transparent, objective, and reliable.

   Trust sets the basis for an organizational mentality where "one team" collaborates toward a bold purpose. It enables the formation of networks of innovators that can grow organically into an inspired innovation community.
2. **Safety**: People need to feel safe to engage with the creative process. It takes courage to share a thought-provoking idea, especially when it is "out of context." The fear of being criticized or "exposed" to upper levels of the hierarchy often excludes people and filters out ideas that could otherwise prove to be valuable. Similarly, when people are asked to provide feedback on ideas by others, they may be reluctant to openly and candidly share their thoughts, especially if the idea is coming from higher levels in the hierarchy or from perceived "authori-

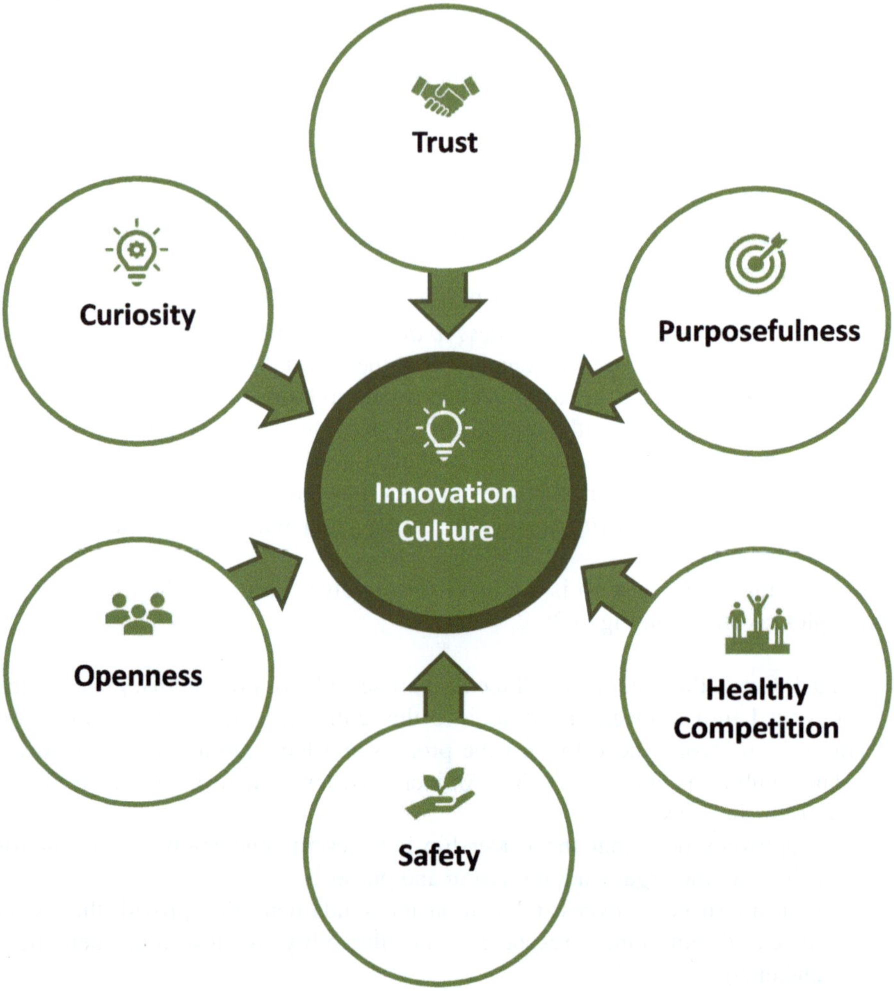

Fig. 3.3 The six components of the innovation culture

ties" in the organization. People must feel safe to ask tough questions and even constructively criticize an idea, regardless of its originator. In fact, justified, *well-intended critique* is what true innovators should be looking for. In a safe, innovation-friendly environment, no courage is required—people feel empowered to share their ideas even if they are controversial and thought-provoking or seem "crazy." The dominant culture is supportive of sharing, contribution, and constructive feedback, and so is the underlying innovation framework. These behaviors are fed into the Rewards and Gamification system as signals of specific behaviors and used to compute innovation performance metrics for individuals, teams, divisions, and the entire organization.

3. **Openness**: Diversity has proven to be a significant success factor for innovation: multidisciplinary teams, with a diversity of thought and a plurality of perspectives, usually perform far better in creative and problem-solving tasks. This applies not only to *disciplines* but also to *characters*: introverts, extroverts, individual contributors, or team players—all innovators should be encouraged to engage with the innovation function and join the self-organizing, inclusive community of innovators. To achieve that, innovation should be *inclusive by design*—people must have access to the innovation process regardless of the team, discipline, or level in the hierarchy. Although this sounds obvious, there are misconceptions that make innovation less inclusive, e.g., the belief that it is more engineering or technology focused. In the presence of such stereotypes, certain groups and individuals may feel discouraged from participating in the innovation movement. Other factors, such as limited bandwidth or time zone constraints of specific teams, may impact accessibility and make the innovation function less inclusive. These can be addressed in many ways, for example, by making innovation processes asynchronous or providing more lead time for people to plan for time-demanding events such as workshops or hackathons.
4. **Curiosity**: To stay innovative, businesses need to have an ongoing "opportunity discovery" thread—a continual search for novel ways that can improve business performance. This requires curious individuals who challenge the current state, go beyond understanding the "how," and ask the "why" of things. They are confident in articulating interesting hypotheses that can be further explored or validated via research and data insights. When curiosity is there, *openness to change rises, and fear of failure drops*. Curiosity is a perfect match with the *experimentation mentality* and the *fail-safe, fail-fast* approach. Combined with the right innovation capabilities, it can lead to great ideas, discoveries, inventions, and remarkable business opportunities. Moreover, curious individuals can play a crucial role in fostering an innovative culture: in a safe and open environment where they feel trust in all directions, curious minds ask tough questions, challenge the status quo, and set the paradigm for new behaviors and thought patterns. They evolve as role models, influencers, and thought leaders, impacting the culture, innovation function, and the entire organization.
5. **Purposefulness**: A well-framed, ambitious organizational purpose can be perceived as *the guiding star of innovation*, giving meaning to the program and inspiring people to engage. When people see the connection between innovation and purpose, they gain a better understanding of the problem space and invest their creative and intrapreneurial efforts in the right direction. In the absence of a clear purpose, innovation may look "empty," fuzzy, or even meaningless. A weak or insufficiently promoted purpose puts the culture at risk, as people may perceive innovation as being disconnected from reality. In such cases, inspiration and motivation drop, and the willingness to innovate and contribute "beyond the job description" fades out. Depending on the business's size and structure, the purpose can be set at the organizational, group, product, or team level. It can be a purely commercial or a societal one, a product vision, a customer promise, or another long-term ambitious goal with enough clarity to inspire people and trig-

ger the creative process. In all cases, it must be communicated clearly and systematically.

6. **Healthy competition**: Corporate environments are inherently competitive in various ways. Internal competition among employees and teams can take the form of frequent productivity benchmarks and recognition of individual or team achievements, which are typically reflected in bonuses and promotions. Competition among employees can drive productivity and short-term wins. Still, it does not always have a positive outlook and a long-term perspective: it can damage the culture and make people more secretive and defensive. There is a trade-off between internal competitiveness and innovation culture. As defined here, the concept of "healthy competition" goes beyond traditional performance metrics and emphasizes qualities like *inventiveness*, *willingness to share*, *ability to execute*, and *eagerness to contribute*, which, when combined, define a set of genuine innovative behaviors. In this setup, people are rewarded both for *individual innovation achievements* and for *helping others to innovate*. Innovators consistently receive the credit they deserve, regardless of how they contribute to innovation. "Healthy" in this context refers to *fairness*, *transparency*, *respect*, and a good balance between *personal ambition* and the *success of the team* and the *organization*. The principle of healthy competition requires trust in the system and its underlying processes.

To illustrate the different mindsets and contribution modes, consider the scenario where an employee has a great idea but lacks the necessary resources or skills to accurately define and drive it forward. In a strictly competitive environment, chances are that the idea remains hidden in the mind of the ideator, under the fear of being copied or leveraged by others with no attribution. In a "healthy competition" environment, the employee from the above example has the option to share the idea through the formal innovation channels and receive credit for inventiveness or creativity without necessarily participating in its exploration or implementation. The employee becomes part of the history of the idea as the "originator," meaning that if the idea is ever built and proves successful, the originator—and all subsequent contributors—gets the recognition they deserve: some for their inventiveness and others for their execution skills.

Similarly, an individual innovator may be recognized for contributing to ideas or innovation projects formed and driven by others. A team may be rewarded for exceptional results in executing an idea submitted by another team or group. Even invalidating an idea may be acknowledged as a significant contribution. In all cases, employees are recognized and rewarded based on their direct or indirect impact on innovation, regardless of the form or the timing of their contribution.

3.6.1 The Healthy Competition Protocol

Healthy competition depends on specific behaviors and a "protocol" consisting of the following principles:

1. Innovation is always on and open to all.
2. People show respect for others' ideas.
3. There are no "bad ideas."
4. Some ideas are better than others in a given context.
5. Great ideas can still fail.
6. Critique is constructive, meaningful, justified, and welcome.
7. Ideas do not have owners; they have originators and contributors.
8. Ideas are free to reuse; attribution is required.
9. There is no single decision-maker for the future of an idea.
10. Originators may not be involved in the execution of their ideas.
11. Rules and resulting decisions are transparent and consistent.
12. There is no space for corporate politics.

The above principles define a framework of respectful competition, which, although it *promotes competitiveness* (there are top performers and some ideas are better than others), also *fosters collaboration and teamwork* (attribution to the chain of originators and contributors). Individual innovation performance is defined on top of dimensions such as *inventiveness*, *openness*, *ability to execute*, and *contribution*. The Innovation Rewards program utilizes these individual performance signals along with the assessment of the associated ideas, to produce an overall Innovation Contribution Score. This score is used to identify the top-performing individuals and teams.

3.7 Blockers of Innovation Culture

In the following paragraphs, we examine the most common innovation blockers that discourage people from engaging in innovation activities and impede or prevent the development of a healthy innovation culture.

- **Innovation is not linked with strategy and purpose**: Companies often invest in expensive innovation programs or fancy labs without clearly linking them to their organizational purpose. When this happens, the failure of the innovation process is inevitable: innovators have difficulty connecting innovation with reality and, eventually, lose interest, feeling uninspired or uncertain about the problems to solve or the opportunities to pursue. The engagement with the company's innovation engine drops, negatively impacting the overall innovation performance and increasing the opportunity cost.
- **Innovation is not linked with career progression**: The value an employee gains from being innovative is not always obvious. People tend to think of narrow job descriptions and understand performance in rather limiting ways. Even when innovation is part of the job description, performance reviews do not always reflect employees' innovation contributions. As a result, it is not always clear to employees how they benefit from engaging in additional innovation activities. Even in contests like hackathons, where people typically join driven

by their enthusiasm, there are often skeptics who are reluctant to share their ideas simply because they do not see value. While a reputation as an innovator might be a meaningful reward, it is not always translated into career progression. Without real-world examples of innovators being widely recognized, appreciated, and promoted, employees may doubt the importance of being innovative in advancing their careers to the next level.

- **"Too Busy" to innovate**: Innovation activities require time and agility. Formal innovation workshops may require valuable team members to commit for hours or days. A concept that is moving through the innovation process may require additional work by the originator of the idea. For example, a patent application needs significant documentation, disclosure meetings, and several reviews of the formal application. People often feel overwhelmed when they realize the amount of work necessary to support an idea through the process, such as presentations or ad hoc activities. In other scenarios, employees may simply want to share their ideas without any intention of researching, pitching, prototyping, or filing patent applications. They may not have the availability to engage or the skills to contribute further. In such scenarios, the absence of a lightweight process to capture ideas can demotivate employees from contributing.
- **Lost in hierarchy and bureaucracy**: The structure of large organizations can become quite chaotic, inflexible, and political. Finding the right stakeholder to influence or the most relevant team to pitch an idea can be daunting. Failure to do so can be frustrating and even misleading regarding the idea's potential and the right next steps. On top of this organizational complexity, the lack of a standard channel or a forum to diffuse ideas and attract attention can worsen the experience and further demotivate people.
- **Fear of exposure and criticism**: In specific scenarios, employees may be afraid or discouraged from sharing their ideas. Even the most experienced inventors and innovators may have second thoughts about new concepts that may look "crazy" or overambitious. Certain characters may prefer to keep such ideas private or wait for the right conditions before communicating them. In general, people may not feel comfortable sharing a "random" idea, which may be perceived as out of context or irrelevant.
- **Lack of tools, templates, and guidance**: In some cases, the willingness to innovate may be blocked by gaps in skills or experience. For instance, people often lack the knowledge to structure and frame a business opportunity. Considering that great but poorly described concepts have limited chances of attracting attention, it is essential to provide guidance, examples, and tools to help people frame and develop their ideas. Or when teams need to rapidly prototype a new concept and expose it to a small audience but don't have the right tools and guidance, chances are that the initiative will be abandoned. Artificial intelligence brings significant improvements in this direction by offering just-in-time assistance and providing highly effective and user-friendly tools for ideation, prototyping, and more, as described in Chaps. 6–8 and throughout the book.
- **Leadership disconnect**: A lack of genuine interest from leadership can demotivate employees. When leaders fail to engage with the innovation function in a

meaningful way, or their message is weak, people may feel disconnected or uninspired. As the term "innovation" is often overused—and sometimes misused—people need concrete examples of ideas that originated from innovators and converted into tangible business opportunities. They need to see executives and leaders as role models, delivering examples, innovation stories, and guidance on how innovation serves the company's purpose. To foster a stronger connection with innovation, leaders should be more present, communicate consistently with clear messages, and provide evidence that they genuinely believe in innovation driven by people. For example, when ideas end up pending in a queue for a long time or are "parked" without proper assessment, ideators doubt the company's interest in innovation and perceive leadership as not paying enough attention to ideas. Situations like these trigger cascading effects that further damage the innovation culture.

- **Blocked by the manager**: This may sound ironic, but it happens frequently: middle managers often do not encourage or permit their team members to spend time on workshops and related events. Even when people find ways to get involved in innovation activities beyond the microcosm of their team, their managers do not always pay enough attention. Under the pressure of deliverables and deadlines, managers may understand "disruptive innovation" differently—as a source of disruption to the smooth execution of a project. From a cultural perspective, middle-level management is typically the layer that requires reform in attitude and a significant shift toward an innovation mindset.

3.8 What Innovators Expect

The promise of innovation raises the bar. Following the announcement of an ambitious innovation program, people's expectations grow fast. Although this is a positive reaction, it may introduce risks if these expectations are mismanaged or not met. To convert this initial interest and energy into engagement, the organization must be *responsive*, *fast*, and *consistent in its approach*. For instance, people who share their bold ideas expect at least a prompt response, constructive feedback, genuine recognition, and the opportunity to develop their ideas further. Failure to respond promptly and meaningfully puts the innovation culture and the overall initiative at risk, especially during the first iterations of the program, where "early adopters" are needed to set the tone and influence others to join the innovation thread. People typically expect the following:

- **Timely, consistent communication**: Innovators are driven by enthusiasm and expect things to move quickly. The moment they submit an idea or a business proposal, they are eager to see things progressing; they need to know "what happens next" and "when to expect what."
- **Transparency on rules and decisions**: Innovators expect transparency—they need to know the "rules of the game," for example, how ideas are being assessed and prioritized, how the company makes investment decisions for new product

development, or the rules and criteria governing the innovation rewards program. Moreover, people need to know "what success looks like" in the context of innovation, and hence, it is essential to provide a transparent definition of innovation performance, supported by examples of how it is being measured. On another front, innovators must be fully aware of the company's intellectual property policies and how they apply to specific cases.

- **The opportunity to pitch ideas**: Corporate environments tend to be challenging to navigate. As a result, reaching the right team or decision-makers to pitch an idea can be a lengthy and frustrating process. The opportunity to pitch is usually one of the key goals of innovators when submitting an idea or proposal—they aim to attract attention from the right audience and explore the options. Hence, presentation and pitch opportunities are expected to be regularly available, along with easy access to stakeholders for presenting ideas and getting constructive feedback and advice.
- **Mentorship and guidance**: The innovation function must be inclusive by design. Employees should be welcome to join regardless of their background, experience in building products, or technical competencies and skills. People expect the innovation process to be equally available and friendly to all. New joiners may need guidance and support to get started and participate actively; they expect to have at least basic assistance, along with appropriate resources such as educational materials and quick-start guides. In a truly innovative environment, people should also have access to mentors—experienced innovators or domain experts willing to provide just-in-time advice to teams or individual innovators.
- **The opportunity to experiment**: A company claiming to be innovative in an open, inclusive way is expected to allow people to explore promising ideas. Exploration can take many forms, ranging from research activities and product discovery to MVP definition and prototype development, as well as proof-of-concept implementations. Innovators expect to get enough time to experiment and access the skills, resources, and technology needed to take a high-potential idea to the next level.
- **Visibility and recognition**: Proud innovators appreciate and expect visibility and exposure as a result of their innovation activities. These may come as public acknowledgments of their innovative thinking, recognition of the impact of their ideas, or contribution to others' ideas.
- **Leadership participation**: Innovators expect leadership to play an integral role in the innovation process, and they appreciate regular communication with corporate leaders through updates, feedback, and guidance. Leaders are expected to demonstrate genuine interest not only in success stories but also in insightful failures, experiments, and key lessons learned.

Leaders have great expectations, as well. They typically expect to see performance indicators that justify the investment in innovation and insights that confirm good progress on the cultural shift toward the Innovation Mode. They expect high-quality outputs from the idea management process, including ideas, product concepts, success stories, and high-potential business opportunities.

3.9 Fixing the Innovation Culture

Culture is a crucial success factor for innovation, and thus, it requires the full attention of the leadership. Fixing the culture is difficult—it takes time and usually involves multiple, long-term initiatives. However, before investing in expensive transformational programs and radical organizational changes, leaders should consider introducing certain inexpensive "fixes" and "hacks" that can bring cultural improvements organically. For instance, known complexities and bureaucratic processes, poor communication practices, lack of educational resources on innovation, and limited understanding of innovation methodologies are all excellent targets for "quick wins" and relatively inexpensive improvements.

Before attempting to improve the innovation culture, it is essential to measure it and understand its current state, including the general perception and attitude of employees toward innovation. An initial measurement sets the basis for a continual improvement process—a framework that allows every cultural improvement attempt to be measured and assessed against a known "starting state" and predefined goals; it brings important insights into how people think of innovation and how they perceive the organization's ability to innovate. Such measurements may lead to interesting discoveries regarding people's expectations, popular misconceptions, or gaps—valuable insights that help shape the plan of action and prepare the first few waves of "cultural hacks."

A simple survey can reveal how employees feel about innovation, such as whether they are encouraged to share their ideas and have the time and resources to experiment with new concepts and technologies. Such insights help understand what is blocking people from innovating and how innovative they perceive the organization to be. This understanding, in turn, enables the identification of quick fixes and the right tactical moves, such as implementing an educational program to update middle management's view on innovation.

Moreover, measuring innovation perception across the hierarchy can reveal critical gaps in how people at various levels and functions in the organization understand innovation. Such insights help the company discover misalignments in how different layers of the organization perceive, contextualize, and prioritize innovation. More specifically, it can highlight the differences in how managers and directors perceive innovation versus senior leaders, thereby identifying potential deviations or divergent views. Such gaps in perception are particularly important since middle and upper management are expected to play an influential role and advocate for the values of innovation. A series of standardized innovation surveys helps the company drive alignment across management layers and shape a strong, consistent innovation message.

By introducing an ongoing "innovation pulse" survey, the company can obtain strong signals about the health of the innovation culture and the associated trends and dynamics. The survey can be combined with other techniques that provide qualitative insights, such as user interviews or focus groups. Based on such insights, the following list of "hacks" may be used to remove obstacles, help people navigate the organizational structure, and make innovation more open and effective.

3.9.1 Define What Innovation Means for Your Company

Novelty, innovation, and success mean different things to people. Even within the same company, people and teams may understand and value innovation differently. Leaders need to bring clarity on *what innovation* is and what *being innovative* means for the company. Beyond theoretical, generic definitions, it is essential to maintain a set of solid definitions of innovation adapted to your company's context. These definitions should be incorporated into the Innovation Playbook and establish a shared *innovation language*. Clearly defining innovation within the company's context enables everyone to understand how it aligns with the organization's vision and connects to its values. When people see how innovation is framed as part of the company's strategy, they engage more and adopt the culture of innovation faster.

To achieve the desired level of clarity, leaders must consistently deliver compelling narratives that explain how the company leverages innovation, how innovation has shaped or impacted the company, and how it is expected to define its future.

- **Connect innovation to the organizational purpose**: When employees don't understand how innovation efforts serve the company's purpose, they're less likely to embrace the innovation culture. To bridge this gap, corporate leaders must consistently demonstrate how innovation is connected to the company's purpose, mission, and future. The primary tool for this is the Innovation Agenda—a "living document" that presents the company's purpose, mission, vision, and strategy and establishes the corresponding "problem space," specific problem areas or opportunities that the company's innovation engine should focus on. The innovation agenda (explained in Chap. 3) translates the company's strategy into a collection of problems and opportunities that, if addressed, will bring the organization closer to its purpose. This provides instant clarity and makes the connection between purpose and innovation clear and compelling.
- **Expand the field of view**: Being laser focused on goals, milestones, and results is beneficial for business, but it also carries the risk of becoming isolated within the company's microcosm. Helping people understand the broader perspective—the environment in which the company operates—makes the company's purpose and vision more meaningful and innovation more strategic. A blend of market signals, competitive insights, and innovation stories from the public domain, when embedded into daily business activities and routines, can change how people think, ideate, decide, and plan. Teams expand their field of view and become more effective in spotting problems and innovation opportunities. When the right mindset is present, these insights help people understand how innovation is connected not only to the company's purpose but also to the broader ecosystem. Resetting the focus and looking at things differently from new angles helps imagine new possibilities, draft novel ideas, and engage with the innovation process.

3.9.2 Redefine Failure

Risk-averse environments are far from ideal for innovation. Without an effective framework to handle failure as part of the innovation process, the organization develops resistance to risk, impacting its ability to pursue novel opportunities. In such environments, failure is an unwelcome outcome, typically implying a "bad" idea or that something went very wrong, such as poor product design or execution. Managers often feel that they must explain and report failures defensively, as a "blame game" is usually involved.

Innovation-led organizations take a different approach: while everything is still optimized for success, they also have the ability to handle failure as part of a culture that promotes experimentation and risk taking. Based on the fail-fast, fail-safe principle, an unsuccessful result is accepted without friction—it may be even welcome—provided that it happens early enough in the process (fail fast) and before significant allocation of resources and prior to any dependencies or commitments (fail safe). This approach enables the consideration and testing of promising but potentially risky ideas, which would likely be overlooked in a risk-averse environment.

Moreover, even when a failure occurs beyond experimentation, e.g., when a product is live in the market, innovative companies have the culture and mechanisms to handle it. They utilize data and feedback loops to explore various solutions, and they are flexible enough to consider pivots or reevaluate their overall strategy. They know when to make tough decisions, such as killing a project or sunsetting a product, and how to be transparent about it by providing strong narratives that explain the logic. This is another strong sign of a healthy innovation culture that accepts failure as part of the innovation process and a learning opportunity; instead of a blame game, this approach focuses on understanding the definitive factors that prevented the initiative from succeeding. Through retrospectives, teams reconsider the initial assumptions and hypotheses in the light of user feedback or other empirical evidence.

What enables those innovative companies to embrace failure as part of the process is the "portfolio approach" they take regarding innovation initiatives: over a sufficiently long period, a company may be experimenting with multiple opportunities. Considering the uncertainty involved in novel ideas and ambitious opportunities, a certain percentage of projects are expected to fail; however, the company may still gain significant positive value and strategic advantages from the few successful ones.

To adopt this approach, companies must reframe failure and help people understand how unsuccessful ideas or initiatives are still valuable for the organization. While in a general business context, failure refers to unsuccessful outcomes, i.e., initiatives that didn't deliver according to expectations or commitments, in an innovation context, a failure should be seen as an initiative that "didn't make it to the next stage." For example, a project didn't meet the predefined success criteria—e.g., market adoption—and as a result, it was "parked" or "killed."

Considering that the purpose of these high-risk initiatives is primarily to validate a concept by testing the underlying assumptions and estimating its viability, a negative result is not a failure: it is an informed decision, e.g., to kill or park the project, that allows the company to focus better and allocate resources among projects wisely. In this context, the fail-safe, fail-early approach provides value in at least the following ways:

1. **Enables learning**: Teams accept failure and conduct retrospectives to review the initial hypotheses and assumptions and understand the real reasons behind unsuccessful outcomes. They embed these insights and lessons learned into the process, allowing them to be considered in future iterations.
2. **Releases bandwidth**: Provided that failure occurs early enough in the process, before significant investment commitments, this approach releases valuable resources that can be better utilized in projects that are progressing or in exploring new opportunities waiting in the portfolio. Through the fail-safe, fail-fast approach, the company's bandwidth to explore opportunities increases.
3. **Boosts the innovation culture**: From a team's perspective, this approach provides a sandbox to pursue high-uncertainty opportunities and get either successful outcomes or insightful failures.

Demonstrating that the company accepts failure in this context sends a strong signal that genuine innovation is indeed happening within the organization. However, adopting this attitude is not easy. It requires extensive and efficient communication of real-life stories about how innovation failures helped the company make better decisions and improve its overall process. Following this approach, leaders present examples of ambitious projects that were "killed" early in the process in light of new insights and outcomes of experimentation. They explain the reasoning, the invalidated hypotheses, the learnings, and how they contribute to continual improvement. For example, leaders may present how an informed decision to "kill" an initially promising project released resources to experiment with other innovation opportunities and helped the company avoid unnecessary development costs.

Another great way to support the updated notion of "failure" is by encouraging the community of innovators to share their "failure lessons learned"—either for specific projects or the cumulative knowledge, e.g., patterns, across a large number of unsuccessful initiatives, for instance, how to state and test assumptions as early as possible in the process or the most important challenges when prototyping complex concepts—all real stories and references from the innovation community. This way, people understand what "success" means in an innovation context and how "failure" is an integral part of the process. By openly sharing such stories, people realize that leaders accept failure too—they see, in action, that *educated risk taking* is well appreciated by the company as an innovative trait.

3.9.3 Add Elasticity to the Organizational Structure

Too much organizational structure constrains and decelerates innovation. Innovation suffers from rigid roles, complex organizational charts, and long chains of command; such environments are challenging to explore and introduce limitations in information flow and knowledge exchange. Under these conditions, the culture of innovation is severely constrained, impacting all stakeholders, as explained below.

Innovators often face the challenge of navigating complex hierarchies and corporate structures to discover the right stakeholders to pitch their ideas. Securing resources, finding sponsors, and opportunities to communicate a proposal can be a frustrating experience. Bureaucracy slows the journey from an idea to artifact generation and experimentation, reducing agility and introducing barriers to information sharing and knowledge exchange.

At the same time, leaders may have limited visibility in the work happening across teams, resulting in inefficiencies and missed opportunities. Non-optimal organizational structures introduce information gaps between teams and divisions, leading to wasted effort and opportunity costs. In large organizations, it is not unusual to realize that two groups have been solving the same problem independently or, even worse, solving one that has already been solved or killed.

Identifying and resolving the root cause of a non-performing organizational structure is a slow, costly, and risky process. Structural changes trigger massive reorganizations and may last for a long time, typically due to corporate politics and broader cultural issues. However, there are "hacks" that can help mitigate organizational problems by injecting some elasticity and agility at the right points of friction.

Flatten Hierarchies, Redefine Roles: Flat, horizontal organizations tend to perform better, at least from an innovation point of view. Although they are proven to work well primarily for smaller companies, corporations can still adopt certain patterns from flat structures that can make their hierarchy more elastic and flexible.

One way to make the corporate structure less rigid is to introduce informal communication channels that connect innovators directly with leadership. A "skip-level for innovation" program enables ad hoc meetings where innovators can present mature, well-prepared ideas to stakeholders for feedback, guidance, and support. These informal, efficient interactions should be encouraged by direct managers and shouldn't require their approval. When properly orchestrated, such programs energize people, bridge information gaps, and promote meaningful communication across all levels.

Building on the skip-level program, employees should be empowered to form virtual, multidisciplinary teams spanning departments to explore ideas and opportunities. Although these are informal initiatives, senior members may participate as mentors by offering strategic advice and fostering cross-level communication across the company. Through these hands-on initiatives, people build professional networks, learn from experts, and experience the innovation culture in practice.

Innovation enablement requires trust in people's ability to self-organize and experiment informally, free from unnecessary bureaucracy and administrative layers.

To support these scenarios, people need time, flexibility, and permission to go beyond their job titles. Moreover, organizations can augment existing roles and job descriptions by adding innovation as an explicit expectation. Leadership can communicate this strategic amendment across all roles, encouraging active involvement in innovation initiatives. Furthermore, by incorporating innovation into performance assessments, the organization sends a clear message to middle management to value and measure innovative contributions, thus fundamentally shifting how they evaluate their teams.

Following this path and assuming that mentorship is available, people become more proactive, take a different view on innovation, and eventually build confidence in their skills and talents. They communicate more frequently with senior managers and leaders, and they feel empowered to innovate and collaborate beyond their levels and seniority.

Break the Silos: Having isolated teams is both a symptom and a cause of fragmented organizations. Teams that are not fully integrated into the organization typically share information on a need-to-know basis—a behavior that contributes to the formation of gaps. This is incompatible with the "one-team" mentality and usually damages the culture of innovation. Even when geographical or other factors explain why teams operate in isolation, basic knowledge exchange mechanisms should be there to bridge the gap and enable cross-team innovation.

For instance, it may seem reasonable for an industry vertical within a large consulting firm to be viewed as "independent," as they may have a different operating model, pace, and business practices. Similarly, two product teams within the same organization may be "naturally" seen as autonomous.

However, significant benefits can be gained in a connected mode, which can be achieved without losing autonomy. In all the cases mentioned above, effective information flows can create considerable value for both the siloed teams and the organization as a whole: by connecting to an internal hub for innovation (see Chap. 4, the Innovation Hub), each team gets access to ideas, resources, solutions, and knowledge produced by the rest of the company; they adopt a standard model for innovation, speak the same "innovation language," and follow proven techniques and methods; they may even "crowdsource" individual problems, by asking the community to find high potential solutions. Most importantly, people become part of a single network of innovators and adopt a system of shared values and principles.

Breaking corporate silos requires strong leadership. Leaders must understand and communicate the benefits of unifying the organization and demonstrate how synchronized innovation strengthens the entire organization as a cohesive "one team."

Long-term success requires systematic, smart information and knowledge sharing across teams. The Innovation Portal serves as this connection hub, where divisions share their innovation agendas and discover knowledge aligned with both local and organizational priorities, as described in Chap. 4.

Remove Bureaucracy: A company may be bureaucratic in the formal sense, governed by strict, multilevel hierarchies and a long chain of commands leading up to authorities to make decisions. In fact, most large corporations tend to be bureaucratic to some extent, as this may have certain benefits, such as predictability and stability. Nevertheless, it is widely acknowledged that a purely bureaucratic environment is not compatible with all the values of the innovation culture, as presented in this chapter. More specifically, bureaucratic setups often suffer from low morale, resistance to change, and a slow pace in decision-making, as everything must go through strict protocols.

In this book, we use the term "bureaucracy" in a broader sense to denote unnecessary complexity in a method or process. Bureaucratic processes may also be present in non-bureaucratic organizations, often resulting from poorly designed or outdated processes. Sometimes, they reflect an intent to avoid change—a bias for stability over action. Due to unnecessary steps, checkpoints, and multiple approvers, these processes are often slow and overly complex, burdened by rules, terminology, and lengthy documentation.

Especially when it comes to the innovation process, the impact of bureaucracy is severe: some companies follow rigid, linear innovation processes, coming with strict rules, checklists, detailed documentation requirements, and formal approvals. When such processes interfere with genuine innovation initiatives characterized by internal drive, passion, a fast pace, and a willingness to change, the culture of innovation suffers, and overall engagement drops, for example, when innovators struggle to get timely approvals for resources that they need to prototype a concept, when they must fill overcomplicated forms and compile lengthy documentation even at the early stages of a raw idea before it gets reviewed, or when they need a manager's approval to perform simple innovation tasks such as obtaining access to the right devices or technology for experimenting with an idea.

Removing bureaucratic processes is not easy—it can be the goal of a long-term transformation plan. To mitigate the problem of overly complex, problematic, and slow processes, leaders need to introduce flexibility and work-arounds explicitly designed for innovation. For example, while the procurement process may be strict, there could be exceptions for the purposes of innovation, intending to speed up the provisioning of the required resources, such as skills, technology, and materials, thus unblocking innovation projects.

Encourage Side-Innovation Projects: Another way to empower the innovation message and improve the culture is by encouraging side-innovation initiatives. This informal program enables employees with the necessary bandwidth to join existing projects or establish their own. This encourages people to self-organize and innovate without requiring managerial approval or other formalities. Employees can discover interesting activities and interact across levels beyond their usual responsibilities. Leadership orchestrates these efforts by maintaining an internal project portfolio, tracking activities, and coordinating presentations and knowledge sharing.

Orchestrate the Formation of a Community: Companies can add flexibility to hierarchical structures and organizational designs by encouraging the growth of an active community of innovators. When such a community is present, people network organically, beyond team boundaries, across organizational divisions and levels in the hierarchy. A good strategy is to identify those self-motivated innovators, builders, and mentors and invite them to establish the community. Empowered by a strong message from the leadership, sufficient resources, and strong branding, this core of innovation enthusiasts can drive a significant, organic cultural shift. The team should focus on popularizing key innovation concepts and lead by example, addressing real problems and ideas. The founding members of the innovation community evolve into "role models" for innovation who can spark people's interest in innovation.

Inject Innovation into Projects: Many teams appear "too busy to innovate" or overprotective of the established pace and rhythm of business—they do not have the capacity to handle the noise of "random" ideas being proposed during execution, which is a valid concern. A good way to embrace innovation without risking existing projects and timelines is by encouraging team members to register their ideas "silently" and asynchronously in a separate backlog. The project manager reviews the ideas backlog asynchronously, consults the stakeholders, and decides which ideas should be considered in the current scope and which to prioritize for future iterations. Considering how easy it is to capture and manage ideas with properly integrated AIs, this approach provides an effective way to promote innovative thinking in a more "conservative" and safe way: ideas are being expressed and registered, and there is a process to review them as part of future phases or iterations.

In other cases, complex, long-lasting projects may need a fresh view and possibly a dose of innovation. To set a new perspective without disrupting the setup and pace of complicated projects, the company may assign an "outside innovator," an employee with relevant expertise who joins the project to identify opportunities for innovation. Acting as an observer, the innovator operates in a "silent mode" and only consults with the project manager and stakeholders when there are justified opportunities to introduce valuable, novel features in subsequent project phases. This way, outside innovators inject novelty into complex, "conventional" projects—not only through feature ideas but also by influencing product development and project management methods to foster innovation.

Benefit from Organizational Slack: Having inspired, motivated employees ready to innovate creates a new challenge: how do we provide time for experimentation without disrupting business operations? There are a few options to consider.

The simplest method is to allocate specific time for innovation, allowing employees to decide how to utilize it. Another option is to embed resources for the winning teams of innovation events, such as hackathons—winners are given the time, equipment, and all the resources they need to prototype their concepts.

A more strategic approach leverages *organizational slack*—the unused capacity within an organization that can be redirected toward innovation. This approach encourages the formation of fluid, dynamic innovation teams that adapt to the availability of skills within the company. To illustrate how that would work, consider a portfolio of innovation projects waiting for implementation, e.g., prototypes, PoCs, or demos. The portfolio is visible via the Innovation Portal and open to anyone with the bandwidth to participate. Using a loosely coupled contribution model, team members flow in and out based on their interests, availability, and skill match.

For example, imagine an innovation project that requires the implementation of a complex software component. The owning team breaks the task into smaller, well-defined pieces and requests help from the innovation community. Developers who happen to have free bandwidth volunteer to contribute to specific tasks according to their interests and skills. On completion of the task, the contribution is automatically registered in the Innovation Rewards system, and the developer receives acknowledgment and, eventually, rewards for their efforts.

This program introduces another dimension of agility, not only in terms of project scope but also from a team composition perspective. In large organizations with the right culture, this model can create a continuous supply of innovators willing to contribute to specific innovation initiatives. With proper orchestration, projects move faster and more smoothly—through informal collaboration. At the same time, this self-organizing approach strengthens the innovation culture since participation is driven by personal interest. This program can evolve into an internal platform for problems, solutions, and talent, where artificial intelligence automatically suggests ideal team compositions and recommends specific individuals based on their skills and availability when a project is defined.

3.9.4 Educate Innovators: Establish an "Innovation Academy"

Providing education and training on methodologies, techniques, and practices is a key enabler for innovation, as it increases general interest, willingness, and readiness to innovate. A smart education program can also drive significant improvement in the culture of innovation: even informal training sessions can help people understand the methods and realize how particular innovation techniques and tools fit into the company's context. This contextualized education program also signifies the importance of innovation for the organization.

The impact of ongoing education at the individual level is evident: individuals become more capable and confident in participating in the innovation effort. At the organizational level, education programs help drive the general adoption of a standard Innovation Playbook—the methods, templates, and tools used to innovate within the company's context. For example, by referencing the playbook, it becomes clear to all what a prototype is, how it provides value, how to build one, or how experimentation adds value to the organization.

Education comes in various formats, including presentations, talks, workshops, and stand-alone training materials. It can be delivered by leaders, domain experts, or anyone from the innovation community. In terms of curriculum, the program should cover the foundational aspects of innovation, starting from the basics, such as terminology and methods and then progressing to more advanced techniques and best practices. As the target audience is typically broad, ranging from junior hires to leaders across multiple disciplines, the program must provide entry points that match the different angles, perspectives, and needs. The following list provides just a few examples that are both inexpensive and impactful.

The Innovation Playbook: This branded strategic document provides a comprehensive guide containing all essential elements needed to drive innovation within your company, from foundational instructions to practical resources, methods, tools, and templates. It stands as your organization's definitive manual on "how to innovate." The Playbook presents clear definitions of innovation, maps out problem and opportunity spaces, and details specific methods, tools, decision processes, and key contacts that your innovators would need to succeed. It introduces a shared language and framework that drive alignment across all organizational levels. Instead of theoretical, generic innovation concepts, the playbook offers a practical guide presenting definitions, methods, and tools as adapted to your company's context; it addresses the innovator's most frequent needs and questions through intent-based navigation, such as "I want to share an idea" or "How to tell if my idea is patentable," and thus it makes innovation pathways clear and actionable by linking processes and innovation tools and providing hints and suggested actions to specific goals. The playbook can be used as the basis for regular live sessions that introduce the innovation function to a broad audience.

As defined here, the Innovation Playbook is more than just a reference document—it is an essential asset that helps transform how the organization approaches innovation by bringing consistency, clarity, and a common understanding of the innovation process. In this sense, the playbook can be part of the official orientation program, integrated into employee onboarding, and recommended training.

In a more advanced form, the playbook evolves into an AI-powered, interactive digital experience delivered through the Innovation Portal. For instance, users can describe their intent, e.g., "I want to build a prototype," and receive rich content experiences with interactive guidance, including relevant resources, videos, documentation, teams, and colleagues with related expertise. Moreover, artificial intelligence can power a conversational experience integrated into the Innovation Portal, where innovators can explain their needs in natural language and receive concrete answers and guidance on how to achieve their innovation goals.

The Journey of an Idea: This training package presents your company's idea-to-market journey, demystifying how ideas are captured, assessed, framed as opportunities, validated, and brought to market either as prototypes or as early instances of a product, such as a minimum viable product (MVP). This package aims to establish a common understanding of the tools and methods for articulating business concepts and exploring the next best steps; it uses real-world examples to explain the idea assessment process. It provides practical tools, frameworks, and templates and presents how AI can be used to accelerate ideation, brainstorming, concept validation, and implementation. This comprehensive approach ensures that every employee understands what makes a good business idea and how to develop and communicate one effectively within your organization's innovation setup.

The Power of Experimentation: This is a special course designed to introduce business experimentation and the prototyping process and demonstrate their strategic value in bringing ideas to market. It is an excellent opportunity to use real examples from your organization to illustrate how prototyping reduces uncertainty, accelerates development, and validates concepts before making significant development investments. The course introduces core prototyping principles, helping individuals and teams understand when and how to prototype effectively. Participants learn about the prototyping methods and tools available in the company and how to select the right approach based on their goals and resources. The course also covers how AI is revolutionizing the prototyping landscape, enabling the creation of functional prototypes via natural language descriptions in minutes and without requiring technical skills. It presents AI-powered prototyping tools and in-product experimentation technologies.

The examples above present a few select foundational training packages that form the basis of a comprehensive, ongoing educational initiative: the Innovation Academy. The program aims to reach all organizational levels and cover an expanding range of innovation topics, from specific methodologies such as design thinking, lean, and agile engineering to advanced strategic approaches.

The Innovation Academy can be delivered through multiple channels and in various formats, such as live events, recorded sessions, and quick-start guides. Live sessions may feature corporate leaders, innovation specialists, or renowned industry professionals who share their unique perspectives, thus further strengthening the message and increasing the impact of the sessions. In a particularly powerful variation, live sessions are led by internal innovators themselves, creating a community-driven learning environment that emphasizes the growth mindset and reinforces the innovation culture. These peer educators receive recognition and rewards for their genuine "innovation behavior"—empowering others to innovate.

Beyond live sessions, the program generates branded content, including articles, videos, and podcasts, which are fed into the innovation knowledge base and thus become accessible through the Innovation Portal and other corporate touchpoints.

This multifaceted education initiative makes innovation more inclusive and effective. By combining methodologies with real examples and success stories, the content reinforces the strategic importance of innovation, strengthens the culture, and opens the program to all. To effectively run this program, the company should form a dedicated innovation education team responsible for content creation, event management, success measurement, and program expansion throughout the organization.

3.9.5 Become Responsive and Transparent

Innovators create and share important content with the company, including their ideas, concepts, proposals, or other artifacts. In their eyes, this content is highly valuable and deserves at least a prompt and meaningful response. However, it is not uncommon for ideators to experience prolonged periods of silence or to receive template-based responses instead of constructive feedback. This ineffective handling of ideas leads to frustration, impacts employee morale, and eventually damages the innovation culture. The minimum expectation from an innovator about a proposal or idea submission is *attention* and *acknowledgment*. In this sense, innovation leaders should consider the following guidelines:

Respond Promptly and Meaningfully: Companies need a framework that explains to innovators *what happens* after submitting their ideas and presents the *typical timeline*, e.g., how long it would take for an idea assessment or an invention disclosure meeting. Timelines should be pragmatic but also optimized to maintain the momentum of innovation. The framework should be included in the Innovation Playbook and also accessible through the main innovation channels, including the Innovation Portal. This way, it can bring alignment and set the expectations for simple innovation cases—e.g., processing an idea and processing a patent disclosure.

Once the framework is communicated, the company must demonstrate consistency—meeting these expectations signals that leadership values people's contributions, while frequent delays impact the innovation spirit and demotivate people from sharing again in the future.

Quality of response matters as much as speed. Dealing with ambitious, passionate innovators who voluntarily share their thoughts and ideas requires carefully designed communication based on well-prepared, insightful, and, depending on the case, actionable feedback. The communication should acknowledge the effort invested and maintain an appreciative tone, recognizing that innovators offer their creativity and passion.

Delivering consistent, meaningful responses requires adequate resources and increased capacity. As explained in Chap. 6, this can be achieved through a streamlined idea assessment process powered by a team of skilled evaluators and AI, which can process large volumes of ideas and provide meaningful feedback while identifying opportunities for the organization.

Act on Ideas and Proposals: While feedback guides innovators and improves the culture, it is *tangible actions upon ideas* that demonstrate the importance of innovation for the company. When there is a flow of ideas but no concrete actions, the entire innovation process risks being perceived as "innovation theatre." "Action" can take many forms, such as idea pitching, prototyping, focused research, or a presentation to leadership and relevant stakeholders. Even when an idea isn't considered beyond this point, showing that it received serious consideration demonstrates a genuine commitment to innovation and thus encourages people to keep innovating. Prompt actions upon ideas contribute to an influential innovation culture.

Make the Innovation Process Transparent: Transparency in the innovation processes builds trust, encourages participation, and helps innovators understand how their contributions align with organizational goals. You can bring transparency by documenting and publishing all the essential innovation processes and rules through the Innovation Portal and the Playbook. This way, aspiring innovators understand the logic behind key processes and can better align with innovation objectives. For instance, presenting the idea assessment process and the involved assessment criteria using real examples helps people understand both the evaluation approach and how it connects to the organizational strategy.

3.9.6 Connect with Innovators

Connecting with innovators is probably the most effective way to prove leadership's commitment to innovation and, thus, a great way to grow a healthy innovation culture. Leaders and managers should take every opportunity to emphasize the importance of innovation and demonstrate its connection to the company's purpose. To amplify the message, leaders can leverage the tools mentioned previously—the Innovation Playbook, the Portal, and the Agenda—to clearly present the company's purpose and how innovation helps achieve it. The following activities can help leaders strengthen their connection with the innovation community:

Ask for Help: Leaders can demonstrate the strategic importance of innovation for the company by regularly inviting the community to tackle significant business challenges. For example, a "call to innovate" from the leadership presents a strategic problem worth solving and asks the community of innovators for solutions. It might involve formal hackathons or simpler pitch sessions where innovators present directly to leadership. These "calls to innovate" send a clear message: the organization seeks innovative solutions from within its own talent pool. They demonstrate leadership's genuine trust in employees' talent and acknowledge innovation as central to solving the organization's most pressing challenges. Such initiatives are low-cost yet high-impact. They can effectively bridge the gap between leadership and innovators and thus strengthen the innovation culture.

Share Innovation Insights: As the innovation process gets adopted, various activities produce engagement data, content, and assets. The core team systematically extracts insights and compiles "data stories" that support the case for innovation. These stories, presented in the right context, can boost the innovation message and attract more interest. For instance, statistics on the volume of ideas handled per month, high conversion rates from "idea" to "experiment" or "prototype," etc. can boost the innovation mindset and reassure them that "innovation is real"—actionable and impactful. At the same time, survey findings, even if they highlight issues and areas for improvement, should be summarized, shared, and discussed openly. Additionally, it is essential to present insights regarding the community of innovators, such as growth rates and dynamics, or top contributors and stories about their impact on innovation.

Recognize Top Innovators: Innovation stories inspire people and bring a significant improvement to the culture. By highlighting great ideas and sharing innovation achievements through events such as all-hands, leaders can acknowledge top innovators and their contributions and make them visible across the organization. People see distinguished innovators as role models who have adopted the innovation paradigm. Recognition may come in additional forms—beyond public acknowledgments—for instance, opportunities for top innovators to present their achievements, distinctive innovation badges, innovation titles, or formal awards at company events. When done consistently, such recognition gestures can create positive reinforcement loops—top innovators inspire others while sending a signal that the organization truly values contributions and that innovation drives career growth and business performance.

Organization-wide recognition programs require specialized capabilities such as the Gamification, Recognition, and Rewards platform described in Chap. 4. At a small scale, this can be achieved through a simple process that tracks activity and selects top innovators, supported by a communication program that regularly highlights top performers and their achievements through corporate and innovation channels.

In every case, it is essential to maintain an objective and robust process when selecting achievements and innovation stories to communicate. The latter requires a solid definition of "innovation performance" in alignment with established cultural values, ensuring the recognition and rewards process is fair and objective to all.

Engage with Innovation: Modern leaders must demonstrate trust in innovation processes and show their belief in ideas as drivers of differentiation and success. Executives, decision-makers, and technology leaders should all actively participate in innovation activities, serving as mentors, orchestrators, and innovators. This engagement naturally flattens organizational hierarchies, creating more frequent interactions between senior leadership and employees. When leaders visibly participate in ideation sessions, hackathons, or opportunity reviews, they send a strong signal that innovation is real. Leadership participation can take many forms: judging innovation competitions, mentoring project teams, sharing their own ideas, or simply being present at innovation events.

3.10 Maintain a Great Innovation Culture

The previous sections presented practical ways to improve the innovation culture, starting by measuring its state and then moving on to several "cultural hacks." It is worth clarifying that these are not one-off actions or projects with a defined lifecycle; they are ongoing initiatives that bring cultural impact through a series of iterations and adaptations. Fixing the innovation culture is a long journey through multiple and diverse work streams and activities; it is a nonlinear process that requires continuity, persistence, and efficient feedback loops. Still, regardless of the sophistication of the approach, the commitment of the leadership, and the strength

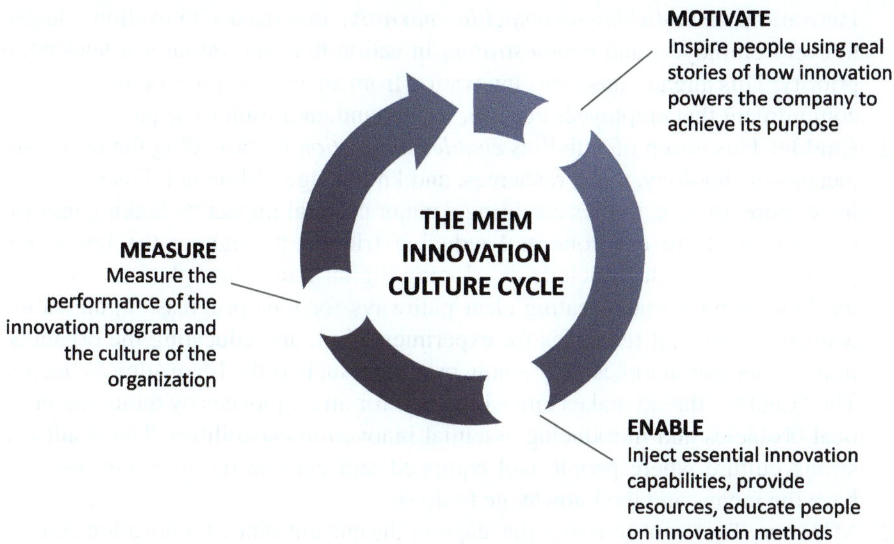

Fig. 3.4 The MEM Innovation Culture Improvement Framework

of the message, the innovation culture may fail to grow. Therefore, a continual improvement model should be followed, an adaptive process that organizes the right activities, not according to a strict plan but instead based on a flexible prioritization that reflects the state and needs of the organization.

The "cultural fixes" presented in this chapter can be naturally grouped based on their nature and intent. For instance, we highlighted the need to systematically *measure* the state of innovation and communicate the importance of *inspiring* people to adopt certain innovation behaviors. Other actions aim to demonstrate the company's *commitment* to innovation. Similarly, some of the recommended actions implied the need to introduce innovation *processes* and *enablers*.

To establish a continual improvement approach, we can abstract these cultural improvement activities and organize them into a simple framework—an iterative process of *motivate-enable-measure* loops where each iteration triggers a dynamic set of actions that aim to improve the innovation culture. This is visualized in Fig. 3.4. The MEM loop can be used to create a custom plan in the context of your organization and orchestrate multiple activities that drive the cultural shift toward innovation. The three threads are defined as:

1. **Motivate**: This group contains activities that aim to *increase the general willingness to innovate* by showcasing tangible impact and real innovation stories that eliminate skepticism and dismiss concerns about "innovation theatre." Activities in this thread provide a broader perspective and position the company's purpose and innovation efforts within the market and the competitive landscape. Key activities include *communicating* how innovation advances the company's strategic objectives, highlighting measurable business outcomes from successful

innovations, *establishing a compelling narrative* that makes innovation relevant to every employee, and *demonstrating* in action that innovation is a leadership priority. This thread transforms innovation from an abstract promise into a strong commitment that employees can see, understand, and want to be part of.
2. **Enable**: This group of activities *enables innovation* by providing the necessary means—technology, tools, resources, and knowledge. While not directly targeting culture, these activities can bring a major cultural impact by making innovation accessible to everyone and reducing friction throughout the innovation process. Key enablers include developing digital innovation platforms such as the Innovation Portal, creating clear pathways for idea progression, allocating dedicated time and resources for experimentation, and educating the organization on innovation topics via training programs such as the Innovation Academy. The "Enable" thread makes innovation real for all employees by removing practical obstacles and introducing essential innovation capabilities. The result is a strong culture where people feel equipped and empowered to innovate—they have the means and the knowledge to do so.
3. **Measure**: These are activities that capture the current state of innovation culture, analyze trends, produce insights, and provide feedback to the Motivate thread for appropriate reaction and fine-tuning of the initiatives. Key activities include deploying targeted innovation surveys, tracking innovation event success, assessing innovation health indicators, quantifying innovation activity levels, and conducting user interviews or focus groups to capture qualitative insights about the innovation function. These data points are analyzed to produce a single view of the company's innovation culture—the current state and dynamics, along with recommended actions, obtained by processing insights and free-form feedback. The measurement thread presents another remarkable case of how artificial intelligence streamlines the innovation process: AI provides the innovation team not only with insights about the innovation culture but also with *a narrative* and *suggested improvements* for subsequent iterations of the cultural improvement loop. This creates a dynamic, responsive system where measurement triggers the creation of meaningful cultural interventions that are then considered for subsequent iterations of the MEM improvement loop.

The Motivate-Enable-Measure cycle—visualized in Fig. 3.4—is orchestrated by the innovation team; they set strategic goals and define the scope of activities across all three dimensions. The individual threads operate continuously, each triggering multiple activities and events that contribute to the improvement of the innovation culture.

During a single loop, typically lasting weeks or months, the *Motivate* thread drives multiple parallel activities designed to energize and inspire. Innovation leaders deliver presentations that link innovation to strategic objectives, host innovation all-hands that acknowledge the contributions to innovation, and showcase tangible examples of ideas that successfully reached the market. Along with the members of the innovation community, they present not only innovation successes but also unsuccessful cases and challenges. These activities demonstrate innovation's strategic importance through real stories and meaningful updates, thus inspiring broader participation. At the same time, the *Enable* thread operates as a foundational layer, with technical teams continuously implementing processes, platforms, and tools that remove barriers to innovation. Meanwhile, the *Measure* thread conducts ongoing cultural assessments through surveys, interviews, and innovation performance measurement. The innovation team analyzes the data to inform subsequent iterations, making data-driven adjustments across all three threads to optimize impact.

As the organization matures, these initially distinct threads naturally converge into a single component of the innovation function of the organization. This integrated approach ensures that motivation, enablement, and measurement work as a single system, creating a continuous improvement cycle that strengthens the innovation culture while adapting to the organization's evolving needs, market conditions, and maturity level. The result is a dynamic, responsive system powered by advanced capabilities, as presented in the following chapter.

Innovation Capabilities: Powered by AI

4

In the previous chapters, we explored how innovative organizations operate and how people and culture set the foundation for innovation success. Indeed, talented individuals with the right mindset can occasionally produce breakthrough innovations. But hoping for the next wave of inspiration or big ideas to appear is not a strategy. To consistently generate meaningful innovations, organizations need not only great people and culture but also a robust *innovation system*: the tools, processes, methods, and technologies that empower people to innovate *systematically* and at scale. This "innovation system" consists of knowledge, human talent, innovation capabilities, technology platforms, tools, frameworks, and specialized services provided by human teams and, occasionally, artificial intelligence.

The capabilities presented in this chapter are the building blocks of a high-performing corporate innovation function. Each of the capabilities contributes to corporate innovation by serving a well-defined objective, such as producing market intelligence, managing ideas, validating opportunities, implementing products, or driving in-market experimentation. When these capabilities exist and work in harmony as a single system, the organization discovers, validates, and takes opportunities to market faster.

The innovation framework introduced in this chapter features a comprehensive suite of AI-powered capabilities that accelerate every stage of innovation. Unlike traditional approaches that rely on intuition and manual processes, this framework operates systematically by taking *environmental inputs*, such as market signals, along with *organizational inputs*, like customer insights and strategic priorities, and converting them into validated opportunities and successful market launches.

In today's hyper-competitive environment, this structured approach isn't just an advantage to have; it is an essential capability. Organizations with a good innovation engine are faster in spotting and evaluating opportunities, responding to trends more effectively, and launching innovations to market. They are adaptive and able to pivot wisely by using data in smart ways.

G. Krasadakis, *Innovation Mode 2.0*,
https://doi.org/10.1007/978-3-032-00835-0_4

This chapter presents a rich collection of AI-powered innovation capabilities that are collectively called the "innovation framework." Seen as a black box, the innovation framework converts *context* to *opportunities* and, eventually, to *in-market innovations*. It contains the mechanisms, processes, and resources that enable the company to react to market signals and internal strategies by forming, validating, and pursuing opportunities at a fast pace.

As seen in Fig. 4.1, various users interact with the framework—each playing a critical role in the performance of the innovation function: the *innovator*, *evaluator*, *business leader*, *market analyst*, and the *product* or *venture* leader. The following explains how they interact and contribute to the overall innovation function:

1. **Business leaders provide the company's context**: These senior leadership members work with the innovation director to set the strategic focus of innovation. They *translate* the purpose and strategy of the company into well-defined problem statements, themes, and focus areas—they shape *the innovation agenda* for the company as the north star of innovation. The innovation agenda sets the focus and thus helps *innovators solve* the right problems, *evaluators spot* relevant, high-potential opportunities, and *product and venture builders make better decisions* about which opportunities to pursue. Beyond setting the strategic focus, business leaders regularly check the performance of the innovation function and intervene as needed to ensure it performs well and remains aligned with the strategic goals and organizational purpose. Business leaders use the mea-

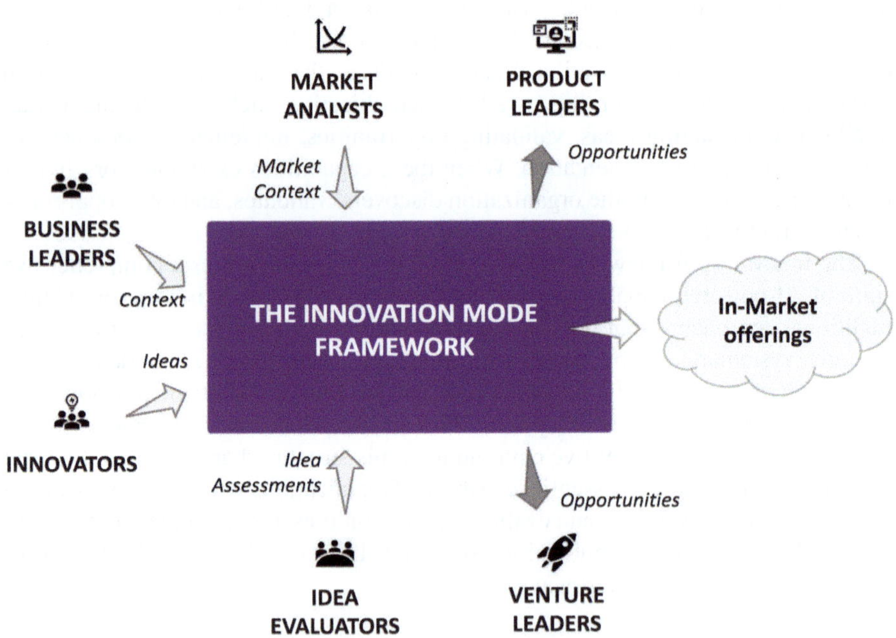

Fig. 4.1 The Innovation Mode framework

surement and orchestration tools of the innovation framework to obtain insights and "health" indicators about the innovation program. They control the pace of innovation to ensure harmony with the operational aspects of the organization. This "context setting" process is led by the innovation director or chief innovation officer, depending on the organizational design, as explained in Chap. 3.

2. **Innovators submit ideas and frame opportunities**: Innovators interact with the framework through *ideation, problem framing*, and *experimentation activities*; they use the innovation agenda to understand what is important for the company and generate ideas or contribute to ideas by others. In many cases, they are also the "builders" who prototype solutions, experiment with technologies, build demos, and participate in user testing and validation activities. The framework provides the methods and all the resources to support the above and help innovators pursue their ideas further, e.g., templates, methodologies, tools, related content, etc. Following the principle of inclusion, innovators could come from anywhere within the company—innovation is open to any employee with a genuine interest and willingness to innovate, regardless of their role, seniority, or skillset.
3. **Evaluators flag opportunities**: Evaluators are domain or business experts who have received sufficient training in validating opportunities and spotting high-potential ones. They continually scan the "solution space" and assess the new ideas by applying the idea assessment model (see Chap. 6) to estimate their potential as business opportunities. The framework provides the tools to speed up the process and make the evaluation of ideas a consistent, streamlined operation.
4. **Market analysts provide insights**: These are experienced market analysts, strategists, or technologists who continually scan the market, the competition, and the technology state of the art to spot interesting changes, emerging trends, and related patterns. They process a stream of facts, trends, and insights reflecting the market dynamics: what users need, where the competition is heading, and what the most important customer pain points are. Market analysts provide regular technology updates along with business reports on what is happening in the industry, the competitors, and the start-up scene. They also produce expert views and perspectives on how emerging patterns, shifting consumer behaviors, and structural changes in the economy are relevant to the company. This is a critical input for the innovation framework, which impacts the innovation agenda and, eventually, the organization's strategy.
5. **Product leaders find opportunities for new product concepts or features**: These are senior product professionals who primarily *consume* the output of the innovation framework, whether or not they actively contribute to the innovation process. They interact with the framework in two main ways: first, by discovering opportunities to enhance existing products or requesting validation reports and market intelligence to explore product expansion scenarios; and second, by leveraging these opportunities and testing them through suitable product experimentation processes and potentially implementing and releasing them as new features or products.

6. **Venture leaders find opportunities for new ventures**: These senior executives leverage the innovation framework to identify and frame bigger, potentially transformational opportunities for the organization. They interact with the framework in two main ways: first, by discovering high-potential opportunities that could become new business units, divisions, or stand-alone ventures and requesting comprehensive market analysis and business model validation to assess long-term strategic value. Second, by developing these validated opportunities through corporate venture processes and potentially launching them as new business entities or strategic growth initiatives within the organization.

The innovation framework uses multiple inputs—company strategy, market dynamics, ideas, and problems—and activates the appropriate functions to maximize the chances of discovering high-potential opportunities, whether new products, services, solutions, markets, or entire industries. It streamlines critical processes such as idea creation, submission, evaluation, concept testing, and prioritization, and thus, it creates faster pathways from an initial concept to an informed decision about its next steps, such as experimentation or implementation. This acceleration enables organizations to evaluate significantly more ideas within the same timeframe, thereby increasing the likelihood of identifying breakthrough opportunities. Beyond efficiency, the framework facilitates intelligent, adaptive knowledge diffusion across the organization. For example, by leveraging AI-powered capabilities, it can summarize the entire market into compact, digestible narratives, thus making it easier for teams to comprehend the market and the broader economic environment. Similarly, it creates smart narratives that present the developments within the organization, thus breaking the silos by connecting people and teams across different levels and divisions.

As presented in Fig. 4.2, the innovation framework consists of 12 core capabilities, which work together as a single system to streamline the journey of an idea, from draft thoughts to a validated proposal and potentially to commercial paths. Properly implemented and operated, the innovation framework supports the entire innovation function of the organization: an efficient system that leverages human talent and technological capabilities to monitor the dynamics of the economic environment, react to signals by identifying promising ideas, and help the organization make timely, well-informed decisions. This framework empowers the company to release high-potential innovations to the market at the right time.

The innovation framework is presented independently of specific technologies. The described capabilities are not necessarily technology systems or platforms. Depending on the company's size, some of the above could be organized as "internal services" powered by simple methods and operated manually by small, effective teams without sophisticated technologies. For example, a team may be

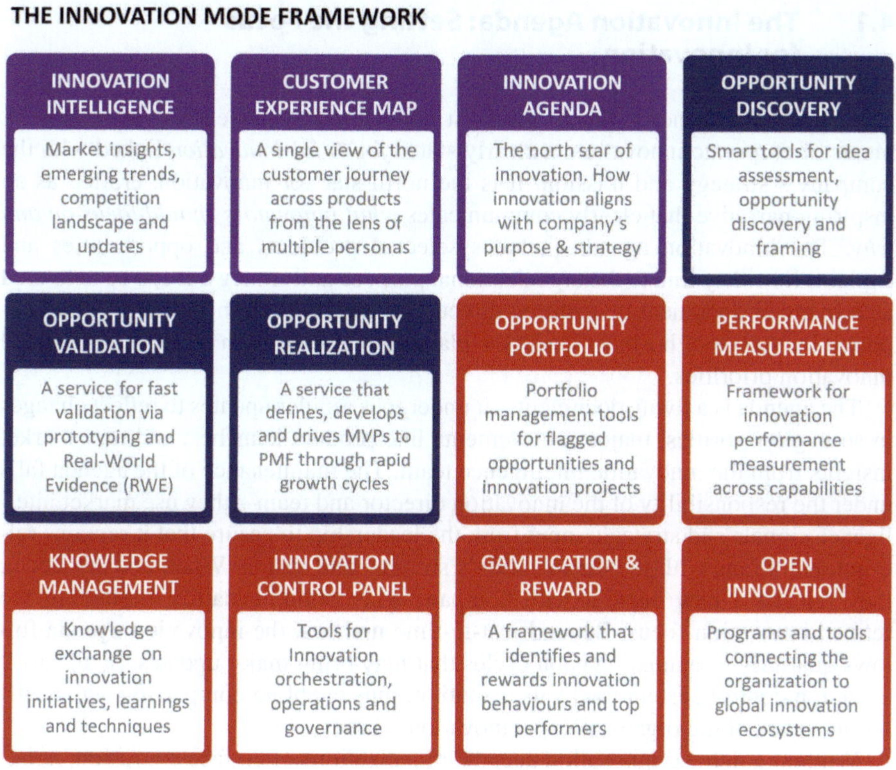

Fig. 4.2 The innovation framework: foundational innovation capabilities

providing the *idea evaluation service*—they look for new ideas, then apply a predefined evaluation method to assess them, and give structured feedback to the ideators. In another example, a company may set up an internal team of experts to do *opportunity validation as a service*, helping product or other teams test their concepts rapidly and efficiently. Similarly, a team of market and product experts may be operating the *innovation intelligence service* to provide streamlined market insights and expert views on trends and structural changes in the global economic environment.

Also, not all of them are required in full to set up a powerful innovation system: leaders should consider the organizational readiness, complexity, and the specifics of their companies to define a plan on where and how to start.

The following describes the capabilities shown in Fig. 4.2 and explains their purpose, along with their inputs and outputs, starting with the innovation agenda, since it sets the stage for innovation.

4.1 The Innovation Agenda: Setting the Focus for Innovation

The innovation agenda is one of the most important yet frequently overlooked elements of corporate innovation: a clearly stated *focus for innovation* linked with the company's strategy and mission. It is the north star for innovation, crafted as an inspiring narrative that clearly communicates *what innovators should focus on and why*. The innovation agenda includes selected problems and opportunities and explains how they link to the organizational purpose and strategy. It can be delivered as a branded document or featured directly on the Innovation Portal, ideally supported by videos of business leaders explaining the innovation focus and the stated innovation priorities.

The agenda is a living document—it undergoes regular updates to reflect changes in strategic priorities, major achievements like product launches, and new market insights from the innovation intelligence team. The maintenance of the agenda falls under the responsibility of the innovation director and team—they use market intelligence signals and strategic input from the leadership to ensure that it remains relevant and aligns with the organization's strategy and vision. When updates occur, they release a new version with company-wide communication explaining the refined innovation focus. Beyond just-in-time updates, the innovation agenda follows quarterly or annual revision cycles that may bring major updates. In all cases, a version control system tracks its evolution, thus enabling comparison across different stages of the organization's innovation journey.

Without a defined innovation agenda, organizations often face confusion, noise, and misalignment regarding innovation efforts: Generic innovation statements instead of well-defined problem areas and the absence of a prioritization framework limit the organization's ability to spot and react to opportunities quickly. Employees and innovation teams cannot effectively focus their efforts on critical problems or identify where the company is placing its strategic bets. When innovation focus isn't well defined, properly articulated, or visible across the organization, people struggle to evaluate whether new opportunities align with the company's direction. This aligns with various failure factors presented in Chap. 2, such as *the lack of strong links between the organizational purpose and innovation programs*.

This lack of clarity around innovation priorities and their connection to company objectives creates significant problems: teams waste time on less important initiatives and struggle to demonstrate how their work advances organizational goals. As a result, the company's innovation resources are used suboptimally, opportunities are missed, and innovation culture suffers as employees lose confidence in the innovation function.

The innovation agenda solves this alignment problem by translating the company's purpose and strategy into a focused set of priority challenges and opportunities for the innovation function to pursue. Rather than abstract mission statements, the agenda presents specific *problems to solve* and opportunities to explore, as carefully selected by leadership based on their strategic importance.

Figure 4.3 presents the structure of the innovation agenda.[1] The element at the top sets the context of the agenda, that is, the division that it refers to and the timeframe. The next element is the organizational, divisional, or team purpose—a short, compact articulation of the impact the team aims to drive. Either at the corporate, product, or team level, the purpose is best understood as an outward statement summarizing the desired long-term value for users, the market or society.

For instance, in a hypothetical corporation developing digital educational services, the purpose could be "to empower people to reach their full potential." Using this simple structure, companies can link the purpose with strategic problem areas that "explain" it and make it more tangible. In the same example, the problem areas

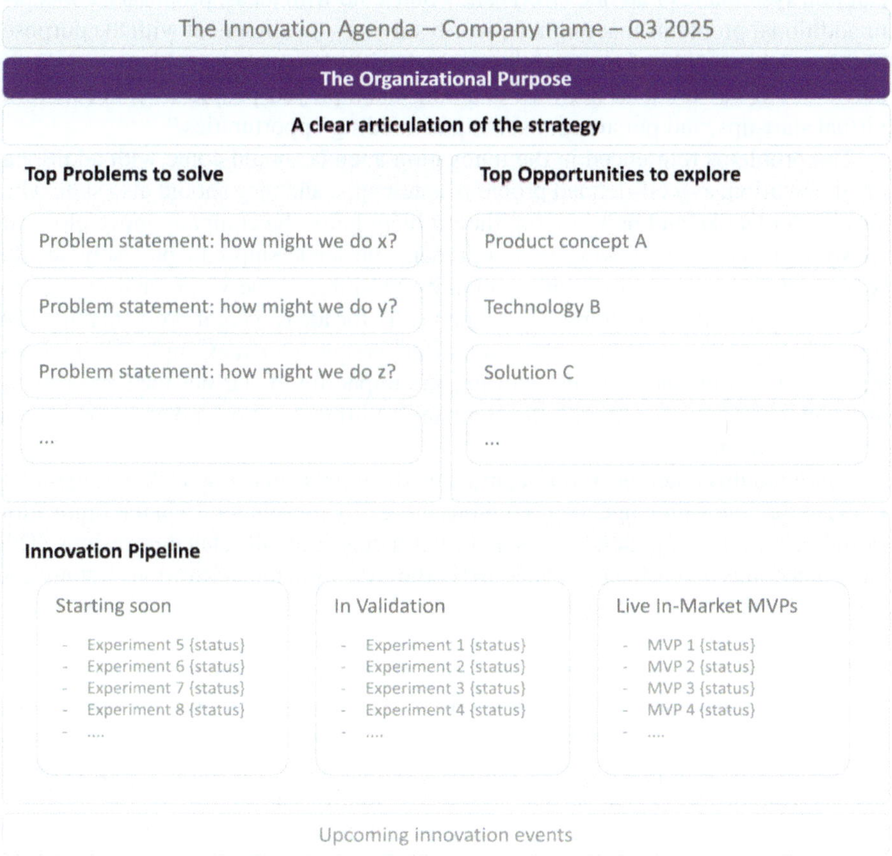

Fig. 4.3 A wireframe of the innovation agenda

[1] Visit the book's Web site, and download a free template implementing the innovation agenda.

could refer to the following: "How might we provide better training and education options for unemployed people?" "How might we enable students to identify their talents?" or "How might we offer a tailored-made, lifelong educational curriculum according to individual interests and talents?"

The third level of the innovation agenda represents the actual defined problems to be solved. This is a dynamic element in the sense that the company may frequently re-prioritize problems or add new ones that, in some cases, come directly from the innovation community. Continuing the same hypothetical example, the educational tech company may have already identified problems worth solving or opportunities, like "lack of effective networking tools for continuing education" or "limited means for discovering business opportunities." These problems are seen as a call to innovate to the innovation community; they can spark ideas, creative discussions, experiments, and prototyping threads: innovators throughout the company can join systematic or ad hoc efforts and contribute with ideas, proposals, concepts, or additional problems that might be worth solving—in alignment with the purpose. For example, an idea for a solution linked with the second problem mentioned above could be "a social network enabling unemployed people to connect, form virtual start-ups, and pursue sponsorship or funding opportunities."

The problems referenced in the innovation agenda should come with additional documentation, as well-defined problem statements, and they should also state what success looks like and how solving the problem helps the company move closer to its strategic goals. Following this approach, the leadership can precisely set the focus and invite the innovation community to embrace the vision and engage by conceiving potential solutions. This "open call" for ideas on real problems that link up to the big purpose of the corporation offers people a great example of how innovation can become meaningful, relevant, and impactful. It clarifies the areas of strategic interest in alignment with the company's purpose and promotes innovation as a means of achieving it.

Although this could be a simple, branded document such as a deck, it is essential to make the innovation agenda ubiquitous—e.g., by presenting it via the Innovation Portal or in innovation newsletters and referencing it on all related occasions. This way, it becomes the primary vehicle for communicating the innovation strategy and a practical guide for workshops, hackathons, idea assessments, and educational sessions.

In addition to communicating the innovation focus, the agenda enables better measurement and steering of innovation efforts: it helps examine innovation projects and potential investments from the right perspective. Moreover, the agenda may include activity and performance indicators at each level, thus providing comprehensive insights into the *focus* and *progress* of innovation.

While the innovation agenda provides crucial direction and inspiration, it should not constrain creativity. Innovation teams are encouraged to explore beyond the defined strategic areas as needed to ensure the organization doesn't miss unexpected opportunities while maintaining its strategic focus.

4.2 Innovation Intelligence: Using AI to Sense the Market

The innovation intelligence service helps the company set the context for innovation in two ways. First by watching the market and the broader economic environment in which the company operates and distilling and providing critical insights about market developments, competitors, technology, emerging market needs, and what customers need and struggle with. Second by looking within the organization and producing equally important insights on what the organization is innovating on, active initiatives, plans, strategies, and the various innovation agendas across the company.

This service distills the vast amounts of information in the market and within the company and helps the leadership obtain an instant and accurate understanding of the competitive landscape, the latest advances in science and technology, the emerging shifts in user needs and preferences, and how these are linked with the agenda of the organization. It provides the insights required to maintain a smart innovation agenda while informing, connecting, and inspiring people through timely insights from both the global economic environment and the organizational microcosm. These two sources—the micro and the macro—are described in the following:

The Market Radar: This crucial service establishes a strong link with the rapidly changing economic environment and technological landscape—a stream of external updates, insights, and market intelligence. The market radar allows the company to "listen" to the market, weigh in on technological trends, predict competitor moves, and detect changes in consumer behavior patterns. This stream of insights helps corporate and innovation leaders to fine-tune their innovation agenda and steer innovation efforts in the right direction. Furthermore, it helps innovators and idea evaluators by providing a broader perspective for idea creation and evaluation, respectively. In general, having a strong connection to the market empowers people and teams to think broadly by continually considering the evolving ecosystem. The content of this stream comes from public domain information and falls into the categories below:

1. **Patent activity**: including published applications or granted patents, provides an important source of information as it reflects, to a certain extent, the technology trends and areas of related investment. However, patents are not "business-friendly"—they come in lengthy technical documentation with a layer of legal abstraction that makes it impractical to use in this context. The market radar offers the "patent watch" service that spots new publications relevant to the business and then produces an executive summary in a business-friendly language. This feeds into a regular *patent activity summary* report that presents and interprets the findings in the company's context.
2. **Research publications**: provide another excellent source of technological and scientific insights that inform both the innovation strategy and specific innovation projects. They provide access to vast knowledge through peer-reviewed journals, academic papers, conference proceedings, research reports, white

papers, and publications from major institutes and global think tanks. They can reveal emerging technologies and methodologies long before they reach the market as commercial applications or even provide signals for upcoming breakthroughs with disruptive potential for industries. However, as with patents, comprehending this content and producing insights is a laborious process—research publications are typically lengthy, highly technical, and written for academic audiences. The innovation intelligence team identifies the right sources in the context of the company, shapes a processing strategy, and produces business-friendly executive summaries on a regular basis.

3. **A stream of technology and business news**: including company updates, product announcements, and news from the broader ecosystem, can prove to be extremely valuable. Sources of such content could be technology publications, industry news platforms, company press releases, business media, or conference announcements. The innovation intelligence team systematically tracks and analyzes these streams to incorporate summaries and key highlights into the regular market updates it produces and distributes across the company.
4. **Market perceptions**: about products and services can unveil interesting insights and dynamics. In today's digital landscape, it is easy to access online reviews, social media threads, media coverage, blogs, and forums for most products or services offered out there. The innovation intelligence team uses such open-source intelligence to track not only the reputation of the company's products but also how related offerings perform and resonate with customers. While respecting privacy regulations, they use publicly available data to capture the dominant sentiment and other interesting product insights. For example, they may be using public domain content such as customer complaints, media coverage, or online discussions to identify emerging user needs, pain points, gaps, and satisfaction drivers. This ethical "digital listening" process converts fragmented public feedback into coherent, actionable intelligence that is valuable to product strategy and innovation initiatives. By focusing exclusively on publicly shared opinions and openly available information, the team maintains high ethical standards while still gaining crucial market insights that can drive innovation forward.
5. **Start-up activity**: provides an additional source of valuable intelligence and inspiration. The team regularly scans the global start-up scene for interesting stories and developments and then distills and contextualizes the information as short "start-up watch" reports that summarize how ambitious start-ups are trying to tackle interesting problems, relevant not only to the organization but in general—as the element of surprise may come from any industry or domain and opportunities may appear from scenarios that initially looked irrelevant to the innovation agenda.
6. **Thought leadership**: including expert opinions and views from industry leaders or influencers in the field, can also provide valuable signals, for example, through public discussions on foreseen disruptions in specific industries. As with previous sources, this goes through the analysis process of the innovation intelligence team to extract the essence, contextualize it, and present it in smart executive summaries.

To systematically collect, process, and summarize the above sources of information is not an easy job—it requires a well-prepared team of market experts and technologists. However, artificial intelligence can be extremely useful in this direction—it can be integrated into the overall process and convert lengthy technical documents and streams of unstructured content from the public domain into sharp executive summaries, which are then interpreted and synthesized by the innovation intelligence team into formal updates for distribution.

Regardless of the use of AI, this team needs to have a good understanding of the market, the competition, and the technology state of the art: they need to be able to filter out the noise by deciding what is critical in the context of the company. The team not only collects, consumes, and summarizes but also *interprets content and signals*: remarkable findings and insights are put in the organization's perspective; then packaged as branded, short market stories; and diffused through the innovation touchpoints, e.g., the Innovation Portal or Newsletters. Occasionally, the team presents such market stories to live audiences, e.g., through an innovation all-hands.

This innovation intelligence capability helps the company's leadership maintain clarity on the company's position in the competitive ecosystem, identify potential disruptions early, and spot opportunities for innovation. It provides critical insights that enable better decision-making about innovation priorities and resource allocation.

The Corporate Radar: As described earlier, internal silos and the resulting information gaps frequently block corporate innovation since fragmentation increases the likelihood of duplicate efforts, misalignments, and missed opportunities. Beyond scanning the market, the innovation intelligence team also analyses the corporation *from within*; it maintains an in-depth knowledge of the organizational structure so it can obtain a single view of the developments and plans across the company. By understanding what other groups are working on and the expertise and innovation priorities of different divisions, the innovation intelligence team can "connect the dots" and facilitate communication among departments in the context of specific initiatives or opportunities. The team processes the individual agendas and creates a virtual, unified one, highlighting potential overlaps and opportunities for collaboration. This report presents a consolidated *corporate innovation story*—a narrative of the organization's activity, planning, innovation focus, and ambition.

As with other capabilities of this framework, the innovation intelligence service does not have to be a high-technology solution from the beginning. It may be offered initially by a small team of experts who use the latest commercial AI tools to search, summarize, interpret, and present the state of the market. However, the higher the innovation pace, the stronger the need for integration and advanced tools: a more sophisticated instance of this service uses automation to *gather the content* and then AI to *semantically process it*. Such intelligence tools remove the noise and offer essential highlights for the team to explore further. With a solution like that in place, the innovation intelligence team shifts focus to interpreting and contextualizing the insights, synthesizing the informative stories, packaging, and presenting them to the organization.

4.3 Customer Experience Map: Obtaining a Unified View of Users and Customer Journeys

Many large product-led companies—especially those with multiple products—face a significant issue that is typically perceived as a product management limitation: they fail to obtain a single, holistic understanding of their customers in terms of personas and how they engage across the full spectrum of offered products, solutions, services, and experiences. I've seen companies doing excellent work documenting user journeys, personas, maps, and features but failing to make them available as universal tools for alignment and customer understanding. Keeping these great insights "trapped" within product or UX teams is a missed opportunity for the organization.

Usually, companies think of user journeys and personas as UX tools helping product design and development, which is true. But in addition to their typical purpose, these assets can drive enterprise-wide clarity and alignment regarding users, personas, and customer journeys across products; hence, they can dramatically improve the innovation program in terms of focus and alignment. Properly captured user journeys and personas empower the entire organization to better understand customers, their pain points, and emotional journeys and instantly identify gaps in products and services. Not having access to such artifacts is a substantial missed opportunity for the innovation function of the organization.

The customer experience map capability aims to transform this fragmented understanding into a powerful innovation driver. Rather than static user insights, the Experience Map provides a dynamic, living representation of well-studied personas and how they engage with the products and experiences of the company across touchpoints and services. This comprehensive view enables teams to identify opportunities in non-optimal user journeys and, on top of them, insufficiently linked products, services, and experiences.

This capability manifests as an *interactive digital experience* maintained by UX and research teams but available across teams. It presents a single unified user journey featuring named personas for each product or experience the company offers. The tool allows for versioning and ensures consistent views, enriched with research findings, plans, and ideas—essentially making the user journey *a canvas for positioning ideas, projects, and innovation activities* within the company. It helps people identify problematic moments in the customer journey and envision how particular ideas would serve different personas involved in each stage.

When people in the company use consistent tools and insights to understand customers, they gain clarity about real user pain points, become empathetic with users, identify important problems, and better focus their innovation efforts. This way, the customer experience map becomes essential for ideation and product framing, helping teams design unified, seamless, superior user experiences across products. Beyond product development, the customer experience map can be an invaluable tool for innovation: teams communicate better, innovation initiatives align more closely with actual customer needs, and the organization develops a stronger, more consistent, customer-centric approach to innovation. Additionally, it provides a new lens to look at business performance, active initiatives, and innovation opportunities.

4.4 Opportunity Discovery: Using Artificial Intelligence to Discover Opportunities Faster

While many companies focus merely on "managing ideas," successful innovation requires a smart *opportunity discovery* capability: an efficient, fast, reliable, and scalable process for spotting and framing opportunities. Opportunity discovery refers to the entire journey from capturing problems and ideas to identifying those with the highest potential for further exploration. This process involves multiple actors and integrated systems: business leaders identify strategic problems and add them to the "Problem Space"—the organization's central repository for maintaining and prioritizing business problems; innovators frame potential solutions and add them to the "Solution Space," the comprehensive collection of organizational ideas; evaluators apply the opportunity assessment model to score new ideas and flag high-potential opportunities. These identified opportunities are transferred to the opportunity validation service (described below) for formal concept validation and estimation of their potential. This ensures that promising concepts receive the attention and resources they deserve. Opportunity discovery is explained in detail in Chap. 6, where we present ways to use artificial intelligence to streamline various aspects of the process and eventually make it *autonomous*.

4.5 Opportunity Validation: Testing Hypotheses with Real-World Evidence

Opportunity validation is the capability that tests the riskiest assumptions of an identified opportunity to assess its potential and inform the next steps. The validation approach varies depending on the concept's nature and the underlying uncertainties. For instance, when considering a novel product concept that introduces a radically different UX paradigm—for example, based on voice and gesture recognition—it is essential to test aspects such as market demand, user readiness to adopt the new approach, and technical readiness. The opportunity validation service is powered by a multidisciplinary team with expertise in building prototypes in rapid mode and using them to establish feedback loops that generate insights that inform decisions and recommendations. The team has expertise in rapid iterations using templates, reusable components, and proven frameworks to accelerate the validation process. They use AI for prototyping, validating, and producing recommendation narratives; they are seen as a "black box", taking as input opportunities and delivering recommendations backed by real-world evidence based on data gathered using thorough experimentation methods. Opportunity validation is covered in detail in Chap. 7.

4.6 Opportunity Realization: Getting from Concepts to In-Market Products and PMF

A powerful innovation setup—especially in a digital product space—needs an optimized *opportunity realization* service, also referred to as the "Venture Studio" throughout the book. This high-performance, cross-functional team defines, builds, launches, and grows MVPs and attempts to drive them to product-market fit (PMF) through experimentation.

The team has deep expertise in taking a high-potential opportunity, as flagged by the Opportunity Discovery service, and quickly identifying the most important features that set the ground for a potentially viable product. Having defined the MVP, the team shapes an implementation roadmap and a go-to-market strategy while identifying the key skills required to build it. They source the right implementation team—from within, through hiring, or by bringing contractors and vendors—and initiate fast, agile development cycles, implementing the defined MVP. When the MVP is ready and stable, the team triggers a staged release to the selected market, typically starting with "invitation only" and then opening up access to a broader audience.

The Venture Team has a very specific objective for the MVP: to establish feedback loops and trigger a series of fast improvement and growth cycles that attempt to get the MVP to product-market fit. They offer deep expertise not only in MVP development but also in product innovation. More specifically, they know how to run effective, in-market experiments from within a live product and steer the improvement process in the right direction.

The Venture Studio can dramatically improve the success rate of those promising products by taking them through smart, rigorous experiment-build-measure cycles that bring the product closer to PMF. Of course, as part of these cycles, the team must often make tough decisions, e.g., to recommend "killing" a project when data and adoption levels indicate that the product is not viable. For ventures that fail to achieve PMF despite multiple iterations, the team conducts postmortems, captures valuable insights, and keeps the leadership informed. In all cases, this capability produces valuable market learnings regardless of individual product outcomes. The Opportunity Discovery service is further discussed in Chap. 8.

4.7 Opportunity Portfolio Manager: Balancing Innovation Styles and Risks

A company may target various types of innovation, e.g., product, process, marketing, or organizational improvements (as defined in Chap. 1), through parallel projects of different degrees of uncertainty, complexity, and expected business impact. Some of these could be radical, while others may be incremental. For instance, along with a multi-year R&D program on breakthrough technologies, the company may be delivering incremental product innovations while experimenting with business models, pricing, and monetization strategies. This dynamic setup requires a portfolio-based approach for balancing risk, managing budgets, and evaluating the performance of innovation projects.

The Opportunity Portfolio Manager enables the definition and governance of multiple collections of innovation opportunities. A portfolio is a named collection of opportunities helping leaders balance various innovation styles across different horizons—from short-term projects focusing on incremental product innovation to long-term ambitious initiatives pursuing disruptive solutions. Companies may maintain multiple portfolios, some enterprise-wide and others at department or product levels—all applying the same structure, attributes, and metrics.

Beyond grouping and exploration, an opportunity portfolio enables effective prioritization, tracking, and governance of innovation initiatives. Through interactive dashboards and visual tools, business leaders manage the synthesis of their portfolios and obtain the big picture of who is innovating on what and how the corresponding innovation projects align with the organizational strategy.

Moreover, the notion of the opportunity portfolio brings a different perspective on managing risk: In this context, *risk* originates from the allocation of expensive resources to innovation projects that have increased levels of uncertainty and, thus, a considerable probability of failure. The portfolio approach sets the basis for perceiving failure as part of the process: a percentage of the contained projects will eventually fail, which is acceptable, provided that the portfolio's overall performance meets the predefined success criteria. Leaders manage this risk by controlling the "exposure" of entire portfolios.

The opportunity portfolio also helps leaders achieve clarity via aggregated metrics that reflect the properties, performance, and dynamics of all the contained innovation projects. For example, statistics at the portfolio level help leaders monitor and control the diversity of the contained projects in terms of risk, themes, and styles of innovation. Additionally, portfolio-level aggregates of the estimated business potential, level of novelty, investment levels, or relevance to the innovation agenda provide instant insights and make the management of portfolios easier and more effective. Overall metrics like *expected* and *realized business value* allow portfolio comparison and analysis of their performance over time.

Leaders use the portfolio capability to track innovation investment returns across their opportunity pipeline and make informed trade-off decisions. The governance aspect of this capability includes the decision-making framework and the possible paths for a project, the resource assignment mechanism, and overall budget control and allocation. By providing a structured approach to managing portfolios of innovation projects, this capability makes innovation more systematic while maintaining the flexibility to make fast decisions and adapt.

4.8 Innovation Performance Framework: Measuring Innovation

This capability provides the means to assess the overall performance of the innovation function. It uses well-defined metrics and powers dashboards that provide critical insights on the levels of innovation activity, engagement, and outcomes. The metrics reflect the size and quality of the corpus of ideas, the level of employee engagement and collaboration, and the efficiency of essential innovation services such as opportunity discovery, validation, and realization. The measurement framework features the opportunity discovery funnel, presenting how ideas flow through the discovery pipeline and occasionally to the market. Moreover, it contains standardized scorecards on how business experiments perform and how in-market MVPs progress toward product-market fit. The foundation of this framework is presented in Chap. 9, "Measuring Innovation."

4.9 Knowledge Management: Creating, Managing, and Diffusing Content

As explored in Chap. 2, organizational fragmentation represents a major barrier to successful corporate innovation. Fragmentation occurs when teams do not communicate effectively, intentionally or not. The consequences are significant: knowledge remains isolated, opportunities are missed, and resources are wasted on duplicate efforts, such as when one team is "innovating" on something another team has already built or, worse, abandoned.

Organizational fragmentation may be caused by cultural issues, e.g., when teams and individuals are overprotective of their ideas and intentionally avoid sharing and prefer to keep information private for their own or their team's agendas and micro-strategies. In other cases, fragmentation occurs due to technical limitations: the willingness to share, discover, and collaborate is there, but the lack of efficient channels eventually leads to information gaps. In both cases, effective information and knowledge discovery tools can help reduce the impact of fragmentation and eventually bridge silos toward a "one-team" vision.

Companies can address both technical and cultural challenges by implementing an integrated system of tools and experiences designed to make information and knowledge more accessible and discoverable across the organization. At its center is the Innovation Portal, a comprehensive intranet hub that connects all innovation components and organizes essential information, content, and innovation entry points in a single location. This capability is enhanced by AI-powered search and recommendation systems that make discovering innovation assets intuitive and personalized.

When effectively implemented, knowledge exchange capabilities gradually break down silos, creating connections between previously isolated teams and even linking disparate innovation centers or R&D departments into a single network. This increased connectivity allows the organization to leverage its collective intelligence, combine diverse insights, and accelerate innovation by setting the right focus and reducing redundant efforts.

The knowledge management capability organizes this stream of innovation assets into the Innovation Graph—a unified content store, making them discoverable and usable in the right context across the organization. Integrated into the Innovation Portal, the knowledge management capability provides templates and tools for creating standardized documents and artifacts, thus ensuring that ideas, opportunities, patents, prototypes, etc. follow consistent models with base descriptors that enable effective indexing and discovery. This growing repository becomes a massive source of knowledge and inspiration where people throughout the company can discover quality innovation artifacts in their context.

4.9.1 Innovation Outputs: A Classification of Innovation Assets

Innovation is ultimately judged by outcomes, but achieving those outcomes depends on specific outputs, both tangible and intangible. The innovation function is a continuous process that generates rich outputs, ranging from ideas, proposals, technical documentation, patents, insights, and experimental results to demos and functional prototypes. Hence, at the core of knowledge management is the ability to *create* and *effectively classify* content that represents the diverse array of artifacts produced by the innovation function.

The output of the innovation function can be classified into three categories: *early concepts* or propositions, such as ideas, pitch decks, and problem statements; *realizations* or product artifacts, such as prototypes, MVPs, and market-ready solutions; and *knowledge assets*, such as market intelligence, experiment results, and intellectual property. These power the innovation process throughout the journey of an idea: knowledge informs the creation of new concepts, which evolve into functional artifacts that contribute by providing data and learnings back to the knowledge pipeline (Fig. 4.4).

Concepts This class of innovation assets contains early concepts ranging from problems and ideas to business experiment definitions and solution proposals. These are not functional—they are just documents that define and describe the underlying concepts. By formalizing these into branded templates, companies can introduce a shared innovation language and thus improve communication among innovation stakeholders. These early-stage innovation artifacts typically include:

- **Problem framing**: A single-page, text-only presentation of a business problem. It targets innovation teams and stakeholders with the objective of establishing a clear, comprehensive understanding of the problem before solutioning. The problem-framing document is essential when preparing for brainstorming or other innovation workshops to ensure participants focus on solving the right problem.

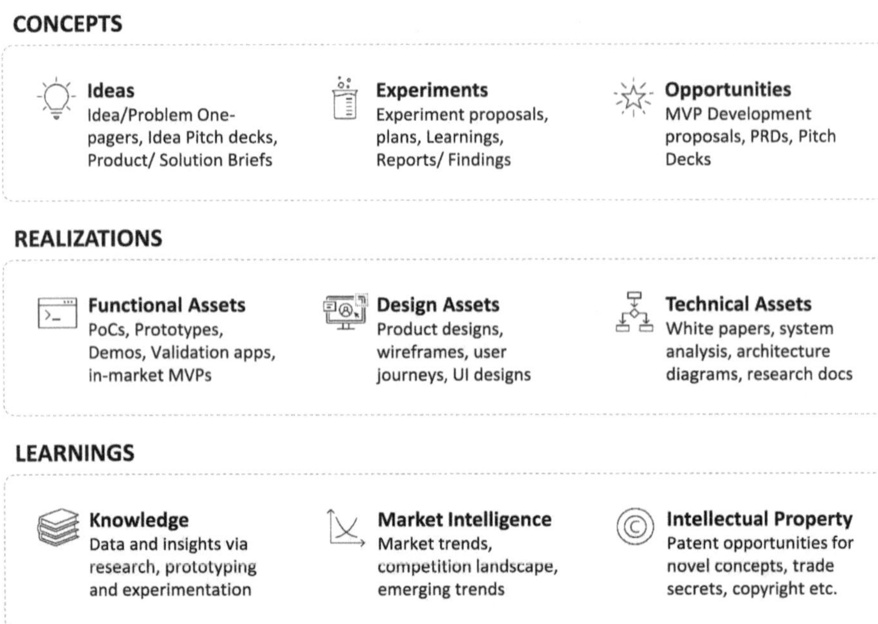

Fig. 4.4 A classification of innovation outputs

- **Idea one-pager**: A single-page, text-only articulation of an idea based on the framing template presented in Chap. 6. The one-pager is valuable when seeking initial feedback from potential collaborators and stakeholders. Its objective is to communicate the key aspects of an idea in a structured, digestible format that allows instant understanding of its core concept.
- **Idea pitch deck**: A thorough presentation that concisely communicates a product concept or solution. It targets senior decision-makers to pitch for funding, support, or resources. Hence, it provides a holistic view of the opportunity while emphasizing the problem, solution, competitive landscape, implementation roadmap, business model, and success criteria. The pitch deck is essential for complex ideas that require leadership's attention and formal support.
- **New product/solution proposal**: This detailed document outlines the implementation plan for a validated opportunity, usually a solution or product. It targets decision-makers and implementation teams and aims to present the opportunity holistically—by detailing the high-level scope, primary features, roadmap, go-to-market strategy, unit economics, and expected financial or other benefits for the company. It also includes validation history and related decisions and may extend into a full MVP definition or solution architecture, depending on the opportunity's nature. The proposal document is critical when exploring validated opportunities for potential implementation.
- **Product requirements document (PRD)**: This is a comprehensive document that defines the complete specification of a product. It targets product and engineering

teams, aiming to provide a clear definition of the product from user, technical, and commercial perspectives. The PRD details functional and non-functional requirements, features, success criteria, constraints, and dependencies; it is the single reference throughout the development of the product, ensuring alignment between stakeholders' expectations and technical implementation.
- **Business experiment proposal**: This document outlines a suggestion for a business experiment or an idea for testing particular hypotheses. It targets product teams that may further enrich the document by formalizing the hypotheses to be tested, defining success metrics, and detailing the experimentation approach, data collection methods, and evaluation criteria.
- **The business case**: A formal document that extends the pitch deck with detailed financial and technical data. It targets senior executives and decision-makers and aims to present the business and financial case of the opportunity and propose investment scenarios. The document includes cost figures, financial projections, feasibility assessments, technical specifications, and implementation, release, and operational plans. The business case is expensive to compile since it requires research, technical assessment, and financial analysis. Thus, it should be produced only for mature ideas considered for significant investments.

Realizations: These are functional or static artifacts that *realize* one or more aspects of a product or solution. The functional assets could be anything from early implementations, such as prototypes or PoCs, to the actual product that is eventually launched to the market. Usually, they take the following forms:

- **A prototype**: A quick, intentionally simplified realization of a concept that can be static or functional—may come as wireframes, user interfaces, dashboards, or digital/physical models, depending on the nature of the idea. It is valuable mostly during product discovery, helping teams test and validate complex concepts.
- **A proof of concept (PoC)**: This is a focused implementation of specific components of a product concept. It aims to test the high-uncertainty features by validating their technical feasibility and proving that they can work as envisioned. The PoC is essential when facing significant technical uncertainty and may be presented as a functional artifact or as a report documenting the approach, tested aspects, results, and associated decisions.
- **A demo of a product or tech**: This is typically a more mature implementation of a product concept or technology aiming to showcase how it solves the underlying problem and how it can provide value to its users and the business. It usually focuses on the end-user experience by highlighting key features throughout the "happy path" and realistic use cases. It is valuable when seeking feedback, general interest, or support for further development.
- **The MVP of a product**: The minimum viable product is an incomplete yet viable instance of a product containing only its most essential features. The MVP is an in-market artifact exposed to real users—early adopters and potential customers. It helps test critical business hypotheses by delivering *just enough* functionality to solve the core problem and enable continuous feedback and learning. The

MVP implementation is crucial since it is the means to go to market and establish fast experimentation and feedback loops. MVPs are discussed in detail in Chaps. 6 and 7.
- **Product architecture documents**: These are technical documents describing a product concept as a complete system—detailing its technical foundation in terms of technologies, architecture, data models, system dependencies, sizing, storage design, and non-functional requirements. These documents are essential when moving from concept to implementation—they provide implementation guidelines and simplify knowledge sharing among technical teams.

Knowledge Assets: This category includes valuable innovation outputs that capture various forms of knowledge produced throughout the innovation process, such as insights, data, ideas, inventions, learnings, and expertise. These assets not only capture findings but also facilitate knowledge sharing and help raise awareness about innovation activities. The most important are:

- **White paper**: A detailed document explaining a sophisticated technical concept to a technical audience and potential collaborators. Its objective is to socialize the topic by providing in-depth technical views such as architectural diagrams, data flows, networks, data models, or algorithm descriptions. This artifact is valuable when introducing innovative technical approaches that require expert validation. It helps capture early feedback and attract collaborators.
- **Market intelligence reports**: These are snapshots of the state of a market or industry—they summarize the dynamics of the market, trends, the competitive landscape, customer needs, and growth opportunities. They help business leaders, product strategists, and innovation teams obtain a clear view of the broader economic environment. Market intelligence reports are essential across the innovation process—from product discovery to in-market experimentation—and hence, they should be produced frequently and made widely available through the Innovation Portal and other channels.
- **Business experiment insights report**: This document presents the results from a business experiment and how data support its hypotheses. The objective is to communicate the findings in a consistent way and recommend the best next steps. The document presents data and insights along with a summary of the experiment design, methodology, and key learnings. It is crucial for product managers and other stakeholders who make product development investments or prioritization decisions.
- **Invention disclosure document**: A formal document that captures the details of an invention or discovery, serving as the first step of the patent filing process. The document describes the idea, its novel aspects, and potential commercial applications—it sets a record of the invention and enables examination of patentability by patent attorneys.

These are the most frequently used assets in the typical innovation process. This typology reflects the innovation journey from initial ideas through tangible implementations to learnings, insights, and knowledge. The specific artifacts may vary for each company—thus, the list above should be expanded and adjusted according to your company's focus and industry. Furthermore, it is important to customize and standardize the innovation documents listed above and offer them to your innovators as *branded* templates. Consistent branding and clear descriptions can drive adoption, improve usability, and reinforce your company's identity.

An excellent strategy for boosting adoption is to incorporate the above classification into your formal innovation education programs and make them easily accessible through innovation touchpoints such as the Innovation Portal. Moreover, you may develop powerful discovery experiences on top of the knowledge store, such as catalogs of functional demos organized by technology, topic, or timelines showing the evolution of ideas and certain milestones.

The knowledge management capability typically requires a dedicated team of experts—content creators and managers—to orchestrate various aspects of the content management lifecycle. For instance, producing and maintaining templates for the assets described above, collecting, organizing, publishing content, measuring content engagement, etc. However, artificial intelligence significantly empowers this knowledge management capability by automating routine aspects of content creation and curation. AI tools can generate initial draft documentation for most of the assets described above or summarize vast amounts of various documents while extracting key insights and automatically classifying and tagging new assets with appropriate metadata. This automation allows the content team to focus on higher-value activities, such as refining content and communication strategies, developing compelling narratives, connecting innovation initiatives, and engaging with stakeholders to better understand their needs. AI can also enhance content discovery through intelligent recommendation engines that learn from the user's behavior and suggest relevant innovation assets.

When properly implemented, these capabilities transform the flow of knowledge throughout the organization. The combination of well-managed assets and effective content creation tools breaks down silos and accelerates innovation by making the collective intelligence of the organization accessible and usable in the innovation process.

4.10 The Innovation Control Panel: Orchestrating Innovation

The innovation control panel functions as a strategic command center that enables leaders to configure, steer, and optimize the entire innovation function as a unified system. By leveraging the innovation performance framework and AI-driven analytics, the control panel provides insights about key capabilities while generating specific suggestions for improving the overall program. It offers a comprehensive view of the innovation function—activities, engagement metrics, planning, feedback, etc.—and the ability to change its various parameters and configurations. For instance, the control panel allows the innovation team to reconfigure components like the innovation agenda, the idea assessment model, or the pace of innovation—as described in the following:

- **The innovation agenda editor** allows leaders to reset priorities at any time. They can refine mission statements, adjust organizational purpose, or add new innovation themes, topics, and problems worth solving to better align with business realities and strategic objectives.
- **The innovation calendar editor** helps maintain a good balance between the rhythm of business and innovation activity and reduces the risk of internal operational disruption. Through the innovation calendar, leaders can control the pace of innovation activities by adjusting multiple aspects, such as the frequency of resource-intensive workshops, hackathons, and innovation expos or their durations. This allows organizations to respond dynamically and adapt to changing conditions and business rhythms. During intense periods requiring operational focus, such as major product launches, leaders can temporarily reduce the pace of innovation, while during periods of organizational slack, they can accelerate innovation to capitalize on available capacity. The innovation calendar helps maintain innovation momentum while preventing the enthusiasm of the innovation community from disrupting critical business operations.
- **The idea assessment model configurator** allows leaders to adjust evaluation criteria and weight factors used in calculating the potential of an idea and flagging opportunities. As explained in Chap. 6, by modifying these criteria, leaders can shift innovation focus to match strategic priorities. For instance, when an updated IP strategy requires more patents, increasing novelty weighting would signal to ideators and evaluators the increased importance of *novelty*.
- **The rewards program configurator** allows leaders to fine-tune innovation incentives by adjusting recognition criteria, the actual rewards, announcement frequency, and reward structures to reinforce strategic behaviors and strengthen the culture of innovation.

In advanced implementations, the control panel incorporates AI to generate recommendations for optimal configuration settings based on performance patterns and organizational goals, creating an intelligent system for managing and orchestrating innovation at scale.

4.11 Gamification, Recognition: Rewarding Innovators

The recognition and rewards capability enables the organization to consistently identify top-performing ideas, innovation initiatives, and innovators and reward them accordingly. The base of this capability relies heavily on the definition of success: how the company understands innovation success and what types of innovation it values the most. For example, one company may pay special attention to patents and give people monetary rewards when their applications are filed, granted, or both. Another company may value ideas that lead to commercial opportunities.

The exact criteria and corresponding weight factors need careful consideration as they reflect the company's values and desired behaviors, and thus, they send an impactful message to the community of innovators.

In Chap. 3, as part of the innovation culture, we explained the importance of recognizing innovators not only for their ability to consistently conceive high-potential ideas but also for their behaviors in reference to *collaboration*, *contribution*, and *willingness to share*. These can all be connected through the reward model, thus linking the culture with the actual reward decisions. This holistic approach celebrates innovators also based on healthy competition principles: *people who consistently help others innovate* are also seen as true innovators.

The recognition and reward capability consists of three major components. The first is about a method to objectively identify *who should be rewarded*—the top innovators and their most impactful content. It implements a model to measure innovation performance at the member level as a function of multiple inputs, including the volume of ideas submitted, their potential as assessed by the evaluation team, their contributions to ideas by others, and more. This results in a numeric representation of the activity of every innovator participating in the scheme—the *individual innovation performance*—which can be then aggregated at the team, group, product, or other levels and define ranking systems, enabling the identification of top innovators in a particular context and point in time.

The second component knows *what reward* should be given to each of the defined classes of innovation achievements. For instance, how many top innovators should be announced, and how often? What should the actual award be? These are all defined via this component—the periods of reference, frequency of awards per period, budget, and type of actual awards, along with the rules and constraints.

The third component is about *communicating* the innovation *achievements* in an optimal way by applying specific templates to create and diffuse innovation *success stories* that present the rewarded innovators and their achievements. The stories reach all integrated systems, from connected kiosks in the smart office space to the Innovation Portal and newsletters.

Receiving an innovation award should be seen as a significant achievement, leading to visibility and substantial benefits. Ideally, the innovation performance should be linked directly to the innovator's career progression and path. For example, an employee's yearly performance review should take into consideration all the formal innovation achievements, as tracked through this program. Additionally, the award could come in one or more of the following forms:

- **Trophies**: These are symbols of achievement, ideally personalized, presenting the name of the innovator or team and the involved idea. They may accompany one or more other items from this list.
- **Financial rewards**: Financial compensation can be particularly effective for acknowledging and rewarding continual innovation contributions, e.g., through annual innovation recognition cycles. Monetary rewards can also be used for individual achievements—for example, when a team wins a hackathon; however, in this case, they should be carefully balanced with other recognition forms and

the right messaging to emphasize intrinsic motivation. When strategically applied, monetary rewards reinforce that innovation is important for the company.
- **Formal innovation titles**: Another way to recognize consistent top performers is by granting additional, formal innovation titles, such as *top innovator*, *distinguished innovator*, *chief inventor*, etc. When this is formal and announced in the company and visible in the organization's directory, it can be valuable from the innovator's point of view, as well as for driving awareness and creating role models for innovation.
- **Innovation badges**: These are digital tokens serving as visible symbols of exceptional innovation achievements. They create a record of contribution that follows innovators throughout their careers. When displayed on internal profiles and signatures, these badges help shape an informal network of innovation expertise within the organization. Gamifying the process with various levels and intermediary achievements can drive continued participation while helping leaders spot innovation talent.
- **Opportunities to pitch**: Top innovators may be rewarded with the opportunity to present or pitch to senior leadership. These opportunities allow innovators to explore their ideas directly with decision-makers who control resources and offer a strategic view. Beyond advancing specific ideas, these sessions build strong relationships between innovators and leaders—they transform organizational dynamics by connecting innovation talent directly with those who can sponsor innovation initiatives.
- **Organization-wide recognition**: Global announcements through high-visibility channels, such as all-hands meetings, company newsletters, and the Innovation Portal, amplify the impact of innovation achievements. This public recognition not only acknowledges the innovator's contributions but also enhances their professional reputation: it expands their internal network, positions them as thought leaders within the organization, and creates opportunities for cross-functional collaboration and career advancement.
- **Resources to "make it happen:"** The most powerful reward for a breakthrough idea or a hackathon-winning project is the *resources* to explore it further: the winners are given the required time, funding, and organizational support to develop their ideas, e.g., build a prototype or perform market tests and validation. The "make it happen" reward creates a path from ideation to implementation and allows innovators to explore further their concepts through early forms of realization. In this context, teams may be invited to present their implementations and insights to the leadership and the entire innovation community, thus providing a concrete example where innovation didn't stop in announcing the winners of an innovation contest. Providing the resources to innovators helps not only to explore high-potential opportunities but also to demonstrate the organization's commitment to innovation.

A well-designed and operated innovation reward program—possibly enriched with gamification elements—can significantly improve the innovation culture across the organization. The actual rewards praise innovation and make it more tangible and visible. The program may be initially implemented based on manual processes or semi-automated solutions and operated by a qualified team. For mature innovation environments, though, certain automation and integration become essential for the initiative's success: it should be powered by the Innovation Graph and offered through the Innovation Portal. The quantification of innovation activity and contributions is further presented as part of the innovation measurement framework in Chap. 9.

4.12 Open Innovation: Expanding Innovation Boundaries

Open innovation expands beyond company boundaries. This capability provides a framework that fosters collaboration, innovation, and co-creation with entities from the broader ecosystem, thus increasing the company's ability to innovate.

To effectively implement open innovation, companies need a multidisciplinary team skilled in partnership development, IP management, and cross-organizational collaboration—professionals who can navigate the complexities of working across organizational boundaries while protecting core interests. This team must maintain active channels for engagement with diverse partners, including start-ups, academic institutions, industry entities, and customers, each offering unique value to the innovation process.

For open innovation to succeed, the team must develop strategies and standardized frameworks, such as well-designed templates for partnership agreements, a clear Intellectual Property strategy, and compelling systems of incentives that make open innovation scenarios meaningful and attractive to all parties. Furthermore, organizations need technology platforms and tools to manage open innovation scenarios such as innovation contests, co-creation with external partners, etc. Governance is equally important—a robust model with clear evaluation criteria for external opportunities, funding mechanisms, and decision-making frameworks for various partnership scenarios. This governance ensures that external innovation activities remain aligned with strategic objectives.

When properly implemented, the open innovation capability significantly expands an organization's innovation capacity by accessing existing solutions, specialized expertise, and diverse perspectives. Open innovation creates pathways to breakthrough opportunities that would remain undiscovered in a closed innovation system.

4.13 The AI-Powered Innovation Portal: Creating a Home for Innovation

Innovation needs a digital home—a centralized, organization-wide source of truth where all innovation-related resources, activities, assets, and plans live and are accessible through smart, personalized experiences. This unified innovation platform is invaluable for any organization—as it connects the dots, breaks the silos, and sets the focus for innovation. More than that, in today's era of remote work and distributed teams, it has become an essential capability: it provides a single destination where remote or on-site employees can discover opportunities, access tools, contribute ideas, track progress, and collaborate seamlessly regardless of physical location.

The Innovation Portal, as envisioned here, is a powerful internal platform that unifies all the innovation resources across the organization. It hosts an array of advanced tools and interactive features powered by artificial intelligence that offer seamless access to the innovation knowledge base—the Innovation Graph. The Innovation Portal brings together all the capabilities presented in this chapter into an intelligent platform that empowers the organization to innovate at scale; it is the primary point of reference for innovation—the organization's most accurate and complete source of innovation assets.

The portal plays a dual role: inspiring people to engage with innovation while making innovation processes more visible, accessible, and efficient. It attracts attention and motivates employees to participate, learn, and become true innovators while simultaneously saving time by intelligently connecting people, teams, and resources. Through AI components and strategic integrations, the portal can answer virtually any innovation-related question by leveraging its knowledge base and, when needed, connecting to other systems or even "collaborating" with the community of innovators.

In its ideal form, the portal offers a dynamic presentation of the innovation agenda, giving everyone visibility into the organization's priorities and strategic focus areas. Moreover, it automatically captures and reflects the latest happenings in the innovation space: even from the very first interaction, the user obtains a precise and fresh summarization of innovation activity across the company—a single view of projects that have just been completed, happening now, or are starting shortly, visualized on the portal's home page. This intelligent "innovation highlights" synthesis is generated by properly integrated AI agents that have access to documents and digital resources about various independent innovation activities across the company. By combining data and content from other corporate systems, the portal's AI agent creates a rich, accurate, engaging narrative on *what* the organization is innovating on and *why*. As part of that, the portal presents highlights, statistics, and interesting insights from the company's innovation function, reflecting its overall activity and aspects of performance.

The Innovation Portal is open to all. However, different user personas interact with it in distinct ways. Experienced innovators use it to stay current on events and resources, share achievements, and engage with community questions. Innovation newcomers engage with the interactive Innovation Playbook and discover pathways to drive their ideas through the pipeline. Innovation leaders leverage the portal as their primary channel for diffusing updates, sharing success stories, communicating innovation activities, and orchestrating the innovation function. To cover these diverse needs, the Innovation Portal must be engaging, current, simple, and contextual—able to deliver fresh content and personalized experiences that adapt to each user's role, interests, and behavior patterns; it enables smart idea discovery and distribution to ensure ideas reach the right people at the right time. For instance, an engineering manager, a sales director, and a software developer would each experience different views reflecting their specific contexts and interests in innovation.

As the home of innovation, the portal also hosts the community of innovators: it is where inspired, talented people connect to discover, share, contribute, learn, and educate each other, e.g., via the innovation blog where innovators exchange thoughts on ideas, technologies, global trends, and potential innovation projects. To foster collaboration, the portal provides intelligent matchmaking that connects the community of innovators with stakeholders and complementary talent across the company, and thus, it helps form virtual teams around promising ideas.

The portal also serves as the place to announce and celebrate top innovators. It connects to the recognition and rewards system and presents the latest lists of successful ideas, distinguished innovators, and most innovative teams.

Normally, the design, implementation and operation of such a system is a massive undertaking. However, AI and related technological advancements drastically simplify the process. Artificial intelligence, APIs, reusable components, and development frameworks have dramatically reduced the technical barriers to such a platform. Companies can approach this as an agile project, beginning with essential features that deliver immediate value and evolving through regular iterations based on user feedback, priorities, and resource availability.

The following sections explore some of the most transformative features of the Innovation Portal and explain how artificial intelligence can dramatically accelerate and enhance complex innovation processes and functions.

The AI Innovation Advisor: Powered by a group of AI agents, this feature transforms how innovators interact with the organization's accumulated knowledge: the AI advisor replaces traditional GUI-based navigation and endless forms with natural language interactions—through text or voice—creating a seamless "Ask Me Anything" experience that spans the entire organization: a gateway to all innovation assets and activities, across the company. Innovators can simply describe what they need in natural language, e.g., "Who is working on project x?" or "To whom should I pitch idea z?" The advisor understands the context and intent and compiles concrete answers, summarizing the related innovation content and, if needed, providing pointers to additional systems or resources. This makes access to innovation far easier and more effective by eliminating tedious navigation menus or endless search results. Moreover, the advisor accesses various knowledge domains and is able to perform smart operations that would previously require hours or days of work. For example:

- **The innovation agent** replaces classic idea *search*, *creation*, and *editing* operations with a smart experience that understands natural language queries and retrieves relevant ideas and innovation content. It takes into account the user's role, team context, and interaction history to provide a personalized experience and set the right context. For example, when a product manager searches for ideas, the agent knows which products they manage and uses this as context to find relevant concepts. With access to the product's feature set, the system focuses on ideas that are *novel to the product* or ones that *complement it* in valuable ways. Moreover, the agent evaluates various signals, such as feasibility, quality, and business potential of ideas. The response isn't just a simple list or a brief; it is a contextual *narrative* that synthesizes the *matched ideas* within the user's specific context, properly framed with market intelligence and recommendations. Additionally, as part of this process, the advisor can automatically generate new, novel-to-the-company ideas and include them in the narrative. Beyond idea discovery, the innovation agent helps ideators by providing instant suggestions during idea creation, e.g., pointing to complementary ideas, relevant prototypes, demos, and videos. Furthermore, it identifies teams and top innovators who are likely interested in the concept. In more advanced scenarios, when defining a new project, the innovation agent automatically interacts with the underlying knowledge base—the Innovation Graph—to synthesize a comprehensive package of ideas relevant to the project being defined, ensuring new initiatives benefit from the organization's innovation knowledge.

- **The team builder** shapes the "perfect" team based on a brief project description. When an innovator describes a concept or picks an idea to work on, the AI agent identifies the required skills and expertise and scans the organization's directory to suggest the optimal talent synthesis—connecting specialists with complementary capabilities across team boundaries and divisions. This capability extends beyond typical "skill matching" by proposing *real teams* and also considering people's availability, interests, and innovation performance.
- **The organization navigator** finds the right people and teams in the context of an idea or innovation initiative. For instance, while the user is working with an idea, problem, or feature proposal, they may ask the navigator to find potential "interested parties," e.g., sponsors, stakeholders, and product teams, or who else is working on that. This helps not only innovators but also all employees navigate the organization based on a business or innovation intent. Beyond answering "who might be interested," it also answers "what relevant workstreams are there" by identifying related work across the organization, e.g., projects, experiments, and initiatives related to the given idea or innovation asset. For instance, when the innovator describes or selects a concept, the Navigator alerts and points them to similar initiatives, whether active, planned, completed, or discontinued. This prevents redundant innovation efforts and also brings opportunities to combine ideas and collaborate with others in the company.

By combining natural language understanding with comprehensive organizational knowledge, the innovation agent transforms innovation from a structured process into an intuitive dialogue, thus making the knowledge of the entire organization accessible in a conversational mode. This remarkable ability of AI to comprehend natural language also revolutionizes idea and problem intake: users simply describe their ideas or problems they want to solve, and they are instantly captured, analyzed, and contextualized within the organization's idea corpus—living in the Innovation Graph—while the user gets actionable feedback and direction within seconds.

The system also recognizes and responds to specific innovation intents, such as "build a prototype," "get advice on an idea," or "file a patent for my idea." Each intent triggers personalized guidance, including links to introductory materials, access to relevant resources, training content, experts to contact, and recommended next steps, thus creating a seamless path from early ideas to concrete actions. This conversational approach makes the innovation process immediately accessible to all employees, regardless of their experience.

Innovation Broadcaster: Powered by artificial intelligence, the innovation broadcaster optimizes knowledge distribution while preventing information overload. Rather than broadcasting general updates to all, this AI agent identifies the right audience before triggering any communication. For instance, when an idea is flagged as high potential, the broadcaster analyzes its content, context, and metadata to identify and notify the most relevant stakeholders, such as subject matter experts who can provide feedback or potential collaborators with relevant skills. Similarly, when evaluators flag an idea as an opportunity, the broadcaster identifies possible implementation teams, business units that could bring the idea to market, or senior stakeholders who might sponsor further development of the opportunity.

The broadcaster may also notify people about external innovation updates, e.g., a new report from the innovation intelligence team, relevant news from the market, or product announcements. For instance, when a patent is published, teams and individuals working in related domains automatically receive executive summaries and updates. This targeted diffusion may take various forms, including standardized reports like "Top Ideas by Business Potential in x" or "Emerging Technology Concepts for z," providing curated views of the innovation pipeline for different contexts.

The innovation broadcaster creates an interconnected ecosystem where opportunities, internal updates, and market intelligence flow seamlessly to those best positioned to leverage them, regardless of organizational boundaries or how users access the platform. To create such targeted notifications, the system leverages deep organizational knowledge across three key domains: first, *employee business profiles*, including title, level, discipline, and role, along with their derived interests; second, *organizational structure* data that describe hierarchy, teams, divisions, product lines, and services; and finally, it uses *global and local innovation agendas* to determine content's relevance and context.

Unified Innovation Calendar: The innovation calendar is an interactive visualization of the scheduled innovation events across the year on a single timeline; it allows users to instantly discover "what's next in innovation," e.g., upcoming all-hands, training opportunities, hackathons, design sprints, presentations, and related happenings, enriched with content and references. Users can browse event agendas and pre-reads, subscribe for updates, and request to join.

Smart Feedback Loops and Support Channels: The portal provides intelligent feedback mechanisms, allowing people to share their thoughts on the innovation process, workshops, and all related activities. User feedback is automatically analyzed and presented through standardized scorecards that measure the perceived performance of innovation events, such as hackathons or workshops. The innovation team obtains a consolidated view of the performance of the innovation function, enriched with AI summarization of user feedback and suggestions. These same channels enable users to submit support requests or questions, which can be addressed by the AI agent, the innovation support team, or the broader community of innovators.

Workshop Designer: A typical innovation year of an innovative organization contains numerous hackathons, brainstorming sessions, design sprints, and other demanding events like expos and demo days. These require significant preparation, communication, and execution—they must be arranged optimally and promoted effectively across channels to attract attention without disrupting the business rhythm. For instance, when planning big events like yearly hackathons, the organizers must consider the company's peak periods and important dates to ensure optimal spacing and a meaningful sequence of events.

The Workshop Designer streamlines this time-consuming planning and promotion process. It enables quick scheduling of innovation events into the portal's unified innovation calendar and accelerates the event's preparation through templates, scripts, and guidelines. The planning team simply sets the title and topic, and then AI handles the rest, e.g., suggesting appropriate audiences, optimal time slots, and content ideas.

Furthermore, the underlying AI leverages predefined templates to generate prereads and essential materials across various workshop types. For instance, when setting up a brainstorming session, the Workshop Designer uses the topic and defined agenda to generate problem and solution spaces with sample ideas and problem statements for context setting and discussion. The system then triggers automated event instantiation: it creates a detailed communication timeline, a branded landing page, and specific email content—announcements, invitations, content sharing, and reminders. Once approved, the Workshop Designer executes pre-configured communication plans, emailing participants according to the timeline. This significantly simplifies event planning and administration while synchronizing seamlessly with the unified innovation calendar.

After the event, the Workshop Designer automatically collects and processes participants' feedback while allowing organizers to upload content generated during the session.

Innovation Onboarding: The Innovation Portal is inclusive and accessible by design: it provides interactive guidance and educational material to encourage those new to the company or new to the innovation function to engage with the process. It uses the Innovation Playbook and real innovation stories to explain the core processes and all the essential resources, including a thorough innovation FAQ—answers to frequently asked questions that can help newcomers discover how they can become part of the effort.

This section presented the vision of the "ideal" AI-powered Innovation Portal—as a comprehensive platform with rich functionality that implements or hosts all the essential innovation capabilities presented in this chapter. In practice, though, not every company will need all these features, and some may need additional experiences unique to their context or industry. Even if this ideal version of the portal is not required in its entirety, a version or adaptation of it should exist in every modern organization willing to drive success through innovation.

4.14 The Innovation Hub: The AI-Powered Network of Innovation

So far, in this chapter, we have covered the essential innovation capabilities of the AI era and explained how they work together to help the organization innovate as a single unit. While the approach of having a single instance of the innovation framework and shared innovation services is best for most companies, there are cases where this is not feasible or not the preferred pattern.

For instance, in large organizations operating multiple products, R&D divisions, or centers, innovation may be happening "independently" across various groups, each following a separate agenda, cadence, methodologies, and tools. While this has certain benefits, such as flexibility and autonomy, it allows and possibly reinforces information gaps and silos; it comes with opportunity cost and eventually with a negative impact on the overall innovation culture. At the same time, using a variety of approaches and methods makes performance measurement and orchestration of innovation difficult.

To illustrate the potential gaps, consider a hypothetical case of two innovation-focused divisions in a large technology company—a central R&D lab and a Product Innovation team. The R&D lab focuses on longer time horizons, exploring emerging technologies, conducting research, and developing breakthrough capabilities. At the same time, Product Innovation runs shorter-term innovation cycles, identifying market opportunities, translating user needs into innovative product features, and developing new product concepts. Typically, in such scenarios, each group adopts its own style of innovation: since they have a different setup, purpose, and leadership, they maintain a separate innovation agenda and follow a distinct approach to innovation—they look at it from a different angle and use various tools, systems, and methods without a consistent innovation tech stack.

While this is reasonable as it allows for independence and speed, it also introduces *opportunity cost* and constrains innovation. Although the two teams are fundamentally different, they both serve the same organizational purpose, higher-level business goals, and, ultimately, customers. Hence, when in this independent mode, they may be missing high-potential opportunities, which would be apparent if there was sufficient information exchange.

For instance, as the Product Innovation team is closely connected to users and has a deep understanding of their pain points, they may be working with problems that could be addressed using the knowledge and technical inventions available in the R&D division. Moreover, insights from the Product Innovation team could influence the direction of future research in the R&D division. In turn, the breakthrough technologies emerging from the R&D division could be a source of inspiration for the Product Innovation team—they could help product managers envision new features, experiences, or product concepts and shape business experiments.

The missed opportunities multiply when we add a third player in this scenario: a Sales and Customer Success team. Typically, such teams accumulate a wealth of market intelligence that is often invisible to other parts of the organization. Through daily interactions with prospects and existing clients, they obtain perspectives on products and how they compare to competitive offerings—they spot product limitations and unmet needs faster than anyone else. When Sales and Customer Success operate in isolation from the company's innovation system, this wealth of knowledge and actionable intelligence remains untapped.

Each of the three groups of the above scenario may own unique insights, learnings, and ideas that, if linked, could create massive business value. Yes, the three groups may meet regularly in all-hands or information-sharing sessions. But still, the lack of a synchronized, systematic knowledge exchange significantly limits the innovation potential. Sales and Customer Success professionals might have the *ideas* but not the expertise or the "responsibility" to explore them further. Product innovators may be working on ambitious features but without awareness of the client-originated signals from the Sales and Customer Success team that could influence priorities or the focus of innovation. Since in this example the Product's and R&D's innovation agendas are not connected, researchers may not be aware of these signals, thus missing important aspects and perspectives.

What if the three teams—and others across the organization—could join an innovation network and automatically exchange ideas, insights, and learnings? Although this might occasionally create noise, *a stream of problems* worth solving or formulated *ideas* could lead to high-potential growth opportunities for products and services.

The fragmented innovation pattern described in the above scenario can be addressed by empowering various divisions in the organization to innovate *independently* but *synchronized*. By adopting and operating instances of the innovation framework, divisions such as the R&D, Product Innovation, or Sales and Customer Success can maintain their autonomy while plugging into an enterprise-wide innovation network. Following this pattern, participating teams use *the same methods, processes, and tools*, such as idea and problem framing templates, the idea assessment model, recognition and rewards logic, etc. and thus are all compatible—they can exchange innovation knowledge fast, with consistency.

This pattern—each innovation team leveraging the *same innovation framework*—defines a great solution that combines the benefits of both worlds. Teams participate in the innovation network through a balanced and meaningful knowledge exchange through the Innovation Portal. For example, if multiple innovation teams or R&D groups follow this approach, they share and discover innovation assets, plans, ideas, and other content in a *controlled* and *contextual* way.

This multiple-instance innovation setup is visualized in Fig. 4.5. At the center of the chart, the Innovation Portal stands as a hub, connecting multiple innovation teams or R&D groups. Each independent innovation team runs another virtual instance of the innovation framework while maintaining its own private knowledge base and content.

All instances utilize the exact same technology and processes—they inherit their capabilities, definitions, rules, and templates from the innovation framework. For example, they measure innovation performance using standard metrics and KPIs, thus enabling consistent measurement of success across the organization. Similarly, document templates, content creation guidelines, and workshop formats all inherit from the same standardized and branded templates. Most importantly, although each of the teams shown in Fig. 4.5 has full control over its own innovation agenda, calendar, and content, all teams contribute to the Global Innovation Agenda. Through the hub, teams diffuse selected innovation content and discover what's happening across the innovation network.

This setup aligns the isolated groups, allows them to speak the same "innovation language," and empowers them to partner just in time—based on opportunities identified naturally through organic knowledge and information exchange. Nodes of this innovation network are compatible since they are powered by shared content models, formats, procedures, and methods. This compatibility makes sharing ideas, content, knowledge, and artifacts seamless. Following this pattern, all the isolated innovation entities in the organization, e.g., labs, discovery teams, and innovation centers, opt into the company-wide innovation network. Nodes "talk" to each other

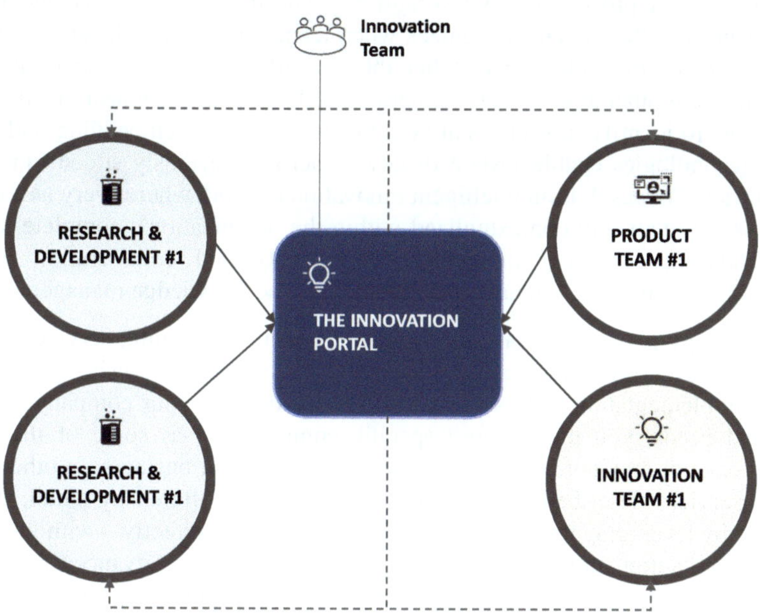

Fig. 4.5 The Innovation Portal as a hub connecting distributed innovation groups

and stay in sync by exchanging their innovation agendas, selected assets, and artifacts.

With this architecture and the Innovation Portal in place, the teams of our hypothetical scenario would receive notifications about relevant ideas or opportunities triggered by certain events, such as the submission of an idea by the Sales and Customer Success team, the release of a new technology update from the R&D team, or a product update from the Product Innovation team.

The teams—and all members of the innovation network—discover innovation assets not only based on rules but also according to the semantics of their innovation agendas. Intelligent background processes maintain an index of all innovation activity and content, which is discoverable by AI agents who facilitate smart information and knowledge exchange among the nodes of the innovation network.

This way, the innovation network can eliminate information gaps and break silos while maintaining a certain level of independence for "local" innovation teams. From a leadership perspective, this unified, scalable innovation architecture simplifies the measurement, steering, and orchestration of innovation.

The concept of innovation at scale with a network of independent innovation or R&D teams brings technical challenges, e.g., regarding the increased volumes of content and, as a result, complexities with its distribution and discoverability. However, with artificial intelligence, this becomes perfectly manageable: Modern natural language components and semantic processing services can efficiently analyze, categorize, and connect vast stores of content across distributed teams. These AI systems automatically extract meaning from ideas, problems, and innovation artifacts, identifying non-obvious relationships that humans would only obtain after extensive manual processing. By leveraging advanced natural language understanding capabilities, the system recognizes when teams in different divisions work on complementary innovations, even when they use different terminology or approach problems from other angles. This semantic matching creates connections that were impossible to identify in traditional systems, while content embedding and vector search technologies enable instant discovery across previously siloed innovation repositories. The result is an intelligent innovation network where every new contribution is automatically contextualized within the organization's complete innovation landscape, creating unprecedented visibility and collaboration without overloading teams with manual content handling and knowledge management.

Technology plays a crucial role in enabling and streamlining services like the above. However, investing heavily in technology is not a prerequisite for kickstarting the implementation of this framework. Depending on your company's current state and needs, you may choose specific components—as some of them may already exist or may not be of immediate priority for your business. In other cases, certain services described in this framework could be offered by small, flexible teams or by leveraging the power of artificial intelligence directly—without system integrations, automation, or AI agents from the beginning. Advanced technology solutions usually can wait to be "injected" at later stages—to extend the first versions of the framework and gradually make it smarter and more scalable. This approach provides flexibility to bootstrap the innovation function in parallel to other preparation work streams or innovation technology integration projects.

Beyond technology and architecture, the innovation framework must be open and inclusive by design. It should welcome not only the "experts" but all individuals and teams willing to make an impact through innovation. It must be accessible by the entire organization, enabling people to engage with innovation activities, access innovation tools, get connected, and apply experimentation approaches in solving strategic problems for the company. The framework aims to flatten the organization through better information sharing, idea discovery, and access to innovation assets, methods, and knowledge. This openness sets the basis for a great innovation culture where good ideas can emerge from anywhere, breaking down traditional silos and rigid hierarchies that often limit creativity and collaboration.

While this framework sets the ground and provides the foundational capabilities, it is the human potential that truly energizes innovation. In the next chapter, we'll explore how strategically designed cross-disciplinary workshops, such as Hackathons, Design Sprints, and Brainstorming sessions, can spark ideas and boost collaboration toward opportunity discovery. Beyond the classic innovation workshops, we will present how to use artificial intelligence to supercharge them and dramatically accelerate the corporate innovation process.

Innovation Workshops and the Impact of AI

5

Innovation events and workshops are at the core of corporate innovation. They serve multiple purposes, such as solving specific business problems, educating and inspiring innovators, or helping orchestrate the innovation function itself. Some aim to *produce innovation*—e.g., workshops that focus on exploring new concepts and solution prototyping—while others seek to *share* knowledge and ideas or *communicate* the company's innovation agenda.

When properly orchestrated, a program of innovation events can improve the performance of the innovation function, help remove silos, boost the culture, and drive engagement with innovation. Workshops bring together powerful cross-disciplinary teams of talented, inspired people and ignite innovation.

However, it is crucial to *maintain the right pace* in terms of frequency, timing, and sequence of events: too many could disrupt the rhythm of business and diminish their own purpose. Too few, and the spirit of innovation will suffer from gaps and start to decline. While some of these events happen regularly, they must not become a routine: innovation events must be well prepared, with a clear agenda and carefully arranged audience. The recurring events need to be well spread throughout the year, with the right frequency and distance from each other. Ad hoc workshops should be associated with specific business triggers to ensure that they only happen when there is a justified need.

The primary class of innovation events is *workshops*—focused innovation sessions with participants across domains and backgrounds collaborating to frame a problem or shape solutions. More specifically, *prototyping workshops* are about materializing an idea or product concept, thus making it more concrete and "real"—helping stakeholders better understand complex concepts and possibly "test" them by exposing the prototypes to specific audiences. Beyond prototyping workshops, this category includes Hackathons and Design Sprints—and also a new, evolving form of brainstorming enhanced by AI—as explained in the following sections.

The following sections present in detail the most characteristic innovation workshops and events.

G. Krasadakis, *Innovation Mode 2.0*,
https://doi.org/10.1007/978-3-032-00835-0_5

5.1 Brainstorming

Brainstorming refers to a straightforward event: in a business context, it is usually a structured session with a simple objective: to generate and discuss ideas on solving a defined problem or addressing a generic need. They typically last up to a few hours, depending on the level of preparation and the complexity of the problem. They can be regular, scheduled across the year, or ad hoc, triggered by specific events and needs. Although simple, brainstorming sessions tend to suffer from the same issues that most business meetings do—they often prove to be "noisy" with no measurable outcome or follow-up actions. The root cause is typically poor preparation and audience synthesis: A brainstorming session without the right people in the room is slower and less productive. Having the right people but not being well prepared probably leads to the same limited outcome. Incompatible personalities, too many people, or too much authority and expertise could diminish the purpose. But even when the "dream team" of ideators is in the session, there are still risks that could limit its value: lack of proper facilitation, poor handling of the generated ideas, and ineffective follow-up can ruin the outcome of an otherwise fruitful and enthusiastic brainstorming.

The following presents what happens during brainstorming, how to overcome these challenges, and what the future of AI-powered brainstorming looks like.

5.1.1 The "Classic" Business Brainstorming

A brainstorming session is typically low-tech, with ideas captured on a whiteboard, sticky notes, or writable walls. Although simple, successful brainstorming sessions require thoughtful preparation.

The first step is to clearly set the agenda by stating the motivation, the theme, and the desired outcome—what the team wants to achieve from the session. Regardless of the formality of the brainstorming, there should be a facilitator who is skilled in driving the discussion and applying basic rules that allow all voices to be heard and ensure that all ideas will be respected.

The next most important element is *the audience*. Selecting the right participants is critical as it can significantly impact success—in terms of both the volume and quality of ideas. When choosing the participants, typically four to ten members, you should consider not only *skills* and *relevance* to the topic but also their ability to bring *fresh perspectives*, e.g., someone who is not directly involved in the problem being solved and able to look at it from a distance and a different angle. Contributions from such participants can act as catalysts for the outcome of the process.

Another success factor is the *preparation of the participants*. An insufficiently prepared team typically ends up having randomized discussions, restating the obvious, and thus spending valuable time. To avoid that, consider compiling a pre-read package with a single pager describing the motivation and desired outcome and a clear articulation of the problem statement. Optionally, there could be a package of inspiring content—e.g., stories from the market and related trends.

Following the kick-off, there is a short discussion of the agenda and the problem statement, which then leads to the ideation phase, where people have a fixed amount of time to prepare their ideas and pitch them to the rest of the group. After the pitch, there is a post-processing step to merge or group similar ideas into emerging themes. Teams often use a voting process to select the most "promising" ideas. However, experience shows that prioritization or selection of ideas *during the event* is far from optimal: unconscious bias, differences in presentation skills among the participants, the impact of seniority or the presence of perceived authorities, and "group think" could severely affect such decisions. A better way is to focus on capturing *all ideas* and processing them *after* the event. Following this approach, the session ends with a package of *raw ideas* as the main output.

The organizer is accountable for coordinating the post-processing of the raw ideas, making them available in a list, and then assessing them based on a robust method, such as the Idea Scoring Model presented in Chap. 6 that allows a more thoughtful prioritization and confident selection of the ideas to be further considered.

With the rise of AI, business brainstorming is evolving into a new form that is less about generating ideas and more about synthesizing and strategizing on top of ideas and prototypes generated by AI during the session. In this sense, AI is there in the brainstorming as another innovator in the room, augmenting human creativity in various ways. Brainstorming morphs into idea synthesis and interactive prototype sessions powered by AI.

5.2 The AI-Powered Brainstorming

Artificial intelligence, and in particular, generative AI, changes dramatically how companies brainstorm. With the current state of the art, an AI system can help set up a brainstorming session in minutes. For example, assuming that the Workshop Designer feature of the Innovation Portal is connected with an AI service, the organizer provides a brief description of the brainstorming and instantly gets a well-defined brainstorming session with an "optimal agenda"—based on the context of the company, its innovation agenda, and related data from the public domain and market intelligence. The portal uses the company's directory to recommend the right participants while generating a dedicated webpage for the brainstorming session, presenting its agenda, rules, and resources.

Instead of compiling multiple attachments and long email texts, the organizer simply confirms the audience and triggers the invite that shares the link to the event's page so participants get an overview and prepare to contribute. Moreover, the AI automatically creates a content package of related ideas, research findings, and "stories from the market" to consider as context and source of inspiration for the participants.

Beyond helping organize the event, AI can play an *active role* in the brainstorming session itself. The following may sound like a futuristic scenario, but it is already feasible: you can have AI in the room that communicates via a smart speaker and interactive screens and contributes by listening, capturing, and organizing the ideas being described—all seamlessly. At the same time, AI acts as an innovator by generating and pitching ideas, matching not only the agenda of the session but also the evolving discussion.

For example, during brainstorming, the AI can take the lead, present ideas, and facilitate the discussion with the team, both in the room and among the online participants. The AI follows the discussion; captures feedback, questions, and answers about ideas; and uses all these to enrich and improve ideas further—seamlessly, simply by listening to the team discussing. The AI facilitator can act autonomously by intervening with key questions or guidelines or providing visual content about the idea being discussed. In an advanced scenario, the AI *visualizes* and *prototypes* selected ideas, which are then presented on connected screens, thus allowing participants to provide verbal feedback and improve them just in time. Through this experience, the team's focus is shifting from *ideating* to *synthesizing* and *estimating the potential* of AI-generated ideas.

The AI facilitator also does the supportive work—it takes notes and organizes the evolving ideas seamlessly by processing the live discussion. At the end of the brainstorming, ideas are automatically reflected in the Innovation Graph, attributed to the identified participant, and enriched with comments and feedback captured in the session. The brainstorming output becomes available via the private event page in the Innovation Portal, allowing participants to access executive summaries and the detailed ideas shaped during the session. The output also contains participants' feedback, prioritization decisions, and links to visuals and prototypes generated during the brainstorming. After the event, AI simplifies things again by processing, summarizing, and potentially scoring human-enriched ideas.

In short, classic business brainstorming is changing dramatically in the era of AI. It is morphing into a "synthesis" session versus a "blue sky" ideation—a hybrid workshop aiming not only to generate ideas but primarily to synthesize, prioritize, and strategize. This changes both the scope and the objective of these workshops—the whole process is accelerated, and the participants can focus their energy on assessing the potential of prototyped concepts versus starting from scratch and framing ideas themselves. Powered by AI and the rest of the innovation framework, this "bionic" brainstorming is dramatically faster in all *planning*, *communicating*, and *running* the actual event.

The organization may streamline and package this modern brainstorming event and make it available across teams as a standard and efficient innovation workshop. These enhanced brainstorming sessions feed into the opportunity discovery pipeline and thus contribute to spotting big, disruptive opportunities. Assuming that all capabilities of the innovation framework are there, more ideas can bring more opportunities and, ultimately, more in-market innovations.

However, this evolution comes with various risks that must be carefully mitigated. There are concerns that overreliance on AI-generated content may diminish human creativity or impact the innovation culture. After all, the *creative process* is the *energizing factor* or, for some, *the fun* of innovation. Organizations must intentionally preserve space for pure human creativity and implement practices that use AI as augmentation rather than a replacement for creative thinking. Additionally, teams should remain vigilant about potential AI biases and critically evaluate AI-generated content rather than simply accepting it.

5.3 Design Sprints and the Impact of AI

A Design Sprint is a fast-paced ideation and prototyping workshop driven by a carefully selected multidisciplinary team. It uses Design Thinking to identify potential solutions to a specific problem and then test them in a rapid, inexpensive way. Testing is usually based on quick visualizations and clickable or functional prototypes that are built during the Design Sprint and exposed to key stakeholders for feedback. Stakeholders may include domain experts, real customers, or users. The team works together with full commitment for 5 days in a row.

As described in the Sprint book (Knapp and Zeratsky 2016), the process consists of distinct phases mapped over 5 days. It starts with *goal setting*, then focuses on selecting and framing the *problem to solve*, and then moves to *ideating* and *sketching* solutions. The third day is about discussing and *selecting the solution* to move forward for prototyping. During the fourth day, the team prototypes the chosen solutions, usually through quick visualizations or clickable wireframes. During the last day, the team presents the prototyped solutions and interviews key stakeholders to capture their reactions and feedback.

The output of the Design Sprint is typically a package of ideas, wireframes, diagrams, answers to key questions, and business insights, along with one or more solutions enriched with insightful feedback from key stakeholders. Depending on the feedback and other insights gathered, the solutions may be then considered for further exploration, prototyping, or implementation paths. The theoretical benefit of this process is that it empowers teams to shape great solutions and make good decisions fast by leveraging the power of the cross-disciplinary scheme.

As with all business collaboration sessions and workshops, the success of a Design Sprint depends on the synthesis of the team, the level of their preparation, and the experience of the facilitator. Considering the Design Sprint's long duration and cost, it is crucial to make the right design choices—plan it effectively and ensure optimal use of its output. The following paragraphs explain how to address the above and other concerns by connecting the Design Sprint to the innovation framework and using AI to make it faster and more productive.

5.3.1 Connecting the Design Sprint to the Innovation Framework

The success of a Design Sprint depends on both the quality of its input and how the organization handles its outputs. Connecting the Design Sprint to the innovation framework presented in Chap. 4 can help in both directions—accelerate its preparation and better use the assets produced. The following paragraphs explain how the Design Sprint can benefit from this "integration" and how certain AI use cases can further empower the team.

- **Market Intelligence Provides Insights**: Preparing for the Design Sprint is demanding—it takes energy and time—but it is also crucial for the event's success. To address that, the organizing team compiles a package of high-quality content to be shared with the participants beforehand—as preparation work that sets the context and provides a shared understanding of the problem space and the broader ecosystem. This is where the *innovation intelligence* service—the team scanning the market for interesting insights, activities, and emerging patterns—can significantly contribute by providing valuable inputs and directional advice. The organizers of the Design Sprint can either reuse existing market intelligence content—e.g., competition or market summaries—or request the compilation of a market report specifically for the Design Sprint. Moreover, the market intelligence team could be invited to present the "market state and dynamic" as part of the sprint kick-off. Using the expertise and unique insights of the market intelligence team saves time from preparation and boosts the likelihood of success—it serves participants with unique market perspectives produced by experts in the company's context.
- **The Makerspace Provides Technology**: In many cases, the solutions proposed in a Design Sprint target special devices or require expensive equipment that is not generally available. A well-equipped Makerspace—detailed in Chap. 7—can cover these needs and thus speed up the prototyping efforts of the Design Sprint. For example, when a solution requires the creation of a physical prototype, the team can leverage equipment such as 3D printing and related know-how available in the innovation community to get a physical prototype fast. In another scenario, the organizers may be able to tell in advance that the solutions are likely to require specific devices, e.g., VR or AR headsets, and thus secure a few of them from the makerspace—possibly along with preset development environments and templates to speed up prototyping.
- **AI Boosts Prototyping**: Design Sprints traditionally emphasize a low-tech approach so people can focus, immerse themselves in the problem, and maximize their contributions. However, especially when it comes to prototyping the identified solutions, it would be a missed opportunity not to use artificial intelligence: with the right AI tools and a library of prototyping resources such as reusable UI components, datasets, services, and APIs, complex concepts could be realized into functional prototypes in a matter of hours.

  One strategy is to introduce a lightweight engagement with AI, e.g., include sketch-to-prototype conversion tools that digitize hand-drawn wireframes into clickable UIs or storyboards and user flows. A more aggressive approach would be to use UI Generation tools along with AIs like Claude or Software Development Agents or interactive Prototype Builders that enable rapid development of functional prototypes. Using such tools, participants describe the desired functionality in natural language, and AI generates a functional experience that can be used to present the solution to stakeholders. However, this could significantly change the character of the workshop—from a focused, deep, cross-disciplinary, intense collaboration to a live prototyping session.

An interesting alternative is to combine the two in parallel: maintain the original character of the Design Sprint and, when the solutions are defined and sketched, "outsource" the prototyping activity to another team that leverages AI tools and builds functional prototypes rapidly. Or, create a breakout session where a subset of the core Design Sprint team works independently for a few hours and uses the latest AI tools to convert the envisioned solutions to functional prototypes. Then, they merge back to the core Design Sprint team to review the prototypes and move on with the intense plan of the workshop. This hybrid approach can maintain the low-tech, focused character of the Design Sprint while leveraging the latest AI tech for rapid prototyping and allowing for parallelism that further speeds up the process.

- **AI Helps Sets Up the Event**: Setting up a Design Sprint is demanding—it requires many tough decisions, good planning, extensive preparation, and effective communication. As with brainstorming, the Design Sprint organizers leverage the AI-powered Workshop Designer to automatically set up aspects of the event, such as the content package, timelines, and communication templates. The Workshop Designer generates a dedicated page in the Innovation Portal that hosts all the key information of the Design Sprint, including critical dates, context, participants, preparation content, and, most importantly, a theme or high-level problem as the primary input for the workshop. Participants receive a link to the event page, accompanied by general instructions that help those new to Design Sprints understand the process and the essential rules.
- **AI Helps Form the "Dream Team:"** The synthesis of the team sets the foundation for a successful Design Sprint. Having the right *skills* and *characters* in the room can make a difference. At least for the former, technology can provide help: the AI-powered Workshop Designer assists the organizers in spotting the right talent and skills, not only based on static profiles and job descriptions but also based on people's overall innovation performance, activity, and the impact of their ideas. The organizers may also obtain a shortlist of specialists on standby in case they are needed during the workshop. Or, they can use the Innovation Portal to find just-in-time help from the innovation community, for example, to unblock a certain thread of the prototyping process.
- **AI Keeps Ideas Alive**: Design Sprints produce plenty of great ideas. However, due to time constraints and the nature of the event, not all of them are properly evaluated. Additionally, the process of selecting the idea to be prototyped is sensitive to many factors, and it may allow for missed opportunities. Idea selection happens under intense, "noisy" conditions, where participants are asked to express their preferences and vote for the "best" idea. But very often, it is not easy to obtain clarity across all the ideas: usually, their articulation on sticky notes is poor or incomplete, and there may be technical complexities preventing

a deep, shared understanding of the ideas. Moreover, increased volumes of ideas do not allow for deeper discussions due to time constraints, and votes can be influenced by strong opinions in the room or impacted by an "information overload"—too many ideas, too fast in a short time frame.

Fixing this is not easy—it is the nature of the workshop, after all. However, the risk of missed opportunities may be mitigated by connecting the Design Sprint with the opportunity discovery pipeline of the organization: instead of archiving or overlooking the non-selected ideas—as it very often happens—the team decodes and feeds the draft ideas directly into the opportunity discovery platform, which then applies the AI-powered processes discussed in Chap. 6, to frame the ideas, de-duplicate them, and make them available for assessment and discovery. Moreover, the ideas are tagged as coming from the particular Design Sprint, and the contributors are attributed and invited to review or enrich them.

Having all the ideas produced during the sprint in the Innovation Graph also allows the organizers to leverage the network of evaluators to obtain an additional assessment from the experts. This way, all ideas conceived during the Design Sprint get enriched and become discoverable and potentially usable beyond the event in different contexts, for example, opportunities for IP or a valuable scenario for developing a demo for a client. Also, the sponsors of the Design Sprint or other stakeholders can take a second pass over the entire set of ideas and rethink them as potential extensions of the selected concept or explore ways to combine them that might have been missed during the sprint.

- **Evaluating the Event**: Considering the cost of having a team of highly paid experts in the room for 5 days, the company must have a level of confidence that Design Sprints happen for a good reason and bring considerable value. Hence, the team needs a reliable way to measure their effectiveness. The obvious way to track a Design Sprint's success is to follow the evolution of the solution defined in the workshop. However, further developing the workshop's solution can last long since it typically involves research, experimentation, and a series of product development activities. Moreover, although a case of a successful product that originated from a Design Sprint is a powerful success story, the opposite is not always true: the lack of progress in developing the solution post-Design Sprint does not necessarily reflect the quality of the event as ideas may be put on hold or even fail for several reasons, independently of the quality and potential of the concept. Nevertheless, having multiple Design Sprints without traction for their solutions signals low performance or a form of disconnect.

  Another source of signals is a follow-up assessment survey: as part of the communication process, after the completion of the sprint, participants and contributors receive an email summarizing the outputs, presenting the next steps, and prompting the completion of a short questionnaire. Participants—including stakeholders and the facilitators—are asked to rate the event's value and provide suggestions for improvement. Feedback is automatically processed and presented as an instance of the standardized event performance scorecard used across all innovation events.

5.4 Hackathons

Hackathons are large-scale innovation contests—usually across a division or enterprise—where multiple self-organizing teams compete to solve a business problem or address an opportunity. They come in many variants—for example, some are private within the corporation, while others are public, and they may be hosted online only, in-person, or hybrid. Their duration also varies—companies often organize regular "mini hackathons" that last just 1 day as well as big, yearly ones across an entire week.

Hackathon participants are asked to do the "impossible," that is, to come up with novel solutions and functional prototypes within a short time frame, typically in the range of a few days. People have to self-organize into cross-disciplinary teams able to perform exceptionally well on a variety of product development activities: they have to *conceptualize* their ideas, *describe and prioritize* what they are about to build, make good technology choices, and execute fast in an agile way, toward a functional instance of their concept.

In parallel, they have to create engaging content that presents their concept in a clear way, emphasizing the business opportunity, ideally with insights and quantitative metadata on the size of the problem and the estimated potential. The deliverable is usually a video pitch of the concept, supported by a functional demo. The entire process is fascinating—from shaping the team and exploring initial ideas to prototyping, wrapping up, and presenting to judges.

Hackathon teams are ideally cross-functional, bringing together expertise from various backgrounds, levels, and organizational perspectives, for example, software developers, product managers, designers, data architects, business analysts, etc.

A series of well-organized corporate hackathons can lead to remarkable business opportunities. Moreover, beyond the winning projects, hackathons feed the entire set of ideas produced into the opportunity discovery pipeline—making them discoverable and usable across the company. At the cultural level, hackathons bring significant value as they promote collaboration, sharing, and a multidisciplinary approach to problem-solving.

Organizing a successful corporate hackathon can be challenging though: selecting the proper format, setting the objective, and orchestrating the process are not always straightforward. The following provides a detailed guide on setting up a great hackathon, not in isolation but in the context of a wider innovation program.

5.4.1 Hackathon Objectives

Establishing precise business objectives for your hackathon helps drive meaningful outcomes and creates the foundation for measuring success. Business objectives may vary significantly. For example, a hackathon may target the discovery of specific *solutions* or *business opportunities*—e.g., a technical solution or a product concept addressing a real, pressing business problem. In another case, the primary objective of a hackathon may be to *improve team dynamics* and *boost the innovation culture*. In other cases, public hackathons may serve outward goals, such as *attracting talent* through publicity. The objective directly impacts the event's *style*, *target audience*, *cost*, and *success metrics*; hence, ensuring alignment with sponsors and corporate leaders is essential. Hackathon objectives typically fall into the following three categories:

1. **Opportunities**: The primary purpose of a genuine hackathon is to produce high-potential, actionable opportunities. A hackathon may address a specific problem space, e.g., in the context of a particular product, or enrich the company's opportunity portfolio with unconstrained ideas—thus introducing the "element of surprise" and empowering the explorations for the "next big thing." Hackathon outputs may evolve into tangible business opportunities in the form of new products, features, R&D initiatives, or intellectual property.
2. **Cultural impact and learning**: While generating opportunities is the primary goal, hackathons can also target cultural improvements—to reshape team dynamics and elevate the innovation energy in the organization. They may also have educational and networking objectives: participants discover emerging technologies, establish cross-functional relationships, and demonstrate skills and talents beyond their formal roles. Hackathons provide opportunities for hands-on learning, expanding people's perspectives, and organic networking—all while addressing business problems that matter to the company.
3. **Public perception**: Hackathons tend to attract attention: energized teams, "cool" technologies, walls full of colorful sticky notes, and sophisticated diagrams on writeable walls—a picture indicating that something major is happening. Inspired by that, companies often use hackathons to create publicity, both internal and external. However, although the "publicity" dimension could also be part of the business objective, it should rarely be the primary one: successful hackathons should be seen as part of an innovation program, not as stand-alone events that are marked as "done" upon the announcement of the winners. When hackathons aim for the "press," people eventually get the signals and recognize them as elements of the so-called innovation theater. Of course, there are valid occasions for meaningful marketing and communication activity on top of a successful hackathon, for example, when it solves a significant problem of societal interest in alignment with the company's social responsibility goals.

Setting the right goals for your hackathon is essential for its success. Clear goals and objectives provide clarity to participants and help the organizing team structure and host a successful, impactful hackathon.

5.4.2 Hackathon Structure

A successful corporate hackathon requires effective orchestration of an array of workstreams and threads, with *communication* being the most important: the success of a hackathon depends on clearly presenting the problem to be solved along

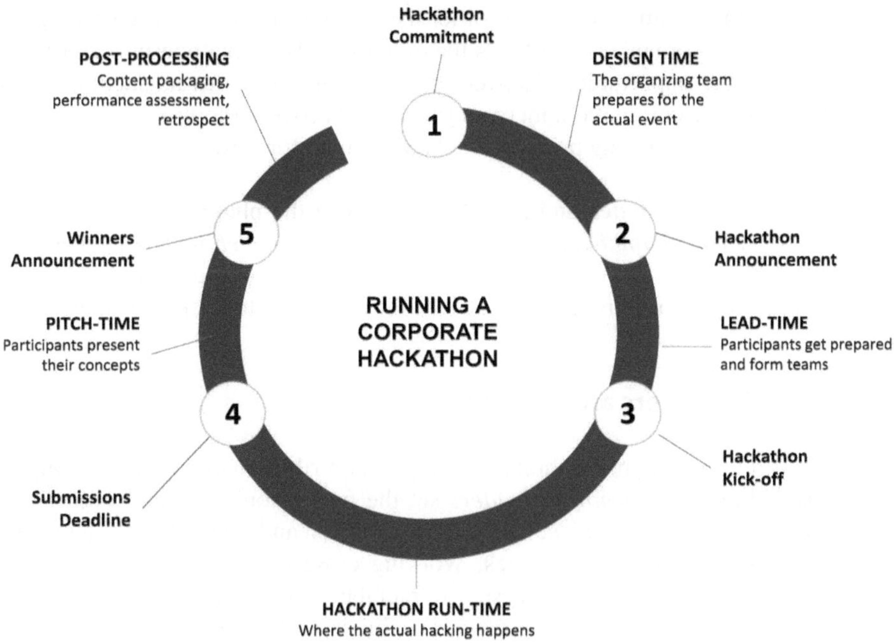

Fig. 5.1 The phases of a corporate hackathon

with the rules and requirements. This falls under the responsibilities of the organizing team, which is responsible for planning and running the entire event.

The organizing team starts by consulting the stakeholders and all interested parties to capture essential requirements, goals, and objectives for the hackathon, which then translates into the proper hackathon format. The lifecycle of the hackathon project can be organized into the following five stages (Fig. 5.1).

Following the initial commitment to host a hackathon, the project unfolds into five stages as described in the following:

1. **The design time** is the phase between the decision to host a hackathon and its announcement. It involves work streams such as the definition of the event, basic planning, and confirmation of the readiness to host it.
2. **The lead time** is the period from the hackathon announcement to the kick-off of the actual event. During this phase, organizers run campaigns to raise awareness, and participants get prepared by exploring early ideas and forming teams.
3. **The runtime** is the effective time of the contest, where teams work together, develop their ideas, and prepare the required minimum deliverables.
4. **The evaluation/pitch time** is the phase between the project submission deadline and the selection of the winners. Depending on the project assessment method, there could be a formal evaluation and/or project pitching to the judges. The winner announcement happens at the end of this phase.

5. **The post-processing time** begins after the announcement of the winning projects. The team organizes and feeds the outputs of the hackathon into other systems, e.g., the opportunity discovery pipeline, and measures its success. After the hackathon's completion, there may be retrospectives or look-back sessions to evaluate progress on any projects that had been put forward.

There are various activities and milestones between the phases presented above, such as the hackathon *announcement*, the *kick-off*, the *completion*, and the *celebration* of the winners. Also, within each stage, there are supportive activities, such as technical assistance or introductory sessions for those new to hackathons, etc.

5.4.3 Stakeholders and Organizers

A successful corporate hackathon relies on the contribution of a diverse group of senior stakeholders. *Corporate leaders* set the hackathon's context, objectives, and overall character—they select themes, topics, and reward strategies that align with the company's priorities. Working closely with the leadership, the *organizing committee*—typically senior members supported by volunteers—designs and executes the event from start to finish while managing expectations, communicating, and orchestrating the overall experience. At the heart of the hackathon are the *innovators* themselves—the eligible employees who participate by forming or joining teams. Finally, the *judges* are senior leaders and domain experts who apply their knowledge to assess projects and provide constructive feedback to teams; *mentors* offer just-in-time advice throughout the event, helping teams navigate obstacles and refine their approaches as they work toward innovative solutions.

Depending on the organization's readiness and the hackathon's scale, the organizing team may need additional roles. For instance, the core team may need *event planners* to organize and manage the activities and all the details of the hackathon or *content creators* to develop the event's branding and create informative, engaging stories before and after the kick-off. Similarly, they may need *facilitators* to orchestrate interactive sessions with live audiences. Additionally, a network of teams and specialists may support the hackathon by offering just-in-time assistance, including *advisors*, *technology experts*, and volunteers from the innovation community.

5.4.4 Design Time: Shaping the *Right* Hackathon

From the viewpoint of the participant or an observer, hackathons are fancy, informal contests. Behind the scenes though, a large-scale hackathon can be a complicated and demanding event. From a leadership standpoint, hackathons are expensive, serious business events that must be planned accordingly. Hence, defining the hackathon with clarity is essential for setting the right expectations. This happens during the "design time," where the organizing committee works with corporate leaders and sponsors to define the hackathon's *purpose* and *character*—they make important decisions regarding the format, eligibility criteria for participants, the project evaluation model, and the minimum required deliverables. In parallel, the committee ensures that all the essential technologies and tools, such as ideation and prototyping systems, are available.

Figure 5.2 presents the key components—the "design parameters" that must be set to define the right hackathon to serve the company's needs. Beyond the practical aspects—time and place—decisions on the *theme*, the *reward model*, *deliverables*, and the *project evaluation* method must be carefully considered and set during this phase. More specifically:

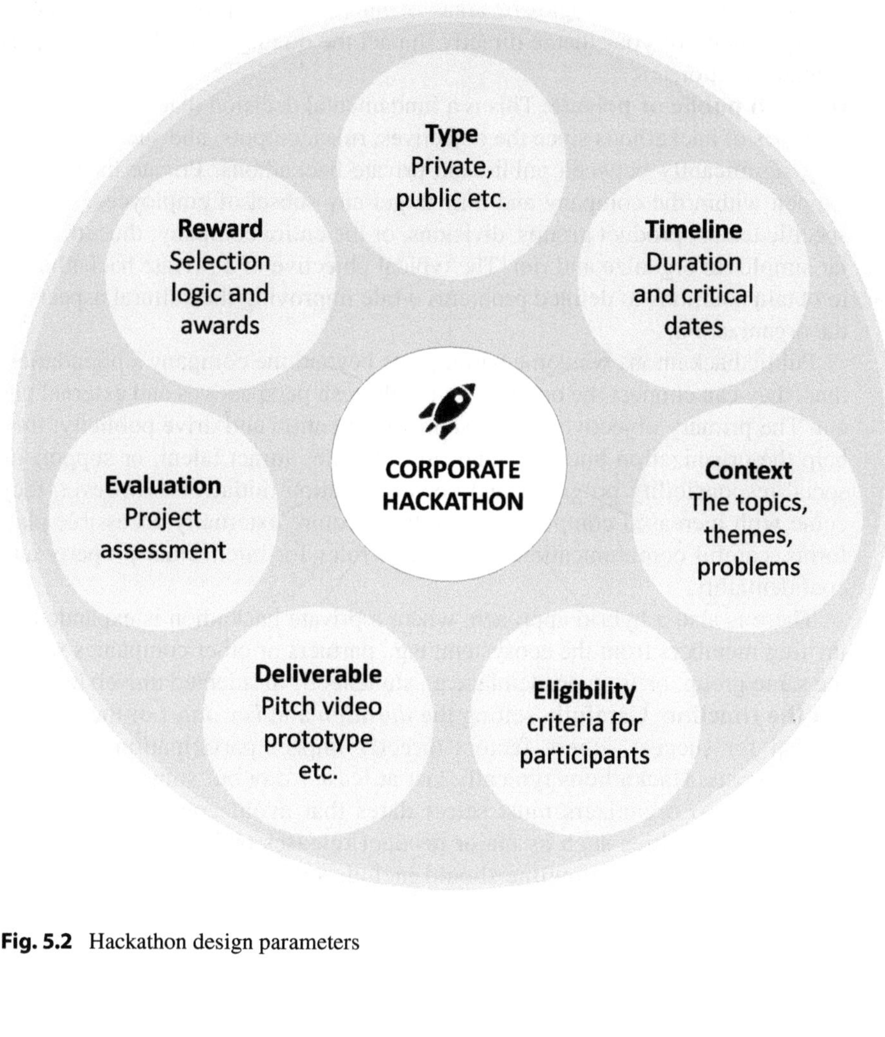

Fig. 5.2 Hackathon design parameters

1. **Name and brand the hackathon**: Effective branding is a key success factor for a corporate hackathon. You will need a smart, memorable *hackathon name* that reflects the event's essence and ambition to attract attention and inspire people. A non-technical executive summary of the objectives—clearly stating the central theme and focus areas—can also raise interest. Effective branding is essential not only for the hackathon's success but also to reinforce the company's innovation culture. A memorable logo, inspiring motto, and consistent digital content add a unique character to your entire hackathon series. Moreover, small things like branded t-shirts, stickers, and stationery can help build excitement, increase the event's visibility, and boost its identity.
2. **Set the context**: The hackathon theme is a critical element that requires careful definition and clear communication: it establishes the *problem space* where participants will innovate. The theme should be shaped in collaboration with the leadership and the event's sponsors. Beyond the core problem, you may also specify relevant technologies or areas of interest for exploration. The clarity and specificity of your theme directly impact the quality and relevance of participant solutions.
3. **Decide if public or private**: This is a fundamental decision that leads to different types of hackathons since the objectives, rules, outputs, and success criteria vary significantly between public and private hackathons. Private hackathons happen within the company and may target any subset of employees, such as specific teams, product groups, divisions, or the entire company; thus, they are far simpler to organize and run. The typical objective of a private hackathon is to obtain solutions to defined problems while improving the cultural aspects of the organization.

   Public hackathons welcome participants beyond the company's boundaries; thus, they can connect the organization with fresh perspectives and external talent. The primary objective is to raise media attention and drive publicity: they help the organization boost its innovation profile, attract talent, or support its social responsibility programs and open innovation initiatives. However, they come with increased complexity since they require externally accessible platforms, careful communication, and special rules for intellectual property and confidentiality.

   There is also a hybrid approach, where a private hackathon is expanded by inviting members from the ecosystem, e.g., partners or other companies within the same group, or from academia, e.g., students from selected universities.
4. **Set the timeline**: Carefully setting the *duration* and *key dates* of the event is critical for success—these factors directly impact participation rates and overall costs. Hackathons typically last at least 1 day but sometimes extend to a week, so organizers must select dates that avoid conflicts with other significant activities such as major product releases or large-scale client or corporate events. The timeline should include sufficient *lead time* for effective preparation and communication to enable participants to discuss ideas, explore technologies, and form teams. For most organizations, depending on the size of the target audience, a lead time of at least a couple of weeks is necessary.

5. **Set the eligibility**: Establishing clear eligibility rules—defining who can participate and how—is also essential. For example, a private hackathon might target full-time employees in a specific team, group, or division. Or it may welcome participation across the organization, including contractors and partners. In this broader scenario, non-full-time employees typically require a different registration process or additional agreements that address intellectual property concerns upfront. Regardless of the approach, these requirements must be explicitly stated and effectively communicated through the Innovation Portal and hackathon updates to avoid confusion and ensure proper governance.
6. **Set the place**: The hackathon's physical and virtual environment influences the participant experience and collaboration. For in-person events, you need open layouts that encourage interaction and also enough separate meeting rooms so teams can focus. The physical space must be equipped with essential tools like whiteboards, digital screens, projectors, and free-form collaboration areas.
7. **Set the minimum required deliverable**: The minimum required deliverable is the *artifact* that defines a valid submission—e.g., what a team must submit to join the project evaluation process. The required deliverable may range from a *concept pitch video* to a *functional demo* or working software—a fully operational prototype along with its source code. Optional elements might include product architecture documents, wireframes, or even physical prototypes. This decision is critical since it determines how inclusive your hackathon will be across organizational disciplines. For instance, a requirement for functional code naturally orients the event toward engineering teams, potentially discouraging participation from non-technical innovators, thus leading to missed opportunities since non-technical innovators can bring valuable ideas. As discussed in the following sections, introducing AI for prototyping can simplify this decision.
8. **Define success**: The success of a hackathon depends on the business lens used to examine its outputs. Sometimes, leaders and organizers appreciate the noise, the vibe, and the energy but do not pay much attention to the actual value of the projects. Others may overemphasize the projects without recognizing the cultural effects. To avoid subjective takes, success must be described upfront, in accordance with the business objective of the hackathon, and always following a data-driven approach: the desired outcome of a hackathon must be defined as numeric targets attached to specific metrics such as *participation rates* across departments, *project quality scores*, percentage of *opportunities identified*, team *diversity metrics*, etc. Such a measurement framework creates accountability and enables meaningful comparison across events, transforming subjective impressions into insights about the hackathon's performance.
9. **Define the reward package**: This defines what the winners will get as recognition of their achievement and possibly support for further exploration or development. This is further explained in the section "Selecting the Reward Scheme."
10. **Define the project evaluation process**: The hackathon is a contest, and thus, it requires a solid mechanism for identifying the winners. The project evaluation method defines *how* submissions are assessed, *who* is eligible to vote, the *project qualities* being considered, and their relative importance. This is detailed in the following section.

Selecting the Project Evaluation Method: The evaluation method must be objective, consistent, and transparent. Objectivity requires ideas to be assessed against *predefined criteria*, according to a robust process, by experts who are not influenced by the team or other "political" dimensions of the submission, such as the group the idea is coming from or its sponsors. *Consistency* means that the assessment protocol is used across hackathons with no exceptions or changes in its core logic. This allows a comparison of ideas across events and ensures familiarity with the process. *Transparency* means that participants have access to the underlying logic—they understand the criteria, the weight factors, and the business reasoning for selecting the winners. Finally, the process must be *robust*, meaning that it should be well thought through, tested, and proven, without the need for workarounds or hotfixes: a different group of judges applying the same evaluation process on a given set of projects should produce similar rankings. The following presents four models for assessing and ranking hackathon submissions, starting from an oversimplistic open voting model and gradually moving to more sophisticated ones:

1. **Open voting**: This model welcomes votes from employees across the organization—they browse the hackathon projects, vote, and comment on them. The organizing committee then aggregates the results to identify the winners. Although this is frequently used, it is rarely a good option: it usually reflects the hackathon team's social influence instead of their project's potential. While it is essential to allow feedback and actions of support from colleagues, their contribution to the final project rankings should be suitably adjusted as one of the many signals considered.
2. **Closed voting**: This is a robust evaluation process based on structured assessments by a predefined group of experts. Each expert reviews the hackathon submissions independently and uses the standard idea assessment model presented in Chap. 6 to score the idea and provide feedback. At the end of this process, every idea has an overall score, as an average across reviewers, which is used to rank the submissions and identify the winning ones. In small-scale hackathons, this process may be supported manually with basic tools. In an ideal scenario though, it should be done through the *Innovation Portal*, where experts can browse the submissions and use familiar tools and utilities to assess projects quickly and effectively. Beyond speed, using the *innovation platform* ensures that valuable outputs from the hackathon—ideas and their assessments—are stored and become available through the standard innovation touchpoints.
3. **Live demos and pitching**: This model is based on live presentations—teams are invited to a live event where they pitch their projects to a panel of experts. Judges play a critical role in this process, so they come well prepared, having studied the theme of the hackathon and the shortlisted projects. Each team pitches its proposal, presents a short live demo, and answers questions from the panel. At the end of each presentation, the panel discusses the project's potential, not in search of consensus but rather to ensure clarity and shared understanding. Then, the judges use the idea assessment model to assess the project—they add their justi-

fication and provide constructive feedback. At the end of this process, scores are aggregated; each hackathon project gets an overall performance score, which leads to the final ranking. The main advantage of this model is the live interaction with the panel of experts: it gives teams the chance to better explain their proposals, answer questions from the panel, and obtain quality feedback and advice. On the other hand, judges may be influenced by factors such as the communication and presentation skills of the team—and their performance on stage—which does not always go as planned and is not strongly correlated with the concept's true potential. Also, the fact that the assessment must be done *in the room* and in *such a short time frame* introduces a risk of bias—for instance, specific reactions of influential or important people in the room could affect the panel and, thus, the outcome. Moreover, this is only feasible for a small number of projects and hence applicable for either small-scale hackathons or the final stage of larger-scale ones.

4. **A hybrid model**: The "closed voting" model has a major advantage: assessment is done independently and in private until the results are announced—thus, the risk of cross-influence is avoided. The disadvantage is that judgment is made only based on the team's presentation or video; therefore, it depends heavily on the quality of the artifacts and the ability of the team to present their concept. On the contrary, "live demos and pitching" have the advantage of live interaction: judges ask tough questions, and teams have the opportunity to explain the strong points of their proposals. But at the same time, depending on the characters in the room, there may be a risk of groupthink or decisions made based on the team's live performance. This hybrid model attempts to combine the best of both—it uses a two-stage process, the first selecting the finalists and the second naming the winners. At the first stage, a large group of experts, including those signed up as judges, goes through a "closed voting" process, where each expert assesses every idea independently and privately, while the results only become available when the process is completed. This quick assessment is used to perform the initial ranking of projects, which is then used to generate the shortlist of projects to be pitched to the panel of judges during the second, final stage. In this model, the judges have already analyzed and scored the projects being pitched and the ones filtered out. Thus, they have the big picture and are more prepared to ask the right questions.

To select the most appropriate model, the organizing team considers the scale of the hackathon, the technical readiness, and the availability of the resources, experts, and judges. In all cases, the selected evaluation method must be well presented and explained as part of the definition of the hackathon.

Selecting the Reward Scheme: The rewards scheme defines how many winners will be announced and what they will get in return. Rewarding the winners may not be straightforward: Should the hackathon have one winning team or more? Should there be category winners? Or special winners such as "best prototype" or most "creative idea"? What should the actual award be?

One could argue that in a truly innovative organization, people do not need special incentives to join innovation activities such as hackathons. When the right culture is there, people naturally participate as a way to support the bigger purpose of the team, the group, and the company. Moreover, personal ambition and longer-term career goals are powerful forces that drive contribution to innovation, possibly stronger than monetary awards or resource provisioning. However, a properly designed reward scheme can indeed drive significant impact: it offers a token of appreciation to the winners while sending a strong message and symbolism about the importance of innovation for the company.

The actual reward could be symbolic, monetary, recognition, a career boost, or a combination of those. In general, I would recommend emphasizing the nonmonetary rewards and focusing on linking the achievements of hackathon winners with their career ambitions, innovation outcomes, and the company's success. This strategy can be supported by combining the following classes of rewards:

1. **Badges and trophies**: Winners receive prizes and special objects, such as cubes with the winner's name and the occasion—as symbols of recognition and acknowledgment of exceptional performance and achievements.
2. **Development resources**: A package of resources supporting further exploration or early implementation of the idea, which is, perhaps, the most meaningful and valuable reward for top innovators. Under the assumption of a truly innovative culture, hackathon participants are passionate about their ideas and eager to find the resources, e.g., time, talent, equipment, funding, and tools, to iterate further and take it to the next stage. Thus, for a genuine hackathon team, securing the resources required to build the project should be the greatest and most inspiring reward of all: the winning team gets the needed skills along with devices, tools, and services to build a functional prototype of the idea and compile a business proposition—which when done is presented to senior stakeholders for further consideration. Even if the decision following the implementation is to "kill" the project, this is a perfect example of innovation, experimentation, and fail-fast culture, proof that the leadership believes in innovation and accepts failure as part of the process.
3. **The stage**: As part of a reward and recognition package, hackathon winners get a presentation slot to pitch their project in a highly visible corporate event or to present a functional version of their idea directly to senior corporate leaders.
4. **Organization-wide acknowledgment**: Winning a hackathon should be seen as a remarkable achievement worth communicating across the organization in formal and informal ways. Therefore, following the completion of the hackathon, winners are announced and celebrated through formal activities; they are featured in the Innovation Portal and the newsletter and referenced in daily interactions—e.g., via email signatures and regular communication. When hackathon work moves on to the subsequent phases, e.g., when the idea is implemented as a real feature or product, hackathon teams get credits through formal attribution. For instance, a product success story may be communicated as "originated from hackathon project x."

5. **Special corporate titles**: Specific innovation titles, such as "Distinguished Innovator" or "Inventor of the Year," help innovators build a reputation and celebrate their hackathon achievements while inspiring others to join the innovation efforts.
6. **Technology**: The winners receive a technology package as a reward, e.g., devices or related products relevant to the hackathon's theme.
7. **Cash awards**: The promise of cash rewards can drive higher participation rates, and as a result, it is a common type of reward, especially in public, open hackathons where the volume of participants is a key success factor. However, if used in an internal hackathon, monetary rewards should be appropriately framed and communicated to motivate innovators without appearing transactional. Cash should be combined with other rewards that have a long-lasting cultural effect.

A well-designed reward scheme provides an excellent opportunity to celebrate top-performing innovators and reinforce key innovation messages. It impacts not only the particular event but also future participation rates, the culture of innovation, and the performance of the broader innovation program.

Making Hackathons Inclusive: Traditionally, it is software engineering teams who organize hackathons. As a result, even if hackathon rules allow all disciplines in an organization to participate, it is primarily engineers or technologists who join. Consequently, it is common for people to perceive hackathons as engineering contests—a perception that acts as a barrier to entry for non-coding employees due to the belief that a strong technical background is a must. Non-technical innovators may feel discouraged from joining or appear less confident that they can bring value to hackathon teams. This misconception makes the event less inclusive and must be handled at design time. The core rules of the hackathon, along with its branding and communication package, must emphasize the openness of the event and dismiss any preconceptions about technical prerequisites. At the same time, the submission of functional prototypes and code should be optional or handled in a different category. To strengthen this message, the organizing committee can use the following points explaining how non-technical innovators can bring significant value to hackathons.

1. **Non-technical innovators bring unique skills**: They complement "classic" engineering teams by providing additional talent and bringing other perspectives, such as commercial thinking, product sense, marketing, or communication skills. In fact, this is precisely one of the great benefits of hackathons: they bring multiple disciplines together in dynamic, agile teams, working intensively to define, build, and present their concepts. Non-technical members can add significant value to hackathon teams by bringing their business, leadership, product management, or scientific expertise.
2. **Non-technical innovators form and lead teams**: People with great ideas may join a hackathon to access the technical skills and resources they need to realize their concepts. For example, a business or marketing employee with an idea about a new product joins the hackathon, forms a team of designers and develop-

ers, and leads the entire process toward a fully functional prototype built by talented teammates. In another case, non-technical employees may join an existing team and lead it to a successful outcome. In this sense, hackathons provide an excellent opportunity for non-technical people to shine.
3. **Non-technical innovators work at the conceptual level**: When the hackathon does not require actual coding, people can provide value by shaping and framing their concepts at a higher level and from other angles. For instance, business users can work together to frame their great idea; define it as a product; emphasize aspects such as monetization, differentiators, or go-to-market strategy; and pitch it through a video or a deck.
4. **AI helps non-technical innovators build technical artifacts**: With the rise of AI, participants can use powerful tools that can convert their product vision into a functional prototype in minutes and by using exclusively natural language. In this sense, the ability to code, at least in the hackathon context, is becoming less important. Hackathon's most critical skillset will soon be about obtaining the bigger picture, sensing products, understanding macro trends, and shaping innovative business models and go-to-market strategies. In this context, functional prototyping will stand more as a way to communicate complex projects and less as a demonstration of execution ability.

The above points can be used to define a strong message that addresses the engineering-only misconception of hackathons. The hackathon organizing team should communicate, share stories, and lead by example to signal the right messages and drive participation across disciplines. Of course, hackathons must also be inclusive in reference to other dimensions, such as gender, roles, and level in the company: innovation is powered by *thought diversity*.

Beyond communication, making hackathons inclusive requires proper measurement. Diversity should be modeled in the metrics and KPIs of the hackathon in order to understand the current state, help design and execute the right communication strategies, and measure their impact.

5.4.5 The Lead Time: Getting Ready for "Hacking"

The period toward the hackathon kick-off is essential for all involved parties. Innovators get familiar with the hackathon's context and engage with lightweight activities such as high-level research, ideation, networking, and team formation. At the same time, the organizing committee ensures that all systems, content, space, and equipment are provided and arranged as planned. In the following, we present the essential steps the organizing team needs to take following the decision to host a large-scale internal hackathon.

1. **Announce the hackathon**: An effective way to start the hackathon preparations is through a formal announcement coming directly from the leadership, ideally in an all-hands or similar, highly visible event. The announcement should come

through as a "call to innovate," inviting people to switch contexts from daily activities to a mode of exploring novel solutions addressing a well-presented problem. It should be backed by a strong narrative linking the hackathon with the broader innovation efforts and the organization's purpose. Early communication of the plan is critical, not only for the participants to prepare but also for managers: they need to have sufficient time to adjust their plans and ensure people from their teams will be available to join. This planning adjustment is essential, especially for multi-day hackathons, which would otherwise introduce a risk of disrupting active projects and commitments.

2. **Provide the necessary resources**: As part of the communication effort, the organizing team releases important information and resources, including planning, context, FAQs, and relevant content such as examples, guidelines, templates, and key contacts. This package of content is also offered via a dedicated page in the Innovation Portal, that also allows participants to register their interests, browse ideas, form or join a team, familiarize themselves with tools and technologies, and connect with the broader innovation community. The event's page in the portal also presents equipment, tools, or devices that are available in the Makerspace, as individual teams might need special resources.
3. **Educate the innovators**: Not everybody is familiar with the notion of the hackathon, and typically, there are plenty of questions. In many cases, people may not understand the terminology and format or be unclear about how they could bring value. Such gaps and limited awareness may prevent people from joining, thus making the event less inclusive. To deal with this risk, the team runs parallel educational activities—e.g., a series of mini-workshops and informal presentations explaining the hackathon's purpose and methods. This can clarify misconceptions, emphasize the multidisciplinary nature of teams, and make the event more productive by allowing participants to join prepared. Consider hosting at least 2–3 open sessions where people can ask questions and get practical advice.
4. **Facilitate team formation**: These informal events bring together people with ideas *looking for talent*, with talent *looking for ideas* to explore team formation scenarios. In parallel, the network of mentors can be activated at this point to allow people to reach the experts for assistance and advice through the Innovation Portal.
5. **Prepare the communications plan**: The runtime of the hackathon—when the actual event is happening—affects the entire organization. Hence, people must be fully aware of the critical dates so they can plan accordingly, either to join, support it, or get ready to handle the disruption. To achieve this level of awareness, the organizing committee prepares and triggers a mechanism of timely updates, reminders, and links to essential resources. Communication happens via the Innovation Portal, emails, connected screens in the office space, newsletters, and quick updates through regular meetings. To drive engagement and anticipation and ensure smooth execution, you should configure the following essential updates covering all phases—before, during, and after the hackathon (Table 5.1).

Table 5.1 The hackathon communication plan

Action	Objectives	Frequency and audience
Hackathon announcement	Raise awareness about the forthcoming hackathon. Share the theme, timelines, and basic rules	Once; company-wide
Join a team	Remind registered users who haven't joined a team to explore the teams looking for talent	3–5 times toward the kick-off date. Targeting registered members without a team
Find talent	Remind users with registered projects who haven't formed a complete team to explore talent looking for projects	3–5 times toward the kick-off date. Targeting registered projects with talent gaps
Hackathon countdown	Update participants with practical information and reminders for signing up	Daily, the last week before the event, company-wide
Raise awareness	Emphasize reasons to join and how the hackathon is inclusive	3–5 times toward the kick-off date; non-registered, eligible
Hints and guidance	Provide practical advice, hints, and content that help participants perform better during the event	Daily, starting x days before the event; registered users
Kick-off announcement	Share highlights from the opening speech	Once; company-wide
Runtime updates	Share highlights from the venues and projects	Once or twice per day during the event; company-wide
Completion	Share highlights from the closing speech, including statistics on participation and project completion	Once; company-wide
Pitch plan announcement	Communicate the plan for assessing the shortlisted projects	Once. Targeting shortlisted teams, judges, and leadership
Winner announced	Celebrate the winning projects and teams	Once. Company-wide
Feedback invite	Capture feedback from participants and stakeholders as signals regarding the success and impact of the hackathon	Once. Company-wide
Retrospective	To reflect on the event, analyze feedback, and identify opportunities for improvement	Once. Targeting hackathon participants and stakeholders

5.4.6 The Runtime: "Hacking" in Progress

The runtime is where the "magic" happens. Following the kick-off, the teams start working on their ideas by framing, visualizing, and implementing their concepts. The organizing team remains available to handle any requests and help the teams achieve their goals. In a typical case, this is how the runtime of the hackathon unfolds:

1. **Registration**: Participants gather at the specified venue, where they register and receive their hackathon badges along with their hackathon-branded material—usually a package of t-shirts, stickers, and other elements reflecting the "hacker culture."

2. **Kick-off**: The organizing committee provides an intro and then invites one or more senior stakeholders to give a short opening speech emphasizing the importance of innovation and explaining the hackathon's focus. The organizing team then briefly replays the rules—the key dates, deliverables, and access to resources; they provide guidance on using the physical space and clarify the options for utilizing specialized equipment, facilities, or devices.
3. **Start**: Following the formal kick-off, teams get together, find a place, and initiate the creative process. Project spaces have signage with the team name, while information points allow quick access to hackathon resources and support services.

Throughout the hackathon's runtime, the organizing team handles all the technical issues and requests—they help teams find people with special skills and point to technical members to help troubleshoot problems. At the same time, video professionals capture random moments, perform quick interviews with teams, and cover important parts of the event. In parallel, advisors and mentors help innovators to focus and speed up their development. Leaders are also present—they demonstrate their strong support and interest in action by sharing their thoughts and providing direction and advice.

As the event moves on, efforts start shifting from development to presentation—teams begin to wrap up to compile their pitches, demos, and other artifacts. When a video is included as a required deliverable, teams use a standard "project pitch script" that helps them prepare their "story"—in a Q&A format—and then compile it as a short, standardized, branded video. Having a consistent script accelerates both the creation of the video, and its consumption—through a list of unified "video project pitches" that all share identical structure, answering the same questions in the same order. The structured, scripted nature of the pitch video allows faster assessment and shortlisting of projects, which may then be scheduled for more in-depth analysis. Following the compilation of their pitch videos, teams prepare their formal deliverable, which may include additional artifacts, such as presentations, wireframes, or source code. With the submission of the deliverable, which should ideally happen via the Innovation Portal, teams enter the waiting mode toward the project evaluation process.

5.4.7 The Pitch Time: Selecting the Winners

As soon as the runtime of the hackathon is over, another intense phase begins: the project evaluation toward the final rankings and selection of the winners. This process is orchestrated by the organizing committee, and depending on the selected evaluation method, it may last from a couple of days to several weeks.

In the case of "open voting," the process is fast since it can be done online through the Innovation Portal. Votes and comments are organized and automatically aggregated into project-level scores. When the "closed voting" system is utilized, the process takes longer as it depends on the availability of the participating experts and advisors. Assuming the right tools are there, for example, the Innovation Portal implementing the "closed voting" process, project assessment can be completed within a few days. If the "live demos and pitching" model is selected, it simply follows as an additional, final stage.

At the end of the process, every idea is enriched with scores and feedback from the general audience, the experts, or the judges. The committee then cross-validates the results, produces the final project ranking, applies the reward scheme, and prepares the formal announcement of the winners. The announcement can be done via a formal email from a senior leader. Even better, it should be delivered through an all-hands, where the winning teams are invited to share their hackathon journey and present their ideas along with their ambition and plans to take them to the next level. This way, the leadership celebrates the hackathon winners openly while explaining the outcome of the hackathon and how it is aligned with the strategy of the company.

Following the announcement, the Innovation Portal presents the winning projects along with stories from all the teams, event highlights, and standardized content such as pitch decks and videos. Teams can browse score aggregates, along with private, summarized input and advice from mentors and judges. The organizing committee diffuses the results via the newsletter, information kiosks, connected screens in the office space, and intranet portals. The entire organization celebrates the winners and the spirit of innovation.

5.4.8 Post-hackathon: Communicating and Measuring Success

Hackathons produce rich content, such as ideas, prototypes, video presentations, and demos, that is valuable beyond the specific event. The organizing team orchestrates the packaging of this content and makes it available through the proper channels. For instance, ideas and project summaries or pitch decks are hosted in the Innovation Portal, along with demos, prototypes, and links to their code repositories. Videos presenting ideas, interviews, or "best moments" of the hackathon become part of the formal communication of the event, shared across channels throughout the organization. At the same time, the team may also invite participants to share their stories through blog posts or informal demos and presentations. Furthermore, depending on the hackathon's scale and success, it may be useful to run a "hackathon project expo," where *all teams* can explain and demonstrate their projects.

In parallel to packaging, the organizing team runs a survey to capture the hackathon's success as perceived by participants and stakeholders. They analyze the results and host a retrospective with a limited audience to discuss and interpret the results. Moreover, they use the predefined success criteria and the actual metrics to compile a narrative of the event's success. The following presents metrics that can be used to quantify the hackathon's performance.

1. **Engagement level**: A set of data points that reflect how people responded to the "call to innovate" and how they engaged with the hackathon. This class includes

metrics such as the *Participation Rate*, defined as the percentage of registered participants over the size of the eligible audience, or the *Active Participants*, defined as the percentage of teams who submitted a valid project over those who registered. While participation may be sensitive to other factors, such as timing, it usually reflects the effectiveness of the communication and promotion of the hackathon and people's general interest in its theme.

2. **Valid submissions**: This is simply the percentage of valid submissions over the total number of joined teams. Submission validity is determined through the formal project evaluation. Low values in this percentage may indicate that some teams abandoned their efforts or did not manage to submit a valid deliverable. Or some teams may have merged their projects.
3. **Opportunities**: The performance of the hackathon in terms of "opportunity creation" can be reflected by the percentage of *opportunities over the total number of valid project submissions*, where opportunities are flagged through the formal assessment process. Such metrics reflect the level of productivity and creativity of the hackathon. Low values may indicate insufficient preparation, motivation, or limited clarity around the problem statement.
4. **Actionable opportunities**: The opportunities are eventually reviewed by business experts outside the hackathon's context. For example, product teams, engineering managers, marketing managers, or patent attorneys may be asked to review the identified opportunities to spot the actionable ones: projects may be flagged as candidate features of existing products or as promising product concepts that are worth experimenting further or valid cases for patent applications. The percentage of *actionable innovation opportunities over the total number of valid project submissions* provides a good indicator of the overall performance of the hackathon.
5. **Validated opportunities**: After sufficient time, some of the actionable opportunities may be realized in early forms and exposed to a limited audience. For example, an opportunity is prototyped and presented to a defined audience for early feedback. The percentage of *opportunities realized for validation over the number of actionable opportunities* is another strong signal for success.
6. **Commercialized opportunities**: A commercialized opportunity is an in-market implementation of a concept offered in general availability—beyond small-scale experiments and beta modes. The conversion ratio to commercialized innovation opportunities reflects the connection of the hackathon with the real market.
7. **Publicity**: When hackathon artifacts reach the public domain, it is useful to quantify their impact, either directly, e.g., via engagement metrics of digital content, or indirectly via innovation perception surveys or other means of quantifying "media attention."
8. **Cultural and team impact**: The cultural impact can be estimated through the feedback from participants and stakeholders obtained just after the event via the hackathon assessment survey. This is particularly insightful since it provides both qualitative and quantitative insights, such as the *overall satisfaction* or the *perceived success score* of the hackathon. The survey may also evaluate specific aspects of the event, such as communication, access to resources, the theme, the

organization, and the support of the upper management. Such surveys provide additional context to the metrics described above and help interpret data and specific conversion rates. Another source of signals regarding the cultural impact of the hackathon is the systematic innovation pulse surveys, where the team may spot changes or certain dynamics that might be explained as the result of the hackathon.

9. **Team dynamics**: While this does not describe performance, it is an excellent source of insights regarding the openness of the hackathon and its collaboration patterns. By analyzing the profiles of the participants and the synthesis of the teams, it is feasible to draw a picture of how diverse and multidisciplinary teams were and, thus, help future hackathons adapt and improve. For instance, the distribution of teams by size, the degree of similarity of the roles within the team, and the range of skills of the participants may lead to important findings that are valuable for further improving the definition, communication, and execution of corporate hackathons.

The above metrics can be used to define specific KPIs and conversion rates, leading to a standardized measurement scorecard for hackathon events. When this is there, the team can build baselines and monitor the evolution of these KPIs and how they correlate with the overall innovation culture. However, some of these metrics can only be obtained months after the hackathon's completion since they refer to realizations of ideas that need time, e.g., validated or commercialized opportunities. Nevertheless, whenever this happens, it is essential to link back to the source hackathon and reflect it on its performance scorecard.

The funnel described above is a special case of the opportunity creation funnel presented in Chap. 9, and it can be fully implemented as part of the innovation measurement capability.

5.4.9 The Connected, AI-Powered Hackathon

Hosting frequent or large-scale hackathons requires a streamlined process and technology that accelerates the preparation and execution of the event and enables its smooth integration with the opportunity discovery pipeline. Artificial intelligence can dramatically improve hackathons from various levels and perspectives.

From an organizer's perspective, the AI-powered Workshop Designer, as described in Chap. 4, streamlines the setup of hackathons by creating high-quality content and material along with the entire communication plan: it uses the initial event brief and the broader context of the company to create branded content that best presents the hackathon and its objectives. As part of the hackathon promo material, the Workshop Designer creates a dedicated hackathon page in the Innovation Portal containing all the essential information. This allows the organizing team to configure and fine-tune a complete hackathon event in minutes, including branding, rules, and associated additional content. Moreover, people can learn about an upcoming hackathon simply by asking the portal's innovation agent. Through a conversational experience, they can explore existing projects and participating teams and express interest in joining, describe their idea to the agent, create a new team, and instantly discover participants who would be interested in joining.

At the same time, the Workshop Designer helps the organizing team execute an effective communication plan: formal hackathon content is diffused through the Innovation Portal, and users receive timely notifications and updates toward, during, and after the event—all based on the content prepared by AI and using the associated high-quality email templates.

AI also helps the organizing committee understand the performance of the hackathon and explore opportunities for improvement. The connected hackathon provides an active channel for people to submit feedback and reviews throughout and after the event. These are automatically reflected in the "hackathon performance scorecard" that provides the organizing committee with a single view over engagement metrics and the general state of the event across phases. Moreover, AI uses the broader innovation context—including the history of hackathons and the entire Innovation Graph—to analyze the event's performance and participants' feedback and suggest next steps regarding the hackathon's projects, themes for upcoming events, or opportunities for improvement.

Another process that gains significant value from a "connected" hackathon is the assessment of the projects. The committee utilizes the network of idea evaluators to either support the panel of judges or "outsource" the entire project evaluation process. This makes the setup of the hackathon more manageable and the project evaluation process faster. Furthermore, as the project scoring mechanism inherits from the idea assessment model (described in Chap. 6), projects can be compared and ranked across hackathons and against the entire corpus of ideas living in the Innovation Graph.

In this connected mode, hackathons output their content directly to the Innovation Graph, thus contributing to the organization's supply of ideas and opportunities. This way, ideas, projects, and artifacts remain discoverable and potentially usable beyond the hackathon, regardless of their ranking. Hackathons become integrated into the broader innovation program—they evolve as connected innovation experiences that feed opportunities to the corporate innovation knowledge base.

From an innovator's point of view, AI-powered functionality brings dramatic improvements. AI prototyping and no-code development make hackathons truly inclusive since non-technical members and teams can create fully functional applications with zero coding. This is feasible through AI tools that can take a concept described in natural language and instantly generate code that implements it—for example, you can describe a digital experience, say a website, to Anthropic's Claude and obtain a first implementation in seconds; then by providing feedback and clarifications, you can experience Claude extending or correcting its own code to meet your exact requirements. In just a few iterations and maybe in less than an hour, you can have a realistic, presentable, interactive experience that matches exactly your requirements. All of these done without a single line of code from the user and without requiring any technical expertise. Moreover, if the team has basic development experience, this scenario can become even more impressive: the code produced by

AI can be embedded as a component into a bigger, hosted application, thus enabling the team to gradually build a fully functional, quality prototype with proper backend and all the essential functions in-place. AI is opening up development to all while compressing development cycles dramatically. This allows hackathon teams to produce realistic, presentable prototypes in a couple of hours rather than days.

Considering the AI revolution, which significantly lowers technical barriers, I see hackathons taking a different path. The emphasis will shift toward bringing great concepts closer to marketable positions quickly—conceiving, framing, and prototyping the concept but also, most importantly, figuring out market entry strategies, hypothesis validation "hacks," and gathering real-world evidence to justify further investments. Hackathon teams will have to focus their energy and creativity primarily on justifying the opportunity around their concept by developing business models, smart pricing, defining partnerships, and intelligent go-to-market strategies. I see hackathons gradually evolving into in-market concept validation contests, with companies awarding high-potential concepts backed by smart market-testing strategies and real-word-evidence of business potential.

5.5 Orchestration Events

This family of innovation events is process-focused, aiming to coordinate the innovation function itself and maintain it in a good shape. The following defines the most characteristic cases:

1. **Idea evaluation sessions**: In modern innovation environments, and especially when AI contributes to ideation, there can be a surplus of ideas and, as a result, noise. To deal with this, companies need a regular, effective idea evaluation process that is configured to spot opportunities. In a simple scenario, the evaluation is done through recurring meetings—*evaluation sessions*—led by a panel of formal evaluators and, potentially, sponsors. The objective of such sessions is to carefully examine and evaluate unprocessed ideas: for each one, the panel applies the idea assessment model and attaches the proposed prioritization, along with justification, feedback, and suggestions to the originators. Moreover, the team attempts to spot high-potential innovation opportunities and, if any, flags them. The frequency of these events depends on the volume of new idea submissions and the availability of the formal evaluators. Ideally, this process should run at least once a month to keep the pace at a reasonable level.
2. **Opportunity portfolio review**: This is a recurring session reviewing the state of the opportunity portfolio and the associated innovation projects, e.g., prototyping, technical assessments, actual implementation, or in-market experiments. The team, consisting of senior stakeholders, sponsors, and members of the leadership, iterate over the contained innovation projects or initiatives, examine their progress, remove blockers, and make tough choices to ensure a "healthy" portfolio; this is the session where *pivot*, *hold*, or *kill* decisions can be made.

3. **Innovation steering**: These meetings are led by the chief innovation officer or other innovation leaders and focus on reviewing metrics and the overall performance of the innovation function. The objective is to spot opportunities for improvement or identify needs to intervene and take corrective actions. In many cases, such meetings lead to decisions about changing the *innovation cadence*, setting new goals or targets, and introducing modifications to the innovation agenda. Any outcomes impacting the nature of the innovation program should be documented and formally communicated through events such as the innovation all-hands. These are typically quarterly meetings.

5.6 Information and Knowledge-Sharing Events

Effective communication is essential for innovation—it inspires and empowers people to engage with the innovation function. This class of events aims to improve information flows and boost knowledge exchange across teams, thus improving the organization's culture and overall innovation function. Innovators participate actively in these events, both to *share* and *acquire* knowledge—such as best practices and learnings on a broad range of topics related to the innovation process. Information and knowledge-sharing events come in various formats, like the ones described below.

1. **Innovation all-hands**: These events allow the entire company to connect with the leadership on the impact of innovation and its alignment with the organizational purpose, vision, strategy, and innovation agenda. Innovation all-hands are led by the chief innovation officer or other members of the leadership team. The style of the event is informal and interactive, encouraging content sharing, short presentations, and Q&A. In a typical instance, the CINO presents innovation performance metrics, achievements, upcoming process improvements, and updates on the subsequent waves of innovation. The CINO explains any recent modifications made to the focus, themes, topics, or priorities and presents the most important problems and opportunities from the innovation agenda. Innovators have a strong presence in these events—they typically get enough time to present their achievements, highlights, success stories, and key learnings from unsuccessful cases. Innovation all-hands happens once or twice per year or on an ad hoc basis, for example, following a reorganization of the company or the release of a new innovation capability, an acquisition, a market update such as a significant competitor move, etc.
2. **Innovation intelligence updates**: These are quick, informal events where the innovation intelligence team presents interesting "market stories," such as competition moves, competing products, start-ups, industry news, technological trends, business insights, and non-obvious patterns and dynamics in the broader economic landscape. Beyond summarizing the market, the team uses the company's lens to interpret the signals and share their unique perspectives on how the innovation engine should react. Moreover, as the innovation intelligence

team also looks inside the organization, the agenda includes internal innovation stories and activities, upcoming innovation projects and plans, and a summary of how local innovation agendas across divisions overlap and could benefit from enterprise-wide collaboration.

3. **Demo days and expos**: Innovation expos aim to showcase tangible innovation by presenting materialized ideas such as prototypes, PoCs, or demos; they allow internal or external stakeholders to interact with live demos or functional prototypes and also meet the innovators—thus acknowledging achievements and inspiring additional innovation threads. These events are generally open to all, but in some cases, the audience may be restricted for practical reasons, for example, to present the innovation artifacts to partners and clients. Additionally, there could be an ongoing innovation expo featuring projects and teams based on a rotation scheme following the company's innovation agenda. And, of course, to deal with the unique challenges of the hybrid working model, this ongoing expo could be implemented as a digital experience and served through the Innovation Portal, the digital home of innovation, as described in Chap. 4.
4. **Innovation retrospectives**: These events enable the innovation team to look back and consider what they could have done differently and how they can learn from inefficiencies to improve the innovation process further. They occasionally invite innovators and use pulse surveys and various data points and signals to drive the discussion toward actionable outputs. The innovation team looks into not only unfavorable cases but also successful innovation initiatives: they encourage innovators to share their thoughts on what they could have done differently to enable wiser decisions faster. In another section of the innovation retrospective, the team analyzes ideas that finally reached the market and compares their real-world performance versus the corresponding initial estimates or early experimentation results.
5. **Technology deep dives**: These are informal events organized by members of the innovation community. Their agenda ranges from in-depth technical topics to development methodologies and design patterns. They may also include quick updates and pointers to new technologies, products, and start-up activities. For example, the agenda could focus on a just-released software development framework, a new class of artificial intelligence algorithms, an innovative cloud computing capability, or anything technology related that is new and potentially useful in the company's context.
6. **Knowledge-sharing sessions**: This is a series of informal events where teams from across the organization present their innovation stories from both successful and unsuccessful projects—with the intent to share, discuss, and learn. Each session features various teams, each delivering short presentations that outline their learnings and results from business experiments and innovation projects, followed by Q&A. As part of the broader knowledge management system, the presentations are captured in the Innovation Graph—the organization's innovation knowledge repository. This way, teams can share their accumulated knowledge, suggestions, and innovation best practices with the entire organization. For example, a team shares a discovery made during a research activity, a pat-

tern found when analyzing the data from a business experiment, or anything linked with an innovation activity. Another team uses real examples to explain the risk of making unrealistic assumptions and how this has impacted innovation projects, or they present pitfalls to avoid when defining MVPs. Teams may also present detailed results from business experimentation and user research regarding the potential of ideas or explanations on why individual innovation projects were "killed." This type of event is fundamental as it demonstrates how innovation is linked to the real world and how failure is celebrated as the means for learning.

Beyond the apparent purpose of information and knowledge sharing, these events play another critical role: they keep the innovation community connected and set the basis for better collaboration. They are organized informally by the innovators themselves—speakers and presenters come from various teams and divisions. Contributions through this program are officially acknowledged through the company's recognition and reward system—innovators are rewarded for sharing their knowledge, insights, and expertise.

5.7 The Innovation Calendar

Considering the remote or hybrid collaboration models and the challenges they bring, it is more important than ever to maintain an innovation calendar—a yearly schedule of recurring events strategically planned to power the innovation process. This calendar is hosted in the Innovation Portal—the "digital home of innovation," as presented in Chap. 4. The innovation calendar provides value to all employees, but it is especially beneficial to remote team members and distributed teams who use it to discover and engage with innovation activities across the organization.

A common challenge in the era of remote working is "providing the big picture"—the single view of what's happening and planned to happen in innovation—a single calendar helping people to get informed, aligned, and inspired in the broader context of innovation. While there are great collaboration tools and digital platforms, each provides a partial view from a specific angle—leading to information gaps and increased context-switching between apps, documents, and internal websites.

The innovation calendar, provided it is properly set up and operated within the Innovation Portal, can address this gap very effectively and eventually bring alignment to the broader enterprise-wide innovation function. As maintained by the innovation team, the innovation calendar is always up to date, offering not only accurate planning information but also an interactive experience that enables users to discover content about scheduled events. For example, innovators can browse the agenda for an upcoming brainstorming session or actual content produced from a past hackathon. This way, the innovation calendar creates an interactive, visual "timeline" of innovation events, allowing access to the underlying content, knowledge, and resources.

By centralizing the innovation schedule, organizations bring clarity around expectations, improve participation rates, and ensure that innovative activities don't get lost amid everyday operational priorities. The calendar also helps leadership teams track the cadence and variety of innovation initiatives, enabling them to ensure a balanced innovation activity throughout the year.

Properly implemented, the innovation calendar transforms from a simple scheduling tool into a powerful guide that demonstrates the bigger picture of innovation and, as a result, the organization's ongoing commitment to systematic innovation.

Figure 5.3 presents a hypothetical arrangement of innovation events throughout the year. The chart illustrates various events of different recurrence patterns, each participating in an orchestrated system of innovation activities. For example, the year starts with an "Innovation All-hands," followed by an "Opportunity Review" meeting, a "Demo Day," etc. Most events are strategically positioned to leverage outputs from recently-completed innovation sessions and provide insights to subsequent ones. For instance, the "Steering Committee" is informed by the "Market Intel," and in turn, it informs the yearly hackathon to set the context according to the latest market intelligence insights.

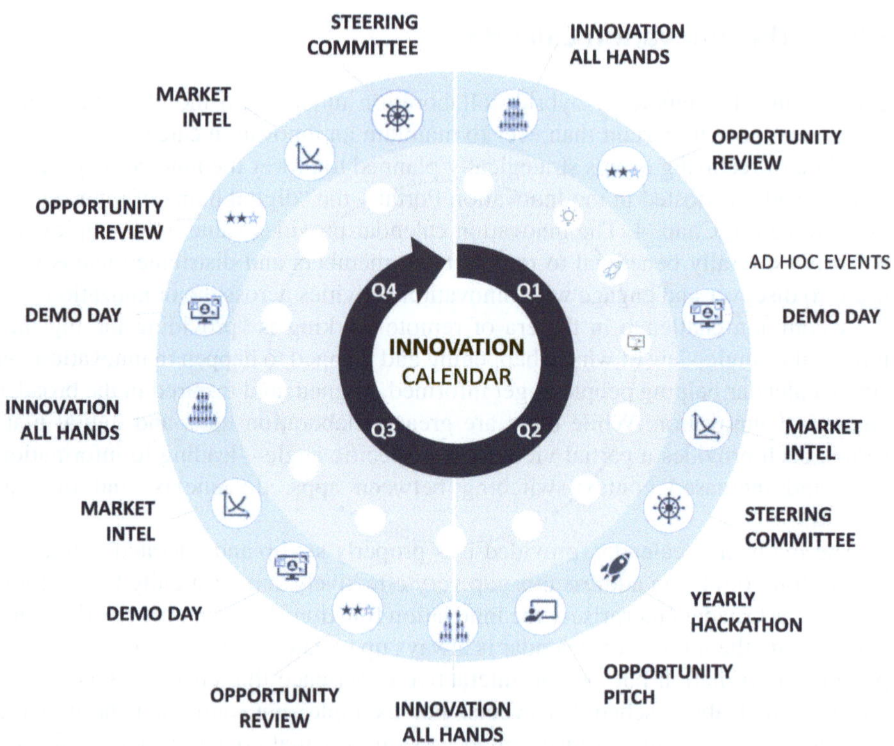

Fig. 5.3 A typical corporate innovation calendar

5.8 Measuring the Performance of Innovation Events

Innovation events, especially workshops, are expensive; hence, measuring their performance and capturing signals of success is essential. This can be done by offering a universal channel for feedback, supported by all innovation workshops and educational events: participants evaluate the event's quality, content preparation, and facilitation, while event leaders can assess participant performance or engagement where applicable. The feedback is automatically processed by AI, which summarizes qualitative feedback, generates insights, and suggests improvements, that are visible to the event organizer and the innovation team. The system produces consistent scorecards across event types, giving innovation leadership a comprehensive view of event performance as part of overall innovation measurement. For example, after a brainstorming session, participants receive a request and assess the event's impact. At the same time, facilitators evaluate the team's engagement—as a single unit. This dual perspective provides a balanced, pragmatic view that goes beyond the typical enthusiasm that is often present in such sessions.

Similarly, all the innovation events can be connected to the innovation rewards program in order to acknowledge innovators who lead certain events, e.g., an impactful innovation talk or those innovators who demonstrate exceptional contributions, as identified by the facilitator's feedback and peer recognition. This integration ensures that valuable participation is recognized and incentivized while providing innovation leaders with rich data on both event effectiveness and individual contributions across the innovation ecosystem.

5.9 Innovation Events in the Remote-Work Era

The pandemic dramatically changed how we work, collaborate, and innovate. Teams are now primarily *online* and often *distributed*, relying on digital tools to collaborate and innovate. Technology offers impressive solutions for online collaboration, co-creation, and innovation—it empowers remote teams to work, communicate, make decisions, shape ideas, and develop systems faster. However, the remote model comes with concerns regarding the cultural impact and, especially, regarding innovation and creative initiatives. Having cross-disciplinary teams innovating together in person can significantly boost creativity, collaboration, and the innovation spirit. When people join an in-person workshop, they not only collaborate; they also develop their business relationships, build trust, and establish stronger connections at the interpersonal level. While these can happen, to a certain extent, in a digital collaboration setting, face-to-face interactions make it easier for people to be empathetic and engage more with creative and innovation activities.

Considering the limitations of online innovation events and the general disconnect that working from home brings to teams, a program of in-person innovation workshops can add significant value. Innovation events can be a great reason for people to get together and spend quality time innovating on challenging problems. This program can be arranged as a recurring in-person innovation meetup, such as brainstorming or prototyping sessions, that brings back the "human factor" into the innovation process and helps teams connect, explore opportunities, and enjoy the creative experience. Such events can boost the innovation culture, team dynamics, networking, and, eventually, the organization's innovation performance. Depending on the geographical arrangement of the teams and the availability of corporate space, these events could be hosted in a dedicated, innovation-optimized space, e.g., in the head office of the company or in a rolling location each time, e.g., a co-working space, a hotel, etc.

Hosting innovation events in a dedicated office space brings various benefits. The innovation-optimized office space serves *practical* needs along with *branding* and *cultural* ones. On the practical side, it provides collaboration functionality—it offers features and technology to boost team collaboration, expression of ideas, creativity, and problem-solving. Moreover, to make better use of the space in a remote world, it is highly adaptive: flexible layout with movable walls or separators, movable furniture and equipment, and multipurpose surfaces along with writable walls to encourage participants express their thoughts and collaborate.

Furthermore, to support hybrid innovation workshops—people in the space but also members joining online—the innovation space is equipped with technology such as large, interactive screens, cameras, and speakers for collaboration and quality interactions between the team and the remote participants. When not occupied by innovation workshop teams, the innovation space falls back to an "always-on" mode—for instance, operating as a makerspace or an innovation expo. In such cases, the space exposes the latest technologies, equipment, tools, electronics, gadgets, and reusable components in the context of the company, allowing people to explore, learn, and prototype solutions—physical or digital prototypes. Similarly, the space could host and present innovation assets such as live demos, interactive apps, and physical prototypes. This scenario can be particularly useful for educational purposes such as live sessions for hands-on prototyping, demonstration, knowledge exchange, etc.

On the cultural side, this special innovation space embeds strong branding and powerful cultural messages that reinforce the principles of innovation and promote the company's purpose, mission, and vision.

Alternatively, innovation events could be hosted in various locations, e.g., collaboration spaces or hotels, according to a rotation scheme that follows the geographic arrangement of the team, bringing people and teams together in a different place or region each time.

5.10 The Cultural Impact of AI-Powered Innovation Events

AI dramatically impacts the innovation workshops and events described in this chapter. While there are significant gains in using AI to organize complex events such as hackathons, the adoption of AI as an *active innovator* changes the character of these workshops and puts the innovation mindset and the broader culture at risk: Extensive use of AI in the innovation process may alter our perceptions of what "being creative" and what "being an innovator" means. When AI can generate multiple remarkable ideas in seconds, innovators may begin to question their own ability to contribute and "compete" with it—a realization that potentially diminishes their role in the creative part of innovation. For example, the integration of AI into hackathons dramatically alters their nature—from an event where talented professionals have the chance to showcase their technical superpowers and come up with solutions that make them proud, it now evolves into a hybrid where AI frames and prototypes ideas in a matter of minutes—faster, better, and done by anyone, with no technical expertise. This fundamental shift creates an existential challenge for classic innovation roles relying on expert coding skills or creative problem-solving abilities. In this context, those talented individuals and teams will have to redefine their roles in innovation and find other ways to stay motivated and energized beyond the excitement of coding or problem-solving under the intensity of the hackathon. The satisfaction derived from overcoming technical obstacles and building smart solutions fast is increasingly being replaced by the general skill of effectively directing an AI agent—something that any professional can do. The rapidly expanding adoption of AI in creative roles introduces a risk not only to the innovation culture but also to people's self-esteem and mental well-being. AI is taking over what many of us value the most in a professional context: creativity.

On the practical side, this also impacts the recognition and rewards engine of the company: when AI is co-innovating with teams, how can we attribute innovation to humans and reward them? Who is the inventor when the core concept is generated by an AI *autonomously*, without a user's prompt? The entire innovation system needs to be readjusted, as the traditional metrics do not apply to solutions that emerge from AI-powered innovation or an AI-first approach.

Companies must adopt new frameworks that acknowledge the distinct value that human judgment, ability to execute, and strategic decision-making bring to corporate innovation. To protect the self-esteem of innovators while leveraging AI capabilities, companies need to follow a balanced approach to AI-powered innovation events: a model that blends AI efficiency with human judgment and empowers people to assume higher-level, more strategic innovation roles, shifting from *ideation* to *opportunity framing, decision-making*, and *in-market experimentation.* This requires acknowledging innovation areas where human insight remains superior, such as understanding unstated user needs, shaping go-to-market strategies, building partnerships, running in-market experiments, driving growth, and achieving successful innovation outcomes.

Companies must be cautious about how they communicate the role of AI in these events and how they approach the AI-human co-innovation model. For instance, I find the popular argument and communication strategy stating that "AI is augmenting instead of replacing humans" only partially true and potentially misleading: We must recognize that *augmentation* often means completing the same work more efficiently with drastically less human effort. For a given demand, this directly translates to fewer positions needed.

We should be pragmatic and courageous enough to admit that when AI augments a role, it will likely reduce demand for human experts in that role—unless the enhanced productivity opens new opportunities or allows us to scale to previously impossible challenges. However, when the scope of work and market demand remain relatively static, fewer human positions will be needed due to the rapidly increasing AI-powered individual productivity.

A narrative built upon this acknowledgment could send a more pragmatic and actionable message to innovators—and professionals in general: prepare for the AI era by upskilling across innovation domains, becoming more adaptive to emerging technologies, and identifying new ways toward professional fulfillment and value creation. Disrupted by AI, innovation itself becomes what we must innovate.

6 Opportunity Discovery: Using Artificial Intelligence to Spot High-Potential Concepts

Opportunity discovery is too vital to leave to chance and just hope for the next wave of inspiration. The ability to discover high-potential opportunities needs more than ad hoc processes and isolated innovation workshops; it requires a systematic method executed with *speed* and *decisiveness*.

A rich pipeline of quality ideas, paired with a robust opportunity discovery capability, increases the likelihood of impactful innovations: the more opportunities evaluated, the higher the chances of spotting those truly game-changing ones—and this isn't merely a numbers game. A *continuous opportunity discovery* process drives a fundamental shift in perspective, creating an entrepreneurial mindset that increases both *willingness* and *readiness* to pursue opportunities.

To achieve this level of readiness and be able to spot and react to opportunities quickly, the underlying processes must be *ongoing* and operating *at scale*. Innovators should always be in this "opportunity discovery mode," and the leadership should be "listening" for opportunities and be open to considering them. Of course, *being able to spot* high-potential opportunities is only the first part: The company must also be *ready to react fast* and *wisely*. When an opportunity is identified, the company must quickly determine the best path forward—which depends on several factors, including the complexity of the underlying concept and the associated level of uncertainty. For example, a flagged opportunity may come with certain risks or unknowns regarding the feasibility of a technical component or increased uncertainty about the market demand. In such cases, the company would want to validate the opportunity by testing the key assumptions and obtaining insights or data that quantify the unknowns. The latter is the purpose of the Opportunity Validation team, as described in Chap. 7, which analyzes the opportunity and identifies the right validation strategy and testing techniques to apply, such as experimentation, prototyping, and proof of concept. Following a successful business experiment, they interpret real-world evidence and recommend how to proceed with the opportunity.

The ongoing opportunity discovery can be expensive, as it requires a steady supply of novel-to-the-company ideas, a strong opportunity evaluation capability, and

G. Krasadakis, *Innovation Mode 2.0*,
https://doi.org/10.1007/978-3-032-00835-0_6

an innovation team to orchestrate the entire process. However, by adopting the latest technologies—and artificial intelligence in particular—the discovery process can be implemented and operated at scale with significantly lower costs. Previously "expensive" idea management operations such as idea articulation and intake, de-duplication, standardization, feedback, validation, discovery, distribution, and communication can now be streamlined by integrating the latest AIs into the corporate environment. A modern AI-powered ideation system can increase both the *volume* and the *quality* of incoming ideas—by *assisting* innovators in ideating or *co-innovating* with them. Furthermore, it can minimize the effort required to *administer ideas* by "understanding" them and triggering the necessary actions. Additionally, AI can boost your organization's ability to *spot opportunities* with accuracy and optimal timing by *helping evaluators* or by *acting as an evaluator* independently, based on the idea assessment model described later in this chapter.

Figure 6.1 presents an overview of the opportunity discovery process and how the primary innovation actors use it. As seen from this figure, the foundation of the opportunity discovery capability is a central innovation repository—the Innovation Graph where all ideas are captured, live, and, in many cases, *evolve*. Beyond ideas, the Innovation Graph encompasses all innovation artifacts and related content generated throughout the innovation process, making it an invaluable source of knowledge for the entire organization and especially important for AI-powered innovation.

Seen at the top of this chart, the stakeholders—product managers, business leaders, or leadership members—steer the innovation process by providing a strategic

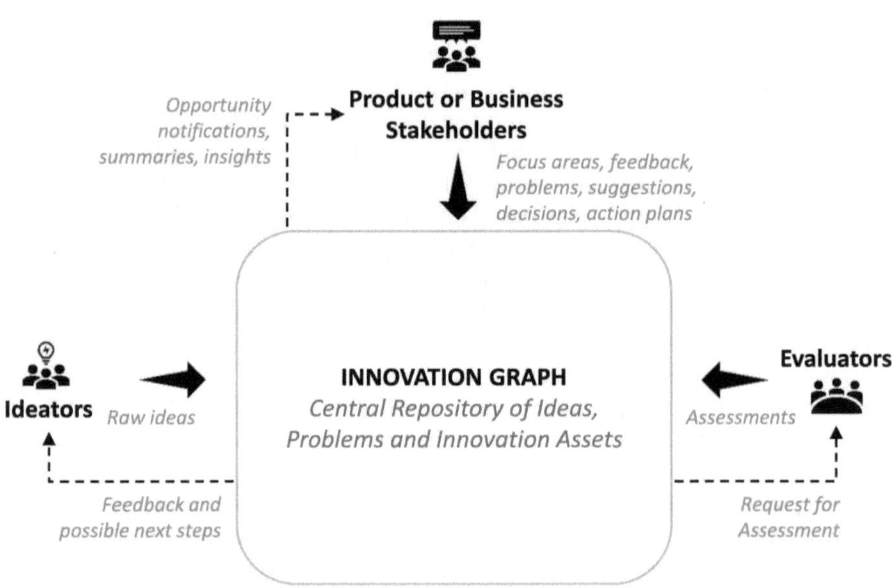

Fig. 6.1 Overview of the opportunity discovery process

view and their vision about products, services, and markets, along with insights regarding known customer problems, the performance of products, and the plans for new ones. Beyond their strategic input—they provide guidance on *where to focus the innovation efforts*—they contribute at the practical level by offering feedback and suggestions on the next best steps for specific opportunities.

On the left-hand side, we see the "ideators"—the ones who, either systematically or sporadically, submit their ideas to the opportunity discovery platform. In this setup, any individual in the organization can act as an ideator without necessarily having a formal innovation title or affiliation with innovation programs and teams. The latter aligns with one of the core principles I have been applying throughout my career: innovation should be open and accessible to all—boosting the culture, helping the innovation community grow organically, and making the process more diverse and inclusive.

On the right-hand side, we see the "evaluators"—employees with specialized knowledge in specific domains, such as technologists, product experts, commercialization experts, and scientists. Beyond their domain expertise, the evaluators bring knowledge and experience in applying *evaluation principles* and *methods* to assess ideas as objectively and reliably as possible.

Based on the pattern presented above, evaluators are notified when there are pending ideas waiting for review. Either in asynchronous or synchronous mode, they apply a formal *idea assessment* model that produces an *opportunity score* reflecting the potential of the idea. The assessment results, along with feedback and guidance from the evaluators, are then communicated to the owners of the idea. Furthermore, when the assessment results indicate that an idea *is* an opportunity, stakeholders are notified so they can promptly review it and identify the next best steps—it could be further discussions, workshops, or the decision to incorporate the idea into a specific opportunity portfolio or directly to a product backlog. For example, a product manager discovers a "flagged" opportunity that matches the context of their product and decides to consider it further as a new feature. In such a scenario, they could add it to their product backlog for further consideration, or if they see increased uncertainty, they forward it to the "opportunity validation" team for formal testing—e.g., through experimentation via prototyping or other ways that produce Real World Evidence (RWE) for the potential of the idea.

What is very important is that *opportunity discovery* should be available as an always-on service, continuously processing ideas that emerge not only from structured innovation activities and events such as hackathons but also from everyday business operations, including routine meetings, product development sessions, and other business interactions. This persistent availability helps capture ideas regardless of when or where they surface. With this always-on approach, the organization becomes more open to "surprises" and welcomes extraordinary, unexpected ideas even when they don't align with its strategic plans. This approach allows ideas to be decoupled from rigid processes and flow naturally across groups and layers of the organization: Evaluators flag opportunities, senior stakeholders discover them, and the opportunity validation team obtains real-world evidence that may take them to the opportunity realization team for implementation, market launch, and growth. All these may be happening for multiple opportunities in parallel, in a fluid way.

Artificial intelligence plays multiple roles in this "always-on" opportunity discovery process: it acts as an *innovator* by generating ideas, an *evaluator* by assessing ideas and identifying opportunities, and a *communicator* by summarizing and diffusing ideas throughout the organization. These are described in detail in Sect. 6.3 later in this chapter. Before explaining the role of artificial intelligence, it is essential to define the foundational components of the AI-powered opportunity discovery process. These include the *Problem* and *Solution Space*, the *Idea Assessment model*, and the *Idea Evaluation* process.

6.1 Innovation Space: Problems and Solutions

"Jumping to solutions" poses significant risks in business and particularly in innovation contexts—and this is not a matter of expertise or seniority: Regardless of their level or their experience in innovation, people often come with preconceived solutions, preferences, and personal agendas that may prevent them from paying sufficient attention to the problem being solved, thus slowing down or even blocking the creative process. Failing to focus on the problem is primarily a mindset issue that needs to be addressed at the educational and cultural levels. However, the right structure and tools can also help. To emphasize the importance of problems in innovation, they should be decoupled from *ideas* or *solutions* and treated as independent innovation assets: Well-framed problems are equally important for innovation as ideas—if not more. A *problem*, as an innovation asset, has its own properties and lifecycle—it exists independently and may be linked with plenty of solutions, each attempting to address it differently.

To further support the decoupling, we introduce the notion of the *innovation space*, where *problems* and *solutions* live independently but are also interlinked. Problems live in the *problem space*—as the objects that link the organization's strategy with the actual innovation efforts. In this sense, the problem space is the translation of the company's strategy and vision into well-defined problems that must be tackled so the company moves closer to fulfilling its purpose. The problem space evolves and expands—it gets frequent updates in terms of new items and prioritization; problems are prioritized as well.

In parallel to the problem space, the *solution space* is where the company's ideas live. As seen in Fig. 6.2, ideas may be linked to one or more problems.

The two combined, form the Innovation Space as one of the essential elements of modern innovation architecture that helps set the *focus for innovation*—what problems the company's innovation engine should solve and what solutions it should prioritize for exploration or realization. It is the basis of the innovation agenda—the strategic tool introduced in Chap. 4 that links *problems* and ambitious *ideas* with the company's *purpose*, helping communicate the company's North Star for innovation effectively.

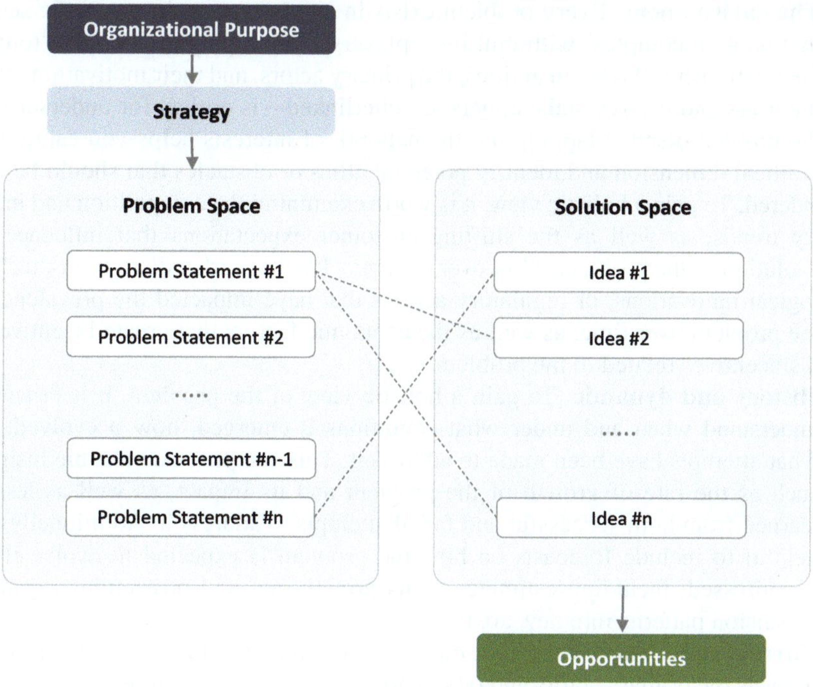

Fig. 6.2 Linking innovation with the purpose and the strategy of the organization

6.1.1 Framing Problems

Framing problems effectively brings immediate benefits to the innovation process: it provides clarity to innovators and all involved stakeholders about the nature of the problem, its importance, the root cause, and the involved parties. A concise problem description drives alignment, allows people to empathize, and shifts focus from solutions to the actual problem. Hence, it is essential to adopt a consistent framework for capturing and communicating problems. While a solid problem statement is a good start, it is often beneficial and inspiring to present additional aspects of the problem, such as its *environment*, *market*, *history*, and *dynamics*. Moreover, it is valuable to contrast the *problematic* and *ideal* states and articulate potential *strategies* to tackle the problem. The problem-framing template described below is a key resource that helps innovators run targeted, engaging, and effective ideation workshops, resulting in more relevant and diverse ideas. It also helps evaluators process ideas in the right context and estimate their potential more accurately. And, of course, a rich problem framing following this format is very useful for artificial intelligence as context for your AI brainstorming partner. In the following, we present the key components of the problem-framing template and explain how they add value to the thought process:

- **The environment**: Every problem exists in an ecosystem, in a specific setting that is often complex, with multiple "players." Identifying the market "forces," the relationships between entities, the primary actors, and their motivation—how the users and the key stakeholders are interlinked—is critical for understanding the problem itself. Mapping out the network of interests helps you capture the political dimension and identify potential allies or obstacles that should be considered. To gain a holistic view, it is worth examining the competition and industry trends, as well as the shifting customer expectations that influence the evolution of the problem. Moreover, you may list the market disruptions, technological innovations, or regulatory actions that have impacted the prevalence of the problem over time, as well as the economic factors that create incentives or disincentives related to the problem.
- **History and dynamic**: To gain a holistic view of the problem, it is crucial to understand when and under what conditions it emerged, how it evolved, and what attempts have been made to address it. This can provide valuable insights, such as the rate of growth of the problem and its impact, as well as lessons learned from both successful and failed attempts to address it. Additionally, it is helpful to include forecasts on how the problem is expected to evolve if left unaddressed, including estimates of its growth rate and projections regarding expansion patterns into new areas.
- **Current state**: This presents the current, non-optimal state and how the problem impacts the primary actors and other entities: certain classes of users may be suffering while others, ironically, may be benefiting. The relationship among entities and actors, as well as the causes and the symptoms, must be clearly stated here. Ideally, this element should contain statistics and references—e.g., frequencies of impacted users, costs, inefficiencies, or other figures quantifying the impact of the current, non-optimal situation. It is also important to think beyond the symptoms and identify the underlying causes and specific triggers or conditions that activate or intensify the problem.
- **Ideal state**: A clear view of the *current* situation becomes even more insightful when contrasted with the *ideal* state: how would the situation evolve if the root problem were somehow resolved? This should be expressed in terms of impacted metrics and success criteria, explaining the dynamic among stakeholders, new collaborations or partnerships that might emerge, and how benefits would be distributed among various groups.
- **Strategies**: This aims to outline potential strategies for addressing the problem. However, this should come without "solutioning" or delving into specific implementations. The aim is to provide directional advice without constraining creativity or prescribing particular solutions. Innovators should focus on describing strategic arrangements for new business models, partnerships, technologies, processes, services, products, etc.

Adopting a structured approach to articulating problems can benefit the company in many ways. Stand-alone problems become assets in the innovation process: they reside in the problem space, and they are evaluated, prioritized, and exposed to the innovation community through the innovation agenda, which provides clarity to innovators and helps leaders set the right focus. The problem space provides *anchor points* for innovation—it answers questions like "What are we innovating on?" or "What problems are we solving and why?" Furthermore, the problem framing template contributes to a *shared innovation language*, enabling people to collaborate on well-defined problems that are linked to the company's overall strategy and purpose. This approach brings various advantages, including:

1. **Increased engagement with innovation**: Problems are more compact and simpler than ideas. They describe a situation and often refer to people's pain points that are easy for everyone to relate to, empathize with, and approach the problem from a user's angle.
2. **A new source of opportunities**: A company-wide, visible problem space helps innovators identify big problems worth solving. Moreover, it can inspire people to engage in the innovation process solely by framing problems without necessarily proposing a solution: innovation is also about spotting significant problems.
3. **Better use of ideas**: When multiple ideas reference the same problem, they are naturally grouped, forming a list of *competing* or *complementary* solutions that could be combined or merged to address it more effectively.
4. **Faster evaluation of ideas**: When the framed problem is evaluated, ideas can be assessed faster because the evaluators only assess *the solutioning part.*

Contributing to the innovation process by framing problems worth solving is an essential innovation behavior that should be recognized via the innovation rewards program.

6.1.2 Framing Ideas

In a business context, ideas refer to any concept or approach that aims to improve an aspect of the business and bring value to the company and its users. A properly framed business idea describes the *users*, references a *problem*, and explains how it attempts to solve it. The *referenced problem* could be anything—from internal organizational issues or known needs to improve the experience of customers to user pain points or market gaps that point to new products, services, ventures, and markets.

Ideas may refer to big, ambitious proposals, such as new products, services, or breakthrough technologies, as well as to small improvements to existing solutions, processes, or business models. The depth of ideas also varies significantly: they may be framed as generic, high-level descriptions of a concept or as very specific, detailed, and accurate pieces of logic addressing the referenced problem.

Considering the above, it is valuable for the company to have business ideas properly framed, using simple and precise language that allows for instant understanding and effective communication. But compiling a concise, executive summary of an idea is not always easy: great ideas are often lost in lengthy presentations or ineffective descriptions. Throughout numerous innovation workshops, I've witnessed teams struggling to describe their ideas effectively and concisely. In many cases, innovators get trapped in the details and provide excessive information on unimportant aspects, making the comprehension and evaluation of the idea difficult and time-consuming. When dealing with technology concepts, this gets worse as people tend to overemphasize the technology itself rather than the *essence* of the concept.

The idea framing template is designed to address these challenges. It is a simple structure that references the problem and describes the situation, the impacted users, the solution, and how users would benefit if the referenced problem is solved—as explained in the following:

1. **Context**: The broader conditions under which the proposed idea has the potential to generate value for its users. It includes a reference to the problem being solved, explaining user pain points, market gaps, business challenges, or a related dynamic in the market.
2. **The target users**: The classes of users or named personas that will interact with the solution and benefit from it.
3. **Value for the users**: The value the target users will get and how their lives will improve if the idea is successfully implemented.
4. **Value for the business**: How the idea is expected to benefit the company and business stakeholders. It refers not necessarily to financial performance and profits but generally to *value*.
5. **The form factor**: Ideas can be realized in various forms—depending on the context, the company's strategy, and the involved personas. For example, a given idea can be developed into *a service*, *a mobile app*, *a connected device*, or an offline experience. When framing an idea, it is essential to briefly describe the envisioned form factors to help stakeholders better comprehend the concept and its potential.
6. **The solution**: A description of the actual solution—*how* the idea solves the problem. It explains the logic, steps, conditions, actors, and entities and how they interact with the solution to achieve the desired outcome.
7. **Definition of success**: A description of what success looks like through the lens of both the user and the business.
8. **Big unknowns and assumptions**: The uncertainties that need to be addressed and the key questions that require answers, for example, unknowns regarding technical feasibility, market demand, and viability. This may also include a brief listing of any critical assumptions or hypotheses that need to be considered while evaluating the idea or in subsequent experimentation and research activities.

The idea-framing template helps teams improve how they capture, communicate, and validate ideas. As with the problem template, this contributes to a shared innovation language and "educates" both ideators and stakeholders on how to think and talk about ideas. More specifically, adopting the idea framing template brings value in the following ways:

1. **Speed**: Ideators can start fast by using the template as a thought framework to construct high-level, compact descriptors of early ideas. It also accelerates ideation and brainstorming sessions.
2. **Clarity**: While analyzing and describing the individual elements, ideators obtain a holistic view of their idea.
3. **Faster comparison and assessment**: Properly framed ideas help AI and human evaluators assess and compare them faster, thus improving the opportunity discovery process.
4. **Faster sharing**: Since the core idea description can fit on a single page, it is much easier to socialize the idea: those who discover it will have to read a well-structured, single-page document instead of a lengthy presentation.

Of course, there are additional elements that help package and administer business ideas effectively. For example, a unique and easy-to-remember *codename* and a compact *title* that reflects the essence of the idea, *metadata* that captures an idea's relationships with other ideas, or *tags* can all improve the discoverability of ideas. Similarly, the *idea scorecard* reflects the overall potential of the idea, while the *chain of attributions* summarizes all the contributors and their impacts throughout its evolution.

A properly framed idea uses simple, non-technical language and is technology agnostic. This makes innovation more inclusive by ensuring ideas are accessible to broader audiences and increases flexibility by avoiding premature technical decisions or directions, e.g., when the idea specifically names technologies to be used in solving the problem. By separating ideas from implementation details, organizations can maintain a clear *master idea* that various teams can reference and extend through different business proposals, prototypes, or technical implementations. This decoupling preserves the idea's adaptability while allowing it to evolve through multiple artifacts and contexts in its lifecycle.

The idea framing template can be implemented as a document, a digital form, or, even better, as a set of prompts in a commercial AI system defining the company's AI Ideator that can be used by anyone in the organization at any time and also in brainstorming sessions to help participants construct and pitch ideas in a more efficient, compact way.

6.1.3 The Intent of an Idea

Ideas may have multiple business intents, and as a result, they require flexible handling and evaluation. The business intent of an idea reflects what the ideator envisions as a possible outcome and how the company may benefit from the idea. It is set by the ideator but then reviewed and possibly extended or reset by the evaluators. Ideas may be associated with more than one business intent—for example, an idea may be aiming for a *patent*, a *prototype*, or a product *feature*. Ideas may follow different evaluation, communication, and discovery paths, depending on the assigned intents. For example, if the intent is *patent submission*, the idea is directly assigned to a patent attorney for immediate review. This way, idea management and evaluation become more flexible: Not all ideas lead to a business proposal or a product requirements document, and only some need a thorough feasibility analysis. Similarly, not every idea needs concept validation through experiments and prototyping. Some ideas may be submitted directly for invention disclosure; others may be added to a product backlog and wait for prioritization—to be validated and possibly implemented as features of existing products. The business intent enables smarter routing of ideas through the company's broader opportunity discovery system. The following covers the most characteristic intents in a corporate innovation context:

1. **File a patent**: The ideator is confident that the idea meets the patentability criteria—it seems *novel* and *non-obvious*, brings *significant value*, and can be *discoverable* if implemented. By attaching the "patent intent," the idea joins the "patent" path for faster evaluation. Alternatively, the idea may be independently discovered by the evaluators or patent attorneys and flagged as *potentially patentable*.
2. **Prove that it works**: The ideator or evaluator recognizes the potential in the idea but also identifies increased *uncertainty*. It may be the nature of the proposed solution, for example, a novel, untested component or a user experience that has many *unknowns* regarding its effectiveness or the expected adoption from real users. In such situations, the ideator or a stakeholder may request the implementation of a Proof of Concept (PoC) to test the critical aspects of the idea and get evidence on how well it could work in real conditions.
3. **Demonstrate to stakeholders**: The objective of an idea could be to present to partners or clients how a new technology or concept could solve a problem more effectively. Typically, such ideas originate from sales or commercial teams that are closer to clients and thus able to better understand their pain points or latent needs. When taking this path, ideas are realized as inexpensive, realistic artifacts that are good enough to pitch the concept or explain the technology to the target audience.
4. **Share and explore**: In cases where the idea is more technical, too radical, or in the early days of exploration, the originator may seek support and feedback from the innovation community. Thus, the intent of the idea submission may be to publish a white paper, an article, or other content that can attract attention and invite innovators to elaborate and contribute.
5. **Propose a product feature**: This intent indicates that the idea proposes an improvement to an existing product. While such ideas typically come from product team members, they can also be conceived by any innovator across the organization who can think "as a user" and propose product enhancements. As with other intents, this may be added by evaluators during the idea assessment: if they see the relevance to an existing product, they add the intent and notify the corresponding product team to review the idea and consider it for their product backlog.

6. **Propose a product or service**: This intent signifies that the idea should be evaluated as a new product or service. In such cases, the idea joins a special assessment queue, and if it is flagged as an opportunity, the related product teams are notified. As with other intents, the ideator may be asked to provide additional, product-specific information and documentation. In such cases, the Innovation Playbook may be particularly useful: it provides tools and resources to help the ideator frame their idea as a new product, such as a template for compiling a product requirements document.
7. **Introduce a process improvement**: Ideas with this intent aim to improve an organizational, production, or commercial process or introduce a new one. This could refer to any enhancement, from a new workflow to an improved business operating procedure or protocol.

Allowing for multiple intents makes ideas discoverable by the right audience and gets them evaluated in the proper context with the most appropriate process and criteria. In contrast to linear ideation and rigid opportunity discovery with stage gates, checkpoints, and strict rules, this multiple-intent approach provides agility and speed: business intents may be assigned or removed at any time throughout the lifecycle of an idea and may trigger different evaluation processes, handled by specialized teams, independently.

The above intents are just the most characteristic ones—the list should be configured and adjusted to match the needs of your organization. Specific intents may also be linked with your innovation rewards program to incentivize intents that serve a priority objective of your company. For instance, if you are aiming for a strong IP portfolio, then ideas that may lead to patents may have more importance than those targeting new products, demos, or process improvements.

6.2 Evaluating Ideas

Idea assessment is at the core of the innovation function since it affects how the organization discovers and pursues opportunities. Moreover, a transparent and fair idea evaluation process can positively impact the culture of innovation: it builds trust, emphasizes the strategic importance of innovation, and provides guidance to the innovation community. To ensure that your idea assessment process is effective both in *discovering opportunities* and in *improving the innovation culture*, consider the following principles:

1. **Ideas receive meaningful feedback**: Beyond spotting opportunities, the idea assessment process serves an educational purpose by providing ideators with advice and constructive feedback. Through this process, evaluators are positioned as *mentors* who provide private, actionable feedback to ideators on how to improve the presentation or other aspects of their ideas, thus proving that ideas are thoughtfully considered. In other cases, evaluators may act as connectors,

helping ideators find the right teams and domain experts to discuss relevant ongoing projects.

2. **The assessment process is robust, consistent, and transparent**: The process itself should be repeatable and well documented. The assessment criteria must be clearly described, explaining what they measure, their importance, and how they connect to the company's strategic priorities. For instance, increasing the importance of the *level of novelty* signals that the company prioritizes disruptive, long-term opportunities or developing an IP portfolio. These settings, rules, definitions, and the entire process should be available via the Innovation Portal, accompanied by an FAQ section.
3. **Evaluation is contextual and time sensitive**: The evaluation process does not "kill" ideas; instead, *it estimates their potential* in a non-definitive manner. An old, low-potential idea might be reconsidered and lead to a radically different result due to a change in the innovation agenda or a shift in the economic environment that makes the idea relevant again. For instance, an idea might be reevaluated due to an advance in technology that makes it *feasible* or an increase in consumer demand that makes it *viable*.
4. **Feasibility is not a constraint**: Overemphasizing the feasibility of an idea, especially at an early stage in its lifecycle, may introduce constraints and limit its potential. Considering the rapid pace of technological change of our times, it is not a good practice to dismiss an idea based on a quick feasibility assessment. Moreover, proper feasibility assessment can be a complex and lengthy process. Hence, it is better to thoroughly examine feasibility and economic viability later in the process, after other aspects of the idea have been confirmed to have remarkable potential.
5. **Evaluators have the right skills to assess ideas**: The plurality of topics and technologies that an idea could reference makes it challenging for a single team of evaluators to *properly* evaluate *every* idea. The evaluation process must somehow ensure that each idea is assessed by the right forum of evaluators who are adequately skilled and have relevant domain expertise.

6.2.1 The Idea Assessment Model

The idea assessment model evaluates multiple qualities of the idea and the associated business problem to provide a single *Opportunity Score*. It uses nine dimensions that help quantify the various qualities of the opportunity and reflect its business potential through a single score. Additionally, it offers insights and partial scores that may reveal certain strengths and weaknesses of the idea. The model uses a weighting mechanism over the following nine criteria:

1. **Importance of the problem**: The evaluator must answer the question "How important is the problem being solved?" This is about estimating the level of significance of the problem in general—independently of the context of the company. This universal view of the importance of the problem enables the organiza-

tion to explore and discover new areas and problems beyond its current focus of innovation and stay open to new, *unexpected ideas*. The evaluator scores the problem and provides justification, supporting facts, and figures, such as estimates on the number of users, companies, or other entities that will be impacted if the problem is solved. This estimation should be quick—it represents what the trusted evaluator thinks the size of the problem is, based solely on expertise and market insights. When the problem is *referenced* instead of *embedded* in the idea, it may be already evaluated, thus making this step easier.

2. **Strategic alignment of the problem**: This aims to quantify how aligned the problem is with the organization's strategy; it is the company-specific view of the importance of the problem based on the current innovation agenda. The evaluator must consider the problem from the company's perspective and score its relevance to the current strategy and priorities. When combined with the universal importance of the problem, this can generate great insights and help to spot opportunities beyond the coverage of the innovation "radar" of the company. For example, it can help identify problems of massive importance that are not currently set in the company's zone of interest, and may occasionally lead to *strategic pivots* and a refinement of the strategy and the innovation agenda.
3. **Effectiveness**: The two criteria above refer to the importance and relevance of the problem. *Effectiveness* refers to the solution—it raises the question of "How effectively can the idea address the referenced problem?" Estimating the efficacy of the idea is probably the most time-consuming part of the assessment, as the evaluator must deeply understand the described solution and how it will work in practice. Moreover, it requires special skills, domain expertise, market understanding, insights, and awareness of global trends and dynamics. Evaluators are expected to reference facts on how other companies have solved the same problem and list the key factors behind successful or failed attempts, as well as the commonalities with the proposed idea.
4. **Feasibility**: The evaluator uses their deep understanding of the technological state of the art, product development, and market analysis skills to estimate the feasibility of the idea and explain the reasoning. They examine whether the proposed solution can be implemented in a reasonable timeframe using current technologies and if it could be economically viable. They also consider *legal* or *regulatory* matters associated with the concept, as these can impact its feasibility. For example, a *technically achievable* and *economically viable* idea may face data privacy constraints impacting its overall feasibility. The level of feasibility should be based on an inexpensive and quick estimation rather than a thorough study; the latter may be conducted at later stages if required.
5. **Ease of implementation**: The evaluator analyzes the complexities associated with *implementing and launching* the idea and estimates how easy it is to drive it to the market. This does not ask for cost estimations, as this is not practical at this early stage. Instead, the score should reflect the evaluator's informed opinion, supported by notes justifying the score and explaining any assumptions made or hypotheses that need to be tested.

6. **Ease of operation**: As with the "ease of implementation," the evaluator is asked to understand the *operational complexities* of the idea and provide a quick estimation of how easy it would be to operate it after it is successfully built and launched in the market. This reflects the evaluator's understanding of the operational requirements and complexities involved, such as establishing and maintaining special partnerships and agreements, onboarding human resources to provide support, the associated costs of maintaining technology infrastructure, etc.
7. **Business impact**: The evaluator estimates the impact that a successful implementation and commercialization of the idea would have on the company. The impact could refer to financial performance, market growth, or expansion in particular ways, such as by building a platform, an ecosystem, or anything that would help the company drive success. As in previous cases, this does not ask for a thorough financial analysis or detailed business cases. Instead, it expects a justified opinion from the evaluator about whether the idea will bring marginal business impact versus being a game changer and market disruptor. Additional information justifying the score, such as the expected impact on specific key performance indicators, is important.
8. **Novelty**: The level of novelty of an idea depends on the point of view: an idea may be new *to the world, the industry*, or *the company*. While it is relatively easy to tell if an idea is new to the company, checking for novelty in a broader context is expensive and time-consuming. Hence, instead of a definite answer, the evaluator is asked to *estimate* the novelty of the idea based on the accumulated knowledge and the available insights about the company, the market, and the state of the art. The question is, "Based on current organizational and market insights, how novel does this idea appear to be?" Novelty is an essential quality of the idea and contributes to its overall Opportunity Score. When evaluators flag an idea as potentially "new to the world," patent attorneys are notified to examine its patentability and possibly trigger a prior art search. Beyond that, novelty is also used by the innovation measurement framework as a signal of the company's innovation performance.
9. **Certainty of demand**: This aims to capture the level of confidence that there is, or will be, sufficient market demand for the solution described in the idea. The evaluator must estimate the current state of the market and the underlying trends, consider the economics of the solution, state any assumptions, and express the *certainty of demand* as a score, where a value of 10 means *sufficient demand* is confirmed. To speed up this task, evaluators may consult the innovation intelligence team to gain insights and evidence regarding the existence or anticipated demand for the referenced solution.

The above criteria should be used by expert evaluators to perform quick and inexpensive estimates of the potential of ideas. They are arbitrary scores, reflecting the knowledge and insights available to the evaluators. Ideas are scored against all nine criteria on a scale of 0 to 10, where 10 represents the best case, the most favorable assessment for the idea. For instance, a value of 10 on *ease of development* reads,

"It can be developed immediately with existing knowledge and resources." The scores should be accompanied by a justification and an explanation of any assumptions made.

The assessments performed by the evaluators enrich the original idea and impact its overall *Opportunity Score*. Parts of the assessments are private to the ideator; others are only visible within the network of evaluators, presenting key points, hints, assumptions, or concerns about aspects of the idea and fostering discussion and collaboration. When a sufficient number of assessments are performed for an idea, and it is *confidently* identified as an opportunity, it gets a public *opportunity badge* and scorecard along with a "narrative" that summarizes the aggregated feedback and explains *why* it is an opportunity. This "Opportunity Narrative" is automatically generated by AI on top of the accumulated individual assessments and feedback from the evaluators.

The idea assessment process should ideally be integrated into the Innovation Portal, with tools that ensure a fast, reliable, and truly asynchronous evaluation experience.

Looking at the Scores Through a Different Lens: The idea assessment dimensions described above are not equally important for every company. Even within a single organization, the importance assigned to each of these qualities varies across teams, groups, and divisions, and it may also change over time as the strategy and business goals change.

Consider, for example, an idea proposing a product concept. The novelty aspect of the idea may not be particularly important in this scenario, as product teams typically seek *value for the user*, *strong business potential*, *feasibility*, and *certainty for demand*. While novelty is a desirable quality in a product development context, it may not be a priority and shouldn't significantly impact the decision to implement the idea or not. But if we look at the same idea from an IP strategy standpoint, *novelty* becomes very important as it is one of the prerequisites for filing a patent. Hence, in the IP context, novelty receives a boost in importance over other idea qualities, which still contribute to the score. Similarly, criteria such as the "ease of implementation" and "ease of operations" that are very important in the product development context are of limited importance in the patent scenario.

The idea assessment model offers flexibility in handling these important nuances by allowing the translation of the *primary assessment* performed by evaluators (column *R* in Table 6.1) into *contextual scores* (shown as *Views* in the same table), which reflects the focus of specific teams. Continuing with the above example, we can define the *Product View* and the *IP View* and set weight factors that reflect what is important for each of them. These configurable "lenses" adjust the primary assessment (shown as *R*) to reflect the importance of certain dimensions for the corresponding team. The scoring remains the same—a single set of scores aggregating the evaluator's assessments—but the interpretation is different according to the weight factors that each team sets.

Table 6.1 Idea assessment criteria with a different lens

			Weight schemes—lens			
Dimension	Description	R	View A	View B	…	View N
c_1	Importance	r_1	$w_{1,A}$	$w_{1,B}$	…	$w_{1,N}$
c_2	Alignment	r_2	$w_{2,A}$	$w_{2,B}$	…	$w_{2,N}$
c_3	Effectiveness	r_3	$w_{3,A}$	$w_{3,B}$	…	$w_{3,N}$
c_4	Feasibility	r_4	$w_{4,A}$	$w_{4,B}$	…	$w_{4,N}$
c_5	Ease of development	r_5	$w_{5,A}$	$w_{5,B}$	…	$w_{5,N}$
c_6	Ease of operation	r_6	$w_{6,A}$	$w_{6,B}$	…	$w_{6,N}$
c_7	Business impact	r_7	$w_{7,A}$	$w_{7,B}$	…	$w_{7,N}$
c_8	Novelty	r_8	$w_{8,A}$	$w_{8,B}$	…	$w_{8,N}$
c_9	Certainty of demand	r_9	$w_{9,A}$	$w_{9,B}$	…	$w_{9,N}$

The various perspectives and priorities across teams and business intents can be reflected via the weight factors $w_{i,j}$ that set the importance of dimension i in context j. Table 6.1 summarizes this configurable idea assessment model.

The first two columns provide the dimension's symbol and name, respectively. Column R represents the aggregated ratings by the evaluators, the partial score in [0,10]. The columns in the "Weight schemes" section represent the *normalized importance* of each dimension for a specific "View"—the *perspective* of each particular team. Each *View* contains the weight factors of all nine dimensions that *translate* the aggregated scores of the evaluators into an overall *contextual* score.

For instance, *View A* in the above table could be named "Patent Opportunity Discovery" and configured to have maximum importance to *novelty* and minimum importance to "ease of operation" or "certainty of demand." This way, while still based on the Opportunity Score, the Patentability Score emphasizes what is important for the patent team. Similarly, *View B* could be named "Product Improvement" and set the weight factors to prioritize "Ease of implementation," "Ease of operation," and "Certainty of demand" while deprioritizing "Novelty."

This does not change the actual rating from the evaluators—it simply translates it to different contexts by applying the specific "business lenses"—the weighting scheme.

The idea assessment scheme can be simplified or expanded to meet your specific business needs. For instance, c_1, c_2 could be combined into a single "Importance of the problem" or c_5, c_6 to "Ease of realization" or even c_4, c_5, c_6 as a more general dimension for feasibility. Similarly, novelty could be omitted or given zero importance if IP is not part of your strategy or is less important.

The Opportunity Score of an Idea: Having the partial scores for an idea allows for aggregation into a single *Opportunity Score*, reflecting its business potential based on the evaluators' estimations. As each criterion, c_i, receives a rating r_i in [0,10] and has a weight $w_{i,A}$ corresponding to *View A*, the contextual score of the idea for View j could be simply a weighted average of the partial scores. That is, for a given *View* or *interpretation* A, the *Business Potential of the idea* is a simple linear combination of the ratings adjusted by the weights across the nine criteria, taking the form $\sum_{i=1}^{n} w_{i,A} * r_i$.

When multiple evaluators have assessed the idea, the value r_i is the aggregated rating corresponding to the criterion c_i over the submissions of independent evaluators.

6.2.2 The Idea Evaluation Team

The "governance" approach—where a team of experts meets to decide the future of an idea—does not scale well and often lacks the necessary expertise to properly assess every idea. Forward-thinking companies need a robust and trustworthy idea assessment mechanism that is *fast* and *scalable*.

Scalability and speed can be achieved by establishing a core team of evaluators supported by a broader network of domain experts who participate just in time—if and when they are needed and according to their availability. The core team is fixed, consisting of senior members who are highly skilled in assessing ideas and spotting opportunities and also have the full context and the "big picture" of the company and its environment: They know well the structure of the company, understand its innovation agenda, and follow business activities and developments across divisions.

Beyond assessing ideas, the team also coordinates a program that connects domain experts across the company who are willing to contribute and occasionally get involved in assessing ideas relevant to their expertise. They onboard new evaluators—taking them through a brief onboarding program that presents the idea assessment framework, explains how to identify opportunities, and provides guidance on giving feedback to ideators.

To illustrate how this approach works, consider a case where an idea picked by the core evaluation team for assessment is technically sophisticated in areas not covered by the core team's skillset. To address that, they route the idea toward the most relevant experts in the network of evaluators. The core team orchestrates the process and collects structured assessments from these qualified evaluators. It then processes the information into the system, prepares the feedback, enriches the idea, and communicates an update to the ideator. A similar scenario would occur when the core evaluation team has the skills but not the bandwidth to handle the incoming ideas; in this case, they would delegate the assessment of the idea to the network and simply oversee the progress.

During this process, evaluators also *flag opportunities*—those ideas with a consistently high Opportunity Score across assessments. When flagged, opportunities become discoverable by senior stakeholders across the company.

With the right tools and proper orchestration, the network of idea evaluators can evolve as a fast, scalable, self-organizing idea assessment service, assisting or even replacing the classic "governance team." These tools can be organized into the Innovation Portal—the home of innovation for the company—to cover *administrative* needs, e.g., helping evaluators explore the coverage of domain expertise, manage the network of evaluators, invite domain experts, etc. but also improve *productivity and collaboration*, e.g., finding, selecting, and assessing ideas, viewing assessments, providing feedback, requesting assessment by a domain expert, etc.

Moreover, the Innovation Portal may include onboarding materials for new members of the evaluation network, presenting the idea assessment model and the evaluation principles, along with examples. The performance and the response times of the idea evaluation service are tracked and analyzed through the innovation performance measurement framework.

When the network of evaluators reaches a critical point, more advanced technology is needed to support its operations. For instance, AI components can automatically distribute ideas to those with the most relevant skills in the network and orchestrate the process until the minimum required number of assessments is achieved. Automation enables independent and asynchronous reviews, eliminating the need for recurring meetings and consensus or majority-based decisions.

Beyond identifying opportunities, the systematic assessment of ideas lays the foundation for measuring the *innovation performance* of the company. Having a repository of scored ideas allows the analysis of specific idea strengths and their potential. For example, a dashboard may present the distribution of ideas by their Opportunity Score and visualize the evolution of high-potential opportunities over time. These insights, properly framed, indicate how good the organization is at spotting opportunities and how effective the related services are.

The following presents the AI-powered opportunity discovery platform; it explains how artificial intelligence enhances the manually operated opportunity discovery function and how this may redefine the role of humans in the innovation process.

6.3 Discovering Opportunities with AI

Opportunity discovery is typically viewed as a loosely defined process, supported primarily by ad hoc activities or independent innovation initiatives, such as a workshop or a Design Sprint, or a specific program that asks the company to solve a pressing business challenge.

In the previous, we described ways to improve this episodic approach to opportunity discovery by establishing an effective, robust process for supplying and assessing ideas: we introduced the *problem* and *solution* space, supported by the *framing of ideas* and *problems*, along with the evaluation team that applies a robust scoring model to assess ideas and route them to the most appropriate paths. These bring a major advancement in the organization's ability to *spot opportunities* and take the right next steps. However, considering the pace of change in our era, additional improvements are needed in order to streamline the opportunity discovery process and make it truly continuous, fast, and scalable: in the era of AI, *innovating sporadically*, based on certain events, short-term programs, and a "manual" approach to opportunity discovery, is not enough to keep products and brands competitive. This is due to two main factors.

First, it is *the rapidly transforming environment* driven by the unprecedented pace of technological advancements of our times, particularly artificial intelligence. We are already witnessing the early stages of an extraordinary market transformation—both in scale and intensity—that will fundamentally reshape entire industries and markets in the coming years. Many products will be transformed or even replaced by AI agents, while others will have to redefine their offerings to differentiate from agentic AI services. At the same time, the demand for certain skills will drop dramatically, while new ones will emerge. Smart companies will pivot and adapt; others will be left behind and vanish. During this rapid, large-scale transformation, it is easy to be displaced, miss opportunities, or suffer massive opportunity costs due to inertia and a lack of readiness to act on great ideas. In such a dynamic and rapidly evolving environment, businesses must be vigilant, constantly seeking new opportunities, and prepared to make the right move when the next significant opportunity arises. To survive in this new reality, companies need to put innovation at their core and adopt *a smart, always-on opportunity discovery system.*

Second, it is the intensified and unpredictable competition. Instant access to knowledge and intelligence enables smaller companies and start-ups to enter domains that were previously inaccessible due to *knowledge barriers*. Established companies will be facing continuous, intense, and new forms of asymmetrical competition from small teams that leverage open access to knowledge and intelligence via AI services. Start-ups and individual developers can now leverage AI to rapidly develop sophisticated capabilities that previously required R&D investments and specialized talent. Asymmetry, in this context, means new competitors can emerge quickly from unexpected directions: With AI, everyone can access great ideas and obtain good-enough "advisory" on implementing them and all at negligible cost. Especially when it comes to digital solutions, these disruption scenarios could be led by tiny start-ups or even single-person companies: in our era, a product visionary with general technical skills and a great product concept in mind can use a few powerful AI assistants, code generators, and cloud services to build, launch, and grow products that would otherwise require entire teams to get them to the MVP stage. This makes the entire market extremely dynamic: the competition will soon be set at a new level, and there will be an increasing number of start-ups disrupting the market and threatening established players and business models. The rules of engagement are changing, and the true competitive advantage of a company is its ability to spot opportunities fast and pursue them effectively—its readiness to discover, experiment, and pivot at scale and a fast pace.

With the rise of AI, *expertise* is becoming a commodity, while innovation tools, methods, and patterns are already more accessible than ever. Take, for example, the case of building a functional prototyping of an app or a website. This would normally require a product architect to capture and convert requirements into a well-defined concept. The product architect would then work with a UX designer and a team of software developers to build the prototype—a process that realistically could take several days or weeks. You can now do the same in an hour or two on your own: anyone with a clear product vision can use commercial, inexpensive services like ChatGPT or Claude to frame a product concept, visualize, and prototype it—using only natural language.

Considering the above, the "always-on" mode of innovation I've been describing in the first edition of this book is more important than ever: the ability to spot opportunities, validate them quickly, and pursue them with speed and agility must be injected into the "operating system" of every company. Organizations should no longer view innovation as a nice-to-have—it has become a critical business priority. To stay competitive in this AI-driven reality, you need a systematic and optimized approach to innovation. Companies must shift from a discrete, event-based approach to discovering opportunities to a continuous, always-on process powered by the latest technologies.

Ironically, the very factor driving broader market disruption—artificial intelligence—can also help companies prepare to face it. AI empowers a company's ability to innovate and can boost most functions of the typical corporate innovation engine. More specifically, AI can be a great *innovator*, *evaluator*, *researcher*, *orchestrator*, *communicator*, *collaborator*, and *thought partner*, helping your company establish a truly ongoing opportunity discovery process.

AI is already a very capable innovator. I've been using AI extensively in the innovation and product discovery process, and its performance as an innovator is outstanding: What could previously take long and expensive brainstorming sessions to achieve can now be done in seconds. In contrast to legacy innovation management systems, which use structured forms and rigid processes to intake ideas, in the GenAI-powered world, ideas come *naturally*—they may be generated instantly as a response to a brief prompt from the user or via a natural conversation between the ideator and the AI, during which the AI collects the various pieces and gradually synthesizes one or more ideas matching the context of the discussion. Even when the generated ideas require further editing, AI makes the process extremely fast and effective, as it can instantly suggest and implement improvements based on user feedback.

Moreover, properly configured AI services, with the right context and good prompts, can create ideas in bulk, all packaged with consistency, using the idea framing template presented earlier in this chapter. AI can also generate ideas in a passive mode—e.g., when accessing transcribed video calls, collaboration chats, or document uploads or by monitoring a collaboration board, such as Miro, Mural, or Lucid. The AI then picks the signals and converts the draft, evolving content into thematic packages of well-structured, consistent ideas.

AI's ability to act as a great ideator makes the ideation process more accessible and ubiquitous. However, having ideas flowing from multiple directions can introduce challenges in managing them effectively. To address the risk of an idea overload and the "noise" that this would bring, we introduce two additional innovation roles for AI: the *orchestrator* of the ideation process and the *evaluator* of ideas.

The following describes how the manually operated opportunity discovery process can be boosted by integrating AI Agents across various innovation roles.

6.3.1 The AI Innovator: AI Ideates and Evaluates Ideas

AI can effectively contribute to the ideation process in various ways, including creating and managing ideas, finding, matching, analyzing, and summarizing them.

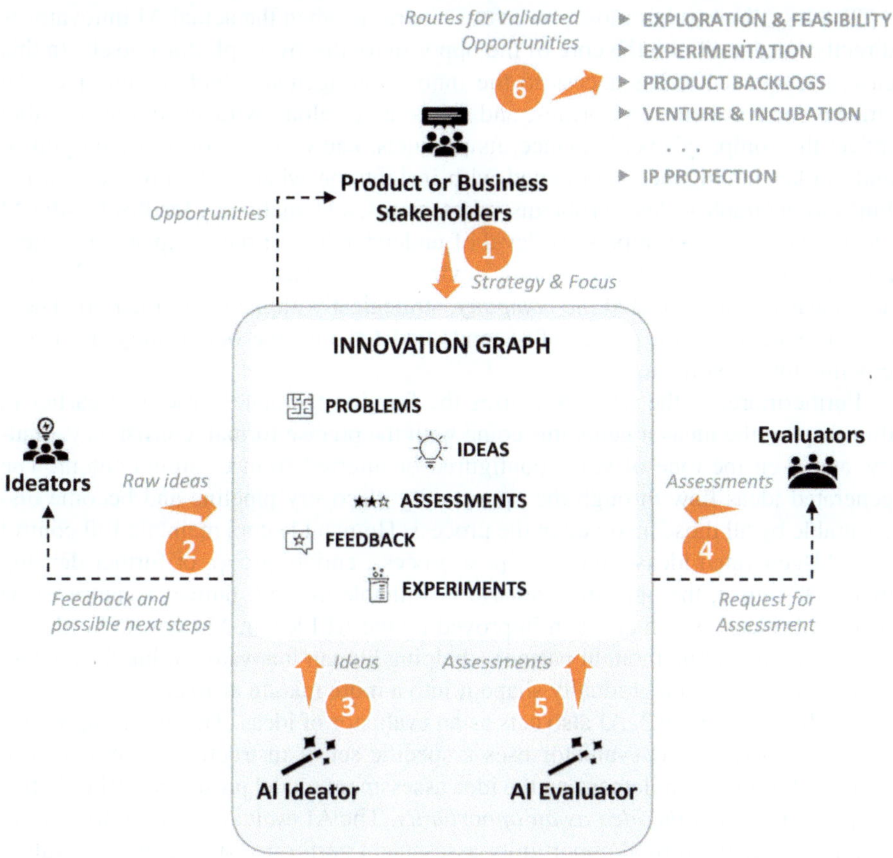

Fig. 6.3 The AI-powered opportunity discovery platform

Moreover, it can assess ideas and thus help the evaluators spot opportunities faster and with less effort. This sets the basis for a superior AI-powered opportunity discovery capability that can drive massive value for the company.

Figure 6.3 presents an expanded view of the opportunity discovery platform introduced earlier in this chapter, featuring two additional actors: the *AI ideator* and the *AI evaluator*. While these may sound like scenarios from the future, they are perfectly feasible with the current state of the art. I have led the implementation of this model in commercial products, where AI serves as the primary, proactive ideator and effective *opportunity evaluator*. Here is how it works.

The most obvious scenario is when the innovator utilizes the AI ideator to create new ideas—e.g., when an employee asks a commercial AI service, such as ChatGPT or Claude, to generate ideas about a specific problem. In this case, it is the human innovator who submits the AI-generated ideas into the opportunity discovery system. The submission of ideas triggers various advanced background operations—e.g., *novelty check*, *semantic linking* of ideas, and more—all powered by AI, which are covered later in this chapter.

The less obvious but most powerful scenario is when the actual AI innovator is directly integrated into the core of the opportunity discovery platform itself. In this case, the AI ideator has access to the innovation agenda, which summarizes the strategy, active themes, priorities, and focus areas, along with select datasets that reflect the company's performance, its products, known issues or user pain points, and market intelligence. Combined with insights on what is already there in the Innovation Graph—ideas, problems, assessments, and qualitative feedback—the AI ideator can obtain an impressive level of understanding of the company, its trajectory, and the dynamic of its economic environment and use it to generate truly valuable ideas that are *novel to the company*, strategically aligned, and focused. These can be generated in a matter of seconds and fed into the opportunity discovery pipeline for assessment.

Furthermore, as the AI ideator uses the framing templates described earlier in this chapter, the ideas it generates come with the precise format, consistency, quality, and even the tone of voice configured or inferred from existing content. The generated ideas flow through the opportunity discovery pipeline and become discoverable by all those involved in the process. Human ideators maintain full control over AI-generated ideas—they can post-process, enrich, group, or further develop them. Of course, the opposite scenario is valuable as well: human ideators shape their draft ideas, which are then improved by the AI Ideator. Moreover, AI plays a role as an innovation thought partner—helping human innovators think through all aspects of an idea and gradually shape it into a more mature artifact.

As shown in Fig. 6.3, AI also acts as an evaluator of ideas. This is an impressive scenario where the AI evaluator uses a specific set of instructions—an advanced system of prompts implementing the idea assessment model presented earlier in this chapter—to *assess the idea as an opportunity*. The AI evaluator is used to support and accelerate the formal opportunity assessment performed by the human evaluators. In more advanced cases, the AI evaluator autonomously assesses ideas and may also orchestrate a series of independent assessments by the evaluation team. When a sufficient number of assessments are performed, the AI analyzes and aggregates the results in the form of an *opportunity narrative*, presenting the strengths and weaknesses of the idea and recommending the next best steps. In another case, the AI evaluator is there as an additional "voice"—an extra member of the core evaluation team. This is a collaborative scenario where human evaluators discuss with the AI evaluator—they collaborate and eventually get more clarity on the AI-generated assessment and the reasoning behind it; they provide feedback to the AI evaluator and challenge aspects of the assessment or share additional context.

In an even more advanced setup, multiple AI evaluators bring different perspectives or personalities to evaluate the potential of an idea from their unique viewpoints. For example, the *AI investor* assesses the idea with an emphasis on monetization, unit economics, and the expected financial performance. At the same time, an *AI product manager* examines the same idea, emphasizing user needs and how it can effectively meet those needs.

The evaluation team can be expanded further by incorporating the voice of the customer into the evaluation process. It is feasible to configure AIs that "think" and "behave" as those well-understood customer personas used by product teams across the organization. Each *AI persona* is built upon accumulated organizational knowledge and insights, including data from user research, identified pain points, and typical user profiles. AI personas participate in the evaluation process, examining ideas from their perspective and contributing assessments, feedback, or even specific asks.

This Agentic AI innovation system is intelligent enough to detect patterns and significant deviations among the multiple assessment scores of a given idea. When conflicting views are detected among the evaluations, the AI agent may trigger additional steps such as further discussions or assessments. Ultimately, all the assessments from both human and AI evaluators contribute to an overall *Opportunity Score* and the creation of the *Opportunity Narrative*, which includes a recommended *action plan* about the idea.

The opportunity discovery loop eventually produces *flagged opportunities* that are presented to the stakeholders for further exploration of potential next steps. Based on the nature of the opportunity and the associated *uncertainties*, stakeholders may assign it to a specific *opportunity portfolio* for further exploration by the corresponding team.

For example, an opportunity for an ambitious new product typically comes with increased uncertainty. Hence, it may be added to the "New Ventures'" portfolio with the intent to validate it through experimentation. This initiates a validation process led by the opportunity validation team that collects Real-World Evidence (RWE) about the idea's potential and its "unknowns." After validation is completed and the collected real-world evidence provides confidence in the potential of the flagged opportunity, the opportunity realization team (Venture Studio) steps in to convert it into a minimum viable product (MVP), build it, launch it, and drive growth toward achieving product-market fit.

If, in another example, the opportunity targets a new feature of an existing product and it is relatively "safe," then it may be added to the backlog of the corresponding product *for consideration* by the product manager. Similarly, an idea may be added to the "IP Portfolio" to be discovered by the legal team for IP filing—e.g., if it is a novel, non-obvious, and valuable technical improvement of the current state of the art.

This AI-powered approach can accelerate the opportunity discovery process and make it ultra-productive and scalable. If properly configured with the right technologies and human support, it can provide a smooth, fast, always-on opportunity discovery platform optimized to generate remarkable opportunities at scale. Moreover, AI reduces the costs associated with generating, evaluating, and handling ideas, as well as the administration of the entire process. Specifically, in the evaluation process, when a strong positive correlation is observed between AI assessments and human assessments, the process can gradually rely more on AI and repurpose the core evaluation team toward more advanced scenarios and decision-making. However, keeping humans in the loop is essential, not only in terms of reliability and robustness of the assessments but also in terms of continual improvement of the AI Ideator—helping them "learn" what ideas are favored by the company and what are not and then use these signals to further improve the qualities of the ideas it generates.

But beyond scalability, speed, and efficiency, this AI-powered, Human-In-The-Loop (HITL) Opportunity Discovery process is an open, accessible, and inclusive process that encourages diverse perspectives and makes spotting opportunities more accurate and robust.

While these may sound futuristic, they are already here. I have engineered solutions featuring both the AI innovator and the AI evaluator, and I have seen them performing extremely well in real-world, demanding innovation scenarios. Solutions like these will soon be adopted by those truly innovative companies, regardless of their size, industry, or type of services offered. However, to run smoothly, the opportunity discovery platform requires additional "smart" elements and features that can handle complexities and operate at scale and fast pace, as described below.

6.3.2 AI Maintains a Corpus of High-Quality, Novel Ideas

Typically, the "classic" approach to idea management suffers from various content quality issues and limitations regarding the discovery and distribution of ideas. Old-school innovation management systems often allow free-form idea descriptors, which introduce inconsistencies and challenges in managing the corpus of ideas. The lack of consistency in articulating ideas leads to various problems including duplication and ineffective idea classification, which impact the overall performance of the innovation process. Moreover, such systems are typically less connected to corporate data sources, thereby failing to leverage the broader *business context* to enhance ideation, evaluation, and opportunity discovery.

Artificial intelligence is making a massive impact in this direction as well. It powers a smart *idea intake* process—the *steps* and *validations* performed before an idea becomes available in the opportunity discovery system. The most significant improvement that AI brings to this process is the *novelty check* of a draft idea—where *novelty* is used here as "new to the company." Consider, for example, a user editing a new idea or describing it to AI. Even at editing time, the user is notified about similar ideas found in the Innovation Graph or related initiatives and projects across the organization. This just-in-time check *prevents duplication* of ideas and *guides the innovator* through smart suggestions on whom to contact to learn more and how the idea could complement existing efforts. This *internal novelty check* is smart enough to identify the source of overlap—e.g., it may be *the problem that the user is attempting to solve* that is already known—not the proposed *solution*.

Furthermore, AI provides the user with an executive summary that explains how existing ideas are relevant and presents an overview of their status, including feedback, learnings, and impact, along with the originators and contributors of these ideas. This way, the ideator can easily obtain a single view of related activities across the company and connect with the right teams. In another scenario, the ideator may discover ideas that are complementary or solve the same problem in an entirely different way. This acts as an additional point of inspiration for the ideator and encourages networking with individuals and teams that have worked on those related ideas.

The above process can minimize the problem of "duplicates" or highly overlapping ideas, which otherwise would be a significant challenge, especially when ideating at scale. Following the submission of an idea, AI brings additional value by "understanding" and enriching its content: it adds smart tags that create associations with named entities, companies' products, features, teams, or departments and may recommend potential next steps, such as *to file a patent* or to consider a *new feature* for one of the company's products.

This way, AI further accelerates the intake process, allowing increased volumes of high-quality ideas to flow smoothly and, most importantly, with consistency, high quality, improved discoverability, and lower operational costs. It also enhances the opportunity discovery process, as it significantly reduces the effort and processing cycles of the idea evaluation team; this is because the ideas that reach the point of evaluation are novel to the company and are consistently framed using the template described previously in this chapter.

Using the latest AI technologies, the *novelty check* could go beyond the boundaries of the company: with proper integrations and a powerful AI-powered semantic analyzer, the opportunity discovery platform could query the "global state of the art" via published patents from offices worldwide, research, and knowledge hubs, in the context of a given idea—leading to an *indication* about the level of novelty of the idea—how new the idea is *to the world*.

A similar intake experience guides the user in creating valid, insightful problem statements using the problem-framing template. Through this process, the innovator obtains an instant overview of existing ideas that attempt to address aspects of the newly created problem.

6.3.3 AI Powers the Innovation Graph

A rich corpus of high-quality ideas and problems sets the basis for more advanced opportunity discovery scenarios. Instead of treating ideas or problems as independent items, you may think of them as part of *an extensive network*. This network links ideas to problems, other ideas, and a range of additional innovation assets. AI plays a major role in maintaining this network by identifying links based on semantic relationships among ideas, problems, and content throughout the organization. This forms a powerful *Innovation Graph* that connects ideas, problems, strategies, priorities, products, business experiments, goals, and market intelligence and provides multiple entry points for opportunity discovery.

For example, to illustrate how ideas can be interlinked, two ideas may be *complementary*: when combined, they provide *a better way* to solve *the same* problem. In another scenario, certain ideas could be *competitive*: each trying to solve *the same* problem but *in a different way*. AI identifies and maintains such relationships within the Innovation Graph based on the degree of semantic similarity of the content. The most characteristic relationship types among ideas are summarized as follows:

- **An idea extends another idea**: This occurs when two ideas *partially* address the *same* aspect of the *same* problem and have an *increased combined effectiveness.* For example, idea A is evaluated as less effective than idea B, but the two combined can provide a better solution.
- **An idea overlaps with another idea**: This is the case when the two ideas address the *same* aspect of the *same* problem in a *similar* way. When the overlap is nearly complete, the involved ideas can be treated as duplicates.
- **An idea competes with another idea**: Two or more ideas *compete* when they attempt to solve the *same* aspect of the *same* problem in a *different* way.
- **An idea complements another idea**: Two ideas *complement* each other when they address *different* aspects of *the same* problem. When combined, such ideas are expected to provide a *better overall solution* to the problem.

Such relationships convert the traditional "idea database" notion into a superior innovation store—the Innovation Graph: *an evolving network* of problems, ideas, insights, and resources from various systems within the organization. The graph is an advanced *innovation knowledge management system* that enables powerful discovery and traversal scenarios and makes the company's innovation process smarter and more strategic. The Innovation Graph is invaluable for building smart user experiences on top of your organization's innovation content and feeding AI systems in the context of continuous improvement and learning.

6.3.4 AI Learns from Everlasting Ideas

Companies tend to abandon ideas that are not actionable in the short term. After all, it may not be apparent how a "rejected" or a non-actionable idea can be valuable to the innovation process. From a strategic point of view, though, there are clear ways that rejected or abandoned ideas can provide significant value to innovation.

"Forgetting" unused ideas is a missed opportunity to shape a long-term memory of the ideas the organization has explored and the associated decisions. A detailed history of all the ideas ever captured and considered within the company lays the groundwork for a powerful opportunity discovery system. Considering AI's effectiveness in searching, synthesizing, summarizing, and presenting content, the entire population of ideas ever produced can remain active, discoverable, and potentially useful without creating *noise* or administration burden. My advice to companies is never to delete or archive ideas or problems. Instead, it is valuable to keep them in a single, centralized "Ideas Store" or, ideally, in the Innovation Graph. Assuming a good design and smart AI integrations, old ideas can be beneficial, especially when they have unfavorable evaluation outcomes or real-world data from experimentation initiatives. The "keep everything" strategy brings various advantages that are especially important in the AI era:

1. **"Unfavorable" ideas provide learning opportunities**: Maintaining those ideas that didn't receive positive, actionable feedback contributes to the formation of a

special type of knowledge, as these ideas may have interesting learnings, stories, and metadata attached. They may reference insightful experiments, bold decisions, interesting debates, or other information and insights regarding the reasoning and the justification of the decisions. Such ideas provide additional strong signals to both AI and human innovators on what to avoid, what to expand upon, and why. This is a valuable context for all the AI agents mentioned throughout this chapter.

2. **Keeping all ideas enables a powerful, "internal novelty checker:"** A new idea that enters the opportunity discovery platform is automatically checked for novelty against *all ideas*. When a new idea is matched with an existing, unfavorable one, the ideator is notified and informed about the learnings and the rationale behind the previous results and is asked to reconsider the submission. This way, the opportunity discovery platform leverages existing, unfavorable ideas to maintain high-quality content without duplication while also informing ideators and helping them focus their innovation energy on new concepts.
3. **It enables the reconsideration of ideas in a new context**: The assessment of an idea might differ depending on the context and the intent for which it is evaluated. For example, the result could vary when the idea is assessed as a *potential product feature* versus an *opportunity for intellectual property (IP) protection*. The Innovation Graph supports prioritization by intent, allowing ideas to be reconsidered in a new context. Beyond intent, the assessment of an idea depends on the rapidly changing global environment. When viewed through the lens of an updated innovation agenda and the latest technological advancements, market dynamics, and evolving consumer trends, previous idea decisions may appear obsolete or even irrational. In light of new evidence, strategy, or market intelligence, an old "unfavorable" concept may be viewed as a high-potential, top-priority opportunity. Moreover, considering the fast pace of technological innovation, the assessment of any given idea might be less relevant or even out-of-date in a matter of months: an idea just characterized as very expensive or not feasible can prove to be a promising and perfectly feasible concept in just a few months' time. What people perceive as a "limited potential" idea now could be a great one that is ahead of its time or not assessed in the right context. As the technological landscape evolves and business priorities change, such ideas may become relevant, discovered by AI, and "naturally" appear again in search results, summaries, or flagged and communicated as opportunities.
4. **It improves the innovation culture**: Treating ideas as *everlasting* and discoverable not only allows rediscovering "forgotten" opportunities in the future but also allows a better narrative to idea owners: instead of communicating the idea assessment result as "not selected" or "archived," the message could emphasize that the idea is only less relevant or feasible *at the moment of evaluation*: ideators know that their ideas remain active, ready to be re-discovered in the right context, at the right time.

The above are just some of the characteristic ways that AI disrupts the opportunity discovery process of modern corporations. With the right implementation, this

AI-powered opportunity discovery platform can effectively manage large volumes of ideas while also reducing operational costs.

However, what we described above is only the beginning. As AI agents become even more capable of processing both organizational and ecosystem data, their impact on the innovation process will be radical. Ultimately, the AI revolution will give rise to a superior opportunity discovery platform that operates autonomously and generates ideas proactively—as described in the following.

6.4 Autonomous, AI-Driven Opportunity Discovery

In the following sections, we delve deeper into how artificial intelligence can further streamline the opportunity discovery function of a company, making it an *always-on, autonomous* process. In this mode, the AI becomes the *orchestrator*, operating an "infinite discovery loop"—a continuous improvement thread with the objective of increasing the rate of actionable opportunities as assessed by evaluators and business leaders within the organization.

As visualized in Fig. 6.4, the autonomous discovery process leverages all the components mentioned so far—including the *Innovation Graph*, the *idea assessment model*, and the AI agents: the AI ideator, who can generate novel ideas in the context of the company, and the AI evaluator, who can assess ideas based on the idea assessment model. It also introduces two new ones: the *orchestrator* and the *market radar* AI agents.

The AI orchestrator agent triggers unattended opportunity discovery loops that use the company's operational context and innovation agenda to generate ideas and flag high-potential opportunities. Each loop may output opportunities as identified by the AI evaluator and appended to the Innovation Graph. The AI orchestrator notifies relevant stakeholders within the company or exposes the opportunities via an opportunity portfolio or through the *Opportunity Board*, where business leaders regularly join to review, discuss, and assess fresh opportunities identified by the AI. This is a learning process in which, in every iteration, the system not only spots opportunities but also learns, adapts, and improves. The AI orchestrator keeps the process up and running and ensures that performance is continually improved. It knows when there are remarkable opportunities to bring to a forum of human experts and also when there are changes in the innovation agenda that need to be fed into the "autonomous opportunity discovery system."

The market radar AI agent uses open-source intelligence to produce insights about market developments and competitor moves. It operates autonomously and knows when new insights must be injected into the opportunity discovery process and daily agendas.

All the AI services in this system, including the market radar, ideator, and evaluator, operate independently as true AI agents: they have their own objectives, success criteria, and a certain amount of autonomy in decision-making and performing predefined actions. But they are always under the orchestrator's direction, who can also modify the "local" objectives of the independent AIs. Furthermore, the entire

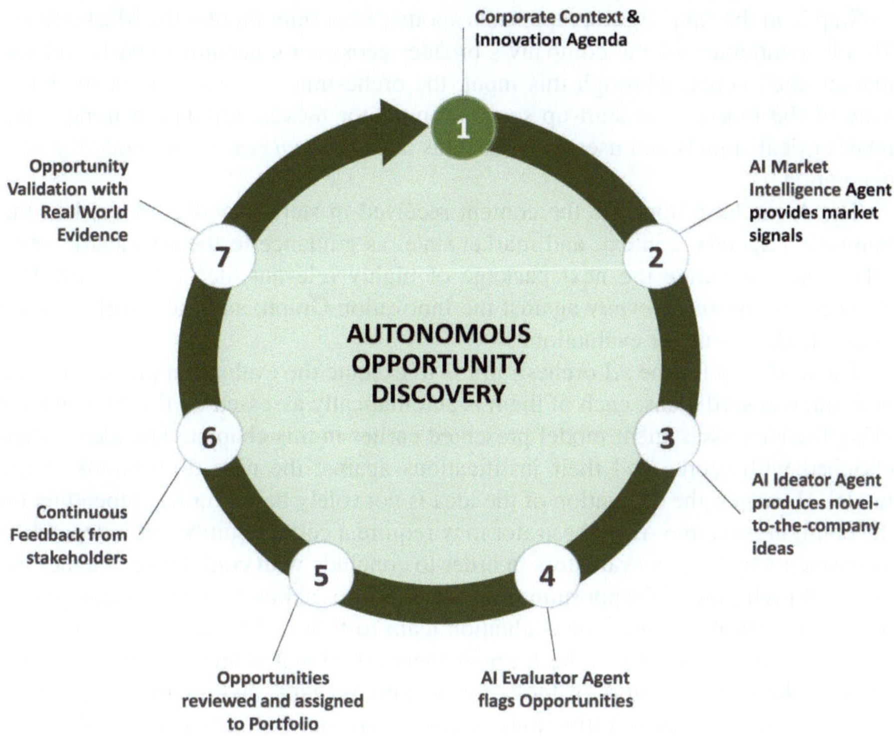

Fig. 6.4 The AI-powered autonomous opportunity discovery process

system and each of the AI agents operate under the human-in-the-loop principle, with a solid mechanism that ensures ongoing monitoring and feedback from humans, along with a statistical comparison of the effectiveness of agent versus human-made decisions. The following briefly describes the steps of the orchestrator, along with the key inputs and outputs. Note that, with the right architecture, each of these steps would require just minutes to run.

As shown in Fig. 6.4, the process begins with the AI orchestrator processing the innovation agenda, which provides the latest strategy and innovation focus, including the major problems to be solved. Moreover, it receives the corporate context, which summarizes the company's marketing plans, financial and product performance, and commercial offerings, including descriptions of products, solutions, and services. It can even include product plans, product feedback, or insights generated about product performance—e.g., user engagement, CSAT, NPS, etc. Simply put, the orchestrator has sufficient knowledge about the company to guide the opportunity discovery process in the right direction. The update of the corporate context is done automatically by connecting to the pre-configured internal data systems, consuming reliable reports and datasets, and processing the latest files available in specific content stores.

Step 2, in the same figure, represents another important input—the Market state. This is a summary of the company's broader ecosystem, accompanied by related market intelligence. Through this input, the orchestrator "learns" about the latest state of the market, the start-up scene, competitor moves, reputation trends, and other critical signals and uses these insights as *additional context* to guide the idea generation.

The AI orchestrator uses the content received in steps 1 and 2 above, i.e., the innovation agenda, context, and market state, as guidance to the AI ideator when asking it to generate the next package of highly relevant ideas. These are then checked for *internal novelty* against the Innovation Graph, and the novel ones are placed in the queue for evaluation.

The next step for the AI orchestrator is to execute the evaluation process for the new, unprocessed ideas: each of them is automatically assessed by the AI evaluator using the idea assessment model presented earlier in this chapter. The idea is then enriched with scores and their justifications against the nine dimensions of the model. However, the evaluation of the idea is not solely based on AI: depending on the configuration, the AI orchestrator may require a certain number of independent assessments by human evaluators in order to conclude with confidence whether the idea is a high-potential opportunity or not. If additional assessments are required, the AI orchestrator invites the evaluation team to follow the standard process and provide them. As the AI orchestrator gathers additional scores and justifications from the human evaluators, it looks for deviations, gaps, and alternative perspectives that might be used to fine-tune or even revise its own assessment. When the evaluation of the idea is robust—e.g., the opportunity score of the idea is above a *threshold*, and there is increased *confidence* about this score—the idea gets assigned to one of the *Opportunity Portfolios* that are visible to the innovation team and the leadership of the company (step 5 in Fig. 6.4).

Following this process, opportunities are discovered autonomously, regularly, or triggered by internal or external events or activities and presented to the company for evaluation. A forum of senior individuals—such as business leaders or evaluators—can then provide signals, detailed feedback, or even guidance for reframing opportunities, thereby guiding the opportunity discovery system and helping it further improve. This constitutes an additional stream of feedback, which, when combined with the evaluators' assessments, powers the continuous improvement of the opportunity discovery process. In every next iteration, the AI takes into consideration the accumulated feedback and uses it to produce better ideas and attempt to hit its objectives.

As opportunities are discovered throughout the company, senior stakeholders may decide to forward select ones to the opportunity validation process and obtain *Real-World Evidence* (RWE) about their potential. The validation team may then conduct experiments that capture valuable data and produce insights, which are subsequently fed back to the opportunity discovery system—thus closing the loop and further empowering the learning aspect of the discovery process by integrating real user engagement data and feedback.

The Agentic AI opportunity discovery system continues to learn even from live, in-market products. By integrating feedback loops, the platform gains access to invaluable insights about user engagement and product performance. For example, the platform may identify opportunities for incremental innovation regarding a live, in-market product triggered by the actual user engagement patterns and other signals coming directly through the embedded feedback loops. In such cases, the discovery platform associates the live product performance patterns with the initial master idea, enabling special retro-analysis that compares initial hypotheses and expectations with real-world performance data. This defines an additional source of learning for both the AI and the organization.

6.5 The AI Sandbox: Designing for Security and Privacy

The possibilities with AI innovation agents are endless. With access to corporate information, such as strategic plans, product roadmaps, product performance, and customer analytics, AI can create powerful opportunities for innovation. However, this comes with significant risks. If not properly configured and managed, these systems could potentially expose sensitive information or, worse, if not strongly secured, compromise the company's innovation or other assets. Without proper safeguards, the benefits of having such a smart innovation system could turn into a significant threat.

Operating an AI Innovation Sandbox is a good strategy to address these risks. Organizations can create isolated computing environments for innovation AIs with carefully controlled data and content feeds, strict access control, and intelligent monitoring systems, allowing AI agents to work with sensitive content in a safe and secure manner. However, to secure smart AI agents, extra measures are needed—beyond the typical data anonymization and standard security strategies. Given that AI agents are able to *perform operations*, there should be strict controls about *what* they can do and *if and how they are allowed to communicate with other systems*, both within the organization and the outside world: imagine a hacked AI agent that silently performs additional operations beyond the ones it was initially configured for.

To prevent catastrophic scenarios like the one described above—AI agents being *hacked*, *misused*, or *misbehaving*—businesses need to implement a modern, layered security approach that combines strong security practices with AI-specific safeguards. The basis of this approach is limiting the AI's access to only necessary systems and data, e.g., via well-defined Model Context Protocol (MCP) servers, and also isolating it in controlled environments while monitoring its actions through detailed logging. Privacy-preserving technologies, such as differential privacy, federated learning, and advanced cryptographic techniques, enable AI models to learn from sensitive data while protecting both the raw data and the insights derived from it. Models should be encrypted, access controlled, and continually tested against adversarial attacks to ensure their security. Robust monitoring systems should be in place, capturing all operations, along with automatic scanning for potential privacy violations and "kill switches" for immediate termination of threads if anomalies or unexpected behaviors are detected. There must be special mechanisms to block manipulation, and critical decisions should always involve human oversight—through a solid Human-in-the-Loop implementation. Secure deployment pipelines, regular security testing, and solid governance policies must be in place to ensure the system remains trustworthy. Securing AI agents is not just about technology; it is about responsible risk management.

By implementing these sandboxed environments, organizations can leverage the transformative potential of AI-powered innovation while protecting their most valuable data assets and strategic content.

Opportunity Validation: Testing Concepts with Real-World Evidence

7

Innovation needs *novelty*, and novelty brings *unknowns*. Uncertainty and risk are, by definition, at the core of the innovation process and are present in every truly innovative concept.

The discovery process presented in the previous chapter is designed to identify opportunities with confidence through a robust assessment process performed by various domain experts and AI evaluators. However, even those handpicked opportunities come with *known* or *unknown* "unknowns" that can prove to be critical success factors. That's the nature of innovation: novelty introduces uncertainty, which, if not understood and handled, becomes an additional source of risk.

Especially in an innovation context, projects and initiatives often embed *silent assumptions* that can prove to be the primary points of failure. I call them *silent* since they are not documented or called out as *assumptions*. Instead, they manifest as *beliefs* and *certainties* that things will work and evolve in a particular way or that users will behave and respond according to specific patterns. Silent assumptions may manifest as over-optimistic expectations and wishful thinking, which are adopted as given, obvious, or normal without being challenged or tested. For instance, a team may be making decisions that rely on unchallenged statements about the effectiveness of a solution, the demand for a product, the underlying user needs, the pricing model, adoption and growth patterns, reactions from the competition, and more. I've seen many cases of impressive business plans that relied heavily on unchallenged assumptions.

When assumptions are left unaddressed, new types of risks emerge. A decision to build a product without testing the underlying assumptions can lead to a failure that incurs financial, cultural, and also opportunity costs. Although innovation is all about *fail-fast* and *fail-safe*, this type of failure *can* and *must* be avoided. Failure is accepted as a learning opportunity when it occurs due to uncontrolled uncertainties or when we deliberately take a risk that we understand and weigh as part of the broader innovation portfolio. Failures that originate from *untested assumptions* denote *poor execution* and must be prevented. When the underlying assumptions are

G. Krasadakis, *Innovation Mode 2.0*,
https://doi.org/10.1007/978-3-032-00835-0_7

identified early in the process and converted into testable hypotheses, the team can launch experimentation initiatives and gather real-world data that reduces uncertainty and sheds light on their validity. This may invalidate the entire business model of the opportunity, unveil the need for additional investments, or indicate a pivot or a different implementation path. In such cases, based on real-world insights, the company can make informed decisions to either adapt its approach or de-prioritize the specific opportunity and invest time and resources in a different one. This "intelligence" and agility at the start of the process boost innovation and increase the bandwidth for truly high-potential opportunities.

Project teams can easily fall into the silent assumption trap simply because these beliefs tend to originate from within—internal biases, a sense of authority in the team, and overconfidence in their skills or limited understanding of the experimentation method and how it delivers value. Very often, silent assumptions hide in plain sight, embedded in the ways of thinking and the collaboration patterns, and they are not even recognized or called out. Beliefs like "users will naturally share this content" or "customers will pay a premium for this feature" should instantly raise a red flag.

This is why a process and mindset that explicitly surface these assumptions and convert them into *testable hypotheses* are so valuable in the innovation process. The ability of the organization to run a fast and scalable *opportunity validation process* is a key success factor for innovation as it increases the chances of investing in the right opportunities at the right time and, consequently, the likelihood of driving impactful innovations in the market.

To establish the experimentation method, the organization needs a superior opportunity validation capability—part of the framework presented in Chap. 4. This is a service operated by a highly skilled, cross-disciplinary team with expertise in experimentation and rapid prototyping. The team is viewed as a trusted partner within the organization, applying the scientific approach and robust methodologies to rapidly validate opportunities and provide critical insights for informed decisions. As defined here, the purpose of the opportunity validation function is to provide *actionable advice* on deciding *if*, *how*, and *when* to pursue an opportunity further. What distinguishes this validation function from a consulting or advisory service is that it uses real-world evidence to ground its recommendations. They apply well-defined methods, tools, and reusable, consistent experimental patterns to obtain data that is then translated into actionable insights and, eventually, valuable recommendations and strategies.

Along with tools, systems, and capabilities that enable experimentation at scale, a cultural shift is also required: A truly innovative environment encourages people to challenge assumptions, identify risks, and handle them as testable hypotheses that join the experimentation pipeline. This aligns with what is described in Chap. 3 as the core quality of the true innovator: the ability to challenge the status quo and question stated or implied assumptions. The most successful innovators and product people I've worked with are skeptical even of their own assumptions and thus always willing to take an experimental approach to validate or invalidate their own beliefs before committing significant resources.

7.1 Risk vs. Uncertainty

Very often, I hear people referring to the validation or experimentation process as *derisking*. However, I find this terminology misleading as it implies two things: first, that the validation process attempts to *eliminate* risks, which isn't a realistic goal in an innovation context, and, second, that it *solely focuses on risks.*

Opportunity validation is not about derisking; it is about concluding with confidence whether the real potential of the opportunity outweighs acceptable risks. Certain risks may be avoidable or manageable, while others may be intrinsic, embedded in the opportunity, or too expensive to handle. There are situations where certain risks might be acceptable after considering the *likelihood of their occurrence*, the *impact* they would have, and the *cost of mitigating or avoiding them.* Ironically, when teams attempt to control all identified risks, they introduce a new one: adding bureaucracy and additional workloads that undermine the objective of the innovation function itself by making things slow and expensive. Considering the above, I would frame the purpose of the opportunity validation function as developing a form of *risk intelligence*—a framework for understanding the source, nature, likelihood, and potential impact of the risks associated with an opportunity and producing efficient strategies to mitigate them.

Moreover, the opportunity validation function is not only about risks; it is *also* about *uncertainties*, which is another misleading aspect of the risk discussion: people often use *risk* and *uncertainty* interchangeably. The two terms represent fundamentally different concepts and require distinct handling and strategies.

7.1.1 Risks, Defined

Risks are possibilities that have a negative impact or outcome that is known or can be estimated with some confidence. For example, the risk of certain technical failures in a product can be identified upfront and assessed in terms of likelihood and impact.

During opportunity validation, risks are proactively identified and assessed to inform mitigation strategies, evaluate alternatives, or determine whether certain risks can be accepted. A decision to take a particular risk or not is based on the context, the probability of its occurrence, the severity of its impact, and the cost of mitigating or avoiding it.

Risks can be technological, financial, reputational, regulatory, and legal—to name a few. For example, for a business opportunity that aims to build and launch a new product or service in the market, typical categories may include:

- **Product effectiveness risk**: The risk is that the product does not adequately solve the target problem or deliver the expected outcomes for users.
- **Market adoption risk**: The risk of lower-than-anticipated customer adoption or demand due to weak product-market fit, poor positioning, insufficient marketing, or low perceived value.

- **Technical reliability risk**: The risk is that the product fails to meet required performance, stability, or reliability levels under real-world conditions.
- **Competitive response risk**: The risk of competitors reacting aggressively through pricing, marketing, or feature development, thus limiting the growth potential.
- **Scalability risk**: The risk is that the product fails to support the growing demand due to system, infrastructure, or operational capacity limitations.
- **Regulatory compliance risk**: These are risks of non-compliance with legal, industry, or regional regulations, which could result in penalties, restrictions, or reputational damage.
- **Reputational risk**: The risk of damaging the brand of a product or the corporate image due to an unreliable or poorly performing product, a perceived failure, or a lack of compliance with specific regulatory requirements.

In all the above cases, the risks are known, and the team can assess them very early in the process: they estimate the likelihood of occurrence, the impact if it occurs, and the cost of avoiding or mitigating the risk. If quantifying the risk is not feasible - e.g. in the case of a new product concept where insights and prior knowledge are not available, these must be framed as uncertainties to be addressed via experimentation.

As defined earlier in this chapter, silent assumptions introduce a special category of risks: When beliefs about customer behavior, market dynamics, or technological capabilities remain unchallenged or even unnoticed, entire business plans and important decisions may rely on an unstable basis. Unlike identified risks or uncertainties, which are documented and considered, these silent assumptions are blind spots and thus introduce various other risks.

7.1.2 Uncertainties, Defined

Uncertainties represent situations with limited information where not all possible outcomes can be explored or defined and the probability of occurrence of certain events cannot be estimated. These are the "unknown unknowns" typically found in a novel concept. In the context of launching a new product, service, or business venture, common sources of uncertainty include:

- **User behavior uncertainty**: This refers to the unpredictability of how users will perceive, adopt, and use a novel product, especially one that offers an entirely new experience. It may be tough or even impossible to articulate such uncertainties in advance. Such uncertainties require real-world user interaction data that can uncover the actual behaviors, needs, and use cases, many of which may not be evident through pre-launch research alone.
- **Technological uncertainty**: This includes uncertainties related to the effect of emerging technologies or unforeseen innovations that may impact a product, disrupt a market, or cancel competitive advantages.
- **Societal and cultural uncertainty**: Uncertainties in this category relate to how evolving social norms, cultural values, or lifestyles may shift customer needs or change what is considered desirable.

- **Ecosystem and market dynamics**: Unpredictable shifts in how partners, platforms, regulators, and competitors interact within the ecosystem could disrupt value chains, incentives, and customer access.
- **Regulatory and geopolitical uncertainty**: Sudden changes in regulation, trade policy, or political conditions, such as tariffs, bans, or sanctions, can disrupt go-to-market plans or operational feasibility.

Unlike conventional risks, uncertainties cannot be addressed through planning or forecasting. Instead, they require two approaches: *experimentation* for uncertainties you can test (user behavior, pricing models, features etc.), and *organizational agility* and readiness to pivot for those you cannot (regulatory shifts, geopolitical events, technological disruptions).

The opportunity validation team represents a special organizational capability designed to navigate this complex landscape of risks, uncertainties, and silent assumptions. Unlike traditional risk management teams that apply standard frameworks uniformly, this team distinguishes between quantifiable risks, explorable uncertainties, and hidden assumptions - applying probabilistic assessment, experimentation, or discovery techniques as appropriate. Their expertise lies in recognizing which type of unknown they're facing and selecting the right approach for each case. They engage early in the process to map the landscape of unknowns and prepare tailored responses: mitigation for risks, experiments for uncertainties, and pivot paths for when assumptions fail.

7.2 Business Experimentation

Business experimentation is the practice of testing hypotheses by obtaining insights and signals under real-world conditions. It acknowledges that innovation inherently involves uncertainty and provides a systematic way to address it through targeted learning activities. The objective is to help draw evidence-based conclusions supported by the collected data and inform related decisions.

Business experiments involve actual customers interacting with realistic prototypes in real market conditions. Typically, the prototype is an inexpensive implementation of a product concept. In this context, however, it is not just a draft implementation presenting "how a product would look." When used to validate product opportunities, prototypes are laser-focused, functional implementations explicitly designed to test the predefined hypotheses. They reflect the essence of the underlying concept and provide the means for capturing *implicit* and *explicit* data. Implicit data refers to information captured while users interact with the prototype, such as telemetry events, which are then used to obtain patterns on how users engage and interact with the prototype and its features. Explicit data refers to direct feedback from users—qualitative data captured from within the product, online forms, or through post-experiment surveys. The data collected is used both to test the predefined hypotheses and to obtain general insights about the potential of the concept being tested. The provisioning of the prototype to real users happens in a controlled manner through a defined process, targeting a carefully designed audience.

There are various other types of experiments and methods used to address the uncertainty around a new product concept or a business opportunity. The following summarizes the most characteristic ones, grouped by the "hosting scenario" of the experiment, e.g., whether it is delivered from within a product or not.

7.2.1 Types of Experiments

Business experimentation can address various types of opportunities, including new products, enhancements to existing products, novel customer experiences, business models, pricing strategies, and more. These generally fall into two experimentation approaches.

When improvements refer to existing products, teams can run experiments *within the live product* itself. Typically, this involves releasing an experimental feature to a small, randomly selected subset of users. This approach allows for direct testing in the actual production environment with real users.

Opportunities may also be tested *independently of existing products.* This approach suggests developing and hosting stand-alone prototypes—not as part of existing products. It is practical when the concept refers to an entirely new form factor or when testing it through an existing, live product would introduce risks of disrupting it. The latter is typically a concern when the feature is complex or requires adaptations across multiple aspects of the product.

In-Product Experiments: These are delivered from within a live product to a subset of randomly selected users who experience either *variations* of a feature or new, *experimental* ones. The system tracks user engagement statistics, which are then used to compute the performance at the feature or variant level. This leads to the "winning" ones that become part of the product and eventually are launched to the entire user base. Most characteristic cases include:

- **A/B testing**: A method that uses two or more versions of a feature or experience to determine which performs better. It requires formal hypotheses and aims to achieve statistically significant results.
- **Multivariate testing**: A method that simultaneously evaluates multiple elements and their variations to determine the optimal combination. It also requires formal hypotheses and aims to achieve statistical significance in identifying the best combination of factors.
- **Feature experiments**: This method involves altering a product's functional characteristics by adding or removing features for specific subsets of users to determine how certain KPIs and the overall product performance are impacted.
- **Pricing experiments**: This involves testing different price points or models to find an optimal pricing scheme or strategy.

Out-of-Product Experiments: These are experiments conducted independently of existing products, either because the core product does not exist or as a strategic choice to avoid disrupting a live product when heavy, demanding experimentation activities are required. Typical cases are:

- **Using functional prototypes**: These are experiments that expose a realistic prototype to a randomly selected group of users. The prototype in this context is carefully designed to reflect the essence of the envisioned product and support the testing of the stated hypotheses. Experiments through functional prototypes can provide powerful insights via telemetry and direct customer feedback.
- **Using "smoke testing**:" These are typically simple, stand-alone digital experiences, such as landing web pages, that create the *illusion* of a product. They attempt to measure market interest before building the actual product. It can provide interesting signals, but it is risky to make decisions based on this alone.
- **Using "service simulation**:" This category includes methods that deliver a user-facing experience that relies on manual human effort behind the scenes. In one case, the delivered experience *simulates* the intended functionality and allows the user to interact with an early instance of the envisioned product, e.g., Wizard of Oz Testing. In other cases, human involvement is transparent—end-users are aware that the underlying service is provided by humans as a way to better understand their needs and how they engage with the concept, e.g., Concierge Testing.

Selecting the right class of experiments is not always straightforward. The team must examine the specifics of the concept and the nature of the associated uncertainties to figure out not only the type of experiment but also its scale—e.g., the *size of the audience* and the *duration of the experiment*. For example, a novel product concept may bring uncertainties about the expected *market demand*. Or a product team might be unsure about the expected *level of adoption* of a radically different UX paradigm. The former can be approached by Smoke Tests and related experiments, while the latter is a typical case of building a realistic, functional prototype and using it to test the UX with real users. In most cases, though, the team must identify the right strategy that possibly combines more than one method.

Functional prototypes often provide the richest data and most actionable insights for opportunity validation, making them one of the most powerful experimentation approaches. While the rest of the chapter focuses on business experiments based on functional prototypes, the core experimentation principles described throughout apply to all cases.

7.2.2 Business Experiment Framing Template

A *business experiment* is a structured method for testing predefined hypotheses through data collected via a controlled, repeatable process involving a defined audience.

The business experiment represents a crucial element in the corporate innovation function and a thinking framework that is central to the experimentation mindset. Adopting a framework for defining business experiments opens up the experimentation process by encouraging people in the organization to frame and submit their experiment proposals. As with problems and ideas, business experiments are stored in the Innovation Graph and become discoverable, not only by the opportunity discovery team but also by product teams who may pick promising business experiments directly from there and initiate the experimentation process. To establish the business experiment as a central component in the innovation process, people need to understand how it is defined and how each specific element should be set. The following describes the structure and can be used as a template that helps people articulate solid business experiment proposals.

1. **Experiment Identifiers**: This is the signature of the experiment. It includes a unique *identifier* along with an informative *title*, *codename*, *description*, and *ownership*—the name of the experiment owner.
2. **Learning Goals**: When designing an experiment, it is essential to explicitly state your learning goals—what the team is trying to learn through the experiment. You may define it as a narrative that sets the general context but also in a structured way, using a list of well-defined hypotheses, as described in the following:
   - **Learning objective**: A free-form description of what the team is trying to learn through this experiment.
   - **Product reference**: The experiment may refer to an existing product or be part of a broader initiative. These should be stated here.
   - **Hypothesis list**: This is the core of the experiment—a list of structured hypotheses, each described by a *name*, *description,* and *thresholds* against one or more *metrics* representing the *belief*, the assumption. They may also contain a reference to a *baseline* for a more effective comparison.
   - **Success criteria**: This is the definition of success in terms of learning objectives—describing when the experiment as a learning mechanism delivered on its purpose, regardless of the validation or invalidation of the hypotheses. An experiment that provides strong real-world evidence to "kill" an opportunity is a successful one.
3. **Form Factor**: To achieve the learning goals, you need to identify the right *medium* and carefully consider how it will collect the required data for testing the stated hypotheses. The form factor indicates the type of experience that will be served to the audience—what the participants will be asked to interact with. It could be one or more of the following:
   - **Landing page**: A webpage that presents an offering, such as a product or a service, in a realistic way in order to capture *signals of interest* by measuring visitor engagement. This can provide valuable insights very early in the process—before making any investments in actual development.
   - **Clickable prototype**: A basic approximation of the user interface of a product, allowing potential customers to interact with core elements and flows of the envisioned solution; typically used to gather feedback on usability and perceived value.

- **Functional prototype**: An inexpensive working version of the envisioned product that enables users to experience its basic features. In an experimentation context, it is used to capture interaction data and direct feedback.
- **Physical prototype**: A draft version of a physical product concept enabling hands-on testing of form, fit, and function with target users in realistic environments. It may also come as a *connected physical prototype*, where electronic components and connectivity allow for smart user experiences.
- **Proof of concept (PoC)**: A small-scale implementation of specific aspects of the envisioned product or solution. It demonstrates technical feasibility and validates particular hypotheses regarding the product's functionality.

4. **Audience**: The audience is a crucial component of the experiment. It must be carefully designed as a list of demographics, each associated with a channel and a communication strategy, with at least the following attributes:
   - **Named demographic**: A name and a brief description of the demographic.
   - **Channel**: This is the communication channel through which users can be contacted and potentially acquired.
   - **Target sample size**: The target number of users for the particular demographic.
5. **Planning**: The experiment plan captures the critical dates, along with the *launch* and *end conditions*, enabling a single timeline for the experiment. Its key attributes are:
   - **Launch check list**: As experiments can be complicated with multiple aspects such as communication readiness, content approval, prototype readiness, and various stakeholders, it is essential to define a "go live checklist" that is part of the experiment setup and visible to all involved parties.
   - **Launch date**: This is the planned start date of the experiment.
   - **End date**: The intended end date of the experiment.
   - **End conditions**: This is a set of conditions over specific performance metrics that signal the early termination of an experiment. For example, when the experiment underperforms and fails to hit the engagement targets, even after interventions from the team.
6. **Decisions**: When designing a business experiment, it is vital to think a few steps ahead—what could or should happen on success or failure and who the key stakeholders are. A description of the potential next steps for each of the primary outcomes is essential since it can bring alignment and clarity across the experiment's stakeholders and contributors. Upon completing the experiment, this may be enriched with the actual decisions and their justifications.

This structured approach enables teams to identify critical hypotheses and focus on the riskiest assumptions associated with a new concept. Defining the key elements of a business experiment early in the process, including the learning objectives and essential hypotheses to be tested, streamlines both the preparation and the execution of the experiment. At the same time, it helps maintain a repository of consistently defined experiment proposals that live in the Innovation Graph.

7.2.3 What Is a Successful Business Experiment?

A business experiment is successful when it serves its purpose: to provide clarity through real-world data and inform important decisions about the opportunity, regardless of whether the decision is positive or negative. In contrast, an experiment based on a prototype that does not accurately reflect the key characteristics of the concept or does not deliver them in a concise way to the users may lead to indecisive situations that require additional iterations, further prototyping efforts, and increasing costs. Even worse, a poorly designed prototype may be misleading: when its users experience a poor UX, they may reflect negatively not *on the concept* but on the ineffective UX of the prototype. This may lead to results that reflect the *effectiveness of the prototype* rather than the *value of the concept being prototyped.*

7.3 Opportunity Validation: The Process

Opportunity validation can be thought of as a well-defined service that adds significant value to the organization by enhancing its ability to *invest in the right opportunities*. The service exists to provide smart recommendations regarding the next steps of an opportunity, backed by real-world evidence, user research insights, and deep expertise.

Following a request to validate an opportunity, the team designs and conducts business experiments aiming to produce actionable insights and knowledge about the future of the concept. The process is fast and agile, with the stakeholders engaged and ready to provide answers, review deliverables, and inform decisions throughout the validation thread.

The section below outlines the team's activities in the various phases depicted in Fig. 7.1, from the *intake of the request* for validation to the *presentation of the validation report.*

1. **Understand Risks and Uncertainties**: Following a validation request, the first step is to determine if the opportunity is described with clarity. The process requires a holistic presentation of the opportunity—the vision, the core concept, target users, uncertainties and big unknowns, the intended form factors, and the market. If properly framed, the team examines the opportunity further with a focus on identifying the risks, uncertainties, and implied assumptions, which leads to one of the essential deliverables: the *list of hypotheses* that require testing—each describing specific metrics, their critical values, and how the overall business opportunity depends on them—how they can impact success. The validation team may consult the market intelligence team to obtain the latest intel from the market and the competitive landscape. Similarly, they may request a quick technical feasibility assessment, as this could be a source of potential risks, e.g., if the underlying technology is not yet mature. The team utilizes this diverse set of inputs along with their cross-disciplinary expertise and accumulated knowledge to frame the opportunity and quantify its business potential.

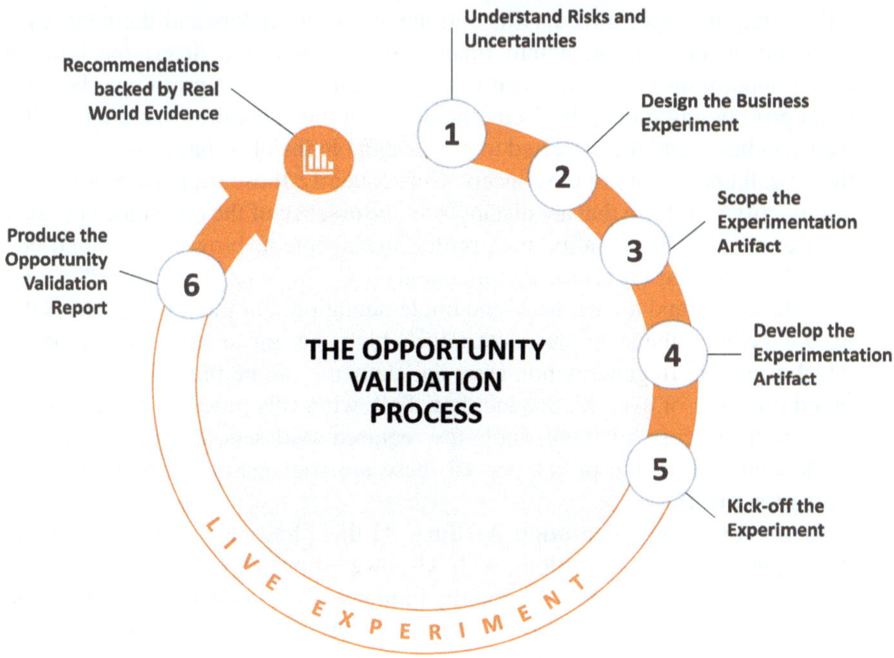

Fig. 7.1 The opportunity validation process

Upon completing this preliminary assessment, the team has a clear view of the type of business experimentation that should be applied. Occasionally, they may conclude that there are no big unknowns and that no further experimentation is required. In all cases, the output of this step is a standardized preliminary Opportunity Assessment Report.

2. **Design the Business Experiment**: When experimentation is needed, the team examines the nature of the opportunity, the referenced problem, the involved personas, and the proposed form factor to identify the best experimentation avenue—*how* to obtain insights and real-world evidence. They explore options ranging from presenting the opportunity to internal forums to get early feedback, organizing focus groups where people interact with a basic prototype, or launching more sophisticated experiments based on realistic, functional prototypes exposed to a controlled audience. The business experiment design must clearly address the following four elements: (a) the hypotheses to be tested; (b) the type of artifact to be used to test the hypotheses and how it can provide the required data; (c) the audience—synthesis and how it will be acquired, e.g., by invite or via campaigns, etc.; and (d) the timeline for how long the experiment will be running and any termination conditions.
3. **Scope the Experimentation Artifact**: This is a critical step that shapes the artifact to be used as the vehicle for the business experiment—what the audience will interact with, e.g., an app, website, or interactive content. Framing the right

artifact requires specialized skills and the ability to understand the nuances of the concept, decompose it into functional elements, and determine how the stated hypotheses can be mapped to certain features in the prototype. When in rapid prototyping mode, the focus should be on those features that are linked to the hypotheses and are expected to bring valuable insights that can help address the overall uncertainty of the concept. Consequently, those supportive or secondary functions or those that are distant from the essence of the envisioned product, such as search functionality, user profile management, browsing content, etc., should be handled via reusable components if available or implemented quickly with static data and no real back-end implementation. For those components that need to be built, the team must determine which ones make sense to develop and which to mock. In general, non-essential elements can be implemented quickly based on static or even hardcoded data. Following this process, the team organizes a clear scope of work, spots the required skill sets, and plans for rapid implementation of the prototype. All these are packaged into the opportunity validation manifest.

4. **Develop the Experimentation Artifact**: At this phase, the team uses internal development capabilities, along with AI-powered prototype builders, or works with contractors and vendors to rapidly implement the defined prototype. Either in-house or with a partner, the team follows a robust, agile process that is optimized for speed. In this rapid prototyping setting, coding standards and process formalities are often less valued in favor of fast decisions, clever work-arounds, and rapid results. The focus is shifting from *code quality* to *user experience*: the team prioritizes a great UX that can effectively support the testing of hypotheses, while behind the scenes, there may be technical conventions, static data, and other limitations that are safe to accept considering the limited scale and lifespan of the prototype. The cross-disciplinary team triggers parallel working threads across the layers of the prototype, including data modeling, content creation, UI/UX design, and communication programs, among others. Sponsors and stakeholders stay in the loop to answer questions and provide frequent feedback. Once this step is complete, the prototype is hosted and presented to stakeholders for initial feedback.
5. **Run the Business Experiment**: This phase begins with a “readiness to launch” check: The team ensures that the artifact is tested and available to be shared with the audience, communication programs are established, the required content is approved, and all necessary operational processes are defined. When readiness is confirmed, the team launches the defined campaigns to acquire users according to the audience specification. Campaigns may be inviting existing users or new ones via social media campaigns or employees within the company. These can be combined to run in parallel or in sequence as part of the staged release, for example, starting internally and opening it up depending on specific conditions. As users start engaging with the prototype, the team monitors a special dashboard that presents essential metrics and aspects of engagement, such as the *experiment funnel*, which shows how users flow from initial interaction to sign-up and actual engagement. It also includes insights about the utilization of spe-

cific features and presents how metrics related to the hypotheses evolve. As users provide feedback, sentiment scores, along with satisfaction signals such as NPS, are also presented in the same single Experiment Performance Scorecard. Moreover, AI automatically generates a narrative presenting users' views on the experience offered by the prototype and the value they get from it. Depending on the insights, the team may intervene to fix issues or make decisions about the business experiment itself, e.g., if there is limited participation, they find ways to onboard additional waves of participants, or if there is no sufficient engagement to produce valid results, they may put the experiment on hold or identify the root cause and attempt to fix it.

6. **Produce the Opportunity Validation Report**: This is about interpreting the real-world data collected during the live phase of the experiment. The team analyzes the predefined hypotheses and their validity in light of the real-world data. Based on objective metrics and KPIs, some may be validated, while others may be far from reality. However, these are not binary checks—usually, there is elasticity, and any deviation between anticipated and actual values triggers further analysis and interpretation. The team applies its deep knowledge in product development to set the right perspective in explaining the results and flag critical issues as well as the major strengths of the opportunity, as supported by the data collected. They use these to identify the recommended next steps, which, in the best-case scenario, would be *to pursue the opportunity* backed by a suggested action plan. The least favorable scenario would be a suggestion to kill or park it. The recommendation may come between these extremes—e.g., suggesting to pivot in a particular direction or performing an additional experimentation cycle. Regardless of the exact outcome, the team compiles and presents the opportunity validation report that provides a solid justification of the suggestions and how they are supported by actual data.

At the end of this process, the prototype is listed in the catalog of functional prototypes, and the accompanying assets, including the prototype manifest, performance report, documents, and references, are stored in the Innovation Graph and become available through the Innovation Portal.

The direct benefits of the opportunity validation service are apparent: when an opportunity is parked based on real-world data, the organization releases expensive resources that can be used to pursue other high-potential opportunities. When the formal recommendation is to proceed with implementing the concept, the company benefits by pursuing the opportunity with confidence, speed, and more realistic expectations, as well as increased awareness of its potential. The insights generated during the business experimentation process play a crucial role in further developing the product as they contribute to knowledge and baselines that can be used in product design, business planning, and performance measurement.

At a higher level, the opportunity validation service enhances the organization's ability to *pursue the right opportunities* by increasing its bandwidth to explore ideas and make informed decisions regarding development investments. Moreover, it helps grow a healthy culture of innovation by involving the community of innovators and putting the experimentation mindset at the frontline, with real examples and actionable outcomes. In the long run, *it changes the way the company designs and builds products, systems, and services*.

The opportunity validation service can bring value across sectors regardless of the type of products, services, or experiences involved. The actual setup, however, could be different to match specific needs. For example, in an innovation center, the prototyping function may be separated from the validation function to allow for parallelism, thereby helping optimize the *prototype-validate-decide* cycle. In this configuration, the prototyping service is responsible for building prototypes, which are then handed over to the validation service to undergo the proper experimentation process.

The success of the service is measured across throughput, speed, rates of successful experiments delivered, and quality of advice provided.

7.3.1 The Validation Team: Synthesis, Responsibilities, Expertise

The opportunity validation process presents distinctive challenges that require an exceptionally skilled, cross-disciplinary team. To perform well, the team needs a core of experts from various domains, including hands-on technologists with diverse backgrounds and skills in software engineering, cloud engineers, DevOps engineers, product managers, market analysts, venture builders, UX designers, and user research. This special team demonstrates a deep understanding of the technology landscape, the market, and the underlying trends and dynamics. They are the best in the organization to examine opportunities from the right perspective and shape effective validation strategies. They maintain a network of additional domain experts within the company for just-in-time advice, such as legal guidance on the regulatory aspects of an opportunity. The team is accountable for running the service and providing timely, quality advice backed by real-world evidence. More specifically, the team offers expertise in all the following:

1. Spotting risks, uncertainties, and silent assumptions and converting them to testable hypotheses
2. Identifying the best validation path for each opportunity and the types of experiments that should be used
3. Designing experiments or research methods for testing the identified hypotheses
4. Identifying the right audiences for the experiments or research methods
5. Scoping, designing, and building inexpensive prototypes—digital or physical
6. Running business experiments and interpreting real-world data
7. Compiling insightful reports with actionable recommendations regarding the strengths, weaknesses, and next best steps for the opportunity
8. Educating the organization regarding experimentation
9. Operating and improving the opportunity validation function

The opportunity validation team also produces and shares knowledge, best practices, and rapid prototyping strategies with the entire organization—they lead the efforts to adopt an experimentation mindset and data-driven decision-making.

The team is powered by the latest technology and AI, enabling them to rapidly build sophisticated prototypes. They are experts in defining prototypes wisely—setting the scope and feature set so that they effectively support the validation of the hypotheses. Once the team has clarity on what the prototype looks like and the features it should contain, they proceed with wireframing, design, and a high-level architecture. Then, they identify existing components that can be reused from their library of assets, e.g., UI components, datasets, models, and APIs. For the rest—the new elements to be developed—they use smart AI-powered development systems that produce high-quality software components in a matter of minutes. They follow a component-based approach for the AI development process, and whenever the generated component meets the specs, they integrate its code into the main prototype. This strategy makes the prototyping process faster than ever: the elapsed time from having a clear scope to releasing the prototype to users can drop to days, or even hours, literally. For example, assuming the prototype features are well defined, they could be developed using AI coding tools, such as Claude or Cursor, in parallel and then merged into the "host" application, the prototype. The team masters this AI-powered process and invests in introducing AI software development patterns, tools, and frameworks that further streamline the production of high-quality prototypes as a means of executing business experiments.

On top of the smart, AI-powered prototype development process, the team uses some advanced tools for designing target groups in the customer base, running campaigns that support the user lifecycle across experiments, monitoring and presenting their performance in a unified way, and exploring and processing the accumulated data, insights, and feedback across experiments.

To scale and increase its capacity, the team connects with internal talent, who, depending on their bandwidth, contribute to the prototyping process with just-in-time assignments. Moreover, the team maintains a network of trusted partners and vendors who provide software engineers on demand helping during peak periods for opportunity validation.

The following provides a deeper examination of prototypes in the context of business experimentation.

7.4 Building Prototypes

A prototype is an *intentionally incomplete* instance of a product that can be used as a means of exploration, experimentation, and learning. This is a straightforward definition. However, to better understand the importance of prototyping in business experimentation, we first need to explain how it differs from other forms of product realization, such as the minimum viable product (MVP), Proof of Concept (PoC), and static prototypes. This clarification is necessary, considering how frequently the above terms are misused or used interchangeably. While they are related, there are important nuances that can prove to be critical when defining innovation initiatives and managing expectations with stakeholders. To clarify the differences, we introduce the notions of *functional completeness* and *production readiness*.

When building a software solution, there is always a target deliverable of a specific *form factor*, such as a mobile application, a wearable device, or a web experience, and a scope that outlines what the application or system will be capable of doing. We may expand this thinking by introducing the notions of *production readiness* and *functional completeness*. These dimensions help the team achieve clarity regarding the nature and purpose of the software deliverable.

Functional completeness reflects how complete a software product is in terms of the features it contains, compared to the anticipated ones—those that would make the product "complete." When developing a software solution, we can define functional completeness as the percentage of *features that are in scope* for implementation *relative to the total number of features listed in the full product definition.* Alternatively, the comparison could be based on the sum of the estimated *value* instead of the number of features. Functional completeness reflects the nature of a defined software deliverable, helping teams and stakeholders better understand and communicate *what they are building* and *why*.

Production readiness reflects how *ready* the product is to be released in the market. It is defined as the product's *compliance* against a list of "go-live" prerequisites. The conditions that define production readiness vary depending on the nature of the product, the market, the industry, and the regulatory frameworks to which the company must comply. Typically, in situations involving technology products and services, production readiness requires standardization and compliance regarding *security*, *privacy*, *reliability*, and quality of the actual implementation, along with the *scalability* of the back-end system. Additionally, it requires *continuity*, *support*, and availability of an array of services. A measure of production readiness can be derived by examining the production-related non-functional requirements that are in scope versus the complete set of prerequisites of a production system of this class.

We may use functional completeness and production readiness to classify certain types of software artifacts, as visualized in Fig. 7.2. The horizontal axis represents the level of production readiness—where values close to zero indicate *internal use only*, while values close to 100% indicate that the artifact is ready for *general availability*. The vertical axis represents functional completeness: artifacts with a value close to zero may be *static prototypes*—they have no functionality—while those close to 100% are close to being *complete products*, containing most of the functionality of the envisioned product. The overlaid elements correspond to frequently used types of artifacts in an innovation context. As seen in the left-bottom area of this chart, a *functional prototype* is an incomplete instance of a product: it only has a limited number of features—the ones that reflect the essence of the underlying product concept and, when used in the context of a business experiment, those that help with the testing of the hypotheses. In contrast, a minimum viable product, appearing in the upper-central area, has increased functional completeness compared to a *prototype*, although still limited compared to the envisioned "*complete*" *product*.

The following provides the basic definitions of the most important artifacts in the context of product development and experimentation:

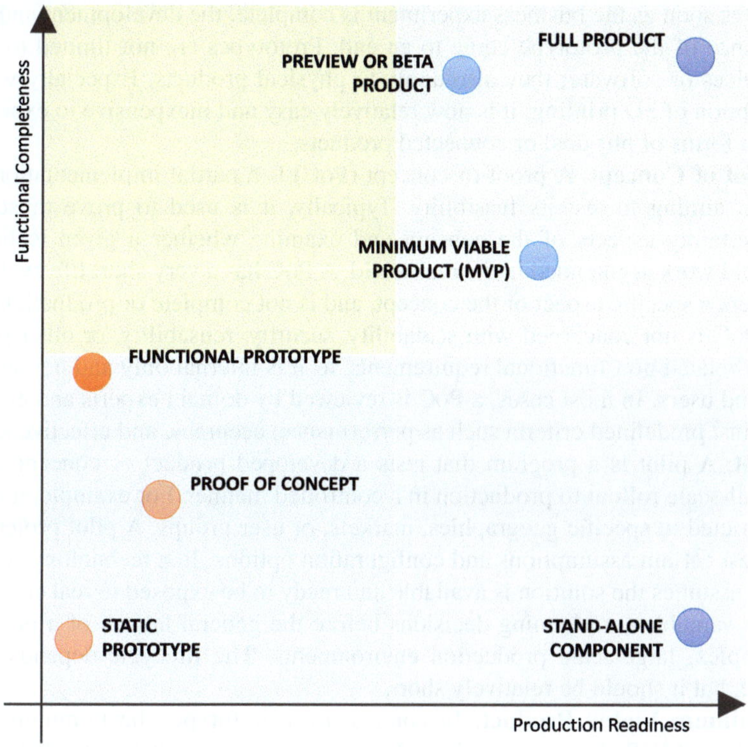

Fig. 7.2 Classification of artifacts based on readiness and functional completeness

1. **Static Prototype**: A static prototype is a non-interactive visual representation of the graphical user interface of the envisioned product. It comes in various levels of fidelity, ranging from wireframes that emphasize structure and information architecture to mockups that feature more polished visual designs, including aesthetics, colors, typography, and imagery. Wireframes, in particular, provide a high-level view of the target digital experience, such as a skeleton of a webpage or a complex workflow or onboarding process. They are very effective in illustrating complex concepts, thereby helping stakeholders, sponsors, and the product team understand the product concept. They are used throughout the product design process—for instance, in innovation workshops, brainstorming sessions, and product discovery sessions—to capture early feedback and inform decisions about features, information architecture, user flows, and other aspects of the product.
2. **Functional Prototype**: A prototype is an intentionally incomplete instance of a product. It is typically used in the product development process to validate concepts before they are planned for implementation. Prototypes are useful as fast and inexpensive realizations of a concept. Although they may look realistic, they come with limited functionality and plenty of conventions. They serve a specific purpose—typically to support a business experiment—and have a short lifecy-

cle: as soon as the business experiment is complete, the development and maintenance of the prototype come to an end. Prototypes are not limited to digital services or software; they also apply to physical products. Especially with the adoption of 3D printing, it is now relatively easy and inexpensive to experiment with forms of physical or connected products.

3. **Proof of Concept**: A proof of concept (PoC) is a partial implementation of an idea, aiming to test its feasibility. Typically, it is used to prove those high-uncertainty aspects of the concept and examine whether a given technology would work as intended in the real world. A PoC has a very short life cycle, only covers a specific aspect of the concept, and is not complete or production ready. A PoC is not concerned with scalability, security, reusability, or other production-related non-functional requirements, as it is internal only and not delivered to end users. In most cases, a PoC is reviewed by domain experts and evaluated against predefined criteria such as performance, accuracy, and effectiveness.
4. **Pilot**: A pilot is a program that tests a developed product or concept using a small-scale rollout to production in a controlled manner. For example, it may be restricted to specific geographies, markets, or user groups. A pilot project aims to test certain assumptions and configuration options. In a technology scenario, this assumes the solution is available and ready to be exposed to real conditions. It is valuable for planning decisions before the general launch of a product in complex, large-scale production environments. The lifecycle depends on the case, but it should be relatively short.
5. **Minimum Viable Product**: In contrast to a prototype, the minimum viable product (MVP) has increased production readiness, as it is intended for real users and customers. Hence, all production-related constraints of a typical commercial product, such as safety, security, availability, and performance, must be adequately addressed. The MVP has limited functionality, according to carefully selected features that are sufficient to solve the core problem and satisfy early customers. In contrast to a prototype that *approximates* the product, the MVP *is* its first instantiation. The MVP is explained in detail in Chap. 8.

All the above are highly relevant to the experimentation and product development process; however, the most important is the functional prototype. The following section explains why and provides principles and guidance on defining and building great prototypes in rapid mode.

7.4.1 Why Prototype?

Prototypes are built as a means of learning and as vehicles for collecting real-world data about the validity of a concept. Prototyping plays a vital role in setting the right focus, providing clarity, and addressing the risks associated with new product development. More specifically, a prototype may bring value in the following ways:

1. **Help drive stakeholder alignment**: A good prototype helps in understanding complex concepts that are otherwise difficult to comprehend. By exploring a

prototype of a complex product concept, people have the opportunity to understand its form factor, gain insight into the experience and interaction patterns, and more accurately estimate its business potential. For example, it is quite challenging to convey an idea about a virtual reality experience that enables analysts to explore multidimensional data in interactive ways. Or a personalized content experience on a mobile device that uses gaze analytics to adapt to the user's behavior. Such concepts cannot be effectively communicated in a descriptive manner. A functional prototype in the above examples enables stakeholders to interact with a realistic instance, gain a shared understanding, and thus help steer the discussion in the right direction.

2. **Power business experimentation**: Prototypes are also the means for addressing the uncertainty of a concept and testing specific hypotheses. A prototype brings significant value when the concept under consideration has increased levels of uncertainty, for instance, when the proposed experience is new to the users, and there is no evidence or signals indicating whether they are ready to adopt it or not. In the previous example, the virtual reality experience may be entirely new to users, meaning the team lacks prior knowledge of what to expect in terms of user engagement. Moreover, there is always the risk that a particular persona or demographic may not be ready or comfortable adopting such experiences. In another hypothetical scenario, a digital assistant providing medical advice through voice-driven interactions could still be ahead of its time for a certain target group: would people feel comfortable interacting with a machine over voice? Given the unknowns, a quick experiment featuring a functional prototype of this concept can provide valuable insights into both the technical feasibility of the concept and the expected levels of user engagement.
3. **Enable user research activities**: Prototypes also serve as tools to gather insights directly from users in an interview, usability testing, or focus group setting. In large organizations, this can be achieved by forming internal groups and asking employees to use the prototype and then gathering their thoughts through a micro-questionnaire.
4. **Showcase innovation**: Prototypes can boost the innovation culture, serving as concrete examples of ideas that translate into tangible outcomes. It is a good practice to maintain visual catalogs of functional prototypes and expos where physical or hybrid prototypes are also displayed and available for people to experience. Prototypes can signal the company's commitment to experimenting with new ideas and accepting failure as part of the process.
5. **Accelerate product development**: Prototyping boosts product innovation and the entire product development process. Business experimentation powered by prototypes produces important insights, influences product development decisions, and helps adopt an experimental approach and mindset.

The increased ability of an organization to build and leverage prototypes provides significant value. However, what makes the difference is the ability to do so in *rapid mode*. The following section explains how to establish such a rapid prototyping capability.

7.4.2 Accelerating the Prototyping Process

Rapid prototyping refers to a streamlined process of building prototypes extremely fast. The factors that allow this rapid implementation include expertise, talent, libraries of reusable assets, and implementation frameworks. Additionally, the adoption and proper use of artificial intelligence in various stages of the prototyping process dramatically improves the speed of prototype development.

The following expands on the enablers of the rapid prototyping capability and presents recommendations for establishing it—including frameworks, templates, and a rich inventory of resources such as software components, data services, algorithms, UI elements, and other internal or external assets.

- **Organize a catalog of standardized data objects**: In an era of privacy concerns, the increasing responsibility and regulation over data management practices make *protecting sensitive data* a top priority. On the other hand, prototyping projects require real or realistic data to approximate the target experience in a convincing way. As a result, data-driven projects are frequently blocked or delayed due to the unavailability of data or a lengthy review and approval process before utilizing an existing data source. To overcome this problem, the team can *sample*, *anonymize*, and *package* small samples of real data representing the most common and potentially useful datasets and processes within the organization. A significant step in this direction is the removal or scrambling of personal identifiers or other sensitive data in accordance with global policies and the company's privacy and compliance programs. Once this is done, the safe-to-use, standardized datasets appear in the catalog as reusable data assets labeled as safe and approved for certain use cases. Items in the catalog come with the following information:

    1. **Identifiers**: The name of the data asset, description, source, extraction methods, and time frames
    2. **Verification of compliance**: Indicators of compliance with privacy and related regulations
    3. **Data profiling**: A compact "data demographics" report presenting the key statistical aspects of the dataset
    4. **Intended use and examples**: A list of characteristic use cases that this dataset could power

The above data descriptor makes it easier for teams to find the dataset they need and gain instant confidence in using it: a developer can check the intended use cases and trust the verification compliance indicator to leverage the data without privacy-related concerns. Furthermore, the catalog provides value when the prototype involves machine learning, statistical modeling, training of artificial intelligence algorithms, etc. In such cases, additional private or public datasets with labeled instances and known benchmarks can accelerate the development of predictive models and AI applications. In addition to the anonymized or scrambled real data, artificial datasets may be generated, standardized, and packaged in a similar way. This can be useful when the desired real datasets are not accessible or certain rules prevent their usage. In such cases, the team may replicate the underlying data model and build scripts that generate artificial but realistic records or objects. This process may be sophisticated enough to even reflect the statistical properties of the original dataset.

- **Embrace artificial intelligence as a prototype developer**: The rapid evolution of AI tools has already transformed the prototyping landscape and the broader software development space. Engineers can dramatically accelerate the implementation of functional prototypes by leveraging AI coding assistants to create applications, complete functions, suggest code optimizations, and even build user interfaces. For example, ChatGPT and Claude are already impressive in generating functional code blocks in response to natural language descriptors and specs. The prototyping team of the AI era can work in a hybrid mode: early drafts, application scaffolding, or repetitive code is produced by AI, while skilled engineers refine and integrate everything to ensure a high-quality deliverable that serves its purpose.
- **Maintain a catalog of APIs**: As with data models and datasets, certain prototyping efforts can be accelerated by integrating the right APIs. A collection of well-documented APIs, along with instructions and quick-start guidelines, helps developers discover services and other building blocks that can be used "as is," thereby speeding up the process. These could expose common functionality within the company, ranging from *authentication* and *telemetry* to *data access*, *machine learning models*, *content discovery*, *AI agents*, and more and more. In some cases, APIs can expose real data; in others, they provide static, artificial data objects. The collection should be dynamic to host new services as they are built and delivered for specific prototyping efforts. Each custom API built, if it is considered potentially usable by other apps, should be packaged and released through the catalog. External APIs could also be listed to allow easy integration of third-party services.
- **Maintain a library of reusable software components**: As in the previous cases, this collection contains standardized software components, libraries, scripts, and frameworks that are potentially useful for prototyping work.
- **Provide AI and ML models**: In the era of artificial intelligence, every new application is expected to leverage a form of artificial intelligence or machine learning capability. Although building new AI/ML models could be challenging and time-consuming, integrating standardized models into an application is straightforward. Thus, for prototyping purposes, a rich and well-documented collection of commercial AIs or APIs for internal machine learning models could accelerate the process.
- **Provide user interface libraries**: Typical prototyping initiatives include some form of graphical user interface. Hence, having a rich collection of reusable UI elements accelerates the development of realistic front-end applications, such as

websites, mobile apps, dashboards, etc. The collection may include more specialized UI components, such as data visualizers, dashboard templates, and interactive charts.

- **Streamline DevOps, automation, and monitoring**: Releasing, hosting, and managing a prototype throughout its lifecycle should also be fast and efficient. Frequent prototyping requires a flexible hosting environment with powerful administration tools, such as standardized dashboards and reports, to track the health of hosted prototypes, activity, resources consumed, and issues raised. Additionally, it is essential to have the ability to query the telemetry and feedback database.
- **Leverage third-party services**: The chances are that for many of the components needed for a technology prototype, there are suitable and readily available commercial services or open-source components. Hence, performing an online search for building blocks before starting development is a great practice: an array of resources, from UI controls and APIs to AI services, datasets, images, and labeled content, could all be available, ready to be integrated—either as commercial services or as open-source projects.
- **Offer tools, equipment, and hardware**: Prototyping projects occasionally require special equipment, computer parts, devices, tools, or machinery. These are described as part of the makerspace, which can be thought of as the technology provider for prototyping efforts in the organization.

The above resources can speed up the implementation of prototypes. However, in addition to technical readiness, it is essential to position the prototyping work properly and address related misconceptions: it is not uncommon among developers to view prototyping work as a "throw-away" and thus less important. While the former might be true—code may indeed be thrown away—prototyping is still valuable as a special mode of software development that serves a different purpose than production software: to boost innovation and help the company make better product development and investment decisions.

In contrast to production software development, where engineers must follow strict rules, coding principles, and protocols, rapid prototyping should allow for technical shortcuts, assumptions, and the use of static or artificial data. Software quality may also be approached differently: In the context of rapid prototyping, quality can be redefined with a bias for UX instead of optimized code and architecture. Although inexpensive and incomplete, prototypes must offer a realistic end-user experience; they must be reasonably stable and of decent quality to serve the purpose. However, because the lifecycle of the prototype and the codebase is relatively short, the team should not be overly concerned about best practices and code structure or spend effort on commenting, documentation, or refactoring the codebase. When prototyping in a throw-away mode, it should be acceptable to hard-code and use static data as needed to move faster. Conventions and shortcuts should be accepted when they accelerate the process but without downgrading the overall user experience or imposing security or privacy risks.

7.5 Building Physical Prototypes: The Makerspace

In the first edition of the book, I described a special "makerspace" as a symbol of innovation within the organization: a place where people self-organize and bring their ideas to life through prototyping using the latest technologies. Since then, digital collaboration and remote work have become the norm, which surprisingly further empowers the role of the makerspace. Having a dedicated space for innovation and creative collaboration is more relevant than ever as it encourages remote teams to reconnect in person, innovate, exchange knowledge, and build cross-team networks. Teams join the space to explore ideas, build physical prototypes, and share back their learnings with their core teams and the rest of the organization.

The rise of smart, connected physical products and related technologies further increases the relevance and importance of the makerspace. Innovators can utilize the makerspace to experiment with physical products, connect them to sensors, program them, and explore the possibilities. In a modern makerspace, an idea can become a 3D-printed prototype, which then can be extended with electronics, connected to services, and offer a realistic instance of a "crazy" idea. Innovators can explore the future of intelligent physical products that seamlessly blend hardware with AI capabilities—from autonomous robots that navigate complex home environments to smart appliances that understand their contents and sense their environments.

Beyond tech, though, the makerspace represents a philosophy of experimentation that encourages the exploration of bold ideas. Its true power lies in growing a community of innovators who try new ideas, learn from failures, share their knowledge, and inspire others.

The makerspace provides a safe, specially designed environment, the necessary technology, essential resources, and a comprehensive framework to make prototyping easier and more accessible. It comes in various formats. The standard is a purpose-specific arrangement in the corporate office space—a large-enough room that hosts specialized equipment. What is typically found in a makerspace is a collection of devices, such as 3D scanners and printers, along with tools, raw materials, and other resources to help innovators craft prototypes in a collaborative and safe manner. It can also provide technology components, electronics, hardware, and software to enable the creation of digital and "connected" prototypes. Occasionally, it comes with a more industrial character, for example, when it houses expensive machinery for specialized tasks and operations.

Regardless of the format, a makerspace is where people explore the latest technologies, connect with domain experts, self-organize into teams, and assemble components into functional instances of their ideas. It is a fundamental innovation enabler that plays a vital role in developing a strong culture of innovation, as it encourages people to get familiar with new technologies by making things.

Basic forms of prototyping in the makerspace can be completed in a self-service mode without the need for an operator or a team. People may work independently or form teams just in time to address challenges or pursue random ideas. In other cases, employees may utilize the makerspace to find the expertise they need and request assistance with prototyping their concept. This self-organizing, community-powered approach, built on top of the makerspace, provides flexibility and speed while promoting the cultural aspects of sharing and collaboration. Furthermore, an active makerspace, with energized people in a creative mode, is a perfect example of *innovation in progress*, where people leverage the facility to pursue their big thinking, experiment, and learn. With such visible, concrete examples of innovative behaviors, the makerspace becomes a strong driver of the innovation culture, showcasing how bold ideas can be realized through technology and effective collaboration. With proper communication, it evolves into a symbol of innovation in the organization—the point of reference for creative discussions, technology exploration, and idea exchange.

The makerspace plays a key role in driving general technology awareness by producing knowledge and great content: provided good orchestration, the community of "makers" and innovators can become very active in sharing their expertise through articles, videos, or live sessions. As individuals and teams build their prototypes and interact with new technologies, they share what they learn through the Innovation Portal and other channels. Success stories, functional prototypes, and live demos attract attention and raise the bar of technology understanding in the organization. Moreover, through scheduled workshops, the community introduces the latest devices and technologies and presents how they can add value in the context of the company and its customers.

7.5.1 Makerspace Forms and Variants

Variants of the makerspace concept can be seen across corporations, academic institutions, and educational organizations. While they all provide access to tooling, equipment, and devices with the intention of empowering users to bring ideas to life, they may differ in their setup, functionality, and operating models. In a corporate environment, a makerspace exists to promote creativity and the spirit of experimentation—a goal that can be achieved in various ways and levels of sophistication and through several formats, including the following:

1. The *Build Space* is typically a "lightweight" makerspace. Hosted in a dedicated area within the company, it provides the necessary tools and resources for physical prototyping and team collaboration. The term *lightweight* refers to the equipment provided, denoting that it is easy and safe to use by anyone without the need for specialized operators. People may also find electronics and components such as single-board computers and sensors, along with essential hand tools.
2. The *Tech Space* is similar to the Build Space but with a focus on providing the latest technologies, digital equipment, and high-tech devices. It also fosters the creation of prototypes and provides a collaboration space and utilities but with an emphasis on developing digital applications or hardware-based solutions, such as those leveraging robotics, IoT, AR/VR, etc. As in the build space, no specialized machinery is involved, and hence, no formal operators are required.

3. The *Demo Space* is less "making" and more "demonstrating." It is the place where functional prototypes—either physical or digital—are exposed to a broader audience. The Demo Space is more of an ongoing expo where anyone from the company can interact with prototypes and demos, provide feedback, connect with the teams, and discover ways to learn more.
4. The *Manufacturing Lab* is a more advanced prototyping facility with expensive tools and systems. Typically, it includes machines like CNC and sophisticated robotic equipment. Such a facility is often found in large organizations that need to prototype mature concepts with increased detail and quality using special materials. Manufacturing labs require specialized personnel and have strict safety protocols.

A modern makerspace can combine elements of the above four categories according to the organization's needs and the state of its innovation function. For the purposes of this book, *makerspace* refers to a combination of Tech, Build, and Demo spaces. The Manufacturing Lab is a more advanced option, which, even if available within the company, requires a different operational and governance model.

7.5.2 The Setup, Equipment, and Technology Inventory

A typical makerspace should be based in a large room able to host activities by two or three small teams concurrently. An optimal setup provides enough space for prototyping and small-scale educational and presentation activities. The arrangement of the space is optimized for exploring and discovering resources in a self-service mode. A makerspace supports non-standard collaboration scenarios and creative activities, and as such, it comes with the following special requirements:

1. **Safety**: The makerspace usually hosts equipment, tools, and devices that require users to follow specific rules or attend special training before using them. Therefore, it demands special safety equipment, clear signage, and instructions for the safe exploration and use of devices and tools, as well as restricted access to materials and equipment that require specialized knowledge.
2. **Soundproofing**: The creative process can become noisy in many ways. A makerspace should be able to accommodate these loud scenarios without disrupting the regular flow in the surrounding office space.
3. **Adaptability**: The space should be flexible with an easily configurable layout to support a variety of collaboration scenarios. For example, it should be able to host an intense prototyping activity with drawing on the walls and designing on workbenches, as well as a hands-on technical presentation event with a small live audience. Adaptive furniture, movable walls, storage units, and toolboxes provide quick ways to reshuffle things and adapt the space.
4. **Visibility**: While the makerspace could be isolated in a basement or a remote spot in the corporate office, it should be placed where it attracts attention and inspire people to get involved, explore, learn, and build. Having a well-branded,

literally transparent makerspace at the heart of the building or on a corporate campus is of strategic importance for its success.

The character of the makerspace is reflected in its equipment and inventory. In one instance, the makerspace can be high-tech, full of expensive gadgets, devices, and robots; in another, it may be low-tech, with basic hand tools and equipment that emphasize crafting physical prototypes. These two extremes can be balanced, defining a generic, functional makerspace equipped with technology and tools from the following categories:

1. **Specialized office furniture**: A set of office equipment designed for adaptability, such as movable workbenches, writable walls, and collaboration desks.
2. **Collaboration and presentation systems**: The makerspace must feature connected, interactive screens and video call systems with multiple cameras, enabling hybrid collaboration, broadcasting, and recording of educational sessions or prototyping and hands-on workshops.
3. **Basic tools and equipment**: Tools and equipment such as soldering irons, hand tools, cutters, design desks, cables, connectors, and anything in between are essential for crafting quick physical prototypes.
4. **Electronics**: A range of components, testing equipment, computer parts, single-board computers, IoT sensors, and cameras. These help prototype experiences involving a physical device enhanced by sensors and logic that leverages back-end services, such as an AI API, to offer smart end-user interactions.
5. **3D Printing**: Scanning, editing, and printing in three dimensions are essential capabilities for building physical prototypes. The makerspace must provide 3D scanners that allow users to capture physical objects as digital models, along with specialized software for editing them and 3D printers to materialize the final designs.
6. **Robotics**: This category includes programmable motors, robotic arms, robots, simulators, and the corresponding tools and programming frameworks.
7. **Consumer electronics**: The latest digital devices in the context of the organization. The list may include smartphones, wearables, smart home devices, smart speakers, connected health devices, and more. These are typically needed for developing mobile experiences, prototypes related to IoT, connected home scenarios, and health monitoring systems, among others.
8. **Virtual and augmented reality equipment**: The inventory should include headsets, glasses, and other hardware that allow the exploration of augmented and virtual reality experiences.

The above is only a sample list of what a typical makerspace contains. The exact inventory depends on the context of your innovation agenda. In practice, the list of devices and tools is expected to evolve rapidly in response to new initiatives, business priorities, or the introduction of new technologies and product releases. As the purpose of the makerspace is to allow people to explore the latest technologies before they become mainstream, it has unique needs in terms of supply management. There should be a straightforward method for requesting new devices or equipment, accompanied by a prompt approval process. Requesting new resources should be open to the innovation community, allowing them to submit justified requests for new supplies in the context of specific innovation efforts.

7.5.3 The Makerspace as a Knowledge Hub

The makerspace can be further enhanced by incorporating a digital layer, fostering an active community, and offering a rich educational program. This advanced version goes beyond a purpose-specific room and becomes a knowledge hub, a technology provider, and a platform for community-driven, hands-on educational activities. The digital layer is particularly useful in the era of remote work—it allows people to engage with the activities and the innovation stories happening in the makerspace remotely and asynchronously. The following outlines strategies to connect and repurpose the makerspace as a strategic innovation asset:

1. **Make it accessible, inclusive, and intuitive**: Given that one of the primary goals of the makerspace is to introduce people to the latest technologies and prototyping practices, it should be easily accessible: individuals should feel free to walk in at any time without needing to book the space or request permission. Furthermore, it should be self-service: apart from advanced equipment or tools that require trained personnel, the makerspace should be intuitive, allowing people to explore technologies and try things in a safe manner. There are numerous ways to achieve this, including smart signage in the space or QR codes on devices that point to high-quality content, providing help and inspiration through examples and recommended use cases.
2. **Build a strong brand**: The makerspace should be rich in symbols and references to inspiring stories and achievements, both from within and outside the company. It needs a logo and a mission statement as the signature for anything produced in the makerspace or by its community.
3. **Establish a digital presence**: This is particularly important, especially in the context of the hybrid work model, as it enables people to connect and follow the developments of the makerspace while contributing remotely. The makerspace is represented in a dedicated section in the Innovation Portal and the newsletter, which allows a flow of information and updates on upcoming events, new equipment, innovation success stories, demos, and accomplishments by the community of innovators. In the same section, users can explore the technology inventory, along with related educational materials and stories or examples of how specific devices or technologies are being used. Additionally, the portal presents key people from the makerspace and the associated innovation community, followed by a support area where users find everything they need to get started in the makerspace—from quick start guides, FAQs, and points of contact, along with safety rules, hints, and guidance on how to use the makerspace.

4. **Extend it as a knowledge-sharing hub**: Powered by an active network of innovators, the enhanced makerspace can evolve as a hub for knowledge and talent. As teams experiment with their ideas, they share their achievements and also interesting failures—prototypes, demos, or outcomes from experiments—which become discoverable by the entire organization through the Innovation Portal and other innovation touchpoints. The makerspace can be further extended as a powerful educational platform on prototyping techniques and technology deep dives to promote prototyping as a means of learning and business experimentation.

In this chapter, we covered the opportunity validation function of the organization, which is powered by a strong prototyping capability that allows the organization to make better decisions about flagged opportunities. Using the recommendations and real-world evidence provided by this team, the company eventually proceeds with investments in building and launching real products, following modern, agile product development methods as described in the following chapter.

8 Opportunity Realization: Building MVPs and Driving Growth

The Opportunity Discovery and Validation services presented in the previous chapters boost the company's ability to identify actionable business opportunities. However, the most important piece of the puzzle is the ability to realize the identified opportunities—to develop products and services, bring them to market, and drive rapid growth cycles.

Opportunity realization can occur on an ad hoc basis. For instance, when there is sufficient bandwidth and resources, a product team takes ownership of a validated opportunity and develops and launches the corresponding Minimum Viable Product (MVP). However, this best-effort approach is limited by definition—as typically, product teams are busy implementing existing roadmaps and rarely have sufficient bandwidth to properly lead additional innovation projects. Moreover, they may not have the ideal synthesis, adequate capacity, or the required tools and knowledge to drive rapid innovation cycles.

To boost innovation outcomes, companies need to transition from this ad hoc implementation approach to a "factory" model that enables multiple opportunity realization projects to be executed simultaneously, at speed and scale. The factory approach streamlines product development, allows for parallelism, and makes opportunity realization scalable, flexible, and effective. We call this capability "Opportunity Realization" or "Venture Studio." Its primary purpose is to rapidly build and ship Minimum Viable Products (MVPs) and drive growth via fast, in-market experiments. It makes innovation real by focusing on driving outcomes through in-market innovations. Moreover, opportunity realization seeks more than successful products; it attempts to shape high-potential *business ventures*.

The opportunity realization capability can significantly enhance the organization's ability to innovate, pursue opportunities, and enable wise investment decisions based on real-world data, accumulated knowledge, and market intelligence. It closes the loop of opportunity *discovery*, *validation*, and *realization* (Fig. 8.1).

G. Krasadakis, *Innovation Mode 2.0*,
https://doi.org/10.1007/978-3-032-00835-0_8

Fig. 8.1 The three most essential innovation capabilities

The opportunity realization service is powered by an exceptional cross-functional team optimized to *define*, *build*, *launch*, and *rapidly scale* MVPs toward product-market fit (PMF).

The opportunity realization service delivers significant value to corporate innovation by transforming conceptual opportunities into tangible products and driving their market adoption. The real value, though, is that they can achieve all that in a *streamlined*, *optimal* way: this highly specialized team utilizes a consistent framework for ongoing, data-driven product innovation; they accelerate the process by using proven frameworks and documented knowledge of similar MVP launches, allowing them to achieve unparallel productivity, quality, and speed. Moreover, this team is elastic—they can expand as needed and even create clones to run parallel MVP launches, thus increasing the throughput of the entire innovation function.

Speed is achieved through lean processes, fast decision-making, and, most importantly, through reusability. The team uses an advanced tech stack that allows rapid integration of *reusable software components* and *shared services*, thus dramatically reducing the effort to build new MVPs or enrich existing ones. Furthermore, they apply *experimentation techniques* and leverage a wide array of specialized tools, as well as the latest artificial intelligence models, to accelerate in-product, live innovation cycles. Similarly, they reuse *analytical* and *operational components*, such as those for telemetry, analytics, and customer support functions, thereby further streamlining the operational aspects of in-market MVPs. Depending on the nature of each venture, they also cover additional product needs such as operational, marketing, go-to-market, business model innovation, pricing experimentation, and business development strategies.

The team maintains a rich knowledge base with accumulated learnings gathered across initiatives and in-market experiments—including performance baselines, adoption patterns, and growth "hacks." They leverage data and insights to make fast, informed decisions; they know when to recommend a pivot or to sunset a product based on well-defined performance and adoption metrics. They utilize a playbook of proven methods and well-prepared scripts, which enable the rapid setup of development teams and implementation plans.

Figure 8.2 presents a high-level overview of the product innovation process that powers the Opportunity Realization service. The left part of this chart visualizes the

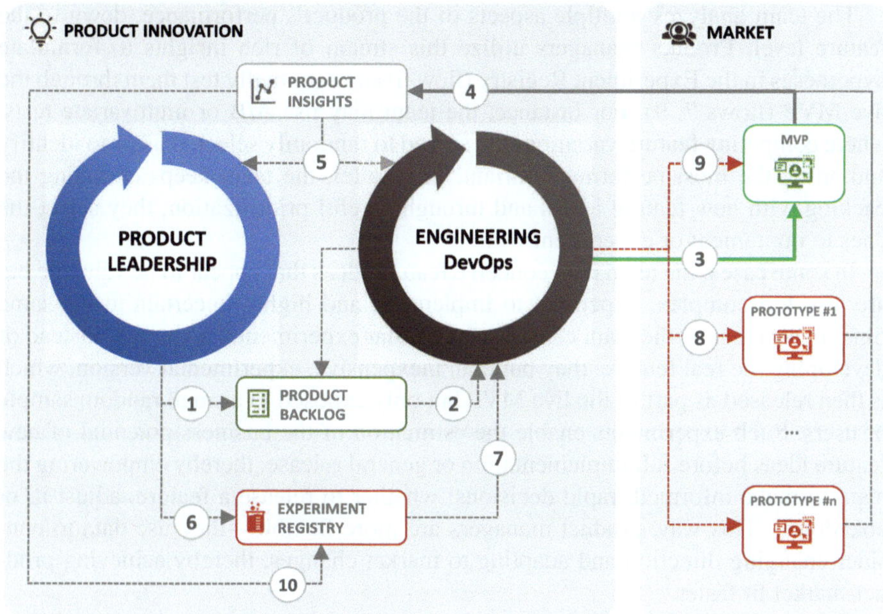

Fig. 8.2 Product development and innovation

key components of the product innovation setup, while the right part shows the market. The Product Leadership loop is where MVPs are defined—they are managed as Epic User stories in the product backlog (flow 1). During this loop, product leaders receive validated opportunities from the discovery pipeline and convert them into effective Minimum Viable Products—they define what needs to be there in the first instance of the product to provide value to its early customers. Additionally, product leaders articulate the big picture of the opportunity, shape the product vision, and define its success. When clarity and alignment about the scope of the MVP are achieved, product leaders set up the right cross-disciplinary *implementation team*—typically a blend of software engineers, designers, product managers, marketers, and any specialized roles required for the specific opportunity—and lead the rapid implementation of the product (happening in Engineering DevOps loop).

Through fast, agile development cycles, the MVP eventually reaches the market (flow 3) and is exposed to real users—initially in closed mode—by invitation only. The live MVP enables a flow of telemetry events and user feedback (shown as flow 4) that feed into the product insights system. These live feeds of user engagement data and feedback are automatically analyzed and converted into actionable product intelligence. Standardized MVP scorecards provide the team with instant clarity about the product's performance, growth, trends, and usage patterns (flow 5). For each MVP, AI summarizes the entire history of data and feedback and produces a product performance overview, enriched with AI's suggestions on metrics to watch and experiments to consider.

The team analyzes multiple aspects of the product's performance, down to the feature level. Product managers utilize this stream of rich insights to formulate hypotheses in the Experiment Registry (flow 6) and eventually test them through the live MVP (flows 7, 9). For instance, the team may use A/B or multivariate tests, where competing feature variations are served to randomly selected users to identify and adopt the most performant variant. In parallel, the team keeps enriching the backlog with new feature ideas, and through careful prioritization, they select the ones to implement or experiment with.

In some cases, the team may conceive feature ideas that appear to be valuable but are also too complex, expensive to implement, and highly uncertain at the same time. In such cases, the team can follow a similar experimental approach: instead of developing the real feature, they build an inexpensive, experimental version, which is then released as part of the live MVP but only exposed to a small random sample of users. Such experiments enable the estimation of the business potential of new feature ideas before full implementation or general release, thereby empowering the team to make informed, rapid decisions: whether to release a feature, adjust it, or abandon it. This way, product managers are more flexible—they use data to consider changing direction and adapting to market changes, thereby achieving product-market fit faster.

The team may leverage an additional experimentation path: they can build standalone prototypes that implement more complex experimental features or digital experiences and publish them in the market independently (flow 8) rather than within the live MVP. These prototypes follow the same pattern—they utilize the same telemetry and feedback mechanisms to provide signals to the team, which then uses standard analytical tools to assess the performance of the out-of-product experiments.

In parallel to the above, the opportunity realization team is also responsible for *operating* the in-market MVPs, which means, among other things, hosting, operational support, customer service, content management, and marketing—all optimized for rapid learning and fast iterations.

This setup enables a fast process that seamlessly integrates product operations, rapid feature releases, in-market experimentation, and informed, data-driven decision-making. The team may be running multiple in-market MVPs simultaneously, with additional instances of implementation teams working in parallel. Each MVP continues the rapid improvement journey until there is strong evidence that product-market fit is achieved or that the product has failed to respond according to the expected growth patterns. In the former case, when the PMF is achieved, the team applies a well-defined and rapid transition protocol to transfer ownership of the MVP to a dedicated product team, allowing them to continue operations and drive growth. In the latter case, where the continued efforts to grow the product have failed to bring the expected results, they trigger a sunset protocol that releases resources and allows the team to take over additional, new MVPs. Such "smart" MVP failures, assuming a well-defined scope of work, design, and execution, should be welcomed since they align with the principles of fail-fast, fail-safe, and continuous learning. The in-market MVPs aim to validate the viability and business potential of promising concepts as fast as possible. While fast PMF is the desired outcome, early, smart failures are welcome.

In all cases, this system generates knowledge and collects rich data in the product insights store while enriching the experiments defined in the experiment registry (flow 10).

The opportunity realization setup is at the core of the innovation framework, as defined in Chap. 4, and benefits from its various capabilities in many ways. For instance, the team may browse the Innovation Graph to discover ideas for new features in the context of their products or consult with the innovation intelligence team to obtain the latest market insights, informing feature prioritization and decision-making. In other cases, the team may use the Innovation Portal to organize brainstorming sessions or crowdsource particular problems and challenges; for example, they ask the innovation community, "How might we improve feature x of the product," or "How might we drive x% up a certain conversion rate."

On the other hand, the opportunity realization service improves the innovation framework not only by establishing a powerful go-to-market capability but also by enriching the accumulated organizational knowledge: the wealth of insights produced by the opportunity realization service become part of the Innovation Graph, and thus discoverable through multiple touchpoints, including the Innovation Portal, the newsletter, and more.

This rapid product innovation process is also beneficial for end-users and customers. While the company continues to innovate and release new or enhanced features, end-users experience a product that improves and remains relevant. Provided that these incremental improvements are delivered smoothly, users are more satisfied with the product since they do not have to wait months or years for massive, monolithic product updates. Instead, through a seamless process, they experience frequent upgrades that should translate to more value and increased engagement.

8.1 Feedback and Usage Patterns as a Source of Ideas

The systematic processing and interpretation of customer feedback and usage data are key in modern product management, as they enable accurate measurement of product performance and inspire innovation. A rich product insights store can trigger the generation of great ideas for new features, services, or problems worth solving; it empowers product teams to keep improving their products through fast *inspiration-implementation-test* loops. The sources that can power this loop typically include the following:

- **Product usage via telemetry**: This data describes interactions between the user and the product, including clicks, page views, feature engagement, content consumption, and navigation access. User interaction data is collected through the product via telemetry. It is an essential source of intelligence that can reveal interesting patterns of how users navigate and utilize the product in real market conditions.

- **Direct feedback from users**: This includes feedback explicitly shared by the user, such as signals during a conversational experience, embedded satisfaction questionnaires, responses to campaigns, or feature suggestions. This source provides both quantitative and qualitative content, which typically reflects the user's sentiment and expectations.
- **Complaints**: This is invaluable feedback that reflects pain points in the user experience. It may manifest in the form of customer support tickets, customer service interactions, online reviews, and social media comments. Complaints are always a valuable source of insights for product enhancement, as they highlight points of failure or expectation gaps.
- **Online reputation**: This is public domain content, including reviews, ratings, and discussion threads on social media, blogs, or news sites that reference the product. They reflect the opinions of actual users and market perceptions.
- **Research activities**: Outbound campaigns that invite users to participate in targeted studies via online questionnaires, user interviews, usability sessions, and feature preference surveys. This provides insights into user needs and expectations that could be useful in parallel with telemetry and other data.

All the above can be streamlined into the product insights store as described above—seen in Fig. 8.3. This store supports not only the opportunity realization service but all the products in the company, evolving as an invaluable resource for customer and product understanding.

It enables product managers to obtain distilled, reliable product performance measurements through real-time scorecards and user engagement funnels. Beyond presenting the current state and performance of an MVP in near real time, the insights store leverages machine learning to identify interesting, emerging patterns in product usage and alert the team accordingly. For instance, a product manager gets notified that a particular functional area of the product is underperforming or that there is a performance exception for a specific, dynamically defined audience: users who meet a combination of criteria engage with the product in a very different way than the rest of the user base. The latter, for instance, could help the team discover certain unstated needs of a demographic or situations where people use the product in unintended ways. This autonomous pattern identification is crucial when the interaction between the product and the user is conversational—based on natural language. Artificial intelligence can identify and interpret such patterns, providing product teams with additional context, suggestions on what to explore, and possible root causes. Moreover, AI streamlines the analysis of both structured and unstructured feedback and usage data. It can correlate usage and feedback streams with the product's actual features, thus creating smart recommendations on what to improve, when, and why.

Findings like the ones described above, along with general patterns in the data, such as non-obvious associations between user feedback and the performance of individual features, are just a few examples that could trigger further investigation and innovation threads. Feedback at scale, combined with usage patterns, is a source of inspiration for product innovation.

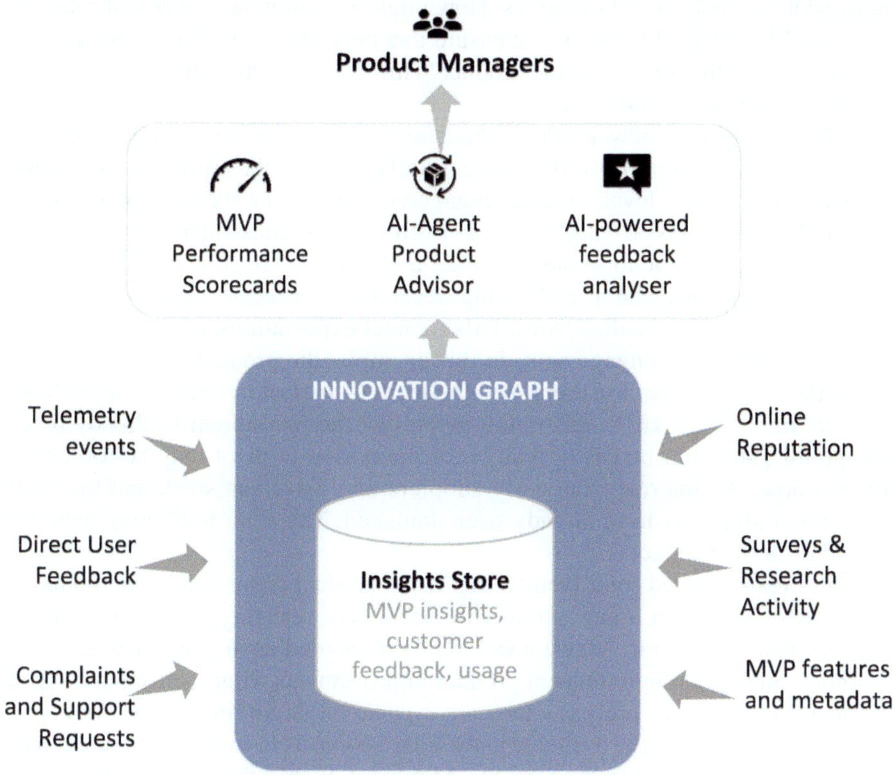

Fig. 8.3 The insights store supporting the opportunity realization function

8.2 The Minimum Viable Product (MVP) Explained

When defining a new product, there is usually a surplus of feature ideas captured as user stories in the product backlog, where they are stored, enriched, and prioritized. In product development, feature prioritization is a fundamental process, as it shapes the initial release of the product and the subsequent increments, the regular improvements that follow the initial launch. Prioritization can be a complex and delicate process that must consider several aspects of the candidate product features, including the *expected value* they would bring to the users, the expected *number of users to be impacted*, the *business impact*, *feasibility*, and *cost*.

When defining a new product, the team faces increased uncertainty of various origins. For example, product managers must estimate the market *demand* for the solution or the *readiness* of a specific user demographic to adopt a new technology or experience. Uncertainty arises from a lack of insights and data, for instance, when a team considers features that have not been validated by users in real-world conditions: novelty introduces uncertainty. Facing such uncertainty, product teams must address fundamental questions: How might we minimize the risk of releasing a non-viable product? How can we ensure that only the most valuable features are included in the first release of the product? How can you tell if the defined product is too big, expensive, and risky?

When building a new product, the real risk is *releasing a non-viable first instance too late*. *Viability* at this stage usually refers to the ability of the product to maintain a good level of user engagement and user base growth that are required to drive broad adoption and, eventually, successful monetization. To illustrate the case of a non-viable product released too late, consider a team that, after significant investment and a long development process, launches an ambitious product only to realize that it fails to meet expectations and, thus, is unable to drive enough user engagement. In this example, the product may be failing to solve the core problem for users, and the team is the last to know; they realize *it too late in the process*. At this point, given that the investment is already made, the product may not be easily fixable, or the option to pivot may be too costly. Even worse, the interest from early adopters may have vanished, and the product's reputation may have already been damaged. The team itself may have lost its belief in the product.

This creates a need for a method that helps product teams minimize the uncertainty associated with a new product by accurately selecting and prioritizing the features that matter most to customers, releasing a good enough product early, and learning quickly through frequent product improvements. High-performance product teams excel in this process—they are capable of identifying *the smallest set of features* that, based on the available knowledge, is expected to satisfy a critical mass of customers. This is the basis of the Minimum Viable Product (MVP), which, according to Eric Ries (August 3, 2009), is the version of the product that can bring the maximum amount of validated learning with the least effort.

Interpreting the above definition, a minimum viable product describes the first instance of a product consisting of select features that are expected to provide sufficient value to early customers so they engage with the product while the company obtains essential feedback and insights to learn, validate assumptions, and steer the product improvement process.

The essence of this approach is the smart identification of the minimum subset of features that solves the problem, which is significantly cheaper and faster to build compared to the full product. Moreover, as this smaller instance reaches the market faster and at a fraction of the cost, it allows the product team to respond swiftly. Following the release of the MVP, the team begins consuming user feedback and usage insights to define improvements and deliver incremental value to users.

This means limited financial damage if the launch fails. It also allows more options to react: the real benefit from an inexpensive and wise start is that the company preserves financial resources, which can be used to improve the product as knowledge becomes available to the team: by leveraging user feedback and insights, an initially unsuccessful launch can be transformed to a successful product through a series of fast development iterations. Given the small initial cost, the team should still have sufficient resources to address issues, reset direction as needed, or even pivot to a new solution: building a good, inexpensive first release preserves degrees of freedom for the product.

By establishing active feedback loops, product development becomes more insights-driven with fewer unknowns and an increased ability to adapt when something is not performing as expected. These feedback channels provide actual usage insights from real users who experience the product in real conditions and, hence, a great source of learning.

Defining the MVP is not a straightforward process. It requires a holistic view of the envisioned product, sound judgment, a deep understanding of the users and their needs, as well as market and technology savviness. The tough questions concern the *prioritization criteria* and the *red line*, for example, how many top-prioritized features define a good set capable of delivering sufficient value to early customers. Obviously, for a given product concept, the definition of its MVP is only an estimation; it is *what the team believes will be proven viable*: the "V" in "MVP" is an additional hypothesis to be tested. Another aspect that needs clarification is that, contrary to popular misconceptions, an MVP differs from a prototype or a proof of concept. Unlike these, MVPs are exposed to real customers, and as such, they must be closer to production-ready (as defined in Chap. 7).

8.3 Defining Great MVPs

This section describes one of the most essential skills of the opportunity realization team: the ability to define great MVPs rapidly. It presents the steps and best practices to move quickly from a *product concept* to a solid *product definition*. The process outputs a product definition document that describes the functionality, outlines what to develop first, and provides a plan for ongoing improvement. This product requirements document also references a prioritized product backlog that contains all the identified features and the cutline that defines the Minimum Viable Product (MVP).

The MVP definition process (shown in Fig. 8.4) is triggered by a sponsor or stakeholder, such as a product leader, who requests the realization of an opportunity that has been formally assessed by the opportunity validation team using real-world data. The following outlines seven core steps that help product teams transform a product concept into a well-defined Minimum Viable Product. The process is led by product managers with extensive experience in conceiving products from scratch and a sound understanding of the corresponding domain. It starts by setting the context, as described below.

8.3.1 Set the Context

Typically, the only artifacts available to a product team at this early stage are problem statements and raw ideas. However, the opportunity realization team works with *validated opportunities*; therefore, they begin with a comprehensive package

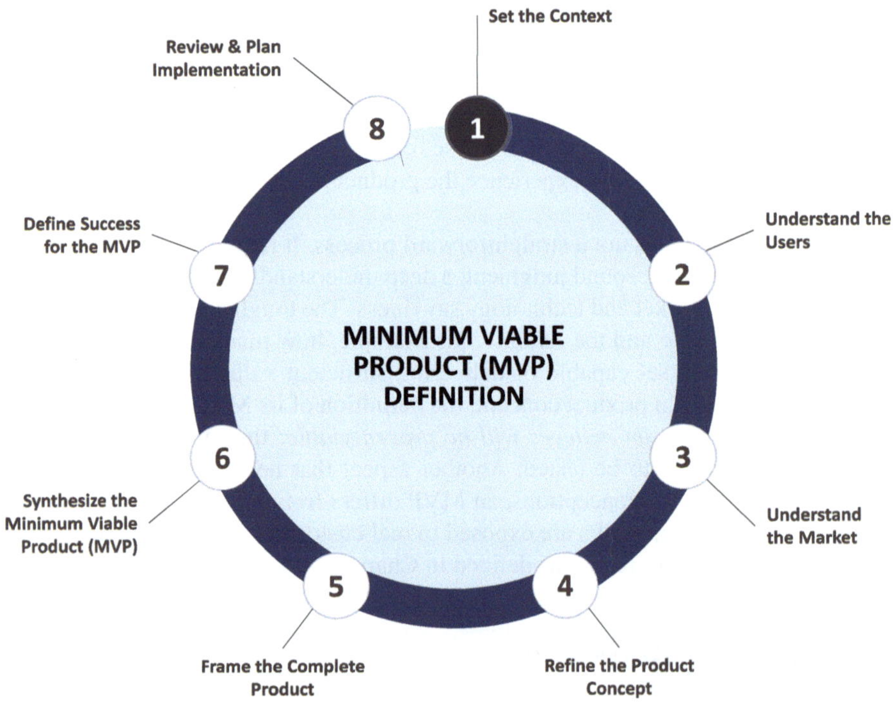

Fig. 8.4 The process of defining a minimum viable product (MVP)

that includes a specific product concept, enriched with valuable insights, product development recommendations, and, in some cases, artifacts such as functional prototypes. Hence, the team accelerates the process and builds on the existing concept: they use the Innovation Portal to organize the MVP definition project and instantly scan the Innovation Graph for related ideas, projects, activities, and knowledge throughout the organization. Moreover, they identify key people—domain experts and stakeholders—who may be needed throughout the steps of this process.

8.3.2 Understand the Users

Understanding the users is a crucial step. However, at this point, this is already performed by the opportunity validation team, and hence, the product manager simply reviews and enriches the existing user framing. They perform a quick meta-analysis of the typical users, profiles, habits, and needs by using existing insights and research artifacts. Occasionally, they trigger parallel user research activities such as qualitative studies, focus groups, user interviews, or surveys to obtain additional data and insights. For example, user research can validate the problem's importance and certain assumptions by asking participants how they are impacted by the problem and how they would describe an ideal solution. The team reviews the identified personas, captures their relationship to the problem, analyzes their pain points and needs, and determines how they would benefit if the problem is resolved, as well as how these translate to specific success criteria.

From the company's perspective, some personas may be more relevant than others. Acknowledging that a good solution does not necessarily benefit all the personas or not all of them to the same extent, the team must identify the most important ones in the context of the product. Having set the focus, the team demonstrates empathy and "thinks as a user" to determine what would bring value to each target persona—a process also guided by the associated success criteria. They analyze various scenarios and user journeys, depicting the flow of information, activities, and experiences of the involved personas in the current, non-optimal situation.

8.3.3 Understand the Market

Another essential element is the market—understanding the demand, the structure, dynamics, and the competitive landscape. The team leverages the prework from the opportunity validation and the unique insights produced by the innovation intelligence team, e.g., reports describing the market, the competitors, the start-up scene, estimates of the market size, the total addressable market, global trends, relevant statistics, and facts backing the importance of the problem. These shed light on certain facets of the opportunity and unveil aspects that may need further exploration or consideration.

Depending on the case, the team may request a thorough competition analysis from the innovation intelligence team, which then conducts additional research and compiles a detailed report of known attempts to solve similar problems, whether successful or unsuccessful. In such cases, they collect information about their approach, effectiveness, and current state. For example, there may be solutions in the market that address the same problem, but only partially or with limitations that customers are not particularly happy about. Sometimes, customers may have found work-arounds and creative ways to mitigate the problem. When existing solutions or products are available in the market, the innovation intelligence team scans the public domain for related user reports, reviews, announcements, patents, and other information that falls under the term 'open-source intelligence'. These are all processed and distilled into a single report, also containing the perspectives and recommendations of the innovation intelligence team. Product managers use this report to gain a deeper understanding of the market and competition and to identify strategies for differentiators and effective go-to-market approaches.

8.3.4 Refine the Concept

At this point, the team has a good understanding of the broader context, the problem, the users, and the market. Normally, the next step would be to trigger an AI-powered ideation thread through the Innovation Portal and obtain an initial set of concepts or potential solutions. Additionally, depending on the nature of the problem, the team may invite specific stakeholders or even the entire community of innovators to review the initial solutions and contribute by submitting their own ideas. Assuming a healthy innovation culture exists, such an open call brings diverse ideas, some of which may be of high potential and entirely new to the product team. For complex problems, the team would also consider running one or more Design Sprints. All these would lead to a collection of *competing concepts*: different solutions attempting to solve the defined problem. The team would then review, combine, and enrich the concepts, gradually synthesizing the overall solution: the product concept to be built.

However, the opportunity realization team receives all of the above from the validation service: the product concept, along with insights and technical artifacts, are all given as part of the package produced during the validation process. Therefore, the team can proceed directly with the MVP definition—they are empowered to start fast and proceed by decomposing the provided concept into features.

8.3.5 Frame the Complete Product

Although the aim is a "minimum" product, it is a good strategy to *think big*, *capture everything*, *prioritize wisely*, and *review often*. The team begins by articulating a solid product vision and the big picture of the product, followed by a lengthy process of identifying key features and describing them as Epic User Stories—compact statements that express user needs. The stories are appended to the product backlog, which allows prioritization and different views of the product and enables the definition of a "small" but effective first instance: the MVP.

Typically, the initialization of the backlog and the definition of the MVP is a long process: the product team gets together to define and capture all the features the product should have to address the underlying problem effectively. They are encouraged to embrace new ideas and innovative, non-obvious, unexpected features, even if they appear out of scope, not feasible, or expensive. The team defines, discusses, and appends user stories to the product backlog until they collectively feel that the product is sufficiently covered. This process may require multiple workshops and extensive post-processing to clean, standardize, enrich, and group the user stories. Eventually, the product backlog reflects the complete product according to the team's product vision, which triggers further enrichment: the team analyzes the Epic stories and adds metadata, such as a rough estimation of its *size*, *complexity*, and *urgency* from the user's point of view. The latter is critical as an indicator of *how early the feature needs to become available* so that the product can effectively solve the problem. During this enrichment and refinement process, the team may also perform an initial draft prioritization. Foundational stories receive higher priority, for example, those with increased urgency, such as the necessary features for the product to serve core, end-to-end scenarios. Less urgent features get a lower initial priority, while those nice-to-have and uncertain features go down to the bottom of the backlog.

In the era of artificial intelligence, though, the backlog initialization and MVP definition are dramatically faster. Instead of the manual process described above, the team uses the Innovation Portal to create an MVP definition project. With a single click, they obtain a detailed backlog of prioritized, grouped Epic User Stories, described accurately and enriched with justification regarding their importance and explanations about the prioritization. Instead of brainstorming and typing in user stories and features, the team collaborates to understand and refine the backlog, enrich it, and debate the initial MVP scope. The AI agent remains in the loop, allowing the team to compile MVP narratives that summarize the scope, how it serves the different personas, what subsequent post-MVP releases would include, and the key performance metrics to track. With a click of a button, the AI creates variations of the MVP and the underlying backlog that focus on specific personas or enforce time or funding constraints. The team leverages these sophisticated AI tools to accelerate the process while making the MVP definition smarter and more accurate.

8.3.6 Synthesize the Minimum Viable Product

The product backlog generated in the previous process reflects what the team understands as the "complete product"—every feature they identified as a valuable part of a good solution. With this superset of features, the product team can synthesize the "best" subset, where best means the one that is *least expensive for the company to build* and *valuable enough for customers to engage with*. It can be thought of as the smallest collection of features that delivers enough value to early customers so they actively use the product. To address frequent misconceptions, selecting a subset of features does not restrict the product by any means. In an agile world, the first release of a product initiates an ongoing process of frequent incremental improvements. Hence, the selection of features *does not filter out items*; it defines what to build first and what may follow through subsequent releases. This initial, smaller instance of the product enables the company to reach the market faster and at lower costs while establishing a channel for feedback and laying the groundwork for a fast, iterative product enhancement process. Future releases eventually deliver some of the features that were initially not selected.

Prioritizing the features to be included in the first product instance is critical and must be done carefully. Releasing a new product with a suboptimal set of features causes trouble for both the product and the team. Too many features can result in a long time-to-market, translating to delays in connecting with customers and getting insights and feedback. Too few features or the wrong ones can result in a product that doesn't solve the customer's problem and thus fails to grow organically. When the first release targets real users and customers, failure to meet their expectations and address their most essential needs puts the product at risk: It can directly impact revenue streams, growth rates, and the reputation of both the product and the brand. Even worse, there may be limited resources left for the company to react fast and attempt to fix the product.

To increase the likelihood of effective prioritization, product managers look through the lens of the customer and think of the value a feature would bring to the user. At the same time, they consider its business impact, the *effort to build it*, and the *expected reach*. As part of this process, the product team identifies and flags special features, such as those having feasibility constraints, high uncertainty, or those that are fundamental or otherwise mandatory for the core user scenarios.

An additional signal helpful in feature prioritization is the *relative timing*, that is, the moment in the product's lifecycle that the feature is more likely to deliver value to the user. For example, a feasible, low-effort feature that is expected to bring significant value to many users could still get a low priority in the backlog: it may have functional dependencies on other features that need to be released and adopted first. In some cases, a feature may depend on the "maturity" of the user, that is, the degree of familiarity and readiness of the typical user to leverage the product to its full extent and benefit from it. A feature may be too advanced during the early days of the product, or it may provide additive value to another feature that needs to be introduced to the market first and achieve a certain level of engagement and visibility. We could name a feature's level of functional or logical dependencies as the *urgency of the feature*.

Having this metadata about the entire set of features in the backlog allows the product team to compute an overall *priority score* for each item, for example, as an average of scores against the above criteria, and use it to sort the stories. This would bring good MVP feature candidates to the top of the list. However, this prioritization should be considered a draft as it still requires thorough reviews, critical thinking, and sound judgment to make informed decisions and navigate trade-offs. The following proposes a six-step method for iterating over the backlog and defining the set of features to include in the MVP definition.

1. **Obtain the high-potential feature set**: Select those features scored as high value and high impact and specifically exclude those with limited feasibility and low urgency. The resulting set comprises those *feasible* and *urgent* features that are expected to be highly valuable to most users.
2. **Analyze the high-potential feature set**: Question any marginal entries and reassess their scores if needed. Review the distribution of features by effort, and analyze the most expensive ones carefully, taking into account both complexity and cost. Make any necessary corrections, and most importantly, try to find cheaper alternatives, such as smaller features and low-tech workarounds, which can still serve the purpose in an inexpensive way. If found, define these as new stories and reprioritize the expensive ones.
3. **Cross-validate the high-potential feature set**: Iterate through the refined set, and try to exclude features. For each feature, answer the simple question: Would the product be valuable (and viable) without this feature? If the answer is not a definite "No," reconsider the entry.
4. **Cross-validate the non-selected features**: Iterate over the items that were explicitly excluded or implicitly filtered out from the high-potential feature set;

for each one, answer the simple question: Is this feature necessary for the first instance of the product? If the answer is not a definite "No," discuss, reconsider, and justify any changes.

5. **Review and refine the high-potential feature set**: It is essential to ask independent reviewers to assess both the high-potential feature set and the remaining set of features. For example, the team may invite evaluators or other product experts in the organization to review and make suggestions on the robustness of the MVP definition. Through short sessions, the team provides quick introductions, setting the context, and then asks the experts to think both as users and as entrepreneurs and evaluate the high-potential feature set. This could provide additional insights and spark creative debates, ultimately increasing confidence in the validity of the MVP definition.
6. **Summarize and validate the scope**: Create a one pager, providing an executive summary of the product's functionality based only on the high-potential feature set. Use it to validate the scope by asking users within the organization to challenge it.

Eventually, this iterative process leads to a robust set of features, defined by the experts and the product team and validated independently. Of course, the cost of building the product must be considered—and this requires input from engineering and technical teams. Regardless, the lack of sufficient resources to build this instance of the product should not lead to "easy" decisions about changing its scope: If the MVP is too expensive for the company to develop, the team should focus on finding less expensive implementation options or technical alternatives or workarounds for the included features. For example, there may be less fancy or less technologically advanced solutions that serve the same purpose. In parallel, features that might have been marginally included in the high-potential feature set must be reconsidered, especially if they require increased effort.

The above process can also be implemented in the Innovation Portal and powered by AI. Product managers collaborate with the AI innovator to set the right priorities, identify dependencies, and make wise trade-offs and scope decisions. This enables the opportunity realization team to develop solid, high-potential MVP definitions quickly and prepare for rapid implementation. The final step is to define what success looks like for the product.

8.3.7 Define Success

At this point, the product team has a structured and validated product concept, along with a prioritized product backlog that reflects the product vision and in-depth knowledge of the users. To complete the product definition process, the team must also define success: what a successful product looks like and how to measure its performance and impact. This involves the definition of specific KPIs that reflect the most vital aspects of product performance for the company, its users, and all major stakeholders.

A product has multiple facets: it aims to solve a problem for customers while also creating value for the company. The definition of product performance must reflect both the value generated for the user and the benefit created for the company. However, *value* is difficult to define; it is not always measured in terms of revenue or profitability. There are cases where a product is a major success as part of an ecosystem of services without necessarily creating direct revenues. In other cases, the cause of the product may not be aligned with the notion of commercial success. Furthermore, products and services evolve and grow. While a snapshot of metrics for a product may not be sufficient to call it a success, an analysis of its growth dynamics could lead to the opposite conclusion.

Part of the process of defining success involves identifying the right KPIs and the metrics they depend on. Metrics typically focus on *user engagement*, *growth rates*, *market share*, *customer satisfaction*, *revenue*, and *profitability* prospects. Success should be defined by assigning goals to the selected KPIs, thus describing how the product should perform in the real world through numbers. A clear definition of success benefits all stakeholders, as it enables objective measurement of performance that guides decisions during development and helps the team steer the product's evolution.

The product definition cycle concludes with packaging all the information produced in a solid artifact: the Product Definition Document. This document contains the problem, the "final" scope of the product, references to the product backlog, and a roadmap, which puts everything in perspective: *what to build first and what is expected to follow*.

Following the completion of this process, the team conducts a rapid review of the MVP definition with key stakeholders and then proceeds with implementation roadmapping, development team formation, and go-to-market planning. This process runs independently from implementation cycles, and when done, it appends the approved MVP Definitions to a special backlog, where they wait in priority for an implementation team to be assigned. This decoupling between *product definition* and *implementation* adds further flexibility to the opportunity realization team.

In the fast-paced world of AI, execution matters more than ever. What defines winning companies in today's competitive landscape is the courage to experiment and the ability to execute, learn, and adapt at speed and scale. In this sense, the opportunity realization team plays a crucial role in modern organizations, as it bridges the gap between ambitious concepts and market reality. While its primary focus is on digital products, it may prove to be equally valuable for connected physical products where software is a key component, such as smart wearables, connected cars, and smart homes that run on software and use telemetry to provide usage and interaction data that help their manufacturers understand how users engage with their products. Although, in this case, software is one component and not the actual product, it can still deliver innovations, such as new features and user experiences, seamlessly over the air.

Innovation Performance Measurement

9

Innovation measurement is a crucial component of the innovation framework. It reveals how innovative the company is and provides critical insights on steering the innovation transformation program. In this sense, consistent measurement of innovation empowers a continual improvement program toward the Innovation Mode. The program itself has an experimental character, which requires systematic measurement and estimation of the impact of various activities, events, and capabilities. To effectively steer the innovation transformation, leaders need a *macro view* of the performance of the innovation function; they must be able to track how the organization responds to the program and how people adopt the new methods and practices. At the same time, it is valuable to have accurate *micro views* of performance at the innovation capability level. This micro view of innovation performance forms the foundation of the reward program, as the latter depends on a reliable stream of data describing innovation activity and achievements.

Measuring innovation is not straightforward. Simple questions like "How well is the innovation function performing?" or "What is the output of the innovation function, and how does it compare with the previous year?" may be hard to answer concisely and objectively. The organization may appear innovative, for example, when it has an enthusiastic innovation community and a surplus of ideas, but a closer look may reveal a limited ability to take action. Very often, companies that *look innovative* struggle with low conversion rates from ideas to opportunities or a slow process for bringing them to market. In other cases, they may be demonstrating remarkable innovation artifacts and achievements while facing issues with their culture of innovation.

Measuring innovation requires a holistic view backed by a deep understanding of the performance of every major component of the innovation function. To obtain this holistic view, organizations need a standardized, unified measurement framework implemented as a system that can capture and process a wide range of innovation activities and expressions. This system needs to be flexible and configurable, as

G. Krasadakis, *Innovation Mode 2.0*,
https://doi.org/10.1007/978-3-032-00835-0_9

the objective of innovation may significantly differ across companies: some may be targeting business impact, while others may be focusing on cultural transformation. Another factor that makes measurement difficult is the large and variable amount of time required for innovation artifacts to mature and qualify for success. A concept being evaluated now may take months or years to reach the market and send back the first signals of commercial success.

The following sections present a top-down approach—we start by defining the *corporate innovation performance scorecard* and then decompose it into measurement areas and specific metrics.

9.1 The Macro View: Innovation Performance at the Corporate Level

Innovation performance in a corporate environment may be defined on top of four distinct performance components, namely, *Impact*, *Output*, *Culture*, and *Public Image*, as illustrated in Fig. 9.1.

These four components reflect what needs to be measured in order to synthesize an overall performance score for innovation. The *Culture* element measures what employees believe about innovation within the organization, thereby reflecting the general mindset and attitude toward innovation. Similarly, the *Output* element measures *what the company produces* through the innovation function, as well as the rate at which eligible innovation outputs move through the pipeline and reach the market. The *Image* component reflects *what the world perceives about the company and how innovative it appears to be in the eyes of its market observers*. Finally, the *Impact* quantifies *how the markets react* and how the ecosystem receives and adopts

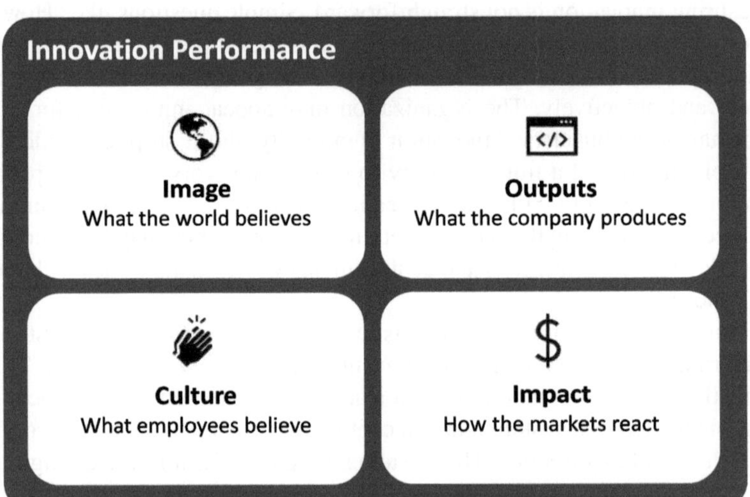

Fig. 9.1 The four components of corporate innovation performance

the released innovation artifacts. The performance scores for these four elements can be aggregated into a single *Innovation Performance Score*, allowing for tracking over time.

To make this more flexible, innovation leaders may assign varying importance to these four components, allowing for a customized version of the scorecard that reflects the company's principles and priorities. For example, when a corporation prioritizes cultural impact as a success criterion for the innovation function, the program leaders assign an increased weight factor to the corresponding component. A company that places greater emphasis on the ability to produce intermediate innovation artifacts, such as high-technology demos, as a driver for business development assigns extra weight to the *Output* component.

Using these weights, the company obtains a weighted Innovation Performance Score that reflects the overall corporate innovation performance. These five scores are presented through the *Innovation Performance Scorecard*, which illustrates the company's performance in these four areas on a simple ordinal scale, ranging from poor to excellent. By adding the time dimension, this scorecard can instantly indicate the company's progress in terms of innovation through trends and dynamics. The following provides a detailed explanation of how to construct the individual performance levels corresponding to the above four elements.

9.1.1 Measuring Output: The Opportunity Creation Funnel

Given the time lag involved between the release of a product to the market and the first reliable indicators of commercial impact, the organization must be able to zoom in and measure innovation *as it happens*. The opportunity creation funnel provides a framework for measuring the outputs of the innovation function, as well as the conversion rates between stages, along with various insightful statistics.

To illustrate the logic of the funnel, consider a flow of ideas becoming available to the organization through an innovation context or generated by the AI agent. These ideas mature and convert into certain artifacts. For example, a happy path for an idea would be to go through the standard assessment, flagged as an opportunity, selected for validation, tested by real users, then built, and released to the market. Such transitions or conversions are tracked for the entire corpus of ideas and can be used to construct a funnel, as shown in Fig. 9.2.

As raw ideas flow into the funnel, they undergo several steps and validation processes, such as de-duplication, enrichment, and merging with other ideas. Consequently, only a subset of these ideas is considered actionable—not all of them will be clean, complete, and eligible to join the formal idea assessment process.

Actionable ideas are systematically reviewed by evaluators through the idea assessment process, during which some ideas are flagged as high-potential opportunities. This means that the experts have identified an opportunity for one or more business intents. Some of the high-potential ideas eventually make it further in the process—they are analyzed, wireframed, and reviewed in terms of feasibility and technology requirements. These mature and high-potential ideas, also referred to as

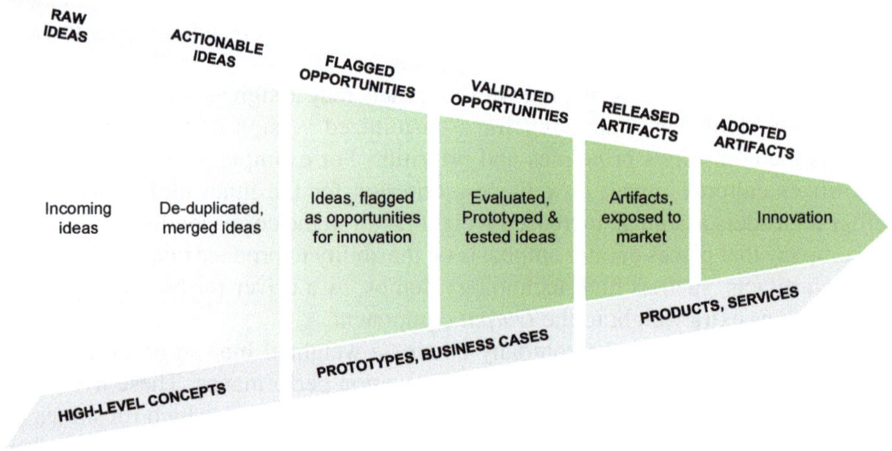

Fig. 9.2 The opportunity creation funnel

innovation opportunities, typically go through the opportunity validation process to be tested using real-world data, producing *validated innovation opportunities*.

Depending on the outcomes of the validation and additional factors such as the capacity of the organization, validated opportunities may be built or compiled as "production ready" and reach the market, thus becoming available to their intended audience under general availability or through a pilot program, etc. In all cases, when they are exposed to real users or customers, they are referred to as *released innovation opportunities* or *released artifacts*.

Some of the released artifacts may be adopted over time, where *adoption* involves various criteria depending on each case. For instance, a business-to-consumer case would require thousands of users and high growth rates to be called "adopted." In contrast, a business-to-business service could only need a few hundred satisfied paying business customers. When this is achieved, we refer to them as adopted artifacts or realized opportunities. Note that adoption does not guarantee commercial success or financial gains. It may be the nature of the service, the initial monetization model, or other factors that explain a wide adoption with no financial impact. The impact of innovation may evolve over the years, reflecting both the market dynamic and related investments made by the company, for instance, in communication, advertising, ecosystem development, and partnerships.

Furthermore, a few of the realized opportunities may grow rapidly and bring a remarkable impact, for instance, changes in how a product is used, a shift in consumer habits, a major impact on the market, or significant profitability for the company. We call them *impactful opportunities*.

The above abstraction covers not only products and services but also other forms of innovation, including processes, monetization models, publications, innovation stories, and patents. All these are considered innovation artifacts or assets, which move through the funnel and are characterized by the level of *maturity* and *exposure*. For example, when a raw idea is flagged as having high potential for a patent, the intermediate artifact is the patent disclosure document, which, in a sense, is *tested* against patentability criteria and prior art. If approved, it converts into a validated opportunity for intellectual property. Then, formal documents are produced, such as the patent application document, which is then submitted to a patent office and eventually gets published in the market—it becomes the *released artifact*. Adoption in the case of a patent could mean a commercialization scenario, such as a licensing agreement or the direct use of the patent in a real product.

The next paragraphs present typical innovation metrics and conversion rates defined using the opportunity creation funnel. They reflect both the quality of the content and the performance of individual parts of the innovation engine.

Conversions. The following simple metrics help measure aspects of performance across the funnel.

1. **Idea to innovation opportunity**: This is the percentage of innovation opportunities over the total number of raw ideas in the cohort. When combined with the volume of incoming ideas, this ratio may reflect the organization's ability or bandwidth to create innovation opportunities. It can be interpreted as the percentage of ideas that have an increased likelihood of converting to valuable innovation assets for the corporation.
2. **Idea to validated opportunity**: The percentage of validated opportunities over the total number of raw ideas. It shows how many ideas reached their intended form factor and were formally tested, e.g., prototyped through the opportunity validation process.
3. **Idea to released artifacts**: This is the percentage of realized ideas over the total number of ideas in the cohort.
4. **Idea to adopted artifacts**: This is the percentage of ideas that have been adopted in the market over the total number of ideas in the cohort.
5. **Validated opportunities to released artifacts**: This is the percentage of released artifacts compared to the successfully validated opportunities. It shows how many of the confirmed innovation opportunities were finally launched. A low conversion rate might indicate capacity issues related to implementation and execution.
6. **Released to adopted artifacts**: This is the percentage of released artifacts that demonstrated the expected level of adoption after a predefined period of time, compared to the total number of released artifacts in the cohort.

The above metrics are just some fundamental conversion rates. The funnel serves as the basis for creating additional ones and analyzing the pace of innovation—specifically how quickly ideas progress through the pipeline.

Pace. Measuring the velocity of conversions is equally important, as it can reveal bottlenecks and opportunities for process improvement. The following presents basic metrics that reflect the speed of processing and decision-making:

1. **Idea evaluation pace**: This may be defined as the average time required for a new idea to be assessed by evaluators or as the percentage of cases evaluated within x days from their submission. It is helpful as an indicator of the capacity of the idea evaluation service.
2. **Opportunity spotting pace**: This is the average time required to identify and flag an idea as a potential innovation opportunity. This is also useful in measuring the capacity of the idea evaluation process and the organization's general readiness to identify opportunities.
3. **Opportunity validation pace**: The average time needed to handle requests to test innovation opportunities through prototyping and real-world data. This reflects the capacity of the opportunity validation service.
4. **Post-prototype decisiveness**: The average time needed for the sponsors of a validated opportunity to make a decision based on the validation outcomes and the experts' recommendations.

The above is not an exhaustive list—multiple metrics may be defined on top of the opportunity conversion funnel. In an ideal scenario, there should be a standardized report presenting the superset of metrics for cohorts of ideas, allowing the user to set a reference period or a specific source of opportunities, such as a hackathon or design sprint. Additionally, selected metrics and KPIs can be combined into a simple dashboard that provides an instant overview of the funnel's state.

Supply. The metrics listed above regarding conversions and pace measure what happens *inside the funnel*, i.e., how fast and at what rate ideas progress to their next state. However, it is essential to also combine the inputs of the funnel and specifically the overall *supply of ideas*: high conversion rates and fast pace would not mean much unless there is a steady volume of ideas coming in. Additional metrics in this category would be:

1. **Ideas per innovator**: This is the average number of ideas submitted per innovator—computed in a predefined timeframe over the size of the active innovation community.
2. **Idea submission pace**: This represents the total volume of ideas submitted through the innovation channels on a monthly or quarterly basis. It is important for capacity planning purposes.
3. **AI-generated ideas**: The percentage of ideas submitted, managed, or handled by AI. The intent is to quantify how AI agents participate in the supply of ideas.

Quality and Potential. The formal idea assessment process provides excellent insights that can be used to analyze the quality of the supply of ideas in association with the conversion rates of the opportunity funnel. For example, a group of ideas submitted within a certain period eventually goes through the idea assessment process, meaning that every idea is scored against the nine assessment criteria presented in Chap. 6, including novelty and expected business impact. These scores can be aggregated to reflect the quality of the cohort of ideas and define various metrics, including:

1. **Inventiveness level**: In its simplest form, this is the average *novelty score* over all the ideas in the package or the percentage of ideas that are assessed as possibly "new to the world."
2. **Level of expected business impact**: This can be computed as the average *expected business impact score* over the ideas in the set.
3. **Level of business potential**: This can be computed as the average of the overall business potential of the ideas contained in the set. As this combines all nine individual scores as set by the experts, it serves as a strong indicator of the company's ability to generate high-potential opportunities.

The above should be combined into a single analytical experience, such as an interactive dashboard that provides current metrics along with time series and also highlights deviations from normality. Such a dashboard should enable filtering to analyze specific cohorts of ideas, time frames, or business intents. For example, it should allow the user to filter the entire funnel for ideas by using an intent or the actual realization, e.g., finding ideas that have resulted in patents, regardless of their initial business intent, etc.

The key question is how to convert all the above into a single number, an *opportunity creation and realization score*, to feed into the corporate innovation performance scorecard. This should be a simple, practical, and generic approach, as proposed below.

Deriving the Opportunity Creation and Realization Score. Assuming a good implementation, the opportunity creation funnel becomes the standard source of insights for innovation leaders. By analyzing these insights over time, leaders establish initial baselines, such as expected conversion rates and levels of idea supply, which are used to define what constitutes a good state of the funnel. They then consider the overall innovation strategy and set numeric targets for the company's opportunity creation ability, e.g., the levels of opportunity creation that the company must achieve in the future to meet its broader innovation goals.

For example, innovation leaders may decide that the *"Idea to Released Artifacts" rate must be increased by 50% and that the overall supply of ideas must double within the next 12 months*. Moreover, they may set targets at specific intents of interest, for instance, to *increase the patent filing rate by* 2× and *reduce the time-to-discover innovation opportunities by half.* Similarly, they may set absolute goals, such as reaching the market with at least x artifacts and filing y patents. This can result in a well-defined scheme of numeric targets, which, provided a suitable measurement framework is in place, are easy to measure and monitor.

In a simple scenario, innovation leaders meet regularly to measure or score the gap between the *current* and *expected states* of the funnel—where *expected* is the state that would indicate good progress toward the corresponding target. This comparison provides a clear understanding of the funnel's performance, allowing the team to derive an overall opportunity creation and realization score. In more advanced scenarios, the scoring process is modeled and implemented as part of the innovation performance dashboard, providing instant *health indicators* of the funnel, progress evaluation, and additional insights.

Regardless of the implementation, the opportunity creation and realization score feeds into the performance scorecard as the *Output* performance component.

9.1.2 Measuring the Business Impact

The opportunity creation funnel, as described above, focuses more on conversion rates, volumes, and pace. From a corporate perspective though, an additional quantification of innovation performance is needed: the *business impact of innovation*. However, as previously explained, it is not easy to measure the success of products, services, or other forms of innovation coming out of the pipeline.

Part of the challenge is the difficulty in defining and measuring business impact in a generic way: impact can come in the form of profit, prospects, process efficiencies, or societal value; it can be based on actual values or projected figures. In some cases, growth rates and widespread adoption are viewed as a major impact, regardless of actualized revenues or profits; in others, the impact is primarily about financial results. Often, business impact is conceived as gains of market share, a boost in brand awareness, intellectual property, or other strategic advantages for the company. The heterogeneous nature of *business impact* and the varying time lags involved in its realization make it very hard to measure. In addition, business impact cannot always be clearly attributed to a specific initiative or innovation project.

Some clarity about the quantification of business impact can be achieved by enriching innovation opportunities during the validation process with business impact figures that define success against a specific timeline. For instance, every idea flagged as an innovation opportunity by evaluators or handled by the opportunity validation service is enriched with an *ideal performance scenario* expressed in terms of financial or other metrics and goals. Experts make quick but thoughtful financial projections and adoption scenarios, setting the goals for measuring success when the artifact is launched in the market. In collaboration with the sponsors, evaluators attach a timeline and specific numeric targets to each of the success criteria.

For example, the evaluators define that a specific opportunity will be considered successful only if it reaches at least x new customers in z months from its release. Or gain y percent market share in a specific time frame. These set the expectations, help the team better shape the strategy, and accelerate future performance assessments of the initiative. As part of the process, the innovation opportunity may also receive a special weight factor indicating its importance for the company.

Assuming all artifacts undergo this process before reaching the market, the impact measurement process becomes simpler and more consistent. A team of innovation leaders and sponsors meets regularly to analyze the progress of released artifacts against predefined success criteria and business impact scenarios.

The assessment of live performance of in-market artifacts may happen early in their lifecycle by comparing their actual, in-market figures with the expected values needed to hit their long-term targets. This way, the business impact can be quantified in various ways, for instance, as the percentage of initiatives from a cohort that met or are expected to meet their success criteria or as an index adjusted by the importance given to each innovation opportunity during the validation process. This hides the complexity and allows comparison and aggregation of projects that have different definitions of success.

In addition, the company may set higher-level goals, such as adoption rates, revenue generation, or market share at the portfolio, division, or even innovation function level. For example, a yearly goal could be to acquire a specific number of new subscribers or generate a given revenue figure across initiatives from various realized opportunities. This means that the measurement of the impact of a set of realized opportunities can be achieved by aggregating their projected impact, such as revenue and subscription figures in this example, and then comparing the total projected figures to the higher-level goals.

As with innovation outputs, leaders consider all the above and estimate the business impact score, which is then fed into the corporate innovation performance scorecard as the *Impact* component.

9.1.3 Measuring the Innovation Culture

The state of innovation culture is a crucial component of the innovation performance scorecard. For some corporations, culture could even be the primary target of the innovation function. Measuring the innovation culture can happen directly, for example, by asking people to share their thoughts through surveys and other research tools; it may also happen indirectly by analyzing associated metrics, behaviors, and patterns. A good process should be able to utilize both sources.

The following is a list of metrics or classes of metrics that aim to answer questions like "What is the state of the innovation culture?" or "How active is the innovation community?"

1. **Innovation community size**: This is the number of innovators—employees who have performed at least one core innovation activity, such as submitting an idea, contributing to others' ideas, participating in prototyping, or engaging in voluntary innovation activities during their tenure with the company.
2. **Active innovation community size**: This refers to the number of innovators who have performed at least one core innovation activity within a recent timeframe, e.g., during the last year.
3. **Innovation community churn**: The number of active innovators who convert to "passive" or opt out from the core innovation program over a period of time. This may indicate cultural, procedural, or availability issues that require further analysis through surveys, interviews, or focus groups.

4. **Innovation morale**: This reflects how people *feel* about the level of innovation within the company, the inspiration provided by leadership, and the importance of innovation work taking place within the organization. It can be measured through ad hoc surveys or via a streamlined innovation pulse micro-questionnaire and expressed as a percentage of those with a positive outlook or as an average satisfaction score.
5. **Employee representation**: The percentage of the innovation community size over the total number of employees in the company at a point in time. It indicates the general interest in innovation—low values may signal limited awareness, insufficient communication, or a less inclusive character of innovation.
6. **Experimentation attitude**: This may be defined on top of various metrics, such as the total number of experiments proposed or conducted over a period of time, the number of prototyping projects, the utilization and engagement of the makerspace, or the volume of requests submitted to the opportunity validation service.
7. **Sharing and collaboration attitude**: Behaviors such as sharing knowledge, contributing to ideas from others, voluntarily participating in innovation efforts, and hosting innovation training events are tracked and can be quantified into an overall *sharing and collaboration index*.
8. **Innovation events engagement**: Metrics in this category capture the performance and influence of various innovation events, as they are often driven by the community of innovators. These may include the frequency, the number of participants, and the satisfaction score per event.
9. **Innovation content engagement**: Similarly, this set of metrics reflects how people engage with the innovation content released via various touchpoints. This may include metrics such as the number of visitors to the Innovation Portal, engagement with named content, educational videos, and the innovation assets catalog, among others.
10. **Perceived innovation ability of the company**: This reflects people's perception of how innovative the company is. It can be measured through pulse surveys or by direct questions such as "Do you think that the organization is able to innovate in meaningful and high-potential ways?" This differs from innovation morale, although it is expected to be positively correlated.
11. **Team synthesis, openness, and dynamics**: This class of metrics reflects how teams innovate and how people form or join teams to experiment and collaborate. Such analytics provide significant insights into the state of the innovation culture and how open, balanced, and multidisciplinary teams are, for instance, in hackathons, ad hoc innovation initiatives, and informal projects.

The above should be monitored systematically through standardized reports and dashboards. Additionally, as in the previous two categories, there can be an overall Innovation Culture Score that summarizes the dominant mindset and attitude toward innovation.

The Innovation Culture score can be obtained in several ways, for example, by building a statistical model on top of some of the above metrics or by involving the leaders to interpret them and infer the state of the innovation culture. The most effective way is to leverage the Innovation Pulse survey and encourage people to complete a micro-questionnaire reflecting their level of inspiration, motivation, and sense of purpose. A background process automatically scores the answers and computes the Innovation Culture Score, which is then fed into the innovation scorecard as the *Culture* performance component.

9.1.4 Measuring Public Perception: The Image

The Innovation Perception Index measures the public's view of an organization's innovativeness. This is particularly important as it could reveal interesting gaps between perception and reality, thus helping the company design more effective communication strategies to increase public awareness and enhance its image as an innovative company. Improving public perception helps the company attract talent, inspire partnerships, and reposition itself within the broader ecosystem; it may also help drive the adoption and growth of its products and services.

The public image of the company as an innovator may be shaped in several ways. For example, participating in open innovation initiatives and actively engaging with the start-up scene can enhance the company's innovation profile. Similarly, getting involved in communities and highly visible open-source projects makes the company more visible to audiences that appreciate innovation. Additionally, it is crucial to establish systematic publishing of meaningful innovation stories, plans, and achievements.

While all these outward innovation activities can be directly tracked, quantified, and used as signals for the company's innovation outlook, it is usually more efficient, cost-effective, and insightful to launch a program of frequent, standardized perception measurement surveys. These can be conducted by third-party research companies to ensure coverage of the right audience, proper questionnaire design, and survey execution. The surveys may target the ecosystem or a general audience that is expected to be aware of the company's business activities. In both cases, participants are asked, among other things, to *rate the company as an innovator*.

These surveys should happen regularly, accumulating results and findings in the Innovation Graph. This enables the calculation of a single number that reflects the public's perception of the company as an innovator. This Perceived Innovation Score contributes to the corporate innovation performance scorecard through the *Image* component.

Figure 9.3 presents a wireframe of the corporate innovation performance scorecard, combining the above-described scores in a single view. Each component visualizes a single aspect of innovation performance. For instance, the *Image* displays the latest score for the perceived innovation ability as captured via the systematic surveys. The rest of the elements connect to the Innovation Graph to retrieve and visualize the current values of the corresponding KPIs. At the top of the scorecard is a single Innovation Performance Score, defined as a weighted aggregation of the four components.

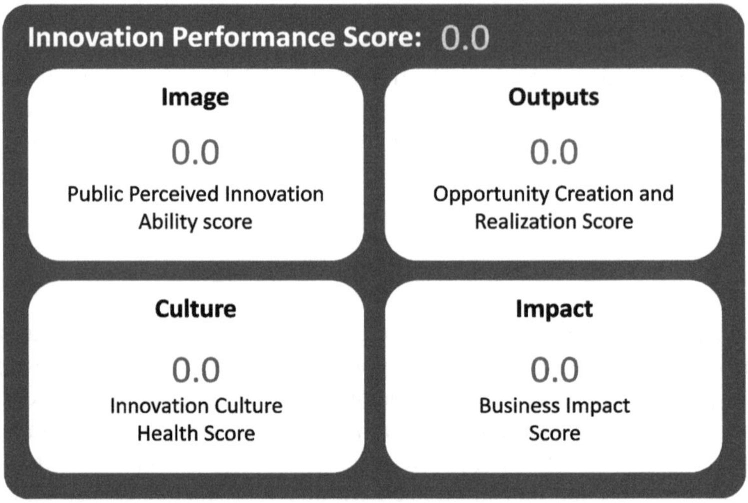

Fig. 9.3 The structure of a corporate innovation performance scorecard

9.1.5 Measuring Cost

The cost of the overall innovation function should also be measured and monitored. In parallel with all the performance measurements, the company should maintain a detailed record of actual costs, including both direct and indirect expenses. Direct costs include investments in laboratories, equipment, specialized personnel, development teams, and associated operational expenses. Indirect costs derive from time spent on innovation workshops, design sprints, and hackathons, along with voluntary contributions and informal experiments. These should be tracked to estimate average figures for the cost per innovation event, prototype, cost of innovation opportunities, cost per participant in educational initiatives, and other relevant figures. Ideally, there should be an overall operational cost for the innovation function with the ability to break it down by process, for instance, the *cost of opportunity discovery* versus the *cost of opportunity validation*, etc. In all cases, the company must be able to separate operational versus innovation investment costs.

Having reliable cost figures enables an accurate view of the overall operational cost of the innovation function and its relationship to performance indicators. It helps set goals and evaluate decisions.

9.2 The Micro View: Innovation Performance at the Innovator's Level

There are cases where innovation activity needs to be tracked at the innovator level, for example, in the context of the Innovation Reward System that aims to identify and celebrate achievements and distinguished innovators. In most cases, the contribution of innovators is tracked seamlessly. For instance, when a user creates an idea in the Innovation Portal, a corresponding event is automatically captured, contributing to the user's innovation impact. Similar events are tracked when people contribute to ideas by others, join innovation contests, give talks on innovation, or volunteer in prototyping projects. In general, all the defined innovation-related activities can be linked with the Reward System, so the various behaviors of innovation discussed in Chap. 3 can be acknowledged and promoted.

9.2.1 Quantifying Innovation Behaviors

Traditionally, innovators are rewarded for "classic" success, that is, for winning a top position in a contest or hackathon or for driving an idea to market. However, in the spirit of *inclusiveness* and *healthy competition*, companies need to also consider dimensions such as *willingness to share and contribute*. The following proposes a scheme of three measurement dimensions that correspond to the values of the innovation culture.

1. **Inventiveness**: This measures the extent to which innovators generate inventive ideas—concepts that have increased levels of both *novelty* and *business potential*. Since every idea that goes through the discovery pipeline is eventually evaluated against these attributes, it is feasible to identify innovators who consistently demonstrate the ability to generate inventive concepts. Another signal of inventiveness can be the volume of patent applications filed or granted.
2. **Eagerness to contribute**: Genuine innovators can bring a massive impact by helping others innovate or by supporting ongoing innovation threads. Often, people prefer to add value by unblocking or advising others in activities such as idea evaluation, brainstorming, prototyping, and participation in design sprints. Most of these activities can be tracked through properly implemented innovation systems and collaboration tools. For example, when a contribution to an idea occurs through the Innovation Portal, the innovator is automatically listed in the chain of contributors as part of the idea's history. Hence, it is easy to quantify these behaviors and consider them when identifying the top innovators.
3. **Willingness to share**: Sometimes, great innovators may be reluctant to share ideas, knowledge, or information—which is usually an issue of organizational culture. This issue can be fixed by measuring and openly communicating the positive impact of sharing and acknowledging those innovators who lead by example. The willingness to share can be quantified in terms of information and knowledge-sharing activity and frequency of sharing.

The above qualities may be associated with specific behaviors and actions that are pre-configured in the innovation framework. For example, assuming that within a month, a user contributes to the evolution of an idea, gives an innovation talk, and files a patent. Each of these three innovation actions assigns a specific number of *innovation points* to the user—where the number of points is configured at the activity level to reflect its importance to the company. For example, the innovator may receive 10 points for *filing a patent*, 5 points for *submitting an idea*, and 3 points for *giving an innovation talk*. Moreover, certain events may happen that also allocate points to the involved innovators. For example, when an idea is flagged as an innovation opportunity, the originators get an additional 20× points. This quantification of innovation activity and behaviors sets the basis for a more objective process of identifying top innovators through a data-driven approach that takes into consideration the values of sharing and collaboration. Furthermore, these performance measurements can be aggregated by team, division, or functional area within the organization and analyzed by skill set, seniority, or profile.

This provides leaders with valuable insights regarding the community of innovators and its internal drivers. Of course, the measurement program should be compliant with corporate policies; for instance, it must provide employees with the option to opt out.

9.3 The Innovation Insights Store

The insights store is one of the fundamental components of the Innovation Graph. It empowers the Rewards System and provides intelligence that helps orchestrate the innovation function and steer the entire innovation program. It allows innovation leaders to understand the state of innovation, set the direction, and iterate fast.

This specialized data store is designed to handle every interaction with the innovation framework. All innovation systems and components, from the Innovation Portal to the Workshop Designer, occasionally reflect their activity by appending interaction data to the insights store. More specifically, the areas of the data stored are summarized in the following:

- **Innovation events**: This is a detailed history of how the company innovates in terms of innovation workshops and events. Every innovation event being planned, from brainstorming sessions to hackathons and design sprints, is appended here, along with subsequent updates on its attendance and performance. This enables rich reporting on event cost, engagement, and impact across event types, topics, and over time.
- **Innovation assets registry and history**: The assets registry contains entries for all the innovation artifacts produced through the various innovation initiatives and workshops. Moreover, it captures lifecycle events, such as sharing, assessment, development kick-off, release, and publication, among others. Additionally, snapshots of performance measurements or testing results at the innovation asset level are also hosted here.
- **Innovator's activity**: This data collection contains actions performed by innovators, including the submission of ideas, patent applications, participation in hackathons, publication of papers, and public talks on innovation. It also includes the history of innovation points accumulation.
- **Innovation capabilities utilization**: This collection of data objects contains a history of operational and utilization data for all the major innovation capabilities and processes. For example, it includes traffic and engagement insights for

the Innovation Portal, the volume of requests and response times of the opportunity validation service, and workload statistics about the idea evaluation service.

- **Surveys and research findings**: This bucket organizes insights generated through systematic internal or external surveys, ranging from the always-on Innovation Pulse to research on perceived innovation ability conducted in the market. It may also capture innovation intelligence reports and findings on the competition and market dynamics.
- **Organizational data**: This class of data reflects the latest organizational information, including the hierarchy, organizational structure, business lines, and corporate calendar. It is valuable in generating interesting views and pivots against the rich data on innovation activity.

At the top of Fig. 9.4 are three characteristic client applications for the innovation insights, as produced in the Innovation Graph. The first one is the *innovation performance scorecard* presented previously. The second is a series of *interactive dashboards* designed to help innovation leaders make informed decisions when steering the innovation program. The third is a class of experiences that implement gamification elements, for instance, *leaderboards* showcasing top innovators and their most impactful ideas.

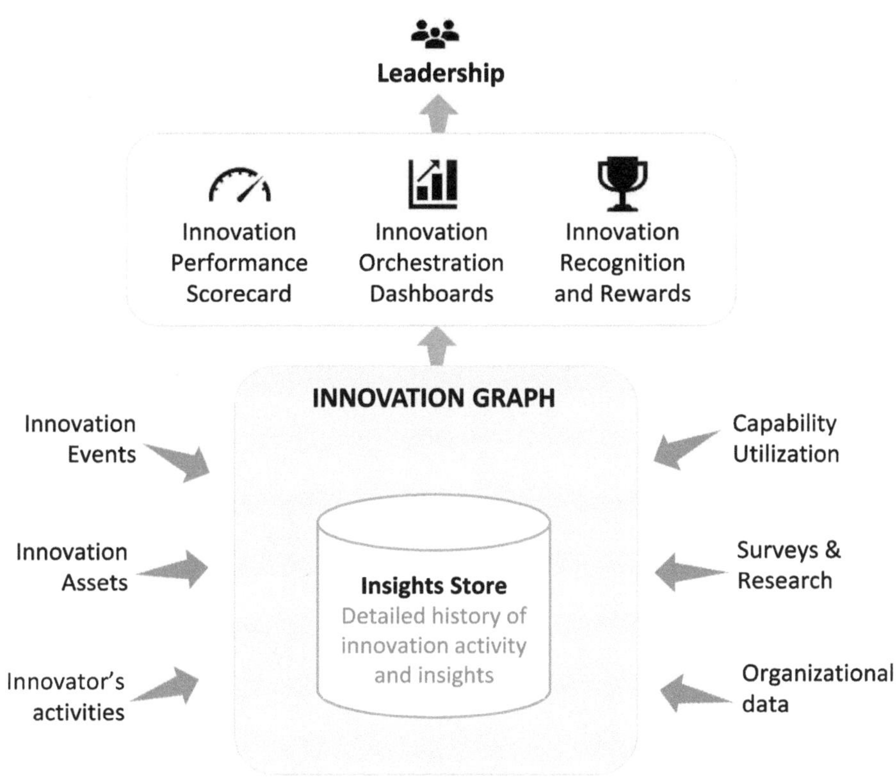

Fig. 9.4 The insights store: part of the Innovation Graph

This concludes the presentation of a powerful innovation measurement framework—an essential capability for corporate success and a cornerstone of high-impact transformation. The next chapter builds on this foundation with the masterplan toward the Innovation Mode.

The Innovation Masterplan: Getting to the Innovation Mode

10

Up to this point, we have presented the key ingredients for establishing *a truly innovative organization*. We covered the principles for building a great innovation culture and introduced capabilities such as *opportunity discovery, validation*, and *realization*, along with the *market intelligence service*. Moreover, we presented how workshops play a key role in driving innovation and how to connect Design Sprints and hackathons to the broader innovation framework. But how do all these fit together? How should a company implement these capabilities, and in what order?

This chapter presents a powerful *innovation transformation program* that can be adapted and applied to any organization, regardless of its size, industry, or level of innovation readiness. The program organizes more than 70 initiatives or activities into *named phases*, each containing a structured action plan to gradually take the company to the next level of the Innovation Maturity Index (presented in Chap. 2) and eventually to the Innovation Mode.

The innovation transformation program defines *what* needs to be done, *why*, *how*, *by whom*, and *in what order*. However, the program is not only about introducing methodologies, launching systems, or integrating technological solutions; it is also about bringing the necessary *organizational, cultural, and process changes* to enhance the company's innovation ability. The multiple deliverables of this program, including systems, processes, and organizational designs, must work as a cohesive system that drives the adoption of innovation methods and improves the organization's ability to innovate at pace and scale.

The program guides an *innovation-inactive* company through the *aware*, *active*, *powered*, and *led* stages, ultimately transforming it into an *innovation-native* organization operating in the Innovation Mode. For this transformation to happen, we introduce a system of six phases—each boosting the organization's ability to innovate—through improvements in *methods*, *culture*, *tools*, and *knowledge*. These six phases provide the structure of the innovation program and are defined as:

G. Krasadakis, *Innovation Mode 2.0*,
https://doi.org/10.1007/978-3-032-00835-0_10

1. **Power-up innovation**: This phase powers up innovation in the company—it raises awareness about the importance of innovation, its methods, and tools. It brings an *innovation-inactive* company to the *innovation-aware* state (Level 2).
2. **Spark innovation**: This phase ignites innovation by providing key enablers, establishing knowledge-sharing initiatives, bringing best practices, and forming an *innovation community* within the company. It takes the organization from the *innovation-aware* to the *innovation-engaged* state (Level 3).
3. **Connect innovation**: This phase connects the various components of innovation with the company's goals and objectives. It establishes a steady flow of actionable ideas, activates the opportunity discovery function, and gradually takes the company from the *innovation-engaged* to the *innovation-active* state (Level 4).
4. **Empower innovation**: This phase is about empowering the organization to make informed decisions about identified opportunities through experimentation and related capabilities. It takes the company from *innovation-active* to *innovation-powered* (Level 5), making it responsive and fast in spotting and pursuing high-potential opportunities.
5. **Scale-up innovation**: This phase enables the organization to *innovate at scale* by making key capabilities more "elastic" and establishing optimal flows of innovation, knowledge, and intelligence across teams, groups, and divisions. It takes the company to *innovation-led* state (Level 6).
6. **Embed innovation**: This phase aims to reach the *Innovation Mode*—the state where the elements of innovation are so deeply integrated into the company's structures and culture that they are perceived as hardwired and embedded (Level 7).

Figure 10.1 presents how each of these phases (horizontal axis) takes the organization to the next level of the Innovation Maturity Index (vertical axis).

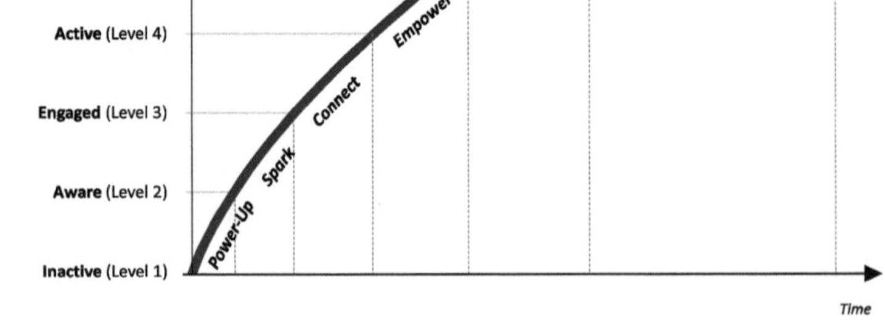

Fig. 10.1 Transformation phases and level of innovation of the organization

To illustrate the journey from *Inactive* (Level 1) to *Native* (Level 7), we may use a hypothetical company that has no innovation programs and initiatives—it is *innovation-inactive*. In this hypothetical scenario, the company's leadership has decided to invest in establishing an innovation capability and driving the necessary changes to make the company truly innovative. They form a *core innovation team* to drive the company through the *Power-Up* phase by launching a series of orchestrated initiatives, projects, and communication events that gradually raise general awareness of the need for innovation and its importance for the company's future. People learn about the process of innovation, the essential tools, methods, and required skills. When this general awareness and understanding of the innovation method are achieved, the organization transitions from the *inactive* (Level 1) to the *aware* state (Level 2).

Being fully aware of the possibilities of innovation, this hypothetical company becomes more open to adopting special tools and innovation processes. The core team advocates for innovation, helps the organization upskill, and introduces new tools and capabilities—innovation enablers. Most importantly, the core team leads by example—showcasing an intrapreneurial mindset, which *sparks innovation* across the company and gradually takes it to the next level: *engaged* (Level 3).

When a basic level of engagement with innovation is achieved, people start showing genuine interest in innovation and begin to participate in programs and events. The core team then triggers the next wave of projects, which bring new tools, techniques, and resources. They explain how the new capabilities support the company's innovation agenda and provide paradigms on how to apply innovation to drive real-world impact and business outcomes. The company gradually becomes *innovation-active*, capable of *systematically producing ideas and opportunities* (Level 4).

Similarly, the *empower* phase introduces advanced capabilities and increases the *readiness to discover opportunities* and build *better products* and *services*; the corporation becomes *powered by innovation* in the sense that innovation has a remarkable impact on the company's overall performance and shapes its future (Level 5).

The general adoption of the innovation tools and methods, the strong innovation culture, and the growing innovation community make the company inherently innovative. Moreover, the adoption of artificial intelligence at various stages of the innovation process enables the company to become more proactive by spotting, testing, and pursuing opportunities faster. The company gradually becomes *innovation-led* (Level 6), meaning that innovation powers not only current business offerings but also opportunities for new products, markets, or business models, influencing various aspects of the company's strategy. At this level, people *understand the company's success as a direct result of being genuinely innovative*. Innovation is now part of the company's essence: it happens organically and gradually becomes indistinguishable from its core business functions. The organization becomes *native to innovation*, which signals the transition to the ultimate state (Level 7): the Innovation Mode.

These six phases can be thought of as "boosters" that aim to improve the organization's ability to innovate. In fact, they are special programs themselves, each consisting of several projects, workstreams, and communication events. They do not have a fixed duration though. Instead, the successful completion of each phase is signaled when a set of success criteria is *consistently met*, which, depending on the phase, may include goals for the cultural shift, adoption of innovation capabilities, or a proven ability to create innovation opportunities.

A phase may last several months or even years, depending on factors such as the organization's industry, the investment made, and the composition of the team that drives the innovation program.

What is presented above is just a simplified version of what happens in the real world. Achieving the desired outcomes, though, is not easy; it requires energy, commitment, persistence, excellent communication, and leadership by example. The program is a demanding, bold, highly visible initiative with multiple stakeholders and occasionally competing objectives. As a result, in many cases, conflicts may arise around prioritization, focus, or decision-making. Hence, the success of the program requires strong leadership—it needs a powerful core team that brings a bold innovation vision and has the ability to execute and steer the program in an agile, fast manner, aligning with the broader strategy. The core team has a challenging role—it must bring together the entire organization across levels, disciplines, and geographies, provide clarity, inspire people, and drive alignment. To deliver on its promise, the core team must carefully set up the program with the right sequence of events, agility in planning, readiness to pivot, data-driven decision-making, and the correct dose and style of communication at each point.

Moreover, the program needs *executive sponsorship* from the top level of the organization. Beyond formal support, corporate leaders are expected to demonstrate their commitment to the program's vision through authentic engagement with innovation experiences and thus send a strong message on the importance of innovation for the company.

The following presents a blueprint for a powerful innovation transformation program, starting with a *preparation phase* followed by an *agile, iterative, and adaptive process* that elevates the company through the levels of the Innovation Maturity Index—from Level 1 (innovation-inactive) to Level 7 (innovation-native). The program uses a solid measurement framework that allows objective assessment of its impact and indicates when the organization is ready to transition to the next phase.

10.1 Preparing the Program

The first step in shaping the innovation transformation program is to identify if the *right skills* are available at the leadership level. What is needed at this early stage is a *deep understanding of the innovation process* and *experience in architecting innovation programs*. The innovation leadership team must have the ability to frame the program—set its purpose, focus, structure, milestones, and pace, among other elements. The following presents a list of the first and most essential steps that set the basis for the program:

1. **Appoint the innovation program director**: If there are experienced innovation leaders in your company—e.g., a chief innovation officer—the decision is

straightforward. If not, you will need to hire people with the required talent and knowledge—professionals who deeply understand corporate innovation and its processes and can help the company prepare for this demanding transformational journey (see also Chap. 3, the section describing the profile of the chief innovation officer).

2. **Set up the core innovation team**: This is perhaps the most important job for the innovation program director: to set up an innovation "taskforce," a highly motivated, autonomous, cross-disciplinary innovation team. The team's purpose is to transform the organization into an *innovation machine*—to introduce the technological, process, and organizational changes that will make it truly innovative and agile. The team collaborates with the innovation director and the organization's leadership to design an optimal, tailor-made program that reflects the company's needs and ambitions. Beyond design, the team assumes full ownership and responsibility for the effective execution of the program. They commit to driving the organization through a continual improvement process that gradually expands its innovation capabilities and improves all aspects of innovation—culture, enablers, and processes. The innovation team is expected to demonstrate effective leadership by inspiring and guiding the community of innovators, transferring knowledge, providing real examples of innovation, and linking innovation with the organizational purpose. The objective is not just to introduce capabilities but *to drive their adoption* and value. The innovation team is data driven, measuring the impact of each iteration and using insights to steer the program as needed. At the same time, the team balances the costs by applying smart prioritization before committing to acquiring expensive technologies and resources. Moreover, the team ensures alignment with the corporate leadership through regular communication of progress, decisions, and insights. As a starting point, the team should have an innovation architect and a program manager working closely with the program director to kick off the program, initiate key threads, and acquire the right resources as needed, according to the desired pace of execution. While initially small, this team is expected to grow fast with additional roles, as described in detail in Chap. 3.
3. **Perform a preliminary assessment**: This initial assessment is one of the primary responsibilities of the innovation program director. The objective is to understand the company's current *innovation setup* and compare it to the ideal innovation architecture to obtain a detailed gap analysis regarding innovation capabilities, resources, skills, and talents. This assessment is essential since it sets the context and the basis for designing the entire program. The program director orchestrates a series of surveys and interviews with key people across the hierarchy to understand *how innovation is perceived*, *what needs to change*, and *what people expect*. The team studies the dynamics of the organization while working closely with leadership members to articulate the innovation ambition and interpret initial findings, gaps, issues, and blind spots. This process typically unveils significant problems, such as cultural blockers, capability gaps, and areas for improvement that the company may not even be aware of. The findings are summarized as a report that also states the company's innovation maturity level, as defined in Chap. 2.

4. **Articulate the innovation vision**: The program director collaborates with corporate executives to frame the innovation vision and ensure it aligns with the organizational purpose and strategy. Moreover, they define innovation in the company's context and what success looks like for the program.
5. **Draft a roadmap and expand the innovation team**: The program director uses the information collected through the preliminary analysis to draft a high-level plan and roadmap for the entire initiative. Moreover, the director identifies any additional key skills required to empower the innovation team to achieve its goal: to drive the company to the Innovation Mode.

10.1.1 The Innovation Masterplan

The Innovation Masterplan is the foundational document for the innovation transformation initiative. It is a "living document" that frames the entire program in terms of objectives, scope of work, leadership model, projects, workshops, and communication plans, along with activities, timelines, milestones, and methods for tracking progress and measuring success. It is the manifest of the program that, at any point in time, reflects the strategy, goals, and current state of innovation.

The program director processes the findings from the preliminary assessment to compile the Innovation Masterplan, which is then used to drive alignment among leaders on the direction of the program. The Masterplan reflects a shared understanding and commitment to the following aspects:

1. **Vision and goals**: The innovation team articulates the program's objectives and how they align with the organizational purpose and strategy. This section provides the context and explains the timing, aspirations, and strategic importance of the innovation program, as well as how it can contribute to the organization's success.
2. **Innovation agenda**: The team compiles the first version of the Innovation Agenda. As explained in Chap. 3, the agenda presents the organization's mid- and long-term innovation focus by referencing strategic problems worth solving, as prioritized by the leadership. It sets the focus of innovation in a practical way—by explaining how solving these problems can bring the company closer to its goals and purpose.
3. **Current state of innovation**: The team positions the company against the Innovation Maturity Index (Chap. 2) and provides a narrative that explains and justifies the assessment by referencing insights obtained from the preliminary analysis. This section also covers both current and previous innovation attempts, known issues, identified blockers, and areas for improvement. It provides an essential snapshot that sets the context and enables tracking of improvements and comparison of future insights.
4. **Innovation team structure**: This section outlines the innovation team that, along with the program director, owns and leads the program. The innovation team is expected to evolve in many ways. Hence, it is essential to document the

team's initial synthesis along with clearly defined roles, responsibilities, target headcounts, and hiring plans.

5. **Budget**: It is important to include initial estimates of the resources needed for the innovation program, e.g., hiring, acquiring capabilities such as innovation management software, initiating educational programs, and hosting events. The leadership must approve the budget and establish a mechanism for requesting additional funding to ensure the required resources are available throughout the program.
6. **Success criteria**: The success of the innovation program can be defined in terms of high-level goals and milestones, such as a shift in the culture of innovation, as well as key performance indicators (KPIs) that reflect the ability to discover, validate, and realize opportunities. The success criteria must be accurately defined and measurable, covering all the key aspects of the innovation program and its desired outcomes.
7. **Stakeholder map**: This serves as the "relationship navigator," presenting the key individuals and groups that influence the program or directly benefit from it, such as executive sponsors, product leaders, innovation champions, and domain experts. The map outlines each stakeholder's role, decision-making authority, and innovation perspectives and illustrates how they contribute to the program and what benefits they anticipate. Moreover, the map may include stakeholder-specific success metrics, communication preferences, potential alignment challenges, and strategies to handle them.
8. **The approach and style of innovation**: Not all companies need to innovate in the same way—what works for one may not work for another. For example, a product-led software company may require a fast, incremental product innovation process to stay ahead of the competition, protect its market share, and keep current product offerings competitive. A technology hardware company may focus on longer-term innovation investments that create intellectual property (IP) and further differentiate its products. A science-led company may require long-term scientific research and development (R&D) programs designed to drive radical innovations. Similarly, a company may be looking for new business models, products, and services while developing an extensive *patent portfolio*. Typically, companies require a specific blend of the above styles and approaches to innovation. The program director and the innovation team consider the company's needs and strategy to determine the appropriate balance between types and styles of innovation.

10.1.2 Prioritizing the Right Innovation Capabilities

The ultimate goal of the innovation program is to enable people and the organization to innovate faster and more effectively, which requires the introduction, adoption, and operation of the right *innovation capabilities*. For example, a system to facilitate the *submission and discovery of ideas* or a measurement framework to systematically analyze the company's innovation performance. The capabilities range from services offered by teams within the company (e.g., market intelligence) to self-service digital tools (e.g., an idea framing tool) or even autonomous AI-powered systems (e.g., an AI agent scanning the market in the context of the company and raising alerts when there are new, interesting developments.) Additionally, there are innovation resources that encourage and empower people to engage with innovation, such as knowledge, methodologies, specialized equipment, and purpose-specific office space.

The challenge for the team is to identify the right resources and enablers and launch them at the right point in the transformation process, according to real needs, priorities, and budgets. A good approach to structuring the innovation transformation program and setting meaningful priorities is to apply lean and agile principles: *start small*, *release early*, *listen to feedback*, *iterate fast*, and *be ready to pivot*.

To start small, the team needs to identify the innovation enablers that can cover those immediate needs, for example, tools or templates that support day-to-day innovation activities such as ideation and brainstorming. These enablers could come in various levels of sophistication, ranging from a paper-based process and digital forms to AI-powered digital experiences. Similarly, the idea review process could be initially delivered manually and low-tech (people gather in a room to discuss ideas, rate them, and decide on potential next steps) or as a sophisticated AI-powered system, such as a digital platform that enables remote and asynchronous idea reviews from both humans and AIs (as discussed in Chap. 6).

Obviously, manual processes are inexpensive (to set up) and easy to start with, but they are slow and expensive (to operate and scale) and may only serve the purpose partially. On the other hand, sophisticated digital platforms come with high initial and operational costs, but they are far more efficient, scalable, and capable of serving innovation at scale. While it is apparent that technology can accelerate specific innovation processes, there is always a risk of overemphasizing its importance and starting with a non-optimal prioritization. Investing in advanced technological solutions from the very beginning allocates valuable resources to components that will only provide value after months of iterations and program improvements. For example, a highly sophisticated, AI-powered ideation system would be of limited benefit for the first few iterations. Such smart systems add significant value but mostly when innovating at scale and when a certain level of cultural and technological maturity is present.

Especially when initiating the program, instead of locking valuable resources for unnecessary components, consider introducing low-tech solutions—implement them manually or with basic tools already in place. Starting small is a wise approach as long as there is a strategy for quick iterations and continual improvement. For instance, you may start with a manual ideation process and, in subsequent iterations, add digital tools for capturing ideas or AI agents that automatically generate and feed ideas into the opportunity discovery pipeline. With this approach, ideas may start flowing in from the very first iteration of the program, while improvements are scheduled to follow at a fast pace.

Selecting the right capabilities requires three primary inputs:

1. **The innovation agenda**: This provides clarity on the big problems the company is trying to solve through innovation and the broader strategic context.
2. **The innovation maturity level**: This represents the current positioning of the organization in terms of innovation readiness, along with a detailed gap analysis comparing existing innovation capabilities with the ideal innovation architecture.
3. **The Innovation Capability Index**: The innovation framework, as presented in Chap. 4, provides the superset of the innovation capabilities. Some of these target early stages in the process, while others are more sophisticated, bringing value in advanced innovation scenarios. The core team must understand the purpose and potential of each of these capabilities, along with their associated costs, lead times, and relative importance within the context of their organization. This allows both to *select the right capabilities to focus on* and *identify the level of sophistication* needed for a successful start.

The above inputs allow the program director and the team to set priorities, identify dependencies, and focus on the most valuable innovation capabilities addressing the actual needs of the organization. The team uses the context captured through the preliminary analysis to make informed decisions on resource allocation and investment trade-offs, also considering the expected pace of innovation and the goals set on engagement and adoption levels. These decisions and their justifications become part of the Innovation Masterplan.

Table 10.1 presents[1] the inventory of innovation capabilities, organized in a way that helps the innovation team plan more efficiently and accurately according to the organization's needs. The first column of the table names the capability, for example, "idea submission" or "idea evaluation." The second column represents a score from 0 to 10 that captures the urgency of the capability, as assessed by the core team, specifically in the context of the organization and the actual timing. The third column captures the level of dependency of the capability on advanced technologies; it reflects the *minimum acceptable level of technical sophistication* required by the capability. The higher the "tech dependency," the stronger the need for a sophisticated technology solution. A low value indicates that the capability can be offered manually without necessarily introducing a technology tool. The basis here is that not all capabilities require the latest and most advanced technologies from the very beginning. Moreover, most capabilities are available at various levels of sophistication, ranging from manual, pen-and-paper processes to specialized commercial software and even AI-powered services. When there is such flexibility, the innovation team should consider *starting small* with the most straightforward approach and follow up with improvements at the right moment in the program. This allows the team to adopt *a progressive approach* and gradually establish more sophisticated and expensive innovation enablers—in an iterative fashion.

[1] Note that this is just a general case for purposes of the book—in practice, this listing should contain the entire set of possible innovation enablers in a corporate context.

Table 10.1 Inventory of innovation capabilities

Innovation capability	Urgency	Tech dependency	Justification
Idea submission	10	2	
Idea evaluation	10	2	
Idea diffusion	…	…	
Innovation insights store	…	…	
Idea store	…	…	
Content discovery	…	…	
Content creation	…	…	
Portfolio management	…	…	
Reward and gamification	…	…	
Hackathon	…	…	
Prototyping	…	…	
Innovation portal	…	…	
Makerspace	…	…	
Makerspace portal	…	…	
Demo expo	…	…	
Innovation measurement	…	…	
Orchestration	…	…	
Patent process	…	…	
…	…	…	

For instance, if the company has no ideation system or process in place, it should be easy to reach a consensus that this is *urgent*—the organization needs a way to accept and manage ideas from the very beginning. However, the tech dependency for the ideation system is low: it can be done using documents or even with sticky notes on a wall. If the conditions or the organization permit it, such a low-tech approach could be suitable as a starting point, provided that there is a plan of action to introduce proper tools at the right time. However, such inexpensive alternatives may not be sufficient in some cases, not even as a quick start. For instance, if the team plans to host a large-scale, company-wide hackathon at the early stages of the program, a robust digital platform is required to effectively capture and manage ideas at a large scale.

The Innovation Capability Index helps the team evaluate the organization's innovation needs, identify gaps, and assign the right priorities for implementation. For each item listed, the team explains whether it is already available within the company and, if so, describes the level of engagement and adoption, along with any known issues and limitations. Similarly, if the team thinks a specific item from the list is unnecessary, they provide the reasoning. Likewise, if it exists but needs improvement or replacement, the team describes the situation. For all those items that are necessary, the team also performs the following assessment, using *urgency* and *tech dependency* as defined above:

1. **Urgency**: The team quantifies the urgency of the capability in the context of the organization and justifies the assessment. A value of 0 signals that "it can wait," and 10 states that "it is needed now."

2. **Tech dependency**: The team indicates whether a high-tech solution is needed in the organization and justifies the assessment—e.g., explaining how the manual process would work or why a sophisticated version would be preferable to the manual approach. A value of 0 means that "it can work manually," and 10 suggests that "it requires advanced technology."

Having completed this quick assessment, the team clusters the capabilities as visualized in Fig. 10.2. In this chart, the horizontal axis represents the level of tech dependency, indicating the required level of sophistication. A low value means that the capability may be valuable in its simplest form—as a no-tech or low-tech implementation to start with. A high value indicates that it cannot be delivered without special tools, technology, teams, and a technology system. The vertical axis represents the item's urgency in the context of the innovation program, as estimated by the core team. High values in this axis indicate that the capability or feature is urgent, i.e., it is "needed now," while low values indicate that "it can wait." Note that

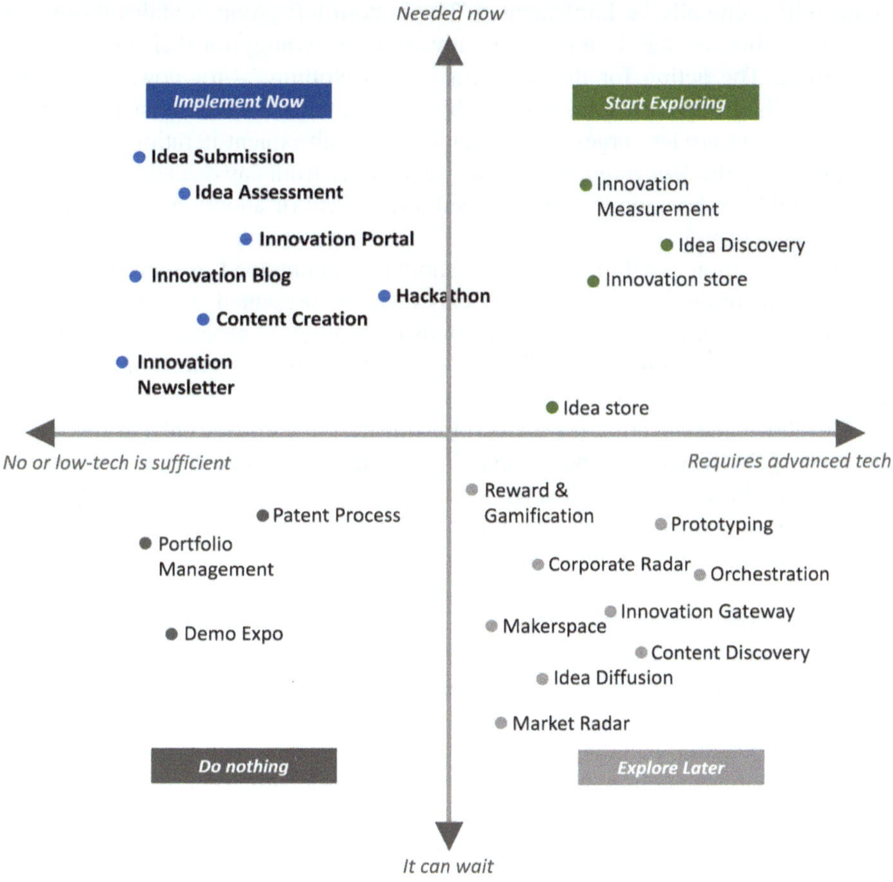

Fig. 10.2 Prioritizing innovation capabilities

this does not refer to the objective importance or value of the capability. Instead, it should only reflect how valuable it is for the company *at the time of assessment*; it is contextual, based on what the company already has in place and what needs to be included in the launch of the innovation program.

We can then use these assessments to cluster the capabilities and simplify the planning and prioritization process. The top-left group, labeled "Implement Now," refers to highly needed capabilities that can be established with a low- or no-tech implementation. Capabilities found in this area should be considered for immediate start. The top-right group contains those highly needed capabilities that require advanced technology and thus considerable investment, even for their most basic form.

For example, *innovation measurement* is indeed highly desirable, but it cannot be provided without a specialized database and related integrations to track and quantify innovation activity. The simplest form it can take is too sophisticated and expensive. Therefore, the recommended action for the top-right group is to "Start Exploring," as this will save time in forthcoming iterations, where some of these items will eventually be implemented. The bottom-left group contains those non-urgent capabilities that do not require advanced technology for their initial implementation. The action for this segment is "Do Nothing"—for now. Finally, the bottom-right group corresponds to capabilities that require advanced and expensive technology but are less urgent—they can wait for subsequent iterations. For example, providing the *Makerspace* or gateway capability from day one adds no value, as there would not be enough content, a sufficient level of adoption, or readiness to derive value from it.

The innovation capability inventory should be maintained in sync by updating statuses and progress. This way, the classification presented in this section will eventually give different results as the innovation program progresses. A "do nothing" item may transition to "implement now" after a few iterations of the innovation loop.

The above classification is provided for illustrative purposes only, as there is no universal prioritization of these capabilities. They all depend on the context, the Innovation Maturity Level of the corporation being analyzed, and the exact phase in the innovation transformation program. You should use this as a guide to assess your innovation capability readiness according to your company's objectives and strategic priorities. Producing the actual innovation capability prioritization for your company allows you to define the exact *action plan* of the six innovation boosters presented earlier, from *Power-Up* to *Embed*.

The preparation phase of the program concludes with the finalization of the Innovation Masterplan—the document that contains the innovation roadmap, project details, resource planning, an index of defined events, and the communication strategy. Upon completion, which comes with the leadership's approval of the entire program, a formal announcement initiates the Power-Up phase.

The remainder of this chapter presents in detail the objectives, structure, and activities of each of the six phases of the innovation transformation program. It describes the projects, communication actions, educational activities, and innovation events that can help your organization transition into the Innovation Mode. The program lists over 70 recommended actions or initiatives that can significantly improve your innovation capabilities. When necessary, I also include best practices and hints for implementing the proposed initiatives.

For simplicity, we assume that the organization joining the Power-Up phase is *innovation-inactive*, meaning that no systematic innovation activity is happening or planned. If your company is already in a more mature innovation state, you can adapt this program to start from the appropriate entry point. Moreover, the program is structured in a flexible way, with relative only prioritization, allowing your team to modify it according to your needs, context, and strategic objectives.

The innovation transformation program starts with powering up innovation.

10.2 Power-Up Innovation: Getting to Level 2

This is the first phase of the program, setting the foundation—it introduces the *essentials of innovation* that turn the power on and trigger the basic innovation processes. The organization enters this phase as *innovation-inactive*, with no established innovation function or systematic activities. The objective is to increase awareness, provide the fundamentals, achieve basic readiness, and mobilize things so the organization gets gradually "upgraded" to the next level in the Innovation Maturity Index: *innovation-aware* (Level 2).

Most of the workstreams in this phase happen behind the scenes, parallel to daily business activities. Some activities are simple communication tasks or workshops, while others are more practical, such as introducing new innovation capabilities. Meanwhile, there is significant activity in fine-tuning the program itself.

As shown in Fig. 10.3, this phase begins with the launch of the Innovation Pulse Survey, which helps the core team understand the state of innovation within the company.

The remainder of the Power-Up phase focuses on communication activities, aiming to attract widespread attention and demonstrate how innovation is linked to corporate strategy. Business and Innovation leaders introduce the program, present the agenda, and emphasize that innovation is crucial for the organization's success.

This phase is content-intensive, involving the development of high-quality artifacts that promote the program and enable educational activities, including the 'Innovation Talks' and the 'Innovation Academy' programs. At least for the first phases of the program, it is the core team that leads the creation of content, ranging from innovation stories and articles to material presenting the innovation program itself. Gradually, they create templates and delegate this process to the extended team or the community of innovators. In all cases, they ensure that the content is of high quality and branded so it is reusable across channels and activities.

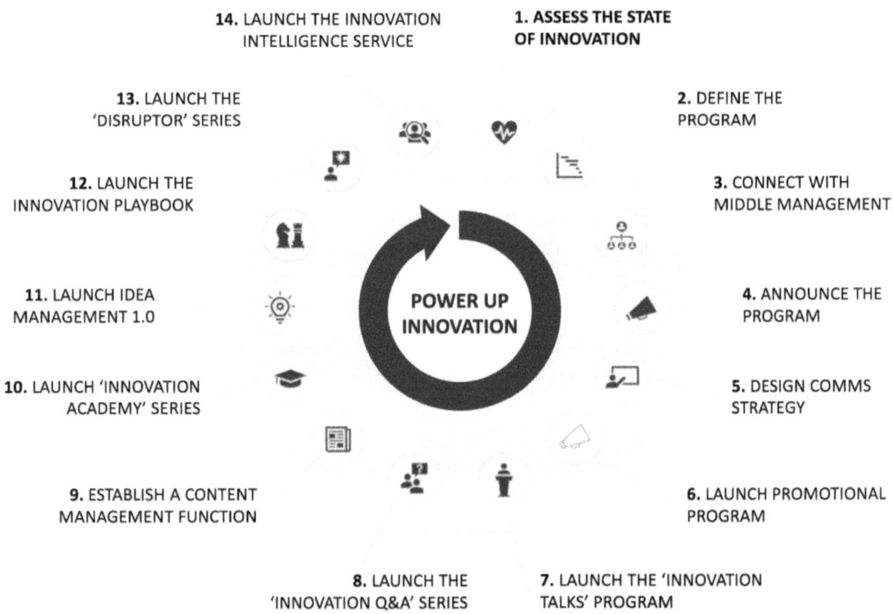

Fig. 10.3 The power-up phase of the program—from inactive to aware

The duration of the Power-Up phase depends on the readiness of the organization, the ambition of the program, and the availability of resources. Provided that the core innovation team is well sourced, it would typically take 3–6 months to reach the required level of awareness and readiness.

During the Power-Up phase, the innovation team establishes the program and, in parallel, performs the following key operations:

1. **Assess the state of innovation**: As the first step of the entire program, it is crucial to understand the organization's *current state of innovation* and, more specifically, *what people believe about innovation* and how they perceive the plans in this direction. These can be done in various ways, including:
   – **Run an innovation pulse survey**: An initial survey, asking people across the company to express their thoughts on innovation, is extremely valuable in *spotting gaps, needs, issues, or misconceptions*. Simple questions like "How innovative is the organization?" or "Do you think you have all the resources you need to innovate?" may reveal critical insights. This initial quantification of innovation perception guides the core team, as it can influence the planning of the program and indicate the need to introduce new activities and communication strategies. It also sets a baseline for interpreting the future states of the organization. The first instance of the Pulse Survey can be conducted in an ad hoc manner, allowing the innovation team to obtain insights quickly while also testing the structure, wording, and framing of the questions. The objective of this first assessment, however, goes

beyond the initial insights. The team uses it as the first step in designing a streamlined version of the Pulse Survey, as an always-on channel that accepts and automatically handles feedback about the innovation function.
 - **Interview people**: In addition to the survey, speaking with people across the organization is essential for gaining a deeper understanding of their needs and opinions across various levels and departments. Hosting user interviews or focus groups on specific aspects of the innovation program may reveal blind spots or new perspectives that can influence the direction of the initiative.
 - **Baseline the state of innovation**: This step enriches the insights obtained through surveys and user research with *evidence* about recent innovation activities. The objective is to collect statistics, reports, and facts, such as patent submissions, the frequency of innovation events, participation rates in workshops, and the number of prototypes or demos built per year, among others. At this stage, most of these metrics will be close to zero, as we have assumed that the company is *innovation-inactive*. However, obtaining this snapshot and repeating the process frequently throughout the program is still important to track progress.

 Survey findings, signals, and abstract themes from user interviews are post-processed and discussed in innovation retrospectives.
2. **Package the innovation program**: The program requires a strong identity and high-quality content that explains its purpose, the importance of innovation to the company, and how it can contribute to achieving its objectives. In its simplest form, this can be a branded deck that presents an overview of the program and its key elements with an emphasis on the innovation agenda. It should also include all the essential definitions, messages, symbols, and references. Moreover, the entire program needs strong *branding*—including a theme and a logo that reflects the program's ambition and helps in presenting innovation workshops and content.
3. **Connect with middle management**: The program requires not only strong sponsorship from the company's leadership but also genuine support from all layers of management, especially the middle layer. People managers play a catalytic role as they can encourage innovation from a practical perspective, for example, by providing time for their teams to join innovation activities or by expressing appreciation for their innovation efforts, achievements, and impact. Therefore, managers should be fully aligned with the program and, if needed, adjust their attitude toward innovation. The team must work with middle managers and present them with the entire program to ensure they understand its goals and the purpose of innovation. This way, managers prepare for upcoming workshops and adopt the correct narrative for daily communication with people. Additionally, this is an opportunity to discuss concerns and explore potential solutions or workarounds to minimize disruptions to schedules and delivery plans.
4. **Announce the program**: The announcement is a critical moment that sets the program's tone and conveys how the leadership understands and appreciates

innovation. Hence, the announcement should ideally come in an All-Hands Meeting where a leadership member presents a bold innovation narrative that goes beyond buzzwords, explaining how innovation becomes vital for the company and how they commit to empowering everyone to innovate. Following the announcement, the program director describes the program's structure and presents the *innovation agenda*. Instead of theoretical, generic notions of innovation, they discuss the *problem space*—the strategic problems the company needs to solve—and explain how *a community of innovators* can help the organization achieve its goals and serve its purpose through innovation. The innovation team presents the values of the innovation culture, emphasizing *collaboration* and *contribution*, and encourages people to join the community of innovators and engage with the program.

5. **Design a communication strategy**: The announcement of the program initiates an ongoing improvement process, which, given the high visibility of the initiative, requires progress reports and regular updates to multiple stakeholders. The innovation team establishes a *communication routine* to ensure alignment among all parties. Beyond the routine, the team shapes a *communication strategy* to manage the growing *expectations* across multiple stakeholders. Following the announcement of the program, expectations can grow in multiple directions. For instance, management stakeholders may expect to see a short-term impact of innovation on products and services and, ultimately, on the company's financial results. At the same time, innovators expect to have more opportunities to innovate, contribute to the company's growth, and further develop their careers based on their innovation achievements. However, in some cases, these expectations can deviate from what's feasible and grow in the wrong direction: business stakeholders might adopt unrealistic expectations about developing new, innovative technologies, while innovators might shape false views about their innovations reaching the market. It is the responsibility of the innovation team to ensure that expectations are *pragmatic* in terms of both *results* and *timing*. The complexity of the initiative and the long time needed for a successful transition to the Innovation Mode require clear, systematic communication: a steady flow of updates containing bold yet pragmatic messages.
6. **Launch a series of promotional activities**: The promotion of the innovation program occurs through a series of live presentations open to all. The intent is to inspire people to engage with the innovation process and join the *community of innovators*. Members of the innovation team present the program's vision and share their stories and perspectives on innovation. They also reference the innovation agenda as the vehicle for explaining *what innovation means* for the company and *what problems innovators should be solving*. They describe the strategic areas and technologies and how they relate to the organization's vision and purpose. The sessions include an extended Q&A section, allowing participants to share their thoughts and receive answers. Beyond popularizing the innovation agenda, these events ensure a strong and meaningful *leadership presence*, which is foundational to the program's success, especially during its

early phases. The primary call to action for participants is to express interest in joining the program and contributing as both innovators and volunteers who support the innovation team.

7. **Launch the "Innovation Talks" series**: One of the primary objectives of the Power-Up phase is to attract attention and gradually inspire people to engage in innovation activities. The Innovation Talks is an information and knowledge-sharing program that, through a series of inspiring events, brings together *those interested in learning more about innovation* and *those with remarkable innovation stories to share*. The innovation team defines and orchestrates this program—they:
   - **Invite influential speakers**: While all aspiring innovators are welcome to submit their presentation proposals, the initial focus should be on the most influential leaders who can set the example and convey the innovation message with clarity. Another great option is to invite speakers from the broader ecosystem, such as start-up founders with a relevant story to share or renowned innovation and product experts who might be interested in sharing their perspectives.
   - **Distribute the content**: The content captured via live events is an excellent source of inspiration, which can be distributed as branded decks or videos across innovation channels and via the innovation newsletter.
   - **Measure success**: The program is open to feedback through a simple online form, allowing participants to share their thoughts or questions with the presenters and also request new topics.
   - **Reward speakers**: Presenting innovation stories is an important sharing behavior; hence, it is considered an additional signal in the overall rewards and recognition system.

   Beyond creating a few successful instances of Innovation Talks, the team develops a standard, reusable format featuring a script that enables the effective delegation of the event preparation. This format allows innovators to prepare their talks and presentations more efficiently, utilizing branded templates, guidelines, and specific rules. After organizing and running the first few instances of the Innovation Talks program, the team delegates it to members of the innovation community.
8. **Launch the "Innovation Q&A" series**: As awareness of innovation rises, so does the need for guidance. Especially in the early days of the program, people have various questions about the innovation process, tools, methods, etc., and it is vital to address them effectively. Initially, this Innovation Q&A service could be provided by the core team, but as the innovation maturity of the organization improves, the service should be delegated to the community of innovators and also supported by self-service digital tools—such as the Innovation Portal—featuring AI-powered components that can answer anything about innovation in the context of the company.
9. **Establish a content management function**: Content creation and management are essential throughout the innovation process. Content may refer to documents that *support the innovation process itself*, such as branded, high-

quality templates, including innovation announcements, event scheduling, a call to innovate from leadership, or regular innovation updates. Content may also refer to *artifacts produced by innovation activities*, such as ideas captured through a brainstorming session or prototypes developed and documented during a hackathon. It is essential to provide the initial templates for all of the above and establish a basic process for organizing such content in a single location where people can access, discover, and utilize the content. Generative AI streamlines this process by creating templates for all communication patterns, emails, documents, and eventually all artifacts involved in innovation, with minimal human effort required to standardize them.

10. **Launch the "Innovation Academy" series**: Igniting innovation requires significant upskilling across the entire company at all levels of the hierarchy. The Innovation Academy is a special educational program that introduces the organization to the latest innovation methodologies and best practices. It is delivered through live, branded events that have a distinctive character as interactive, informal, and practical sessions. An essential aspect of this program is that it places innovation knowledge within the company's context rather than just presenting generic innovation content. Another important aspect—and success factor—is that the Academy program is *led by the innovation community*: volunteers who are passionate about innovation and willing to learn the latest topics and share back with the team. Beyond the initial setup, the innovation team acts as an orchestrator. Instead of running the events, they empower the community to do so by providing guidance, along with detailed scripts for creating training material and hosting the actual session. In terms of orchestration, the innovation team:
    - Monitors the demand for education needs through the feedback processes and maintains a prioritized list of topics for future sessions.
    - Supports innovators in preparing their presentations with just-in-time advice and guidance.
    - Organizes "learning threads" on new topics—e.g., by asking the community of innovators to study a new topic, create the educational material, and present it back to the company—and get rewarded for their innovation activity via the recognition program. This not only amplifies the program's positive impact but also makes it scalable and efficient. In another scenario, when the required knowledge is not available within the organization, the team coordinates the provisioning of training services from the market.
    - Provides standardized, reusable templates that accelerate the preparation of events, such as live presentations, hands-on training sessions, or workshops.
    - Promotes the program through innovation touchpoints—e.g., scheduled events are announced early enough, and content is distributed following each session. The program features a dedicated document library where innovators can access content, submit topic requests, connect with presenters, pose questions, and engage with the community.
    - Measures success. As with every event, it is essential to systematically measure performance and quantify success in a consistent and comparable man-

ner. After each event, participants are invited to rate it and submit their thoughts. This allows a satisfaction score per training session, along with qualitative feedback or suggestions for improving the innovation education program. Moreover, the core team tracks simple metrics such as the number of participants and engagement level.

This Innovation Academy program provides an excellent opportunity to energize people, drive awareness, and increase anticipation for applied innovation work. Done correctly, it serves both as an *enabler* and a *source of inspiration*.

11. **Launch the Idea Management Process 1.0**: Despite the program's early phase, it is essential to include at least a basic version of an idea management process to enable the team to handle the initial waves of ideas. It also allows the team to configure, validate, and adjust the foundational entities and methods of capturing, handling, and assessing ideas. By applying the capability prioritization method presented earlier in this chapter, we classify the ideation process as "urgent" and "can start manually." Thus, the first version could be based on simple digital forms—documents that implement the framing templates for ideas and problems. Another approach is to directly implement these templates as context for standardized AIs that receive briefs from the user and produce ideas in a consistent and compact format. This basic idea management process enables people to quickly express their ideas in the standard format and submit them via digital channels or even via a simple email or chat channel. As the core team receives this first wave of ideas, it applies the assessment process described in Chap. 6 and estimates their potential, thus acting as an *idea evaluator*. Then, the team compiles and provides feedback to the originators of the idea. This simple, inexpensive (to implement) process handles the initial wave of ideas and, at the same time, allows the team to test and fine-tune the assessment process itself—e.g., set the right weight factors for the idea assessment, adjust the templates, etc. These components get improved through iterations across the program and, eventually, upgraded to a full-blown digital innovation management system.
12. **Launch the "Innovation Playbook**:" Although this is only the beginning of the program, and things are still relatively simple, providing a high-quality, thorough Innovation Playbook is essential. The playbook is envisioned as the single resource that an innovator would ever need to get started with innovation: it serves as the primary point of reference for the methodologies, the innovation calendar, problem and idea framing templates, opportunity evaluation criteria, guidance on experimentation, patent submission process, product development essentials, innovation terminology, key contacts, venture-building paths, and more. Moreover, the playbook establishes a shared language and principles for innovation. It emphasizes the key messages from the leadership and reinforces the connection between the company's purpose and the innovation process. The innovation team orchestrates the design and production of the playbook, ensuring that it accurately describes the *specific* innovation process as it is designed and planned for the company. It should be accompanied by a branded short

video featuring statements from the innovation team, the leadership, and select innovators across the company. The innovation team ensures that the playbook becomes available to all and gets adopted as the primary innovation asset.

13. **Launch the "Disruptor" series**: The Disruptor is an information and knowledge-sharing program that combines education with challenge-based learning to keep innovation teams at the cutting edge of technology. Innovators are invited to select an emerging technology that is relatively unknown to the company but has the potential to be disruptive. Then, they conduct preliminary research, learn from it, and then present their findings back to their teams through hands-on demonstrations, where applicable. The presentations focus on the company's context rather than providing a generic introduction to technology—the presenters offer perspectives on the potential applications of the technology in the organization's products and services. This way, presenters and the audience learn together, creating a collaborative environment that encourages learning and exploration. Topics of the Disruptor program must meet two criteria: they should have a strong potential to disrupt the company's market and be new to the innovation community. This ensures the program continuously pushes the knowledge boundaries of the organization. The program establishes a cadence of updates on emerging technologies and strengthens cross-team relationships through shared learning experiences. It contributes to developing an *early-warning system for disruptive technologies* while, at the same time, boosting the innovation mindset and breaking silos.
14. **Establish the innovation intelligence service**: As presented in Chap. 4, innovation intelligence is a crucial capability that provides actionable insights from both the market and within the organization. The innovation team establishes this capability by forming a team of analysts or researchers who use the latest technologies to scan the market, the competition landscape, the state of the art, and the dynamics in the broader environment. They generate valuable insights that help the company set the proper focus for innovation and product development and make better decisions in general. The team offers expert views on the competition and emerging trends, which can also be delivered as just-in-time advice, e.g., when collaborating with teams in workshops or product road mapping sessions or by distributing regular updates and market briefings to the entire innovation community, e.g., via the Innovation Portal, newsletter, presentations, etc. Furthermore, market intelligence insights enhance the evaluation of ideas, inform the innovation agenda, spark ideation, and help the innovation community align with business reality.

Exit State and Criteria: The phases in the innovation transformation program are not time-boxed, and there are no deadlines or transition dates. There are no checkpoints that control the transition. Instead, what signals the transition is the overall state of innovation, the organization's general readiness, and the level of adoption of the recently introduced capabilities. For example, the Power-Up phase aims to increase awareness of innovation, commitment from upper management, and a growing community of innovators. Hence, indicators for assessing its progress are:

1. Ongoing, well-adopted education programs
2. Ability to systematically capture feedback on innovation
3. Ability to capture, handle, and assess ideas
4. Significantly improved perceived innovation ability score
5. Ability to effectively respond to innovation support requests
6. Branded material reflecting the purpose of the program
7. An active core of the innovation community
8. A well-sourced core innovation team

The innovation team should frequently assess the above against the goals set or the baselines derived at the beginning of this phase. To be ready for the transition, these should be consistently satisfied over a period of time. In any case, the transition from one phase to another is neither formal nor announced; it is an integral part of a management tool, a method for self-assessment, progress evaluation, and tracking. It helps identify gaps and issues and take action to improve the program in the right direction.

10.3 Spark Innovation: Getting to Level 3

The company is entering the Spark phase with growing interest in innovation—it is now *innovation-aware*. The previous phase introduced the fundamentals of innovation, such as a simple ideation process, educational and information-sharing initiatives, and strong branding for the program. The Innovation Talks and Disruptor programs are now active, with multiple instances happening throughout this phase on various topics.

The objective of the Spark phase is to further establish the innovation program by providing key innovation enablers, with a focus on *information and knowledge sharing*. A characteristic capability to be introduced in this phase is the *Innovation Portal*—the single point of reference for all innovation activities within the organization. This phase is rich in *communication* and *educational* events, featuring a wave of talks and presentations, as well as a series of updates regarding new capabilities and training programs on various innovation topics. The innovation team continues to present the program and advocate for its goals. At the same time, business leaders demonstrate their commitment and genuine support through strong, consistent innovation messages, their presence, and contribution to the process.

As part of the preparation, the innovation team conducts a survey to capture people's thoughts on the recently introduced capabilities, asking them how they view the initiative and what their expectations, concerns, or suggestions are. This survey is run once in each phase on small, random samples of employees across the organization. The results help the team refine the innovation program and inform specific decisions.

As with all phases of this program, Spark has no fixed duration; the innovation team orchestrates as many iterations as needed to transition the organization from *innovation-aware* to *innovation-engaged.* Regular measurement activities presented in the previous phases continue to happen and are standardized as elements of a performance measurement framework.

Visualized in Fig. 10.4, the Spark phase begins with an assessment of the current state of innovation, as described in the previous phase, followed by the first Innovation Steering meeting. The following presents the key activities the innovation team must perform:

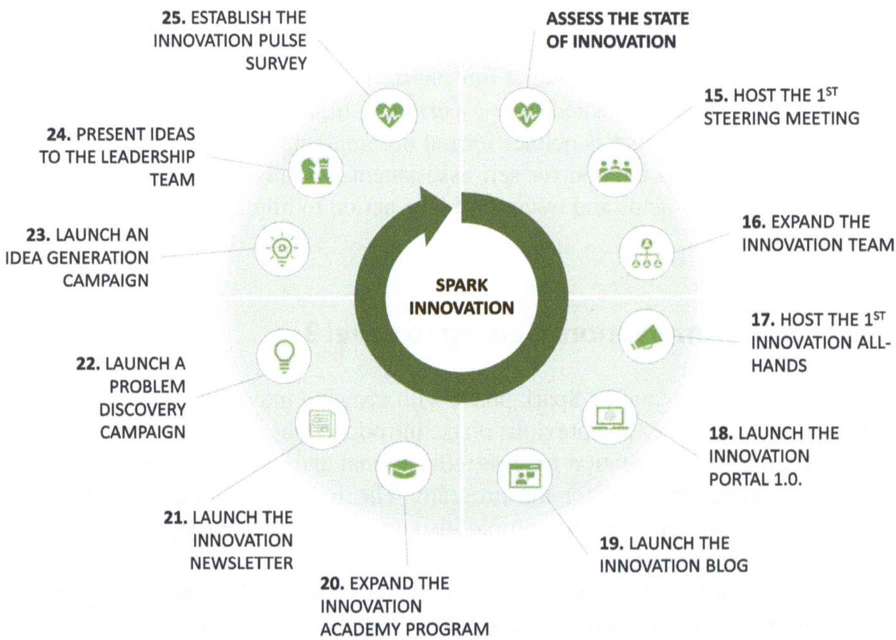

Fig. 10.4 The Spark phase of the program

15. **Host the first innovation steering meeting**: The innovation team hosts the first meeting of this class, establishing a critical governance checkpoint to evaluate the program's progress and effectiveness. This structured session brings together key stakeholders to review program metrics against defined targets and previous performance benchmarks. In preparation, the core team produces a report that contains the updated baselines, performance indicators, insights into the current state of innovation, feedback highlights, success stories, and known issues, gaps, or problems. The report highlights items needing leadership attention, such as resource constraints, cross-functional friction points, or approval delays. During the meeting, the leadership and the innovation team review the

topics and occasionally make decisions that help keep the program on track or pivot as needed. These might include interventions in the portfolio of innovation projects, such as prioritization or budget adjustments, as well as decisions regarding organizational structures, technology investments, timelines, or the innovation process itself.

16. **Expand the innovation team**: As the program becomes more demanding, visible, and busy, expanding the innovation team and increasing its capacity is crucial. Beyond the initial core scheme, which comprises an innovation leader, program manager, and communicators, the program also requires *technologists*, *event organizers*, *product leaders*, and *venture builders*. At this point, the team estimates talent needs for subsequent phases and creates a plan that outlines the required skills and available sourcing options, including internal moves and external hiring.
17. **Host the first innovation all-hands**: A classic all-hands meeting provides an effective way to share general updates on a wide range of topics. The innovation all-hands is a similar event but with an innovation focus—allowing people to spend dedicated time exploring and discussing a series of innovation-specific topics. This special all-hands is recurring but less frequent than the typical, general one—a good starting pace could be two to three events per year. The first innovation all-hands meeting is especially important, as it sets the context and expectations for the rest of the program. The following presents ways to make it valuable and boost the level of engagement with your innovators:
    - **Reflection**: The leadership team presents the progress since the announcement of the innovation program and then invites the core team to provide detailed updates on the progress, forthcoming upgrades, events, and activities.
    - **Call for ideas**: Following the updates, the leadership presents one strategic, big problem worth solving, asking everyone to contribute by sharing their ideas and potential solutions. This is not a hackathon or a formal innovation contest, as the capability to host such a large-scale event is limited at this point. Instead, it is a genuine *call for ideas* targeting a fundamental problem from the innovation agenda, with no deadlines, formats, or award promises. The aim is to inspire people by amplifying the innovation message: *the company truly believes in innovation and values ideas*. The leadership commits to reviewing the ideas with the intent to identify the promising ones and explore them further. This initial call for innovation makes the program real and actionable from the very beginning.
    - **Q&A**: The innovation all-hands features an extended Q&A section, allowing people to share thoughts and questions.

    Upon completion, the core team sends an email update summarizing the key points and providing instructions on how to respond to the call for ideas. The team also evaluates the event and summarizes the feedback captured.
18. **Launch the Innovation Portal 1.0**: The launch of the Innovation Portal, as envisioned in this book, is a key milestone in the entire innovation program. In the post-pandemic world, with many companies working remotely or on a hybrid

model, it is more important than ever to have a "home for innovation"—a single place that is always up to date on all innovation-related matters within the organization. The Innovation Portal, as described in Chap. 4, provides a digital platform for innovation, incorporating various AI-powered features that simplify the innovation process like never before. However, as explained there, the Innovation Portal can get quite complex, with multiple types of content, sources, and tools it can host. Hence, it is essential to follow agile and lean principles—start small and iterate fast by launching various improvements throughout the program. Following this approach, the core team focuses on the immediate needs that shape the first version of the portal: a simple, internal website providing strategic messages (the innovation agenda), practical information (how-to guides, FAQs), scheduling information (forthcoming events), and innovation content (stories, ideas, whitepapers, etc.). This first version of the portal aims to socialize the innovation program and allow everyone in the company to discover, learn, and connect. To introduce a valuable first version, consider the following tactics:

- **Start small**: As described in Chap. 4, the Innovation Portal has a long list of rich features, but not all are needed at once or from the beginning. A basic version presenting the program, the team, and the key innovation capabilities would serve the purpose of the Spark phase.
- **Focus on content**: The content is critical in this context and should be of high-quality. However it may be static in the initial release of the platform, provided that there are at least manual processes for content updates and a plan is in place to gradually streamline the process by leveraging a content management system.
- **Enable communication, feedback, and networking**: Even from the very first version, the portal should provide ways for people to express interest in the innovation program and provide their input. It should also present the members of the innovation team and key points of contact.
- **Assign a single owner, but also involve the community**: As an essential piece of the innovation puzzle, the Innovation Portal must have clear ownership, with a single individual or team operating it *as a product*, ensuring it is up and running, featuring fresh, high-quality content, and demonstrating a growing level of engagement.
- **Build a roadmap**: Starting small is a good strategy, provided that there is a plan for improving the initial, limited version. The innovation team prioritizes a list of features that enhance the Innovation Portal and extend its impact on forming an active innovation community.

19. **Launch the innovation blog**: The innovation blog can play an important role in shaping and fostering the growth of the innovation community. It is where innovators describe their experiences and share insights and stories about their achievements, failures, and lessons learned. Articles about new technologies, market developments, proposed innovation methods, and product announcements are all examples of great blog topics. The innovation blog is driven primarily by the community. Still, content from the innovation team and the company's leadership is also important, for instance, to explain the strategy or

describe an update on the innovation agenda. The key requirement for a blogging platform is to be fast in authoring and publishing—with no approvals for posting content and no moderators. This is a private corporate space where responsible innovators communicate under a simple set of rules that match the values of the innovation culture. Blogging activity may also feed into the rewards system as a knowledge-sharing behavior that inspires others to engage with the innovation program.

20. **Expand the Innovation Academy program**: The innovation team leverages the Innovation Academy program established in the previous phase to help people familiarize themselves with the terminology, concepts, techniques, and methods of innovation. The team schedules and orchestrates various Innovation Academy events covering not only elementary topics but also more advanced ones—for example:
    - **Innovation Masterclass**: These structured events help new innovators understand the company's innovation capability. It covers what innovation is, what it is not, and how it is relevant and important for the organization, with real examples from within and from the market. It also covers the essential tools and methods for corporate innovation and references the Innovation Playbook as the primary entry point for the company's innovation ecosystem. Moreover, there can be various specialized instances of the masterclass, each covering an aspect of the innovation process or a specific method, for example, "what a Design Sprint is," "how to prepare for a hackathon," or "how to define an MVP." These are beneficial for new joiners or anyone who might be uncomfortable with innovation terms and methods.
    - **A primer for ideas**: An introduction to framing problems and ideas, presenting through real examples how they are valuable for innovation, how they are used within the company, and how to effectively articulate and communicate them. The program also explains how AI can be utilized in the ideation process to empower innovators to generate and develop innovative ideas.
    - **A primer for experimentation**: This specialized package explains how business experimentation adds value to innovation and product development, when and how to define experiments, and how to make decisions using the insights captured.
    - **A crash course on prototyping**: Introduces the techniques for building prototypes fast and explains when to build one and how to benefit from it. It also presents how to use AI tools to accelerate the prototyping process.
    - **A primer for Intellectual Property**: This package helps innovators understand when and how Intellectual Property should be protected and obtain an overview of the patent application process.
21. **Launch the innovation newsletter**: This phase introduced the first version of the Innovation Portal as the go-to resource for all things innovation. A well-prepared company-wide innovation newsletter can boost engagement with the program and drive more traffic to the Innovation Portal. Typically, the newsletter includes innovation highlights, success stories, profiles of top innovators, plans, and upcoming events, along with program updates and a "What's New"

section to present recently introduced capabilities and resources. The innovation newsletter is owned by the core innovation team, which utilizes the content of the Innovation Graph and advanced AI tools to regularly produce and distribute new issues.

22. **Launch a problem discovery campaign**: As explained throughout the book, spotting problems worth solving is essential for the innovation function. Inviting people to participate in this process is an excellent opportunity to promote transparency in the innovation program and foster an evolving innovation culture. This campaign invites people to spot dysfunctional scenarios, challenges, gaps, user pain points, or other situations that would benefit both customers and the organization if solved. Innovators use their ability to "think as a user" and their business understanding to identify problems worth solving or other themes worth considering. Submissions are fed into the problem space and then enter a framing and prioritization process. The selected ones become part of the innovation agenda—the document that serves as the guiding principle for innovation. The innovation team orchestrates this process; they announce the campaign, provide the means to frame the problems, gather and post-process submissions, and update the innovation agenda, which is then presented to the company through a dedicated session or the next innovation all-hands.
23. **Launch an idea generation campaign**: At this point, the innovation agenda contains all the top problems that are important to the company's strategy, including the ones captured during this phase. The innovation team triggers another *call to innovate*—this time asking for *ideas*. The innovation community is challenged to generate ideas attempting to address the specific problems listed in the innovation agenda. This informal initiative brings value by connecting innovation with corporate reality—referencing real, pressing problems as prioritized by the company's leadership. It proves the engagement and interest of business leaders, as they actively seek help from the innovation community and contribute by providing valuable feedback to ideators. Moreover, by promising to sponsor further exploration of selected, high-potential ideas, the leadership demonstrates their commitment and trust to innovation. This open call is intentionally unstructured, with no deadlines, complex deliverables, or special requirements; teams or individuals can submit their ideas at any time using the basic ideation process introduced during the Power-Up phase.
24. **Present ideas to the leadership team**: Throughout this process, the innovation team manages the ideas submitted in response to the various calls to innovate. Since there is no unified innovation management platform yet, the processing, selection, and presentation of ideas require significant manual work. More specifically, the innovation team has to:
    - **Collect ideas**: In the absence of an innovation management platform, the team must manually gather ideas, organize them in a single location, acknowledge the submission, and potentially enrich them with feedback. They utilize the idea assessment model (as explained in Chap. 6) to identify the most promising ideas and compile a shortlist, along with an executive summary, to serve as a briefing for the leadership review meeting.

  - **Review ideas**: The core team hosts idea review sessions with leadership and, if necessary, with domain experts and facilitates the review of the shortlisted ideas, capturing feedback and suggestions.
  - **Communicate feedback to the originators**: Depending on the volume of submissions, the core team provides feedback via brief private meetings or via a compact form that summarizes their assessment and recommended next steps.
  - **Present selected ideas**: Even though this is not a contest—there are no demos, winners, or deadlines—public acknowledgment from the leadership is essential. The originators of the selected ideas are invited to present them at one of the most visible events, such as an all-hands meeting. The leadership team introduces the shortlisted ideas, explains why they have high potential, and asks the innovators to present them followed by open discussion on the potential next steps.

    This step closes the loop from the initial call for ideas to the acknowledgment of selected ones that are being considered by the leadership. This manual process will be automated and optimized in subsequent program iterations.

25. **Establish an ongoing Innovation Pulse Survey**: The Innovation Pulse Survey was introduced in the Power-Up phase as one of the tools to capture the initial state of innovation. Considering the expansion of the innovation program, the team standardizes and streamlines the process by adopting commercial survey tools and making the Pulse Survey available via all the *innovation touchpoints*. This way, people can proactively submit their feedback about any aspect of the innovation process at any time. The process allows for comparing overall scores against time, enabling effective monitoring of the program's "health." This essential process can reveal issues or inefficiencies within the program and lead to calibration or changes, such as improving the recurrence of certain events.

Exit State and Criteria: The Spark phase introduced various capabilities and programs aimed at raising awareness, educating, and clarifying the business potential of the innovation function. The effectiveness of these interventions is expected to be reflected through several key measurements, including the activity of the innovation community, participation in the initial call for ideas from leadership, and engagement with the Innovation Portal. To be considered as ready for the Connect phase, the core team must ensure the following:

1. Strong evidence of innovation community and culture growth.
2. The Innovation Portal is operational, with increasing engagement.
3. The innovation blog is actively growing in adoption.
4. The innovation newsletter has been launched.

As discussed earlier, the transition from one phase to another is informal; it is neither decided nor communicated. Instead, it is used as a form of internal assessment by the innovation team, which frequently evaluates the exit criteria of this and previous phases, along with other performance metrics, to conclude the health and progress of the innovation program. The level of "compliance" against the above criteria is also used to steer and manage the program and effectively communicate the state to the leadership.

10.4 Connect Innovation: Getting to Level 4

The organization enters this phase with a growing community of innovators and the first version of the Innovation Portal that serves basic communication needs. People gradually realize that innovation is connected with tangible business outcomes and serves a bigger purpose. The goals of the innovation program are now well understood, and people are familiar with the foundational innovation methods and tools.

The Connect phase aims to link the basic pieces together and establish a steady flow of *actionable ideas* and *opportunities*. The core team upgrades the manual idea management process used in previous phases by introducing "Idea Management 2.0," a technology that streamlines the end-to-end process and enables smart opportunity discovery: ideas start to flow into the opportunity discovery pipeline, where evaluators look for opportunities and recommend next steps.

This is the phase during which innovation gradually becomes more tangible as it takes shape and is seen in action: applied and connected to the business reality.

As the innovation program progresses, the community itself becomes a source of inspiration: people collaborating on ideas, sharing innovation stories, and exchanging knowledge. The innovation team empowers the community of innovators and promotes activities such as blogging and information sharing. They orchestrate the submission of posts and, in some cases, advertise topics of interest, such as proposals for writers or focus areas or themes for new articles. As illustrated in (Fig. 10.5), the key activities performed by the innovation team are:

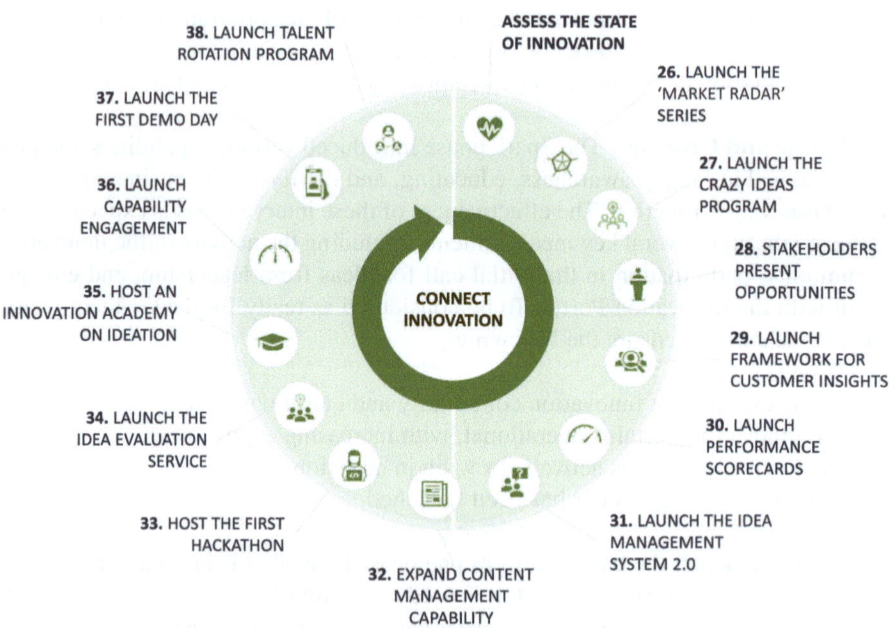

Fig. 10.5 The Connect phase of the program

26. **Launch the "market radar" series**: This is a special program hosted by the market intelligence team. In a live session, they present their market insights—a synthesis of the market and competition landscape and the company's current position and strategy. The session begins with an overview of the market, highlighting any recent market shifts and emerging trends. Among other updates, they discuss and interpret key developments, including competitor moves, product announcements, reputation trends, changing customer sentiment patterns, start-up activity, and acquisitions. They also explain how these are relevant and important in the company's context and how they could influence innovation efforts. Moreover, they use side-by-side comparisons of the best offerings in the market versus the company's current roadmap, thus identifying gaps and framing potential reaction strategies. Finally, they present key emerging technologies with the highest potential to impact the industry in a mid-term window. The innovation program director concludes the discussion, emphasizing how these insights influence the innovation agenda and encouraging people to utilize this market update in their innovation efforts.
27. **Launch the "crazy ideas" program**: This informal program is designed to promote unconventional thinking from across the organization while helping ideators upskill in framing and pitching their ideas. The program provides a safe space for employees to propose highly ambitious concepts without being constrained by feasibility or costs, thus allowing exploration of potentially breakthrough concepts that traditional ideation processes might otherwise filter out. Ideas can be relevant to the innovation agenda, but they can also be entirely new. The innovation team orchestrates the program and also serves as a mentor, providing ideators with just-in-time advice. The program is simple—based on ideation-assessment-pitch cycles that repeat every few weeks. Innovators submit their "crazy" ideas through the Innovation Portal to enter the queue for the next assessment iteration, where the evaluation team reviews submissions using the idea assessment model presented in Chap. 6. Selected ideas are then refined and packaged, and their ideators get the chance to pitch them to the most relevant stakeholders in the company. The program is linked to the recognition and rewards system to acknowledge innovators and their achievements.
28. **Invite stakeholders to present opportunities**: An effective way to highlight the importance of ideas is to invite senior stakeholders to present real cases that had a remarkable business impact or potential. For example, a product leader could present flagged opportunities with high potential for their product vision or ones they are actively experimenting with. Providing such concrete examples of ideas being considered for production scenarios is an excellent way to prove that innovation is genuine. Similarly, high-potential ideas or flagged opportunities may be selected through the Innovation Portal and included in Innovation Talks presentations, where the presenter explains why they are promising, how they were assessed, and the potential next steps.

29. **Launch a framework for customer understanding**: The innovation team collaborates with product leaders to develop a framework for gaining a deep understanding of their customers or users, including their profiles, preferences, needs, and pain points. The team uses quantitative or qualitative insights to create diverse personas representing different markets, demographics, needs, and user journeys for each of the company's products or services. They orchestrate cross-functional journey-mapping workshops to identify specific pain points, moments of truth, and unmet needs across each persona's journey. They present this to the innovation community and incorporate *persona references* in the problem and idea framing templates and all the innovation proposals. Especially in a product-led company it is crucial to associate ideas and proposed features with specific personas, their needs, and expected improvements on the user journey. The framework can be implemented as a visual, interactive tool, empowering people across the company to interact with it and align their projects, ideas, and initiatives with certain moments in the journey of well-understood personas.
30. **Launch performance scorecards**: Measuring the performance of the various aspects of the innovation function is the basis for continual improvements and fast iterations. The team introduces various scorecards, including:
    - **Live "Innovation Pulse" Scorecard**: Continuous feedback is essential for innovation, not only for ideas and projects but also for the process itself. In previous phases, we described the Innovation Pulse as an ad hoc research activity executed manually by the core team. This workstream implements an always-on version of the pulse survey, which can be used by any employee at any time to submit their thoughts on the innovation function through a fast experience consisting of a few questions. The goal is to establish a stream of insights that reflect the performance of the innovation system along with the perception and expectations of employees and teams. In contrast to the ad hoc versions used in the previous phases, this is fully automated: the incoming answers are handled on submission and contribute to the overall *innovation culture health score*. This process powers a live scorecard, presenting the innovation perception as a time series, which is a particularly useful tool for the core team and the leadership as it summarizes what people think of the innovation function over time. By leveraging AI services, the system automatically analyzes the free-text feedback and enriches the scorecard with highlights, key themes, and even suggestions for improvement or things to investigate further. AI automatically analyzes current versus previous snapshots to highlight interesting patterns or changes and produces a concise "story" that clearly presents the health and dynamic of the innovation system. The Innovation Pulse Scorecard can be embedded in larger dashboards used by the leadership to steer the overall innovation program.
    - **Launch the Innovation Portal Scorecard**: As described above, the Innovation Portal plays a crucial role in driving awareness and engagement with the innovation function. Hence, the innovation team must ensure the portal performs at a good level, which, in turn, requires objective measure-

ment. The core team orchestrates the implementation of a simple, well-defined scorecard, providing a comprehensive view of the performance of the Innovation Portal. The performance reflects user engagement, e.g., conversion rates, the volume of engaged users, content performance, and direct user feedback. The entire process is fully automated, resulting in a live scorecard similar to the one defined for the Innovation Pulse, where AI automatically converts user feedback into recommendations and opportunities for improvement. Similarly, the blog's performance can be captured in terms of content engagement and content creation activity. These independent scorecards can be integrated into an overall *innovation performance measurement* dashboard.

- **Launch the Event Performance Scorecard**: The innovation program is rich in various types of events. Innovation workshops and information-sharing sessions can be highly effective if conducted correctly or a waste of resources if not done with the necessary preparation. Hence, it is essential to incorporate a universal *event performance tracker* that captures feedback across all types of events, such as Innovation Talks, Design Sprints, hackathons, Innovation Academy sessions, or brainstorming workshops. Following the same principles applied to the innovation pulse and portal scorecards, the team orchestrates the design and implementation of a simple *event performance view* powered by a micro-questionnaire, which becomes available to participants immediately after each event. While the questions can be generic, the scorecard uses the metadata of the referenced event to break down the performance by event type and theme. As with other scorecards, AI consumes user comments to produce suggested actions and executive summaries of what participants thought of the event, as well as how the dominant sentiment compares with that of other events of the same type. This feedback loop is essential as it allows the core team to experiment with new event formats, content, recurrence, and other parameters. Then, they can make decisions and necessary adjustments based on the analysis of the impact on engagement and perceived success. In the case of educational events, this channel also allows the team to "listen" for topics and learning needs directly from the participants.

31. **Launch the Idea Management System 2.0**: Up to this point, ideation has been based on a manual and possibly oversimplified process—following the low-tech, "start small" approach. As innovation gains traction, this process becomes ineffective, slow, and eventually a bottleneck: although innovators may be using the latest AI technologies to frame their ideas, there is a lack of a single system to capture all the ideas and foster collaboration and smart opportunity discovery. Without such a system, ideas often end up being stored in multiple locations within the organization, waiting for manual handling and with no clear expectations for possible outcomes or timelines. To enhance the ideation capability, the core team introduces a robust mechanism based on a centralized repository of ideas residing in the Innovation Graph. This mechanism refers not only to technology but also to supporting services, such as idea assessment by

evaluators. Idea management is viewed *as a service* operated by a designated team. As described in Chap. 6, idea management feeds into the opportunity discovery pipeline, forming a smart system that takes as input ideas and outputs flagged opportunities. At this point, the core team must decide whether to purchase specialized software, subscribed to a SaaS offering, or, if internal talent is available, build a custom solution. The latter would typically be the least preferred option. However, with the current state of technology and the tremendous capabilities of artificial intelligence, it is easier than ever to organize a single repository of ideas and use AI to interact with it: building software in-house becomes an interesting option again. An in-house implementation also offers important safety and information security advantages, as software and data are hosted on corporate systems and cloud environments. The decision depends on the case, as pros and cons must be evaluated in the organization's context. Regardless, the innovation team must make sure that at least the following are provided:

- **Idea and problem management and collaboration functionality**: The ideation system must model the entire process from AI-powered idea creation and editing to collaboration, enrichment, and distribution. The ideation system should adopt a consistent model for ideas and problems, like the ones described in Chap. 5.
- **AI-powered search and discovery functionality**: Beyond legacy search and browse experiences, a modern ideation system must support smart, semantic search that, based on a prompt or business context, can retrieve, summarize, and present relevant ideas in the user's context.
- **Idea evaluation and feedback provisioning**: To streamline the idea evaluation process, the platform must offer effective tools for assessing ideas, enriching them with scores and feedback, and communicating recommendations to the originators. The platform provides a configurable model for scoring ideas, similar to the one described in Chap. 6. The experience is optimized for speed, helping evaluators submit their assessments and feedback quickly. It also provides effective tools for managing the workload of ideas awaiting assessment.
- **Reporting and insights**: This is a collection of reports and dashboards that presents activity, performance, and levels of engagement with the ideation system—used by the core innovation team to steer the process.
- **Integration capabilities**: This is a collection of APIs that allow other corporate systems to query innovation content, including ideas, problem statements, and innovators, and present them in a different business context.

The above can be thought of as the minimum requirements for an effective ideation platform in the era of AI. Launching such a system is more than delivering the technology though. It is about providing a reliable, scalable, and fully operational service that the corporate innovation process can rely on. Hence, before flagging this as "done," the core team must ensure the following:

- **The ideation service is fully operational**: This means that the technology is integrated, tested, and ready to be offered as a production-ready service, that is operationalized and reliable, with performance and health reporting and tracking, as well as processes in place to ensure high availability.
- **There is clear ownership**: The service requires a clear ownership model—an individual or team that operates the services, measures its performance, and drives adoption and growth.
- **There is user support**: The necessary end-user support process is in place, along with help materials and a feedback mechanism that could be primarily or entirely AI powered.
- **It is properly communicated**: The release of the ideation service must be followed by systematic communication across all available innovation channels. Content must be diffused through the Innovation Portal, the newsletter, and blog posts. The new capability must be mentioned in regular meetings and presented through innovation or leadership talks. The entire ideation and review process must be demonstrated through how-to guides tailored to different scenarios, for example, one targeting the *ideator* and another targeting the *evaluator*.
- **There is growing adoption**: Following the release and announcement of the service, the owners and innovation team must monitor adoption levels and usage patterns, which should grow rapidly toward a predefined target. For instance, the target could be articulated as "At least *x%* of the employees to be active users of the ideation platform," where the "active user" could be defined as one having at least two or three sessions per week. The exact definition depends on the environment, but there should be a target indicating sufficient adoption.

If any of the above is not met, the ideation service should not be reported as "successfully launched." Especially if the adoption is poor, the team must react fast and consider ways to boost the platform's visibility while initiating user research threads to test its usability and probe for any latent adoption blockers. Given the importance of ideation in the overall innovation function, failure to improve adoption within a considerable amount of time, e.g., in a few months, should trigger a thorough investigation to understand the blockers, associated behaviors, or cultural issues preventing people from engaging.

32. **Expand the content management capability**: During the Power-Up phase, we introduced the content creation function to cover the essential needs of the program. However, the newly introduced content-driven experiences, such as the Innovation Portal and the newsletter, require additional content. Moreover, events like hackathons heavily depend on engaging content and efficient communication. Thus, it is essential to empower this team by providing the technological means to streamline both content creation and distribution. At this point, the core team coordinates the provisioning of a content management technology to be used along with powerful generative AI services with at least the following capabilities:

- **Content creation and collaboration**: Features enabling fast, AI-assisted content authoring and lifecycle management.
- **Named templates**: Configurable templates for the creation of new instances of specific classes of content. For example, there could be preconfigured, named templates for articles, idea descriptors, newsletters, announcements, and innovation artifacts, among others. This accelerates the process of creating branded, high-quality digital content.
- **Content APIs**: Instances of content created by the team are stored in a centralized repository and accessible via standard APIs. Authorized systems, such as the Innovation Portal, can utilize these APIs to retrieve fresh content in its native format, which is then presented as part of the portal experience. This way, the content becomes reusable not only from the integrated channels but from any application or corporate system in the organization. For example, an innovation story created for the monthly newsletter may also be featured in the Innovation Portal, listed in the newsletter, or even promoted on the home page of the corporate portal.

33. **Host the first hackathon**: The idea management service, combined with the Innovation Portal and an empowered content team, boosts the organization's innovation capability and sets the right conditions for the first corporate hackathon. The core team utilizes the model described in Chap. 5 to frame the hackathon. In parallel, they consider the organization's readiness to host such a large-scale workshop. In all cases, unless an experienced team is available to ensure smooth execution, this first hackathon should start small by targeting a specific group or division rather than the entire organization, which makes the project more manageable and safer. To accelerate the process and increase the likelihood of an impactful hackathon, the team must follow these steps:
    - **Assign an owner**: The event requires clear ownership and strong leadership. Hence, the team must name an experienced senior member to assume responsibility for designing, hosting, and evaluating the event.
    - **Create the hackathon manifest**: The owner follows the hackathon setup guidance provided in Chap. 5 to define the right hackathon for the organization's needs. The hackathon manifest lists all the essential attributes, e.g., the topic, dates, judges, evaluation protocol, and the event's target audience. The owner presents the manifest to the core team and the leadership for refinement and approval.
    - **Create a hackathon leadership team**: Upon approval of the hackathon's manifest, the owner forms a project team consisting of members of the innovation team and volunteers. This project team provides planning and support throughout the hackathon, from the announcement of the event to the announcement of the winners.
    - **Confirm and communicate**: The event's announcement should be made only after the final confirmation of its validity and feasibility. For instance, it is crucial to ensure that both the ideation system and the idea evaluation service are fully operational and able to handle the expected increased usage levels. The announcement should be accompanied by a clear timeline, sup-

ported by scripted communication; for example, reminder emails are automatically triggered at specific points leading up to the event. This first hackathon is an excellent opportunity for the core team to configure the proper format, refine it, and package it as a named template that can be leveraged to reduce efforts and speed up the setup of subsequent hackathons. Additionally, a templated hackathon allows other teams to reuse it as a script to independently set up their own smaller-scale events while inheriting the official hackathon's structure, rules, and mechanisms.

34. **Launch the "idea evaluation service:"** As described in Chap. 6, the idea assessment is crucial for the opportunity discovery process and the overall innovation program. Up to this point, the submitted ideas have been handled through the manual start-small approach introduced during the Power-Up phase; it was the core team that performed the assessment and provided feedback to the ideators. As the volume of idea submissions increases, the core team needs to "outsource" this process for two reasons: first, to free up its resources and focus on more strategic work required for the program and, second, to ensure that a more diverse group of experts participates in the evaluation process. Following the familiar agile pattern, the network of evaluators described in Chap. 5 can start as a small, virtual team of experts who commit to assessing incoming ideas at a predefined rate or volume per week. They perform the assessment independently and asynchronously. If additional skills are required, evaluators may request assistance from other members within the organization, for example, when an idea requires specialized technical expertise to be properly evaluated. The actual assessment and provision of feedback are conducted through the Innovation Portal.
35. **Host an Innovation Academy on ideation**: Using the established Innovation Academy program, the team orchestrates introductory courses on the new ideation process and the recently launched tools, including the opportunity discovery pipeline. They explain the possibilities and clarify what people should expect after submitting an idea. The package emphasizes the assessment process, clearly explaining the criteria, rationale, and how idea evaluation is linked to the organization's strategy. The same material is packaged as quick-start guide videos, articles, or recorded training sessions and served through the Innovation Portal. The training may also take the form of hands-on workshops and brainstorming sessions that present in action the new capability to capture and discover ideas.
36. **Launch a capability engagement program**: The mandate of the innovation team extends well beyond the initial selection and implementation of innovation capabilities; it also includes *driving adoption* throughout the organization. This holistic approach requires the team to actively promote, support, and continuously refine innovation capabilities based on engagement data and qualitative feedback. To achieve this, the innovation team establishes a robust feedback mechanism that systematically captures insights, challenges, and improvement suggestions from the community of innovators who use these capabilities. By taking this proactive, data-driven approach to identify issues and react with

focused interventions, the innovation team gradually improves the innovation function, drives the required level of adoption, and empowers innovators to achieve more. Insights may lead to non-technical interventions, such as training programs, documentation, and informal community-driven activities that create psychological safety for experimentation. With this approach, the team treats the innovation framework *as a product* and demonstrates the principles of *agility*, *user-centricity*, *data-driven experimentation*, and *continuous improvement*.

37. **Launch the first Demo Day**: The team organizes the first Demo Day, a vibrant, in-person event where innovators proudly present their latest achievements in an informal, energetic atmosphere. Teams share not only their technical accomplishments but also their innovation stories—in a variety of formats: functional product demonstrations where people from various teams interact with prototypes, deep dives exploring complex technical aspects, and talks that socialize early-stage concepts and upcoming innovations. Demo Days boost the innovation culture by celebrating both successes and failures, reinforcing the importance of failure as a vital part of the learning process. The innovation team ensures that the digital version of the event is available in the Innovation Portal, where people throughout the organization can discover standardized materials, videos, and, when applicable, interactive demos.
38. **Launch the Talent Rotation Program for innovation**: The innovation team introduces a scheme designed to accelerate the transformation process through *talent mobility* and organic *knowledge exchange*. The program offers a rotation scheme that enables individuals from across the organization to join the core innovation team for focused assignments typically ranging from 1 to 4 months in duration. This scheme serves multiple strategic purposes. On the one hand, it helps spread knowledge of innovation and accelerate the adoption of new processes, methodologies, and practices across the organization. Rotating team members gain hands-on experience with design thinking, rapid prototyping, and customer-centric methodologies while working directly with innovation experts on real projects. When participants rejoin their original teams, they utilize and share the knowledge and methods they have acquired, thus becoming "promoters" of the innovation process. On the other hand, bringing highly motivated domain experts to the core innovation team also brings diverse and fresh perspectives to the innovation process. The talent rotation scheme enables the innovation team to increase its capacity while sharing knowledge and the innovation spirit throughout the organization. This scheme is particularly effective in hybrid or remote working environments, where digital collaboration tools enable the seamless reassignment of distributed team members. In general, this model can help break down barriers and silos within the organization, thus, boosting the innovation mindset and culture.

Exit State and Criteria: In the *Connect phase*, organizations are upgraded with a streamlined idea management and evaluation service, as well as advanced content creation capabilities. Educational and information-sharing threads, along with the first hackathon, drive awareness and adoption of the newly added capabilities. These have a significant impact on the perception of innovation and contribute to a shift toward a culture of innovation. To be considered *innovation-active* and thus to move to the next phase, the following should be true:

1. The Idea Management 2.0 service is adopted.
2. The idea evaluation service is operational and reliable.
3. There is strong evidence of improvement in the innovation culture.

In practice, the exit criteria of each phase should be monitored regularly by the core innovation team, at least on a monthly basis. This routine can provide valuable insights and highlight issues that require the attention of leadership. Especially when attempting to drive adoption for new capabilities, multiple iterations, research activities, quick fixes, and experiments may be necessary. The core team is in a *try-measure-learn* loop, orchestrating activities to raise adoption and readiness until the above criteria are met. When this happens, the program moves on to the next phase, where additional innovation capabilities aim to *empower* the organization.

10.5 Empower Innovation: Getting to Level 5

Being at this level means that the company has implemented advanced innovation capabilities, including a first instance of the opportunity discovery process, and has mobilized people to engage with the innovation process. The leadership fully supports the innovation program, and the company benefits from a healthy innovation culture. Meanwhile, the innovation function is clearly linked to the organization's strategy and purpose, and teams have clarity on what problems they should focus on and why.

The next most important set of capabilities for a company at this level is about *business experimentation* and *prototyping*: an innovation-powered company knows how to react when high-potential opportunities are identified. We may refer to this as the *reflex advantage*: the ability to rapidly transition *from a problem* to *validated ideas* and make swift, informed decisions, such as whether to park or move them forward. The decisions are backed by data, evidence, and signals gathered by exposing inexpensive prototypes to real users. To reach this point, the company needs both a *cultural* and *technological* boost.

The goal of this phase is to introduce the technological capability, organizational flexibility, and the right mindset needed to adopt the experimentation culture—and thus advance the company from innovation-active to *innovation-powered* (Fig. 10.6). At the cultural front, people must adopt this new attitude and apply it in their working routines, planning, and decision-making processes. Adopting this mindset requires systematic efforts to educate people and demonstrate how experimentation can add value to the business. But most importantly, the company needs to make prototyping and validation easy, effective, and scalable.

To enable fast and informed decisions regarding the next steps of identified opportunities, the core team introduces a specialized capability: the *opportunity validation service* that offers real-world validation through rapid prototyping and other concept testing methods. It can be thought of as a *black box* that receives as input an opportunity and outputs a validation report with recommendations backed by data, thereby enabling teams to make better decisions quickly. The opportunity validation function empowers the organization to explore more opportunities and select *with confidence* those to investigate further. It accelerates the ideation, validation, and decision-making cycle, thus increasing the throughput of the overall innovation system. In addition, the "makerspace" empowers individuals and teams to get involved with prototyping, either through self-service or by requesting to join specific prototyping initiatives.

During the *empower phase*, the innovation team orchestrates various activities, including content creation, blogging, and workshops in the makerspace to promote the experimentation mindset and help teams reframe risk and failure. Furthermore, the team coordinates leadership talks, training sessions, a compilation of educational material, and blogging activities designed to shift the dominant mindset toward business experimentation. More specifically, the team performs the following:

Fig. 10.6 Empowering innovation: getting to Level 5

39. **Host an Innovation Academy on experimentation**: Experimentation and prototyping require special educational programs for both innovators and business leaders. The core team coordinates the provision of hands-on training sessions, along with courses specifically designed for upper management and corporate leaders to demonstrate how business experimentation can enhance the innovation process. They use the well-established Innovation Academy program to deliver multiple educational packages including:
    - **The fail-safe, fail-fast principle**: This special package features various leaders promoting a shift toward a data-driven experimentation culture. They explain how failure needs to be redefined as part of the process and provide concrete examples of the fail-safe, fail-fast principle. They describe how the newly supported *prototype-validate-decide* cycle can serve the organization's purpose and encourage people to adopt the experimentation mindset in their daily business routines.
    - **Business experimentation methods, applied**: These are more practical sessions, presenting real cases where experimentation made a difference. Innovation leaders, technologists, or other experts demonstrate the entire journey from an idea to a prototype, including the definition and setup of the experiment, the testing process, results evaluation, decision-making, and, ideally, the resulting product. Similarly, product managers may present how experimentation can be part of a product's continuous improvement process.
40. **Run an innovation retrospective**: Given the complexity of the innovation transformation program, it is essential to regularly assess the overall progress, recognize mistakes and missed opportunities, learn from them, and make improvements. The innovation retrospective enables the core team to collect and evaluate feedback on the execution of the program and the impact of its capabilities. The retrospective can be organized through the following steps:
    - **Ask for feedback**: The team invites people to evaluate the innovation program by submitting their ratings, suggestions, or comments. This is a time-boxed campaign communicated through the Innovation Portal and the newsletter.
    - **Process feedback**: The core team analyzes and interprets the survey results, along with all the insights gathered since the program's initiation, and compiles an executive summary highlighting key findings. The team gathers, discusses the findings, and shares additional feedback and perspectives. This meeting outputs decisions, suggestions, or even immediate actions.
    - **Present findings to the leadership**: The team presents highlights and actionable results to leadership to ensure alignment, seek direction, or propose solutions to identified problems.
    - **Communicate back to the community**: In the spirit of transparency and openness, the core team shares an update, including highlights and actions or plans to improve the innovation process. These may be delivered as an article through the Innovation Portal or presented at a subsequent all-hands meeting.

The above process has significant practical value—it helps the core team improve by identifying gaps, blind spots, and issues that require attention or intervention. Sometimes, this process may signal the need to alter the program by removing or adding new activities, changing the pace, or the communication patterns. At the same time, the innovation retrospective carries an important connotation—it emphasizes that the company seriously considers the views and opinions coming from the innovation community.

41. **Announce the innovation rewards program**: Simply put, the rewards program is the logic that measures innovation activity and gives predefined awards to top-performing innovators. This is a good point to launch this capability for several reasons. First, it requires a solid framework and reliable technology that is becoming available during this phase. Second, at this point, the company has sufficient data to properly design the logic of the program and more accurately estimate its impact. During this phase, the innovation team orchestrates the implementation of the framework, configures the rules to identify top performers, and determines the type of awards to be given, along with their recurrence and the associated communication strategy. Establishing the rewards program is a demanding project, and it should only be announced after thorough testing of the model's robustness and the reliability of the results. The content team should also be involved in this process to prepare and compile effective material explaining and promoting the entire innovation rewards program.
42. **Launch the Innovation Project Portfolio**: As described in Chap. 4, the Innovation Portfolio is implemented through dynamic visual dashboards that present multiple innovation projects in a clear and interactive manner. It offers a holistic view of innovation projects and their progression through the opportunity discovery pipeline, offering senior stakeholders a comprehensive single-view perspective. The dashboards display critical metadata, including resource allocation, risk metrics, progress indicators, and estimated market potential—all aggregated at both the individual *project* and *portfolio* levels. This portfolio approach fundamentally shifts organizational attitudes around risk by normalizing failure as an expected component of a balanced innovation portfolio. When projects are viewed collectively rather than individually, stakeholders can clearly see that while specific initiatives may not succeed, the portfolio's overall performance and value can still be strong. This perspective enables more objective decision-making about continuing or terminating projects based on portfolio-level metrics. The visualization tools also facilitate pattern recognition across projects, revealing which approaches or domains consistently bring better results, allowing for continuous refinement of innovation strategy and resource allocation. By implementing these visual portfolio management tools, organizations establish a framework for discussing innovation investments, creating greater alignment between innovation teams and executive leadership. This transparency increases trust in the innovation process, reduces political influences in project selection, and fosters a more sustainable innovation culture that balances short-term wins with longer-term transformational opportunities.

43. **Inject innovation in the daily agenda**: In parallel to introducing strategic capabilities, the core team finds ways to inject innovation into the daily agendas—so that innovation gradually becomes part of the core business thinking and normal daily activities. The team drives this lengthy process by providing instructions and essential training to middle managers, enabling them to incorporate innovation tactics into their business routines. For example, people managers should be fully aware of ideation and prototyping tools and encourage people to leverage them. Moreover, they should seek opportunities to get value from the established innovation capabilities. For instance, a project manager facing a difficult decision about a new, complex feature should consider experimenting with it through prototyping. Or when new, "random" ideas come up during a daily standup, people should be guided to submit them to the opportunity discovery pipeline. In all cases, people managers should encourage team members to explore and learn by participating in presentations and educational programs about innovation.
44. **Measure adoption, engagement, and utilization**: The innovation team systematically analyzes metrics and KPIs that describe the performance of the innovation function, including the level of engagement and the effectiveness of the idea assessment process. Furthermore, they establish metrics on the health and growth of the idea corpus, the level of prototyping activities, a framework to capture the utilization of the makerspace, and the performance of the opportunity validation service. For all the above, the team coordinates the creation of performance scorecards, analogous to the Pulse and Innovation Portal ones introduced in previous phases. Occasionally, they host user interviews to gather qualitative data on the newly added capabilities. Triggered by findings, the team may also organize ideation sessions to improve the innovation process itself.
45. **Launch the makerspace**: As covered in Chap. 7, a properly established makerspace brings significant value in many ways and eventually becomes a symbol for innovation and a reference point for experimentation and prototyping. Setting up a successful makerspace is a complex project in its own right, and it deserves sufficient attention and careful design. It consists of multiple workstreams and must meet specific requirements regarding the layout of the space, safety precautions, accessibility, and operational procedures, such as inventory management. Moreover, the success of the makerspace depends not only on the included resources and its operational state but also on a layer of programs and activities that add value and help shape a community of innovators. The innovation team oversees the overall project, from ordering equipment and devices to ensuring compliance with safety standards in the space. The approach described below helps innovation leaders introduce a "small" yet fully operational instance of the makerspace, which can then be expanded in an iterative manner. Key guidelines include:
    - **Start small**: Define the minimum version that matches your organization's needs (see Chap. 7 for variations). Find a suitable space, apply a flexible layout, and provide the fundamental equipment and resources. Collaborate

with your marketing team to establish a strong character and a signature for the makerspace through a logo, branded artifacts, key messages, and mottos.

- **Design the key processes**: Document the core operational procedures, for example, how to manage the technology inventory, maintain devices, book the space, handle requests for devices, communicate activity, and host events.
- **Form the leadership team**: Set up a team of technologists and delegate aspects of the project and specific workstreams. This team should gradually assume ownership and operational responsibilities; they should be the ones that ensure the makerspace is up and running and that it serves its purpose in a safe and effective manner.
- **Involve the community**: Call for volunteers to help set up the makerspace and organize a series of subsequent events, including training sessions and workshops.
- **Establish core operational processes**: The makerspace team implements key processes, such as controlling the tech inventory and maintaining a unified catalog of resources.
- **Prepare a program of events**: Following its announcement, the makerspace should begin to evolve into a platform for educational, training, and presentation activities. The innovation team orchestrates the preparation of a rich program of events and activities.
- **Establish a feedback channel**: As with all the innovation capabilities, it is essential to allow people to rate the value of the makerspace and make suggestions. This should follow the same pattern and reuse the technological solution already adopted from other components of the framework. The makerspace should also get its own performance scorecard.
- **Launch the makerspace**: As soon as the first version of the makerspace is ready for business, the team announces and promotes it throughout the organization using a strong narrative that invites people to familiarize themselves with the business experimentation process. The announcement comes from the leadership and active members of the innovation community, backed by bold messages regarding the mission of the makerspace. The launch could include the presentation of selected ideas waiting to be built in the makerspace.
- **Drive engagement**: Following the launch, the space requires operational support and a well-planned growth program. The team must not only operate the makerspace but also drive engagement and foster a community of "makers."

46. **Communicate the makerspace**: Beyond the formal announcement, the core team must effectively communicate the makerspace, as it is a unique construct, a new entity that people may not be familiar with. Additionally, its various functions, such as *making*, *exploring*, and *learning*, may confuse people regarding its intended purpose. Therefore, systematic and continual communication is essential for driving adoption, growth, and success. To set up a good communication plan, the team should consider the following:
    - **Leverage the established innovation touchpoints**: Introduce the makerspace, and diffuse content through the Innovation Portal and the newsletter.

- **Announce a series of makerspace events**: Promote upcoming events, such as training sessions, workshops, or technology presentations, and invite participants to register.
- **Mobilize the innovation community**: Invite innovators to explore the makerspace and blog about its potential, the technology and equipment it offers, and how it boosts the company's innovation capability.
- **Distribute material presenting the makerspace**: Coordinate the creation and distribution of branded content that presents the purpose, the supported use cases, and a summary of the tools, technologies, and resources provided. Consider including a short video introducing the key functions of the makerspace. Ideally, a dedicated page in the Innovation Portal should host all this content, along with frequent updates and stories from the "makers."

Beyond an enthusiastic launch, the makerspace must swiftly become part of the innovation discussion and get listed in all relevant communication threads. This way, the makerspace is set up to evolve as the symbol of experimentation and prototyping—the place where innovators meet, collaborate, and make things happen.

47. **Launch the opportunity validation service**: To further empower the organization to pursue opportunities, the core team establishes the first instance of the opportunity validation service, as described in Chap. 6. This new organizational entity is capable of creating optimized validation strategies according to the nature of each opportunity. When needed, it builds and leverages functional prototypes to capture real-world data and validate the stated hypotheses. It is offered as a service operated by a dedicated, self-sufficient team of experts. The opportunity validation connects the "opportunity discovery" with the "opportunity realization": it empowers the organization to decide which opportunity to pursue and how. The following provides high-level guidance on how to introduce and establish this service:
    - **Set up the prototyping and validation team**: Rapid prototyping requires a dedicated, purpose-specific, and multidisciplinary development team consisting of technologists, software engineers, designers, scientists, and product experts. Hiring for this team is challenging, as it requires encapsulating technical expertise, product sense, and the right mindset to accelerate the prototyping development process, including the ability to leverage AI for software development. It also requires commercial acumen and research skills to drive the testing process, interpret user feedback, and make recommendations for the future development of the concept being tested.
    - **Provide the right technological setup**: The technology stack is critical; it should include specialized equipment, technology, methodologies, tools, and access to advanced AI-powered software development platforms.
    - **Educate the organization**: The opportunity validation service is probably new to most people. As part of the effort to educate the organization, the team coordinates a series of presentations and activities based on real cases of transforming an idea from a one-page description into a validated opportunity with recommended next steps backed by real-world evidence. They

explain the process of exposing a prototype to users, capturing feedback, and using it to suggest the next steps. They also highlight the gains in terms of better resource allocation and increased opportunity discovery bandwidth.

- **Establish an intake protocol**: For good utilization of resources, the team applies a consistent assessment to determine whether any submitted opportunity qualifies for formal validation—whether it *can* and *should* be validated. In some instances, there may be no reason to validate an opportunity, or the required means may not be available. Thus, the team may reject a request for validation or assign a low priority. The organization must understand when to request opportunity validation, what to expect, and how to use the information provided.
- **Ensure online presence**: To raise awareness regarding the new capability, the team must ensure a strong presence of the opportunity validation service through the Innovation Portal, the makerspace, and the related newsletters. Additionally, the new entity must be enlisted in the content creation process of updates and innovation stories.

48. **Expand the Innovation Academy**: **training on Design Sprints**: The core team introduces Design Sprints as another method for solving big problems through design thinking, rapid prototyping, and testing. They produce special content to educate the upper management and stakeholders. Beyond presenting the process, the team also sets up a quick start guide for organizing Design Sprints, covering how, when, and why to host one. These may be offered as branded videos presenting real cases and how teams reached a promising, validated solution through a fast-paced sprint. To make Design Sprints a valid option, the organization trains or hires professional facilitators who can organize and host such demanding workshops.
49. **Host prototyping workshops**: This is a series of hands-on workshops for developers and "builders" as a way to popularize and demystify rapid prototyping and experimentation. It leverages the capabilities of the makerspace—it is hosted there to allow crafting artifacts, using resources, equipment, and tools as needed for the training session, all in the "natural" environment for prototyping. The core team defines the format and delegates the creation of a series of workshops, branded as "makerspace events," where innovators build something real in front of a small live audience, which also participates through a Q&A section. The event is captured and distributed as a branded, high-quality video via standard innovation channels and through blog posts that summarize the workshop, inviting questions or comments from the community. As with all community-driven educational events and training sessions, this initiative is also connected to the rewards program, allowing the team leading the prototyping workshop to be recognized for their contributions. The actual prototype could also be exposed as a demo in the makerspace.
50. **Run the first Design Sprint**: At this point, the core team seeks business problems that are challenging and significant enough to be addressed through a Design Sprint. When such a case arises, the team schedules the very first Design Sprint, also aiming to demonstrate the power of time-boxed, intensive, cross-disciplinary collaboration. The team conducts stakeholder interviews to gain a

holistic understanding of the problem and then forms the appropriate cross-functional team for the sprint. It is the core team that organizes the sprint, but the facilitators orchestrate it. Upon completion, they communicate the outcomes and highlights to the innovation community, serving as an example of hands-on, cross-disciplinary collaboration.

Exit State and Criteria: The *Empower phase* aims to boost the company forward by introducing new methods for testing ideas and making decisions. As with all phases in this program, launching the technology or capabilities themselves is not enough to move the program forward; success and maturity should be measured in terms of *adoption* and *engagement*. During this phase, the innovation team regularly measures several aspects of performance and growth. Depending on their state, the team may change the focus of the initiatives in an attempt to meet the minimum expectations on the following:

1. The opportunity validation service is operational and adopted.
2. The makerspace is operational and has been adopted.
3. There is a general awareness of business experimentation and its value.

Assuming a continual improvement of the capabilities presented so far, the organization eventually becomes *innovation powered* and moves further toward innovating at scale.

10.6 Scale-Up Innovation: Getting to Level 6

Companies entering this phase have an increased ability to innovate. They can move fast, from ideas to opportunities, by leveraging capabilities such as the makerspace and opportunity discovery and validation services. They run innovation workshops, such as hackathons and Design Sprints, to solve significant problems. The innovation function is driven by an engaged community of innovators who also contribute to multiple educational and communication threads.

As the innovation function scales up, the organization must manage a vast amount of artifacts and knowledge generated through innovation operations, such as ideas, proposals, prototypes, experiments, and insights. These are valuable assets that must become discoverable and usable across the organization. To address this content overload, the organization needs to streamline knowledge management processes and make the discovery and distribution of content *smart* and *seamless*. The latter can be achieved by expanding the Innovation Portal as a hub that brings together isolated teams, innovation centers, or different R&D divisions across the organization. Additional AI-powered features in the portal allow various entities to synchronize their innovation agendas, exchange knowledge and ideas, and innovate using the same tools and protocols. This setup enables the smart discovery of innovation content by the right individuals, teams, partners, or the ecosystem at the right time and in the right context—supporting an optimal flow of innovation, knowledge, and intelligence across teams, groups, and divisions.

Fig. 10.7 The fifth set of iterations of the innovation loop—from powered to innovation *led*

Beyond knowledge management, the Scale-Up phase introduces additional capabilities that empower the company to reach the market quickly. A core capability in this direction is the *opportunity realization* function, which specializes in defining and building minimum viable products (MVPs) and taking them to market for rapid experimentation and growth. Moreover, the innovation team introduces the VC Funding program as an additional path for opportunities to reach the market. In parallel, the team extends the performance measurement framework to include metrics and KPIs for the recently established capabilities, such as the makerspace and the innovation intelligence team.

The Scale-Up phase, as shown in Fig. 10.7 above, is communication-heavy, since one of the goals is to connect different divisions, groups, or innovation labs. The innovation team hosts several all-hands events to demonstrate the value of innovating as "one team"—they present why *orchestrated innovation* is important along with the goals, ambitions, and expectations of an *organization-wide innovation system*. The team emphasizes the importance of a consolidated innovation agenda featuring priorities and problems worth solving across the company. In parallel, as part of the organization-wide innovation system narrative, the team announces the first group of *distinguished innovators*.

This is an exciting phase of the program, where many advanced capabilities come together to form a bigger innovation system. Innovation becomes more visible across the organization through workshops and information-sharing activities such as innovation talks on real success stories, learnings from prototyping efforts, interesting market updates from the innovation intelligence team, technology presentations in the makerspace, and live prototyping sessions. An additional source of inspiration comes from the gamification layer, which increases visibility and access to innovation content while promoting aspects of *healthy competition.*

This phase is about scalability-which is achieved in many ways. At the technical level, it is enabled through a modern stack and infrastructure with smart integration of AI in crucial operations, such as market intelligence, content discovery and distribution, opportunity validation, and software prototyping, along with decoupled, flexible services and AI agents. At the talent level, inspired individuals from a wide network of innovators voluntarily participate in innovation activities, such as prototyping and testing, according to their availability and bandwidth. They empower functions such as opportunity validation, prototyping, and MVP development, and they are rewarded for their contributions.

Companies that progress successfully through this phase become innovation led—they can scale their innovation efforts and demonstrate an enhanced ability to discover new products, services, and markets. They use innovation not only to stay competitive but also to expand into new business areas and territories. The following outlines the key projects that enable the organization to scale up innovation. During this phase, the innovation team plans to:

51. **Announce the first of the innovation awards**: The previous phase introduced the recognition and rewards program, a vital component proving that the company appreciates innovation efforts. Following a period of data collection and processing, the team is ready to announce the first group of *distinguished innovators*. This first announcement is of increased importance: it allows the team to properly introduce and justify the program, set the tone, and address questions and concerns with clarity. The celebration of the top innovators takes place through a highly visible event, such as an all-hands meeting, where the innovation team introduces the top-evaluated ideas, names the distinguished innovators, and gives them the stage for brief presentations. Following the announcement, it is essential to explain the assessment process and the rationale of the program to underline its robustness, objectivity, and ultimate goal. It is also important to emphasize that the program is not only about ideas and inventions but also about *contribution and openness*, which aligns with the values of the innovation culture and the healthy competition presented in Chap. 3. Distinguished innovators and their ideas are also communicated via the innovation channels throughout the organization.
52. **Launch gamification experiences**: Besides the formal announcement of top innovators, which should happen once or twice a year, the core team introduces a gamification layer that allows frequent, informal views on trending ideas and top performers across categories and from various angles. This consists of a series of digital experiences, such as the Innovation Leaderboard, which showcases the top-performing innovators and their recent achievements, as determined by the reward model. These experiences are delivered via the Innovation Portal and other means, e.g., selected connected screens in the corporate office. The purpose is to make innovation more interactive and engaging. The gamification system is rich, ongoing, and interactive: the rankings are

refreshed frequently and are available at all times. In addition, it allows the recognition of non-standard achievements in reference to particular behaviors, which, although informal, can be impactful and influential. For example, it could include special categories that take into consideration how the community engages with the innovator's content, allowing titles such as the "Most Influential Innovator" or "Top Innovation Blogger" of the month. With proper implementation and communication, gamification elements can inspire people and promote behaviors such as contributing, sharing, providing feedback, or mentoring. This dynamic set of innovation rankings supports various experiences, including the following:

- **Leaderboard of innovators**: This is a live listing of top innovators based on their recent performance scores across a system of *categories*, *topics*, and *behaviors*. The multiple categories and levels of awards allow a greater number of innovators to be recognized.
- **The Innovation Hall of Fame**: This is the ultimate recognition, as it features a *permanent* listing of innovators who have demonstrated remarkable achievements. Members do not join on a schedule; instead, they only enter if and when an extraordinary achievement is met. Hence, there may be long periods with no new additions to the list. The criteria for identifying achievement depend on the company's strategy and the specific behaviors or directions it wants to promote. For example, one company could define the entry achievement as "any employee who ranks as a top innovator for three years in a row." Another company may focus on patents and thus set the entry criterion as "any employee with more than x patents granted in a z-year window." When a new member joins the Hall of Fame, it is formally announced and celebrated as a major milestone. This distinctive recognition is accompanied by monetary awards, badges, and extended visibility in the organization.
- **The Wall of Great Ideas**: This timeline highlights those remarkable and impactful ideas that have shaped the organization's history. For an idea to get featured on this "wall," there must be an inspiring story backed by data that proves its outstanding impact. Ideas pinned on the "ideas wall" stay there forever as a *permanent distinction*. As with the Innovation Hall of Fame, it is not easy to reach this point, and there may be periods with no new entries. When an idea is accepted, the entire chain of contributing members is invited to a highly visible event to present their story—their journey from *conception* to such an achievement. All contributing members receive an award and a prestigious badge. The Wall of Great Ideas may be presented as a digital experience within the Innovation Portal. It may also be delivered in a more innovative manner, such as via an actual digital wall in the office space, allowing the audience to interact with those Great Ideas through gestures and voice.
- **The connected office space**: As with the digital wall of ideas, the connected office itself can be leveraged as a surface for celebrating achievements and recognizing top performers. Interactive screens and information kiosks in public spaces within the corporate office, such as corridors, meeting rooms, and collaboration rooms, can become part of the company's content distribu-

tion network, which, among other content, presents curated *innovation stories* and news. While the smart building can be an excellent canvas for sharing innovation updates, in our remote or hybrid world, it is equally important to integrate similar experiences into digital collaboration and communication platforms—e.g., automated summaries or announcements via team collaboration tools such as Slack or MS Teams.

53. **Launch the digital instance of the makerspace**: The makerspace is expected to be a very busy and productive space, with frequent events, scheduled activities, and spontaneous happenings that generate artifacts and interesting innovation stories. The significance of the makerspace justifies its own section in the Innovation Portal, dedicated to everything happening in there, including experiments, planned prototyping work, innovation stories, and upcoming educational events. The core team coordinates the implementation of the makerspace channel, incorporating the features described in Chap. 7, and ensures a slot in the innovation newsletter. The content and communication team creates the necessary branded templates and enlists makerspace events in the overall innovation planning.
54. **Launch the unified innovation insights store**: The team drives the efforts to build and launch a centralized repository of innovation activity metadata and insights, as described in Chap. 9. The purpose is to enable a *unified view of the performance of the innovation function*, which empowers better orchestration of innovation activities and initiatives.
55. **Expand the Innovation Portal as a hub**: The innovation team encourages innovation at scale by inviting different groups or divisions to adopt the innovation framework (Chap. 4) and create their own "instance." This way, they opt into a "single innovation system" consisting of standardized terminology, event definition, tools, methods, and templates, making the exchange of knowledge and innovation assets faster. While each group can maintain its own innovation agenda, it feeds into a single, all-up corporate innovation agenda that presents a unified view of "who innovates on what." Although this contradicts the notion of "one team," it provides a great way to innovate at scale by offering independent innovation agendas while connecting and orchestrating activities through the hub. Following this strategy, individual teams and divisions maintain the flexibility to innovate on their own terms within their private digital space while allowing signals from other teams to come in and their own updates to go out. This setup is particularly valuable in connecting independent business lines, research and development centers, and complex structures across geographies. Furthermore, it makes innovation consistent and measurable across the organization by applying the same methodology to translate innovation activities, events, and outputs into unified innovation performance metrics. For example, the innovation rewards program inherits the same rules and configuration options, utilizing the exact same metrics and KPIs that are well defined and understood across the company. Thus, it defines a consistent and more objective way to recognize and reward innovators both within and between teams and divisions. This way, while maintaining "local flexibility," each division supports the "one team, unified innovation" vision. To drive this long process, the core team focuses on the following:

- They coordinate the setup of additional, independent instances of the innovation framework. In parallel, they ensure that new instances are only introduced when there is a valid reason. For example, when a division or team has an entirely different agenda and business rhythm. In such cases, they assist with setup and perform the necessary knowledge transfer to help the new member get started with innovation and join the hub.
- They educate local innovation leaders through rapid knowledge transfer, where members from the innovation team train their counterparts to establish, configure, and operate local but connected innovation frameworks.
- They monitor usage patterns across the instances. The core innovation team has access to higher-level metrics and KPIs across the instances—members of the hub. This oversight is important to ensure that the extended innovation function operates at the desired level of performance.

The hub significantly boosts the organization's innovation ability. As such, it should be further defined as a separate program run by a dedicated team with the mission to influence, educate, and finally onboard all major groups and divisions of the organization.

56. **Launch the innovation heatmap**: The team delivers the innovation heatmap as a smart visualization tool that maps the intensity and distribution of innovation energy across the entire organizational landscape. It is hosted in the Innovation Portal as a visual navigator of innovation activities happening across the organization. Unlike typical portfolio views that focus solely on formal innovation projects, the heatmap reflects all innovation activities, including workshops and innovation events, thus creating a comprehensive view of where innovation happens within the company. Color-coded activities and intensity levels reveal "innovation hotspots," enabling innovators to delve into and discover innovation agendas, ideas, and unexpected opportunities for collaboration. The heatmap provides unique visibility and an insightful perspective into the organization's innovation ecosystem. In addition to intensity, it overlays themes, products, ideas, enabling technologies, and strategic innovation agendas, creating a powerful, interactive "innovation navigation" experience that makes corporate innovation visible and accessible.
57. **Launch the opportunity realization service**: The team launches the opportunity realization service, a cross-functional team that takes validated opportunities to market with exceptional speed and powerful experimentation and growth strategies. This sophisticated unit is uniquely skilled in rapidly *defining*, *developing*, *launching*, and *refining* minimum viable products (MVPs) until they achieve demonstrable *product-market fit*. This capability significantly boosts the innovation function by connecting it with the world and enabling multiple parallel in-market experimentation threads.
58. **Launch the internal "VC Fund:"** The internal Venture Capital Fund is a financing mechanism within an organization that applies venture capital principles to provide resources to promising, validated opportunities. The fund aims to accelerate the development of promising innovations beyond standard budgeting cycles and foster a culture of entrepreneurial thinking within the organi-

zation. The Fund maintains its own portfolio and governance model to support promising opportunities that do not fit in the digital product space or are less relevant to the organization's strategy.

59. **Launch the "market radar" service**: Until now, the market intelligence team has been providing ad hoc market insights and competition summaries. However, as the company's innovation capabilities mature and the opportunity discovery process becomes always on, companies need faster, automated, and more comprehensive market intelligence systems. The team recognizes the need and empowers the market intelligence function in two ways: first, by adding talent to the team—experts with both strategic vision and a deep understanding of the organization and its competitive landscape—and, second, by introducing advanced AI technologies—services that scan, comprehend, and summarize market changes and dynamics within the context of the organization. Beyond summarization, AI agents can proactively share "breaking updates"—e.g., when a new competing product is released, a new competing start-up is funded, or a related patent is published. Depending on the configuration, the AI agent can notify the market intelligence team to take action or directly alert the most relevant stakeholders. This service becomes the company's "market radar," continuously scanning the public domain for open intelligence content, including patents, product announcements, research publications, and competitor movements, and distilling unique insights, opportunities, and emerging patterns that might otherwise remain hidden. It transforms how the company *senses* the global environment and *responds* to market dynamics, boosting both the opportunity discovery and validation processes—the former by influencing the problem-solution space and the latter by injecting the latest market and competition insights into the opportunity validation process. By systematically processing this wealth of information, the team can identify changes in consumer demands, spot threats from potentially disruptive startups, or discover opportunities for collaboration or acquisition.
60. **Launch the "early adopters" program**: This new program invites employees to opt in and voluntarily participate in using early implementations of innovative concepts, such as functional prototypes. This defines a "sandbox" that allows early feedback from trusted people—employees only—without the concerns associated with exposing ideas in the market. This program does not intend to replace research activities or usability studies; instead, it provides a fast and safe way to obtain additional quantitative and qualitative feedback earlier in the process. The structure of the early adopters program is simple: people are incentivized through the rewards program to join and occasionally spend a few minutes evaluating prototypes as they become available or by invitation. Participants provide feedback, which is automatically processed and presented through the Concept Performance scorecard. Provided an extensive network of early adopters, this program can generate the first wave of meaningful insights in minutes, thus significantly enhancing the opportunity discovery process. This program could also raise awareness of innovation activities by exposing prototypes to different teams across the company.

61. **Announce the "Innovation Mentor" program**: The team utilizes established tools and channels to form a network of mentors to assist individual innovators and teams with their innovation initiatives. The program encourages innovators to submit requests for advice or mentorship, which are then identified and addressed by more experienced members who are willing to help. This program is also connected to the innovation rewards program, thus recognizing mentorship as a significant behavior in the culture of innovation.
62. **Launch the Innovation Portal 2.0**: As the home of innovation, the Innovation Portal plays a critical role, especially in our remote or hybrid world. The first version of the portal, introduced in the Spark phase, offered only the basics—it required manual content updates and had limited integration with other systems. This enhanced version of the portal features additional capabilities that leverage artificial intelligence to simplify innovation and deliver exceptional, personalized experiences to all parties involved in the process. For instance, the advanced version of the portal offers the "AI Innovation Advisor," a powerful agent that can answer any questions related to innovation. Similarly, the "AI Team Builder" is aware of the talent within the organization and can recommend teams based on a specific project or innovation context. The "Unified Innovation Calendar" also utilizes AI to help the team maintain, present, and communicate a single timeline of innovation activities throughout the year. The Innovation Portal becomes a truly intelligent innovation platform, capable of answering any question on innovation and even innovating on behalf of the company.
63. **Launch the innovation workshop designer**: At this stage, the frequency of innovation workshops is expected to increase rapidly. To simplify the process and save resources, the innovation team coordinates the implementation of the "Workshop Designer," as described in Chap. 4. This AI-powered capability enables teams to streamline the setup of various events, including brainstorming sessions, workshops, hackathons, and design sprints. It also helps participants prepare by sharing relevant content upfront. Most importantly, all events organized through this process support the same feedback mechanism and thus contribute to optimizing the entire innovation system.

Exit State and Criteria: The Scale-Up phase is expected to elevate the organization to a new level, where it innovates as a unified system, synchronized and capable of identifying, validating, and driving multiple opportunities to market in parallel. It becomes a trailblazer led by innovation. Beyond contributing to the overall innovation maturity and introducing advanced capabilities, this phase established the opportunity realization and the Innovation Hub as the key enablers of innovation at scale. The enhancement of the innovation capability should be reflected in the following criteria.

1. There is a scalable and widely adopted opportunity realization service.
2. The innovation intelligence service is operational.
3. Additional instances of the innovation framework adopted.
4. There are increasing rates of knowledge exchange via the hub.
5. There is a highly engaged and fast-growing innovation community.

When the above criteria are consistently met, the organization should be ready to transition to the ultimate state: the (Autonomous) Innovation Mode.

10.7 Embed Innovation: Getting to AI-Powered Autonomous Mode

At this point, the organization is innovating at scale. Reaching this level means that all major innovation techniques and methodologies have been successfully launched and widely adopted, with a measurable impact. Innovation has evolved from independent components and isolated projects to a sophisticated system of knowledge, technology, and culture that powers some of the organization's most critical functions, including strategic planning and new product development. This system is orchestrated by various specialized teams and a growing community of innovators. Innovation is supported by a blend of activities throughout the year, from hackathons and Design Sprints to Innovation Talks and educational programs. The corporate innovation function relies on a sophisticated opportunity discovery pipeline powered by artificial intelligence. In parallel, a robust measurement framework enables leadership to gain insights, steer the innovation program, and coordinate a range of innovation initiatives. Meanwhile, the generalized reward and recognition system promotes top performers and strengthens the message of innovation.

In this concluding phase, illustrated in Fig. 10.8, the core team plans to:

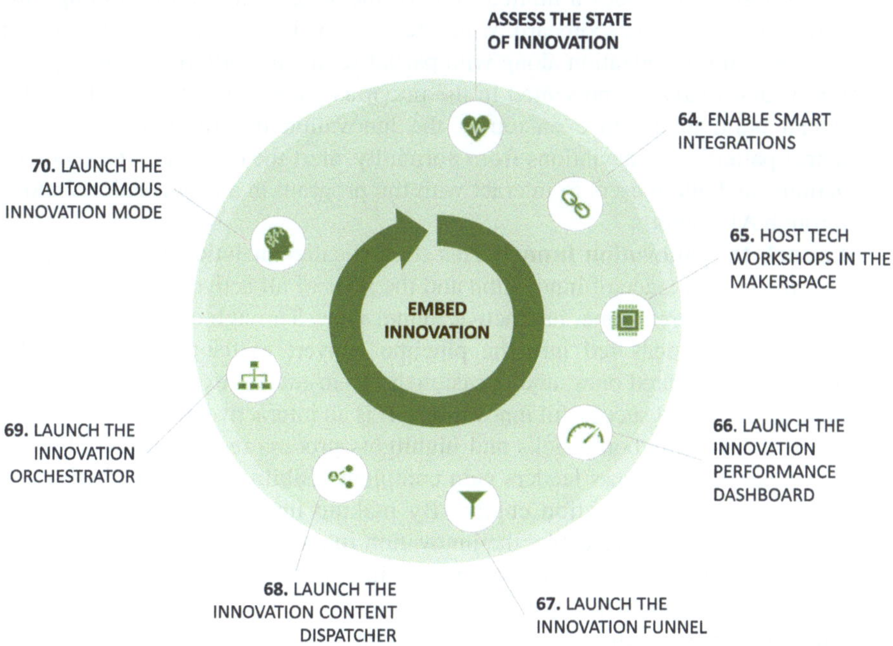

Fig. 10.8 Getting to the AI-powered, autonomous Innovation Mode

64. **Enable Smart Integrations**: The team orchestrates the implementation of specialized APIs that allow authorized systems within the corporate environment to get metadata about innovation activities, for example, "The time series of idea submission volumes for the last 6 months" or "The top 10 most highly scored ideas tagged as #robotics" or "The Innovation Funnel for the previous year." As this API layer responds with standardized data objects, it opens the innovation platform, providing insights and content to support various scenarios, from composite dashboards to integration with Agentic AI systems.
65. **Host technology ideation workshops in the makerspace**: The core team orchestrates a series of events as hands-on, contextual explorations of new technologies. For example, a practical introduction to 3D printing or designing augmented reality experiences. These workshops may be driven by a specific real problem that is of interest to the company. For instance, how could AI improve the quality of a production line? Or how augmented reality could help visualize complex multidimensional datasets? The core team sets the agenda and probes for support from the community. As with all educational and training events, these workshops generate branded content (video, articles), which is then shared via established communication channels such as the Innovation Portal, newsletter, etc.
66. **Launch the innovation performance dashboard**: The team coordinates several projects that integrate innovation activity measurements into the insights store (part of the Innovation Graph). The latter empowers a series of analytical capabilities, including advanced reporting and interactive visualizations. Most importantly, it provides a unified view of the state of innovation through the corporate innovation scorecard, which features a single performance indicator for the entire organization along with partial scores for *culture*, *impact*, *opportunity*, and *image*, as presented in the previous chapter. Other projects in this thread build intelligence on top of the innovation insights store—e.g. they detect patterns and deviations from normality, alert the core team, recommend actions, and allow users to interact with the program in a conversational mode through AI agents.
67. **Launch the innovation funnel**: This sophisticated analytical capability presents the performance of innovation and the state of all active innovation initiatives through a real-time, interactive funnel view. Through conversion rates, it presents how ideas fed into the pipeline convert to flagged opportunities, through to validated ones, and occasionally to in-market experiments and ultimately to adopted successful innovations. It is an interactive management dashboard that reveals bottlenecks and highlights process inefficiencies. Through this capability, business leaders gain complete visibility into the effectiveness of the corporate innovation engine. By making innovation progress visible, measurable, and manageable, the innovation funnel transforms what was once considered an ill-defined creative process into a disciplined, powerful innovation engine that improves over time.
68. **Launch the Innovation Content Dispatcher**: This technology enables smart diffusion of innovation updates to those who need to know. It leverages the

indexing capability of the Innovation Graph to ensure better discovery and circulation of innovation content throughout the organization in autonomous ways, initiated via a system of internal and external triggers. The team gradually integrates this technology into all innovation touchpoints to make content experiences more intuitive and contextual. As a result, people discover interesting innovation material in their context; innovators publish their contributions and are confident that their content will be discovered by the right people.

69. **Launch the Innovation Orchestrator**: This is the "control panel" for innovation—a special system that allows the program director to review and change the configuration or direction of the innovation program with just a few clicks. The innovation team configures the orchestrator to enable a 'click-and-steer' approach which dramatically simplifies strategic adjustments: leaders can modify the innovation agenda, change the pace, update the calendar, revise the rewards model, and change other key program parameters — all with the click of a button. The Innovation Orchestrator is proactive: it leverages the Innovation Graph to access patterns and accumulated knowledge to make recommendations for improving operational and strategic aspects of the program.
70. **Launch the Autonomous Innovation Mode**: The innovation team launches the ultimate AI-powered scenario in the corporate innovation context: the autonomous AI innovator, as described in Chap. 6. To leverage the most advanced innovation capabilities and services, the innovation team activates the autonomous Innovation Mode to further accelerate the opportunity discovery process. This mode is literally autonomous. It "listens" for signals coming from the market and from within the corporation that, depending on the accumulated knowledge that lives in the Innovation Graph, may trigger a thorough ideation process that produces novel-to-the-company solutions, also assessed by multiple AI personas. The flagged opportunities are served to a network of senior stakeholders who can react by providing feedback (to AI) or picking certain flagged opportunities to be further handled by the opportunity validation team by acquiring real-world evidence.

This is an open-ended phase, and hence, there are no exit criteria. From this point onward, innovation evolves as a system, holistically and organically. The innovation teams and leadership focus on optimizing the entire innovation system, streamlining processes, and integrating them deeply into the organization. Every iteration of the innovation loop makes innovation more "natural" and tightly connected to other business activities.

This phase brings the company closer to the Innovation Mode—the state in which the elements of innovation are so deeply integrated into the corporation's structures and culture that they are perceived as hardwired and embedded. Innovation becomes a durable attribute of the character of the corporation—a foundational capability that is everywhere. When this is achieved, the organization becomes native to innovation in the sense that no specific effort is required for the company to be innovative; there are no processes named as such, and there is no distinction between corporate and innovation culture. The community of innovators continues to grow, while the hierarchy becomes increasingly flattened.

At this advanced level, innovation activities blend seamlessly with everyday business operations. Although there are still innovation activities and events, these are perceived as typical, business as usual; they are part of regular communication and information-sharing behaviors. At this level, there is no need to assert the importance of innovation; it is proven and acknowledged as the *driving force* of the organization. Similarly, the need to take specific actions with the intention of inspiring people gradually fades away. The innovation culture is at its peak, and the innovation community is actively working on a plethora of opportunities and challenging problems. The constant flow of innovation intelligence, news, and stories from the market inspires people and sparks autonomous innovation threads. The rewards program continually recognizes top performers and remarkable contributions, thus maintaining a thriving innovation culture and further empowering the innovation community. However, all the above are *blended* into regular communication, training, business events, and collaboration activities: inspiration comes naturally through the bold purpose of the organization and the dominant mindset. In addition to this powerful setup, by leveraging the superior AI innovation capabilities presented throughout the book, the company is gradually transitioning into a state of "autonomous Innovation Mode."

This chapter covered an extensive program and bold initiatives that can drive any organization from an *innovation-inactive* to the ultimate *innovation-native* state. It provided the timeline, the arrangement of the main work streams, and key activities that gradually allowed the organization to innovate at scale and pace.

To put this plan into action, innovation leaders must adapt it to match their organization's specific needs and circumstances. Adaptation may refer to reordering or skipping some of these recommendations, adjusting them, or adding others as needed. In all cases, it is important to ensure good prioritization with clear objectives in terms of engagement and adoption. Even more important is the continuous measurement and improvement process: some initiatives will work well, others will not, and in all cases, the innovation team needs to know as early as possible, with facts and actionable insights. Being decisive is a crucial trait of the innovation team—they should know when to pivot or "kill" an initiative or project and how to communicate their decisions.

Steering this ambitious and long program—each phase could last several months—requires rich insights and precise measurements of impact, engagement, and performance. In a sense, the innovation team is also experimenting with improving the innovation function by continually testing new features, methods, and innovation tools. Therefore, the innovation leaders implementing this program should prioritize the analytical components presented throughout the book, such as feedback loops and performance scorecards. These set the basis for fast iterations—they are essential management tools for the program and the entire innovation function.

The primary success factors for the innovation transformation program refer to *culture*, *pace*, and *leadership*. Although the enablement of innovation through technology and processes is essential, it is *culture* and *adoption* that drive success.

Throughout the book, we emphasized the need to invest in educational and information-sharing programs as drivers of cultural change. In parallel, we proposed several programs that involve the innovation community in core innovation functions, such as the elastic team for the opportunity validation and realization services.

The above, combined with leadership commitment and a fast-paced, consistent approach, provides an excellent recipe for driving cultural change and, thus, the adoption of new capabilities and engagement with the overall innovation function. The fast-paced approach does not mean rushing through the program to reach milestones sooner, as this would introduce risks of disrupting the company's operational aspects and allowing for unrealistic expectations. On the contrary, fast-paced refers to prompt response times in regular innovation activities and interactions between innovation actors, including innovators, innovation consumers, and leaders. Consistency comes through solid behaviors, protocols, response patterns, and rules, helping people know what to expect and when.

The right pace of innovation is also a critical success factor, for example, the frequency and density of events and initiatives throughout the year or the parallelism in conducting in-market business experimentation. The pace and scale of innovation must be balanced with the business reality to maintain a steady output of innovation artifacts while respecting the operational needs and commitments of the company. Therefore, innovation leaders need to adjust the pace of innovation frequently, as required by the business occasion.

11 Final Remarks

In the first edition of this book (written in 2019), I concluded with this comment:

> The corporation of the future will evolve as a platform for innovation. In a fully digitized environment, powered by Artificial Intelligence, operational aspects get streamlined, efficient, and eventually fully automated. The distinct parts of the organization connect to a digital backbone in real time, forming a living entity that captures signals from its environment, consumes information, decides, and reacts. In this environment, the focus shifts from running the business to pursuing opportunities. In the future organization, effective leadership will be about directing and fine-tuning the innovation machine, a complex system that converts signals to ideas and then opportunities to realized innovation, in a fast, adaptive way. In this system, humans will play a substantial role in forming opportunities through business creativity—one of the few areas that AI has not outperformed us yet.

The future I am describing above is here. Artificial intelligence has already dominated many functions and operational aspects of a modern, digitized business, and it is now rewriting the fundamental rules of how companies innovate, operate, and compete. The underlying technology is advancing at a rate that makes its broader impact difficult to predict or even comprehend. Very soon, we will be partnering with AI agents that, beyond executing complex tasks, will be able to achieve business goals under the orchestration of other, higher-level AI agents. Every business role that relies on digital content and technology will be augmented and profoundly impacted by AI, and eventually, most roles will be redefined. Moreover, AI is taking control of creative tasks that, until recently, we thought were AI proof, such as creative innovation, complex reasoning, and strategic thinking.

The impact of artificial intelligence on the innovation process is profound: it not only augments corporate innovation but also fundamentally changes how it works. Considering the breadth and depth of knowledge that AI uses when generating ideas, it is apparent that humans will soon have a secondary role in the creative part of innovation. Although human-conceived ideas may still occasionally have certain qualities and superiority, the comparison to AI is already "unfair," as AI can provide hundreds of high-quality, relevant ideas in a matter of seconds. Consequently, ideas

G. Krasadakis, *Innovation Mode 2.0*,
https://doi.org/10.1007/978-3-032-00835-0_11

as an innovation asset will be managed primarily by AI. Moreover, implementing ideas as functional prototypes or demos of digital experiences has become easier than ever: AI can generate high-quality, interactive digital assets without requiring a single line of code from the user and with minimal or no human supervision. Hence, activities such as prototyping and experimentation will eventually be taken over by powerful AI agents able to build impressive functional prototypes—inexpensively and within minutes. Workshops, such as brainstorming sessions, Hackathons, or Design Sprints, will be redefined or repurposed to accommodate the new reality.

Artificial intelligence makes innovation dramatically faster and more accessible: a non-technical business user may design and prototype an app they envision simply by describing it to AI using natural language. With some technical skills, users can *build fully functional prototypes in hours*, *entire digital products in days*, and *go to market in weeks*—and this is becoming increasingly faster and smarter rapidly.

Realizing AI's central role in innovation raises various challenging questions, such as "Are human innovators still in the loop?" "What is the impact of AI on the innovation culture?" and "How will we be innovating in the future?"

The deep integration of AI into innovation processes creates an existential challenge for traditional innovation roles and undermines several key qualities of the innovator's identity. When AI can generate dozens of remarkable ideas in seconds and produce functional prototypes in minutes, human innovators inevitably question their ability to contribute and compete with the "AI Innovator." This new reality may trigger psychological consequences since the fulfillment derived from technical mastery and the sense of pride that comes with creating value through novel solutions are now under threat. Organizations face not just process disruption but also risks to the innovation culture, employee self-esteem, and psychological well-being.

Given the rapid advancement of AI models, their expanding knowledge base, and real-time web access, we must prepare for a future where AI challenges human superiority in creative innovation. This reality, though unsettling, requires a pragmatic stance: we must explore *how to ethically integrate AI* into innovation processes while defining *new, valuable roles for human innovators*.

The role of innovators will shift fundamentally: it will be more about bringing *judgment* and *wisdom* in making bold *innovation investments*, allocating resources to the right opportunities, and creating innovation ecosystems. We will be partnering with AI agents to serve higher-level innovation objectives—*setting the purpose* and strategy, *steering* the opportunity discovery function, *seeking* high-potential opportunities, and *shaping* the appropriate exploration and execution paths.

However, this transition will not be smooth. Business leaders should prepare for this new reality by shaping a strategy and taking proactive steps to become more flexible and adaptive. We must define and adopt *new innovation roles*, *collaboration patterns*, and *career paths* that value human contributions and our unique qualities, such as critical thinking, judgment, and the ability to execute. We need to link these behaviors and outcomes to corporate recognition and reward systems and create role models that demonstrate how talented people, powered by AI agents, can push real innovation to the market and create value through growth and adoption. In this context, it is essential to provide strong narratives on how human innovators assume new responsibilities and add value by converting innovative concepts into in-market, adopted innovations. In parallel, it is crucial for companies to establish ongoing *upskilling* and *career advisory programs* and introduce the mindset of *adaptive roles*, *flexible career paths*, and *new models of engagement*.

Innovation roles of the future will inherit the characteristics of today's *intrapreneur profile*: ambitious, autonomous, and entrepreneurial individuals with strong product and business sense will thrive as innovators in the AI-powered organizations of the future. Companies will increasingly rely on intrapreneurs and their teams to take high-potential opportunities, launch them to market, and make wise investment decisions to drive adoption and business impact.

Beyond the corporate world, AI-powered innovation brings promises for addressing humanity's most pressing challenges. The acceleration of scientific discovery through AI-augmented research is already driving breakthroughs in medicine, biology, environmental science, and materials science that would have taken decades to achieve through traditional methods. If properly directed, the AI-powered innovations emerging from research laboratories can enhance our well-being and quality of life, optimize the production and distribution of goods, mitigate climate risks, and expand access to education and opportunities globally. By emphasizing the ethical use of AI-powered innovation, organizations can provide their teams with a *sense of purpose*, *social responsibility*, and *bold vision* to serve humanity's most aspirational goals.

At the same time, we must acknowledge the major societal concerns that come with AI's transformative potential. Questions of *equity*, *bias*, *privacy*, *social discord*, *technological unemployment*, and *concentration of technological and political power* require our thoughtful consideration and, ultimately, innovative solutions. Although these challenges demand government intervention and global policy frameworks, organizations must take proactive responsibility. While adopting AI-powered innovation, business leaders must consistently incorporate ethical frameworks, transparent governance, and regulatory tools to ensure that AI innovation serves both business and human goals in balance, with respect for human values and ethical systems. After all, it is not AI that needs regulation; it is *businesses and their leadership*.

As a personal note, my hope is that this unprecedented access to knowledge, tools, and AI capabilities will empower waves of talented individuals to innovate not just products and services but the global status quo—by creating better societies, political systems, businesses, educational institutes, healthcare solutions, and, ultimately, a more fair and prosperous humanity.

References

Chesbrough H, Bogers M (2014) Explicating open innovation: clarifying an emerging paradigm for understanding innovation. In: Chesbrough H, Vanhaverbeke W, West J (eds) New frontiers in open innovation. Oxford University Press, Oxford, pp 3–28. Page 17

Anil R. Doshi, Oliver P. Hauser (2024). Generative AI enhances individual creativity but reduces the collective diversity of novel content. Science Advances, 10, eadn5290. https://doi.org/10.1126/sciadv.adn5290

Eric Ries (2009) Minimum Viable Product: a guide. https://www.startuplessonslearned.com/2009/08/minimum-viable-product-guide.html

Knapp J, Zeratsky J (2016) Sprint: how to solve big problems and test new ideas in just five days. Simon & Schuster, New York

OECD (2016) Defining and measuring innovation in all sectors of the economy: policy relevance

Vuori TO, Huy QN (2015) Distributed attention and shared emotions in the innovation process: how Nokia lost the smartphone battle. Admin Sci Q 61:9–51

Further Reading

Cai, Y., Lattu, A. Triple Helix or Quadruple Helix: Which Model of Innovation to Choose for Empirical Studies?. Minerva 60, 257–280 (2022). https://doi.org/10.1007/s11024-021-09453-6

Cheng, J.L.C., Love, E. Designing chief innovation officer positions: a strategic contingency framework. J Org Design 11, 115–128 (2022). https://doi.org/10.1007/s41469-022-00126-6

Curley, M., & Salmelin, B. (2018). Open Innovation 2.0: The New Mode of Digital Innovation for Prosperity and Sustainability. Springer International Publishing.

European Commission (2016). Open Innovation 2.0: A New Paradigm.

Meng An, Jiabao Lin, Xin (Robert) Luo, The impact of human AI skills on organizational innovation: The moderating role of digital organizational culture, Journal of Business Research, Volume 182, 2024, 114786, ISSN 0148-2963, https://doi.org/10.1016/j.jbusres.2024.114786.

Mauro Cazzaniga, Florence Jaumotte, Longji Li, Giovanni Melina, Augustus J Panton, Carlo Pizzinelli, Emma J Rockall, and Marina Mendes Tavares. "Gen-AI: Artificial Intelligence and the Future of Work", Staff Discussion Notes 2024, 001 (2024), accessed May 14, 2025, https://doi.org/10.5089/9798400262548.006

EY India (2025): Agentic AI: The next frontier in automation https://go.ey.com/3S1GWlC

How AI Can Drive Innovation in Your Industry (HBS Online, 2024)—https://online.hbs.edu/blog/post/ai-innovation

G. Krasadakis, *Innovation Mode 2.0*, https://doi.org/10.1007/978-3-032-00835-0

Jones, G., Chirino Chace, B., & Wright, J. (2020). Cultural diversity drives innovation: empowering teams for success. International Journal of Innovation Science, 12(3), 323–343. https://doi.org/10.1108/IJIS-04-2020-0042

Meng, X.-L. (2023). Data Science and Engineering With Human in the Loop, Behind the Loop, and Above the Loop. Harvard Data Science Review, 5(2). https://doi.org/10.1162/99608f92.68a012eb

Microsoft—Work Trend Index Annual Report: 2025: The Year the Frontier Firm Is Born—https://www.microsoft.com/en-us/worklab/work-trend-index/2025-the-year-the-frontier-firm-is-born

OECD/BCG/INSEAD (2025), The Adoption of Artificial Intelligence in Firms: New Evidence for Policymaking, OECD Publishing, Paris, https://doi.org/10.1787/f9ef33c3-en

OECD/Eurostat (1997) Proposed guidelines for collecting and interpreting technological innovation Data, Oslo manual. OECD, Paris

Palepu, S., Nitsch, A., Narayan, M., Kim, S., & Osier, N. (2020). A Flat Organizational Structure for an Inclusive, Interdisciplinary, International, and Undergraduate-Led Team. Frontiers in Education, 5, 102. https://doi.org/10.3389/feduc.2020.00102

Quarterly research and innovation literature review: The impact of AI on R&I (2023) https://research-and-innovation.ec.europa.eu/knowledge-publications-tools-and-data/publications/all-publications/quarterly-research-and-innovation-literature-review-impact-ai-ri_en

Ries E (2011) The lean startup: how constant innovation creates radically successful businesses. Penguin Books, London

Index

G. Krasadakis, *Innovation Mode 2.0*, https://doi.org/10.1007/978-3-032-00835-0

MIX
Papier aus verantwortungsvollen Quellen
Paper from responsible sources
FSC® C105338

If you have any concerns about our products,
you can contact us on
ProductSafety@springernature.com

In case Publisher is established outside the EU,
the EU authorized representative is:
Springer Nature Customer Service Center GmbH
Europaplatz 3, 69115 Heidelberg, Germany

Printed by Libri Plureos GmbH
in Hamburg, Germany